THE RISE OF MODERN EUROPE

A SURVEY OF EUROPEAN HISTORY
IN ITS POLITICAL, ECONOMIC, AND CULTURAL ASPECTS
FROM THE END OF THE MIDDLE AGES
TO THE PRESENT

EDITED BY

WILLIAM L. LANGER

Harvard University

THE

COUNTER

REFORMATION

1559–1610

BY

MARVIN R. O'CONNELL

University of Notre Dame

ILLUSTRATED

1817

HARPER & ROW, PUBLISHERS

New York, Evanston, San Francisco, London

FIRST EDITION

Library of Congress Cataloging in Publication Data

O'Connell, Marvin Richard.
    The Counter Reformation, 1559–1610.
    (The Rise of Modern Europe [4])
    Bibliography: p.
    1. Counter-Reformation.   I. Title.   II. Series.
D6.R5 vol. 4 [BR430]   940'08s   [270.6]   73–14278
ISBN 0–06–013233–7

For

ANNA MAE KELLY O'CONNELL

A Valiant Lady

CONTENTS

CONTENTS

ILLUSTRATIONS

These photographs, grouped in a separate section, will be found following page 142.

MAPS AND CHARTS

———

INTRODUCTION

Our age of specialization produces an almost incredible amount of monographic research in all fields of human knowledge. So great is the mass of this material that even the professional scholar cannot keep abreast of the contributions in anything but a restricted part of his general subject. In all branches of learning the need for intelligent synthesis is now more urgent than ever before, and this need is felt by the layman even more acutely than by the scholar. He cannot hope to read the products of microscopic research or to keep up with the changing interpretations of experts, unless new knowledge and new viewpoints are made accessible to him by those who make it their business to be informed and who are competent to speak with authority.

These volumes, published under the general title of *The Rise of Modern Europe,* are designed primarily to give the general reader and student a reliable survey of European history written by experts in various branches of that vast subject. In consonance with the current broad conception of the scope of history, they attempt to go beyond the merely political-military narrative, and to lay stress upon social, economic, religious, scientific, and artistic developments. The minutely detailed, chronological approach is to some extent sacrificed in the effort to emphasize the dominant factors and to set forth their interrelationships. At the same time, the division of European history into national histories has been abandoned, and wherever possible attention has been focused upon larger forces common to the whole of European civilization. These are the broad lines on which this history as a whole has been laid out. The individual volumes are integral parts of the larger scheme, but they are intended also to stand as independent units, each the work of a scholar well qualified to treat the period covered by his book. Each volume contains about fifty illustrations selected from the mass of contemporary pictorial material. All noncontemporary illustrations have been excluded on principle. The bibliographical note appended to each volume is designed to facilitate further study of special aspects touched upon in the text. In general every effort has been made to give the reader a clear idea of the main movements in European history, to embody the monographic contributions of research workers, and to present the material in a forceful and vivid manner.

Most histories of the Counter Reformation have been written by Protestants, and even the most scholarly can hardly be called free of prejudice. For this reason it was decided, at the very initiation of the Series, to entrust the stormy period from 1559 to 1610 to a competent Catholic scholar who would be able to write understandingly of the determined efforts of the Catholic Church to reform itself, to stem the advances of Protestantism, and if possible to recover the lands lost to heresy in the earlier sixteenth century. Unfortunately, work on the project was twice interrupted, first by the death of the Reverend Robert Howard Lord and in 1967 by the demise of Monsignor Philip Hughes, the distinguished historian of the Reformation in England. Each of these scholars had done considerable work on the volume, and its present author, the Reverend Marvin R. O'Connell of the University of Notre Dame, has made what use he could of the materials left by his predecessors. As a disciple of the late Monsignor Hughes, Father O'Connell has written clearly and succinctly of a very confused and controversial period. To say that the reader will be unable to detect, from the text itself, whether it was written by a Catholic or a Protestant is to pay the highest tribute to the author's depth of understanding and truly unusual objectivity.

WILLIAM L. LANGER

PREFACE

When Monsignor Philip Hughes died late in 1967 he left unfinished his work on this volume of the Rise of Modern Europe Series. The Series' editor, Professor William L. Langer, asked me to try to edit and complete what Monsignor Hughes had written so that the contribution of such an eminent scholar would not be lost to the historical community. This request was seconded by Mrs. Margaret Laing, Monsignor Hughes's executor, and I was more than happy to agree, out of regard for the memory of a beloved mentor to whom I owe so much as well as because of my affection for Mrs. Laing. After eighteen months or so of very hard work I concluded that the task was beyond me. Rather than present to the public a distorted patchwork of scissors and paste, I offered to write the volume myself from an entirely new beginning. Both Professor Langer and Mrs. Laing concurred. What is here, then, is my own, though the genial ghost of Philip Hughes haunts its pages, and my fondest wish is that the book is one of which he might have approved.

My debt to Professor Langer, for his trust in me and for his astute and kindly supervision, cannot be adequately expressed. I am grateful to my friends and former colleagues at the College of St. Thomas: to Professor Robert P. Fogerty, chairman of the Department of History, who encouraged my work at every stage and made practical arrangements to facilitate it; and to Professors George V. Martin and William Delahanty, who read the text in typescript and gave me the benefit of their advice. The maps and charts which enrich the text and, hopefully, in some places clarify it were prepared by Mr. Peter Kooyman. This is the third book Mrs. Kathleen Boyd has patiently and skillfully typed for me; I can only say that like good wine she improves with age.

MARVIN R. O'CONNELL

Notre Dame, Indiana
February 19, 1973

THE COUNTER REFORMATION

1559-1610

Chapter One

THE QUALITY OF LIFE

"ALL the world's a stage, and all the men and women merely players." The drama of European history, acted out between 1559 and 1610, was dominated by a handful of kings, popes, soldiers, diplomats, and savants. Indeed, the violent death of one French king conveniently marks the beginning of this era commonly called the Counter Reformation, and the violent death of another French king marks its end. During these hectic years, of which Shakespeare was a witness, as were Cervantes and Montaigne, a small elite made the decisions and dreamed the dreams which affected their contemporaries and, in some instances, all the generations that came after them.

But however much actors like the Cardinal of Lorraine or Queen Elizabeth I or the Duke of Alba occupied center stage, one cannot forget the roles played by other nameless millions, a huge chorus of gentlemen, peasants, priests, and artisans. In a sense every era is the era of the common man, who is concerned more about his children and his sheep than about ideology. And he will have his way in the end, because, if for no other reason, the laws of inertia are on his side. So we must look at him and at the setting in which he played his part, even though he had little to do with the colorful and decisive histrionics which were reserved for the leading actors; we must look at him and at the quality of his life.

I. LAND AND PEOPLE

The land, then as now, stretched from the Sierra Nevada in southeast Spain, across the Pyrenees and Alps and Carpathians, through the basins of the Dnieper and the Volga, until it reached the western slopes of the Urals, which stood a modest barrier to the vast Asiatic plain beyond. Lesser mountain ranges—like the Apennines and the Balkans—crisscrossed the European continent and cut off one region from another, one people from another, though for thousands of years peddlers had picked their way through obscure mountain passes and

I

with their wares had proved that, when it comes to appetite, all human beings are pretty much alike.

Europe's 3,750,000 square miles constituted only a small percentage of the earth's land mass. What perhaps distinguished it significantly from other continents—the nature and even existence of which Europeans in 1559 were only dimly aware—was that except for its northern fringes it was almost entirely habitable. Of course the amount and quality of resources differed markedly from place to place. Some exceedingly fertile soil, as in the Lombard basin of northern Italy and the lush wheatland of the Hungarian plain, could make life relatively easy. The list of produce dispatched regularly to London by a Middlesex housewife sounded like a happy litany: "milk, butter, cheese, apples, pears, frumenty, hens, chickens, eggs, bacon and a thousand other country drugs."[1] But starkly different were areas like the rocky plateau of old Castile, where hot winds withered the grain fields and left the countryside pocked with dry waste.

More of the land, then as now, was simply ordinary, imposing the burden of wringing a livelihood from it on a man's toil and ingenuity. Speaking generally, in the south where the Mediterranean climate prevailed—cool, wet winters and blindingly hot summers—the dominant topography was one of hillsides and small valleys. Advantage had to be taken of every scrap of arable land, of every drop of water. Low-yielding grain crops had therefore to be planted sparingly, and in bad years (like 1591) thousands of tons of cereals had to be imported.[2] The scraggly grass that grew here up the sides of steep slopes was fit for strong-legged sheep and goats, but not for cattle. Here the staples remained olives, grapes, and other fruits, like the fig, which came to harvest two or three times a year.

To the north, on the other side of the Alps and the Pyrenees, was more useful land, but also more swamp and forest, more severe and unpredictable weather. An immense plain stretched from the Atlantic eastward, along the southern shores of the North and Baltic seas. Here, in France, Germany, and Poland, flourished grain fields and dairy herds, and in the valleys of the Loire and the Rhine, vineyards, orchards, and hop fields. Here men feasted, when times were good, on

1. A. L. Rowse, *The England of Elizabeth* (New York, 1951), p. 72.
2. Fernand Braudel, *La Méditerranée et le monde méditerranéen à l'époque de Philippe II* (Paris, 1966), I, pp. 386–87.

bread, cheese, and great hunks of red meat, washed down with wine or beer.

Beneath the ground lay a variety of other treasure which, if not yet widely exploited, sixteenth-century Europeans could use to enrich their lives, provided they were lucky enough to find it and industrious enough to ferret it out. Spain had its iron, Italy its alum; in various places were copious supplies of copper, lead, tin, and zinc. And perhaps most significant in the long run, there was abundant coal.

A score of rivers gave Europe, then as now, not only broad valleys rich in alluvial soil but also bustling avenues of inland trade. Quite incalculable was the overall impact on the lives of sixteenth-century Europeans of the barges which plied the Vistula, the Rhone, and the Danube and carried their cargoes of grain, wine, furs, salt fish, and cloth to every corner of the continent. It was no coincidence that Antwerp, located where the River Scheldt flowed into the sea and close to the Meuse and the lower Rhine, became the greatest commercial depot in the world; perhaps it would have remained so for a long time had it not been ravaged by war.[3]

The number of people who lived in Europe during the second half of the sixteenth century must have ranged between the seventy and eighty million mark. This figure, like those which follow, can be advanced only tentatively, not from an absence of data but from an unevenness of it and from an uncertainty as to the precise meaning of the available statistics.[4] Some broad generalizations can nevertheless be safely made. The continental population increased steadily through the century, but it did so by fits and starts, here more and there less and in some places not at all. Deaths in a particular region or country might outnumber births during a plague year or over the course of several bad harvests in a row. The full demographic effect of such events would not be felt until twenty or thirty years later. The same

---

3. See Hermann von der Wee, *The Growth of the Antwerp Market and the European Economy* (Louvain, 1963), especially Vol. III. The prodigious Spanish siege (1584–1585) and its aftermath are described succinctly in Henri Pirenne, *Histoire de Belgique* (Brussels, 1919), IV, 189 ff., and at great length in Leon von der Essen, *Alexandre Farnèse* (Brussels, 1933–35), Vol. IV.

4. For a discussion of the statistical problem, see E. E. Rich and C. H. Wilson, eds., *The Cambridge Economic History of Europe* (Cambridge, 1967), IV, pp. 5–95, and Roger Mols, *Introduction à la démographie historique des villes d'Europe du XVIe au XVIIIe siècle* (Louvain, 1954–56).

might be said of the calamities attendant upon the French religious wars which over four decades may have caused as many as a million casualties, and of the more or less continuous fighting that went on in the Netherlands after 1566. Battlefield fatalities may have been paltry by twentieth-century standards, but the armies of Coligny and Farnese left in their wake famine and disease as lethal as their new cannon.

Despite some pronounced fluctuations, the population of France hovered near sixteen or seventeen million. That of German-speaking lands was about the same or possibly a little larger, but it was spread over a much wider area.[5] Still, German observers were dismayed at the swollen numbers which everywhere drove up the prices of land and food, and they noted, with a kind of proto-Malthusian melancholy, that war was a useful technique in a society in which couples married young and never seemed to have fewer than eight healthy children. But Switzerland provided evidence that war, even when it was the chief national industry, could not alone check the rising population. About a million people lived in the Swiss cantons by 1600—an increase of about 50 or 60 percent in a hundred years—even though at least a quarter-million young men, at the height of their vital powers, had emigrated during the century to fight as mercenary soldiers for foreign governments.

Across the Oder to the east, 6 million Poles merged politically with perhaps 4 million Lithuanians, whose Grand Duchy sprawled from the eastern shore of the Baltic to within 170 miles of Moscow and down the Dnieper to the southern Ukraine.[6] North of the Baltic inhabitants were scattered thinly across a cold, bleak countryside, though here too population steadily rose, except in Sweden, where interminable wars and crop failures left considerably less than a million people by 1600.[7]

At the same date there must have been about 13 million Italians, of whom some 2 million lived in the Papal States, a little less than that in the Republic of Venice and about a million and a quarter in the duchy of Milan. The population of southern Italy (the Kingdom of Naples)

---

5. Hajo Holborn, *A History of Modern Germany: The Reformation* (New York, 1967), p. 37.

6. W. F. Reddaway et al., eds., *The Cambridge History of Poland to 1696* (Cambridge, 1950), p. 441; George Vernadsky, *Russia at the Dawn of the Modern Age* (New Haven, 1959), p. 176.

7. R. B. Wernham, ed., *The New Cambridge Modern History*: Vol. III: *The Counter Reformation and the Price Revolution* (Cambridge, 1968), p. 425.

increased by 28 percent between 1545 and 1595, while Sicily passed the million mark by 1573. On the other side of the Adriatic, in the Balkans, Hungary, and Greece, dwelt another 8 million Europeans. Here too urban and rural population grew steadily through the sixteenth century. One reason was that most of this area had been incorporated into the Ottoman Empire, and the Turkish regime, however onerous it might have been, did bring to its subjects the inestimable benefit of prolonged peace.[8]

Spain's population reached perhaps 8 million by the end of the century, three-quarers of it in Castile, where the total doubled in a hundred years. Neighboring Portugal, by contrast, probably fell beneath the 2 million inhabitants she might have counted in 1500. Besides the common crises of plague and dearth, the Portuguese suffered from the results of an overextension of scanty human resources in the military and commercial adventures of empire, which led to chronically severe labor shortages at home and finally (1580) to political collapse.[9] There was a striking difference in density between the Italian and the Iberian peninsulas: 114 inhabitants per square mile in the former and only 44 in the latter. The density in the Netherlands—104 per square mile—was also far greater than that of their Spanish overlord. The total population of what is now Holland must have been just over a million, of Belgium just over two.

In the British Isles, Scotland and Ireland together supported less than 2 million people, while England and Wales by 1600 counted a little under 5 million.[10] This latter figure represented an increase of some 20 percent through the long reign of Elizabeth I.

By far the overwhelming majority of sixteenth-century Europeans were rural dwellers, but the pattern was neither so static nor so consistent as one might expect. Though only five of every hundred Swedes lived in towns, the percentage was four or five times as high among the English. In Germany there flourished more than 3,000 towns; most of these indeed were small, but the influence they exercised in their localities was not insignificant. A chronicler in 1600 listed, besides 25

8. Braudel, *La Méditerranée*, I, 361–71; Henri Hauser and Augustin Renaudet, *Les Débuts de l'Age Moderne* (Paris, 1956), pp. 46 ff.

9. Herbert Heaton, *Economic History of Europe* (New York, 1948), pp. 262 f.; H. V. Livermore, *A History of Portugal* (Cambridge, 1947), pp. 250 ff.

10. Carl Bridenbaugh, *Vexed and Troubled Englishmen* (New York, 1968), p. 218.

English and Welsh episcopal cities, 641 market towns. London's population at Elizabeth's death (1603) probably exceeded 200,000.

There were more large cities in the Low Countries and Italy, areas which had long been devoted to commercial activities. Antwerp, despite its many tribulations, grew through the century to over 100,000 and Amsterdam was about the same size. Naples was the largest city in Italy with upwards of 250,000 people; Venice in 1600 had 140,000; Rome in 1592 had 97,000 and more than 100,000 a decade later.[11] Paris kept pace with London and Naples, while in Germany, Augsburg, with more than 50,000 inhabitants, was slightly ahead of Cologne and Magdeburg.

The levels of urban population also indicated the presence of considerable human mobility. Thus of thirty-one good-sized towns in Castile, eleven declined in population between 1530 and 1594 and twenty increased. During the same period Seville doubled in size to 90,000.[12] But not only in Spain was there this kind of internal migration. War and religious persecution certainly prompted it in the Netherlands, where harassed Calvinists, or artisans simply weary of the endless fighting in the south, made their way to Holland and Zeeland, which were relatively secure from Spanish armies behind the barrier of their great rivers. So as the cities of Flanders shrank in size—in some instances as much as 50 percent—a Dutch town like Leyden quadrupled its population in forty years.

As Castilians moved generally from north to south,[13] Poles moved from west to east and Germans from south to north. As early as 1500 southern Germany was relatively overpopulated, in the sense that landholdings had become fixed and industry had not developed enough to absorb the overflow of people from the countryside. Another factor of mobility and urban growth was the conversion of large estates, especially in England and Spain, from farming to pasturage. And so the lucrative possibilities of the woolen trade sent streams of landless peasants into the towns. Finally, some evidence points to intranational migration, once more affecting Spain, particularly to which Frenchmen flocked during the heyday of Spanish imperialism—by the end of the

11. Jean Delumeau, *Vie Économique et Sociale de Rome dans la second moitié du XVIe siècle* (Paris, 1957), I, 123.

12. J. H. Elliott, *Imperial Spain* (New York, 1966), pp. 289 f.

13. Jaime Vicens Vives, *An Economic History of Spain* (Princeton, 1969), p. 333.

century 20 percent of the population of Catalonia was said to be of Gascon origin. The Genoese, shrewd businessmen, technicians, and mariners, also settled in Spain in large numbers, while 100,000 Spaniards in their turn left home for the colonies in America.

The rising population totals represented in one sense a recovery from the demographic crisis of the fourteenth century when the European peoples had been decimated by repeated visitations of the Black Death. One direct result of the recovery was the opening of new land to cultivation, or rather the reoccupation of land unused for two centuries. "In our times," observed a sixteenth-century chronicler, numbers of people "are greatly augmented and increased, whereby the land has been opened up more than within the memory of men, and hardly a nook, even in the bleakest woods and on the highest mountains, is left uncleared and uninhabited."[14]

Yet, even so, much of the land of Europe remained starkly empty during the last half of the sixteenth century. Many a Castilian city stood like a lonely oasis in the midst of a blank, hot plain, and one traveler in Aragon reported that he journeyed for days without seeing a single human being. In Provence bears roamed through wide open spaces, while in Corsica pitched battles had to be fought with wolves and wild boars. Impenetrable forests, with fen and marshland, were common in Germany. In England the calculated destruction of forest preserves had the similar result of emptying the land, since those who lived on the edges of the woods were deprived of fuel and building materials. The vast expanses converted to pasturage meant that the only human voice to be heard for miles around might be that of a shepherd calling to his flock. A witness noted, in 1574, that Serbian Christians did not try to run away from their Moslem masters because, among other reasons, they feared to flee through a wilderness filled with wild animals.

Some of the predatory beasts which lurked in these barren, deserted areas were human brigands whose cruelty and rapaciousness exceeded the simpler capabilities of lower beings. Every forest, every marsh and mountainside, swarmed with them. The sixteenth century was a time of much law—royal decrees, acts of parliaments, judicial edicts—but not much order. Catalonia, southern Italy, and Albania had the worst reputations in this regard, but the phenomenon was universal, and

14. *Cambridge Economic History*, IV, 25.

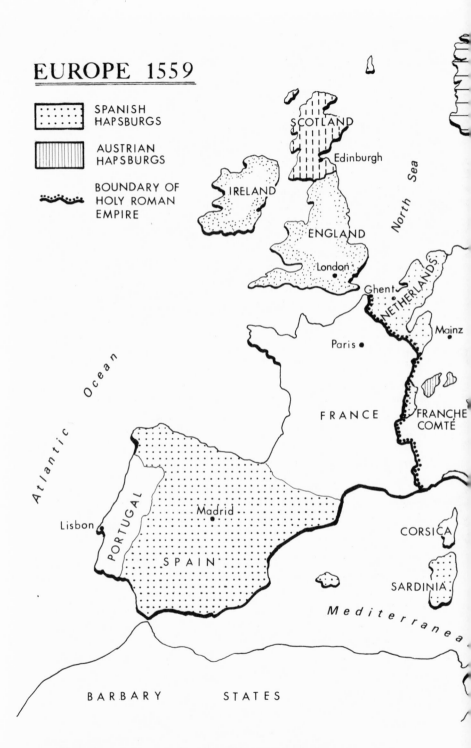

EUROPE 1559

SPANISH
HAPSBURGS

AUSTRIAN
HAPSBURGS

BOUNDARY OF
HOLY ROMAN
EMPIRE

SCOTLAND

Edinburgh

IRELAND

North Sea

ENGLAND

London

Ghent

NETHERLANDS

Mainz

Paris

FRANCE

FRANCHE
COMTÉ

Atlantic Ocean

PORTUGAL

Lisbon

Madrid

SPAIN

CORSICA

SARDINIA

Mediterranean

BARBARY   STATES

hardly a man or woman, of whatever station, did not share the Psalmist's fear of the arrow that flieth by day and the terror that creepeth by night.

The end of the long Hapsburg-Valois conflict in 1559 loosed upon European society not only soldiers for religious wars but also men-at-arms for whom brigandage was a more congenial and lucrative profession than any other. Central governments, which were only beginning to exercise any meaningful control outside the limited royal domain, lacked the resources to mount an anticrime program which was both vigorous enough and sustained enough. Even relatively well-policed states like Venice had serious difficulty combating the bandits. Weaker ones were plagued by them. At various times expeditions scoured the Neapolitan countryside with the pledge that banditry would once and for all be stamped out; but the outlaws back in the hills knew that the government could not afford to apply large force for long. So they waited until the gendarmes went away, as they invariably did, and then it was business as usual. In the Papal States at least until the time of tough old Sixtus V (1585–1590), bandit gangs roamed practically at will, and not even the extraordinary measure of burning out woodland in the Campagna, as a means of depriving them of cover, did much to curb their activities.[15]

Often enough legitimate governments had to adopt the humiliating expedient of recruiting into their armies criminals they could control in no other way. Similarly, resistance to centralization by a feudalism, which was dying but not yet dead, provided outlaws with opportunity for profit and status. Great lords, who thrived on a tradition of violence toward each other and toward the pretensions of a king, easily evolved into robber barons, condottieri, surrounded by increasingly motley crews of men-at-arms. From their crumbling castles they watched the slow withering away of those judicial and executive responsibilities which had in past times furnished a noble pretext for the violence they habitually practiced. Now noblesse oblige had come to mean not service of others but survival for themselves.

How numerous the bandits were no one can say with certainty, but their depredations were universal and brought untold misery to those least able to bear it. The tale told at Naples in 1578 was typical: farmland ravaged, trade interrupted, travelers murdered, churches

15. Ludwig Pastor, *History of the Popes* (London, 1932), XXI, 76 ff.

desecrated and burned, people kidnapped and held for ransom. As the Turks expanded across the Balkans into Hungary, the inhabitants suffered a double scourge: hordes of brigands were routed from their lairs and pillaged their way westward ahead of the advancing armies. It was not unknown in Calabria for robbers to descend upon a town at midday and sack it. For many years no courier could travel safely between Barcelona and Saragossa.

Indeed, the incidence of brigandage was on the rise all over Spain during the last years of Philip II (d. 1598), and it spread even more rapidly during his son's reign.[16] Wherever it flourished the poor suffered most. During years of scarcity and high prices the bandits grew bolder and more vicious, and their chief victims were the peasantry. It is little wonder that in a place like Portugal, where agriculture was in a chronically depressed state anyway, large numbers of peasants gave up resisting and became robbers themselves. In more industrialized areas, like Flanders, a similar phenomenon took place; a depression in a trade or craft could turn some workers into vagabonds, others into beggars, and still others into outlaws.

More often than not it was simple men like these, rather than hardened criminal types, whom hunger or other dire necessity drove into highway robbery or the like and then into the toils of the law. In 1613 a laborer from Chelmsford was hanged for stealing twenty-three pounds, and the same year, also in England, a spinster suffered the same punishment for purse snatching—despite her plea for clemency on the ground that she was pregnant. The statute law, with its hundreds of capital crimes, reflected the attitude of societies driven to penal savagery by the cruelties inherent in a situation verging on anarchy.

2. LORDS AND PEASANTS

Still, one must not overdraw dramatic disorder; the countryside harbored many more industrious husbandmen than thieves and murderers. Most people made their living on the farm, and though in many ways it was a harsh existence, it was not without its compensations. The land possessed a spaciousness, a sense of physical freedom and openness, which must have been conducive to a serenity often lacking amid the crowds and bustle of later times. Fields stretched toward the horizon unmarred by the heaps of refuse which disfigure industrial

16. John Lynch, *Spain Under the Habsburgs* (New York, 1964), I, 300.

societies. Sixteenth-century towns seemed somehow an extension of the placid rural scene as though, like the trees, they had sprung up naturally out of the earth. The dreary round of work and worry was broken by country pleasures: by Twelfth Night, by shearing feasts and ale of Whitsuntide, and, above all, by dancing.

But what Professor Braudel calls "this universe of peasants" was no idyllic place. Housing was mean and ramshackle, damp and cold in winter, stiflingly hot in summer, unventilated and redolent in every season of body odors. And as for rational sanitation procedures, practically none existed. Once an infectious disease began to spread, little could be done but to let it run its course (though in this regard the countryside was better off than the towns). Infant mortality was astronomical, and so life expectancy remained correspondingly low. Statistically a man was lucky to survive his fortieth birthday. Sketchy evidence suggests that wives tended to outlive their husbands, despite the fact that so many women died in childbirth.[17]

Agrarian techniques and forms of land tenure differed little from those of the Middle Ages. With the simple and indeed primitive implements at his disposal, the sixteenth-century farmer worked mostly by the sweat of his brow and the muscles in his back. Here a more efficient iron plow was put in use, there mules substituted as draft animals for oxen; but such improvements were modest in scope and overall impact. So was the introduction of new crops—maize, potatoes, and beans—from the Americas.[18]

One momentous development, however, did occur or rather was accelerated: as the century wore on, subsistence farming—the habit of a thousand years—was making room for an agriculture directly related to the market. This process moved too slowly to be termed a revolution. Yet its ultimate consequences altered profoundly the direction of European society. If Mr. Rowse is correct, "the sixteenth century, and in especial the second half of it, saw a rapid and concentrated transition from the more static conditions of medieval agriculture, that express themselves so deeply in the medieval experience of life and religion, to the freer, more mobile conditions of agriculture carried on on the basis

---

17. Braudel, *La Méditerranée*, I, 387, 379; Delumeau, *Vie Économique*, I, 423.

18. Only later than 1610 did these and other new crops become economically significant. For the potato in Ireland as an example see J. H. Parry, *The Age of Reconnaissance* (New York, 1963), p. 304.

of money. . . ." What this amounted to was the emergence of free labor in place of bond.[19]

The basic reason for the change was quite simple. Larger towns, larger military establishments, more overseas expansion and commercial activity—all these stood in greater need of food and fiber. Obviously behind these and similar proximate causes was the gradual but very real increase in European population. There were more towns and more people living in towns because there were more people, which meant for agriculture more mouths to feed and more limbs to clothe.

The results were many and various. Responding to a more intense demand, agricultural produce and the land in which it grew increased steadily in value through the last fifty years of the century. It was a good time to be a landlord unless, as was the case in some places, ceilings were fixed by law on rents, and then it was a good time to be a tenant.[20] In either case, during an era of unfaltering price rise, a good deal of money was to be made down on the farm.

The prosperity, however, was far from even, and it carried in its wake not a little social dislocation. In Poland, where most of the land was held by the king and the aristocracy, a sharp rise in profits was registered from increased production in grain, breeding cattle, poultry, and garden vegetables. But the peasant masses, though perhaps they ate better or at any rate more regularly due to a more efficient exploitation of the land, paid a high price in the loss of their traditional tenure rights. And the Polish monarchy did not benefit much either in the long run, because if the king's revenue increased significantly, that of the unruly baronage increased considerably more. Peasants who worked a nobleman's estate were virtually his subjects; in eastern Poland it was not unusual for a lord to hold a score of peasant villages under his sway.

A similar development took place in Germany east of the Elbe, in Pomerania, Brandenburg, and Prussia, where the gentry—Junkers as they came to be called—eliminated the free peasantry and created in its place a rural proletariat. Since like their Polish counterparts the Junkers enjoyed judicial powers over those who worked their land, their control over local economic life went practically unquestioned.

19. Rowse, *England of Elizabeth*, p. 80.
20. For England see Christopher Hill, *Reformation to Industrial Revolution* (New York, 1967), pp. 48 f.

They played the role of agricultural entrepreneurs whose profitable business was exportation of grain to the west.[21]

In other parts of Germany the pattern was less consistent. Free peasants flourished in Friesland and lower Saxony, and in the duchy of the Tyrol they even had representation in the estates. In the populous southwest, amid the glut of tiny principalities of Swabia and Rhenish Franconia, land tenures, mostly hereditary and with fixed rents, were favorable to the peasants, who for all practical purposes enjoyed the status of proprietors. But to the north the situation was again quite different. Near Bremen old forms of feudal bondage survived into the seventeenth century, while elsewhere landowners with ruthless dedication to efficiency merged the small medieval holdings at a ratio of about four to one and turned over these larger tracts to farmers called *Meiers*. The result, as in Poland, was heightened productivity at the cost of a large, restless mass of evictees.

Everywhere in Europe some movement of this sort was going on, as the pressure of growing population provided opportunity for agricultural profit. But, as in Germany, local conditions dictated a variety in mood and tempo. Tenure, for example, was relatively secure for a peasant in Catalonia; his Castilian counterpart, on the other hand, could count on no such security, and his tenancy was in any case so expensive, so burdened with debt and ecclesiastical tithes, that he often had to sell his produce at low prices well before harvest time. He likely considered himself not much better off than the laborer who worked on a vast latifundium owned by a nobleman or a monastery.

England, too, at this moment when the sands in the manorial glass were running out, presented many faces of rural organization. To the south lay fertile soil adjacent to and stimulated by the huge London market; here, in Essex and Hertfordshire, prosperity bloomed for farmers of every social class, and preoccupation with subsistence disappeared. Elsewhere, however, the story was far otherwise. North of the Humber, where they still "knew no other prince but a Percy," the Middle Ages had not yet ended; still valued were the old ways of the earls of Northumberland, and a deep suspicion prevailed about the

21. A Junker was a *jung-herre*, a young nobleman. He was a "working entrepreneur," according to Hans Rosenberg, "The Rise of the Junkers," *American Historical Review*, XLIX (1943–44), 1–22, 228–242.

bustling enterprise, smooth manners, and new-fangled religion of the south.

The incidence of change, then, was checkered and uneven. Seignorialism lingered next to an increasingly bumptious capitalist agriculture. The steady rise in food prices, sparked by population pressure, may have predetermined which kind of rural life would win in the end, but many factors conspired to make the process of change a sluggish one. Mixed husbandry, for one thing, came only very slowly. German farmers raised grain almost exclusively; without even beets or potatoes to fall back on, a single bad harvest could be calamitous, not only to the hungry inhabitants but to the development of a genuine market economy. Cattle breeding was limited in Germany for lack of meadow—only forest land and, in the autumn, empty fields were available for grazing—and in England for lack of winter fodder. Manure was therefore scarce and haphazardly applied, and the need for fertilization, like that for crop rotation, was only partially understood.

Still more serious was the universal tendency to answer demand for more agricultural produce not by increasing yields but by cultivating heretofore unused land. Not that the rescue of waste areas was itself a bad thing; but without an accompanying improvement in production techniques and methods of distribution the rise in consumptive output was often illusory or temporary. Not enough waste land could have been cleared to meet the steadily growing demand even if—which of course was not the case—that land had been of the highest quality. The result was that per capita productivity lessened rather than increased.[22]

And often thoughtless diversion of agricultural resources further compounded the problem. This happened perhaps most dramatically in Spain, where so much cultivated land was converted to sheep pasturage to serve the export woolen trade. Throughout the century Spanish farmers struggled with the powerful combine of sheep breeders called the *Mesta*. The animals trampled the grain fields, the farmers complained, and their pasturage, with its thin grass, intensified erosion. For a long time the government, which leaned heavily on *Mesta* taxes, supported the sheepmen and followed the short-sighted policy of discouraging grain production by imposing a low ceiling

22. See the penetrating analysis of Braudel, *La Méditerranée*, I, 384–389. But see also Rowse, *England of Elizabeth*, pp. 96 f.

price on it. In the end, however, the *Mesta,* and indeed the whole Spanish economy, had the worst of it, when Spanish wool became too expensive to compete in the international market.

Perhaps the most basic reason why the commercialization of agriculture proceeded so slowly was simple inertia. If, for example, upwards of 15 million tons of grain were consumed each year by the peoples of the Mediterranean basin, with a market value a hundred times that of the American silver received annually in Seville, one can appreciate how completely agriculture, with its deep medieval roots, still dominated the economic life of Europe. And if, of that grain total, half were consumed on the spot where it was grown and another 10 to 20 percent were collected in kind for rent payments, tithes, and interest charges, that left a relatively small proportion to the dynamics of the marketplace. The inert body needs an external stimulus to get it moving, and the gradual rise in population during the sixteenth century served that purpose. But the pace of economic change would remain leisurely until some technological breakthrough released a significant amount of human energy from preoccupation with producing low-yielding cereal grains. In fact agricultural methods altered hardly at all through the century, and, ironically, the capital investment necessary to develop genuine technical improvements was itself almost exclusively tied up in the inflexible land.

Here was a clue to the basic social phenomenon of these years: though many things had changed and many more were in the process of changing, still the major fact of life continued to be land and the uses of land, and therefore the pattern of social relationships did not alter very much. It is not enough to say that agriculture remained the overwhelmingly important sector of the various European economies, though this perhaps should be said first. Beyond that fundamental consideration, or rather intertwined with it, was a whole psychology, a whole system of ideas and values which went back a thousand years. Despite the emergence of strong kings, an aggressive middle class, and a new religion, the quality of life was still largely determined by the age-old rhythms of planting and harvest, and this meant in effect that the dominant tone in society was still set by the rural aristocracy.

Feudal vigor did not disappear during the sixteenth century. It was challenged indeed and modified; it had to adjust to new realities like gunpowder and inflation and a philosophy of divine-right monarchy. A certain political ambiguity undermined the former status of the barons, who had to surrender many prerogatives their ancestors had enjoyed. But the paradox was that a king, anxious as he may have been to curb feudal independence, could not do without the services of the lords because as yet he lacked the resources to govern as completely in fact as he did in theory. Whenever possible he incorporated the lords into the royal system and gave them responsibilities and rewards commensurate with their rank.[23] Now when they exercised jurisdiction they did so not in their own but in the king's name, with fortresses and soldiers not under their own but under the king's banner. This amounted to a significant constitutional development, but it made little practical difference to most people, who continued to regard the local baron as the source of order and the guarantor of stability. As for the lords themselves, the latter part of the sixteenth century was a moment of transition between the rough and ready medieval days when they bowed to no man and the era of accomplished despotism, soon to come, when they would be reduced to a decorative and parasitic court nobility. During the reign of Philip II the grandees of Castile came to court with increasing frequency, though not without some reluctance. If they resented the base-born civil servants who framed the king's policy, they took what consolation they could in the knowledge that their estates were growing larger and wealthier and that the most important offices of the kingdom—vice-royalties, governorships, army commands—were strictly reserved for themselves.[24]

It would be oversimple to see the almost primeval relationship between lord and peasant as dissolved by the economic and religious revolutions which were in progress during the sixteenth century. If anything, the economic power of the lords increased, at least vis-à-vis their own peasantry. The irony was, as Professor Vives observed, that the nobleman, "who disdained labor and refused to lower himself by engaging in business, was the only one who did not lose money during the price revolution."[25] He may indeed have spent himself into bankruptcy by a sumptuous style of life which increasingly came to be a

23. "The notion of a close marriage between the sixteenth century monarchies and the parliamentary bourgeoisie scarcely exists outside the text books," writes Professor Hurstfield. See *New Cambridge Modern History*, III, 132 ff.

24. Gregorio Marañón, *Antonio Pérez* (London, 1954), pp. 62 ff.

25. Vives, *Economic History*, pp. 338 f. See Delumeau, *Vie Économique*, II, 584 ff., for Pius V's attempts to control the rapacity of the Roman barons.

substitute for vanished political power. But just as often he was a working entrepreneur who took advantage of the growing value of his land by cultivating and selling more produce in an ever expanding market.[26]

That the tiny wellborn minority of the population should have continued to dominate European life cannot in any case be explained by simple economic categories. There were at the same time other and perhaps deeper causes at work. Men still saw the whole universe as a great chain of being whose order was stable and right and divinely sanctioned. In this chain everybody had his foreordained place. A man was not noble because he was rich; he was rich because he was noble and because it was God's will and therefore right. Hierarchy was something without which people thought they could not live or at least could not live in peace. They had no particular sense of history which could trace social relationships back to economic arrangements arrived at in the Dark Ages. Things were as they were because that was the way they were supposed to be. The dynamisms of monarchy, Protestantism, and capitalism all tended to dissolve the hierarchical structure or, perhaps more accurately, to modify it. The dissolution, however, was far from swift, not least because the land itself, endless and unchanging, gave an almost hallowed sense of permanency.

3. THE PRICE REVOLUTION

Prices, however, and particularly food prices, were anything but inflexible: they rose steadily, if unevenly, all over Europe. The last half of the sixteenth century fell in the middle of what economic historians have come to call the "price revolution." This inflationary cycle began about 1475 and continued for almost two centuries. Many factors contributed to it, the most spectacular of which was the expansion of the money market. Before 1500 new sources of precious metal were discovered in central Europe: gold near Salzburg, silver in the Tyrol and Bohemia. The Portuguese accelerated the process with the gold their mariners brought back from the East Indies and Africa, especially from Senegal. The supply of available money thus expanded, but with

---

26. See Lawrence Stone, *The Crisis of the Aristocracy* (Oxford, 1965), for a brilliant and exhaustive study of the English peers, and Davis Bitton, *The French Nobility in Crisis* (Stanford, 1969), a much shorter work.

no corresponding increase in domestic production, prices were bound to go up.

And so they did dizzyingly after 1550 when, thanks to a new technique applied to the mines in Peru, the Spanish treasure fleets began to dump huge cargoes of silver on the docks at Seville.[27] The price rise went out like shock waves which struck Andalusia (where Seville and its port San Lúcar were located) first and hardest, then Castile, then the rest of Spain. They crossed the Pyrenees and passed through the English Channel with military payrolls and payments for imports. For Spain was burdened not only with a chronically unfavorable trade balance—she depended upon northern Europe for wheat, tin, copper, timber, hemp, textiles of various kinds—but also with imperial adventures on a massive scale. All this cost money, and so the silver flowed out of Seville to the north and east and penetrated to the heart of the continent, so that, for example, it contributed to the tripling of wheat prices in far-off Saxony. The English price index was 150 percent higher in the last than in the first decade of the century; France's went higher than England's and Spain's of course higher than France's.[28]

Recent research suggests that prices reacted not so much to the amount of silver dumped into Europe from 1550 to 1600 as to the velocity with which that silver circulated. It used to be thought that European bullion holdings prior to the Peruvian and Mexican silver rush were negligible. There is less certainty on that point now. But what does seem clear is that as much as it would have liked to do so, the Spanish monarchy could not restrain the outflow of bullion. Every time a treasure fleet approached San Lúcar the tremors were felt all over Europe. "The money from Seville circulated from one money market to another, in settlement of commercial and financial transactions often to a value of ten or a hundred times its own value, and then passed on to the next money market for a fresh period of cash advances and trading settlements. Whether as coin or as bills of exchange,

27. The fundamental work on this subject remains Earl J. Hamilton, *American Treasure and the Price Revolution in Spain, 1501–1650* (Cambridge, Mass., 1934). Refinements and revisions have, however, been offered by, *inter alios,* Braudel, Delumeau, Lynch, and Vives, whose works have been cited above. For a brief but authoritative statement of Hamilton's views, see his article, "Price History," *International Encyclopedia of the Social Sciences* (1968), XII, 473 ff.

28. Vives, *Economic History,* pp. 377 ff., says Spain's price index quadrupled during the century, although the rate of increase was slower after 1550.

money cascaded from person to person and from money market to money market."[29] Rome handled as much coinage as Seville; Venice during the last quarter of the century minted a higher volume of gold than that of the total bullion receipts at Seville.

The Mediterranean was traditionally an area of high prices, and the proximity of the Spanish silver guaranteed that it should remain so. Thus, by 1600, though the price of grain in Poland had risen significantly, it still cost there only 20 or 25 percent of what it cost in France. But important as the silver imports were, other factors worked toward the same end. In Italy, a large-scale building boom to repair the devastation of seventy years of Hapsburg-Valois war sent prices up. Elsewhere, notably in France and the Netherlands, almost constant warfare meant scarcity and inflation, and the enormous credits advanced by bankers to sustain Philip II's various military involvements accelerated the spiral. Universally governments debased their currency and minted more coinage than they could support. (It was not the least of her contributions to the well-being of her people that Elizabeth of England was the one notable exception of this rule.) And everywhere population outpaced productivity with the inevitable consequence of dear bread and hard times.

Wages from this period are harder to trace than prices, because they were often paid wholly or partly in kind. Yet, although wages rose, they doubtlessly lagged behind prices, perhaps in terms of real purchasing power as much as 50 percent. In England the overall wage increase was only 30 percent, in France more like 25. The increase in Spain was considerably higher, but never high enough to match the relentless march of prices. For a hundred years after 1540 wages paid in the neighborhood of Munich could not keep pace with the cost of rye.

What this amounted to in the long run was that the rich got richer and the poor poorer. The rewards for the provident, the lucky, the wellborn, and the efficient agricultural producer were almost unlimited. But for the poor man, like the dispossessed peasant who worked for a salary, the times were grim indeed. He knew nothing of the subtleties of statistical charts on the standard of living, but he remembered ruefully and in bewilderment that his grandfather—a man no more industrious or thrifty than himself—had more often than not put meat and

29. Fernand Braudel and Frank Spooner, "Prices in Europe from 1450 to 1750," *Cambridge Economic History,* IV, 447 f.

beer on the table, while he had to scramble to provide even enough black bread for his family. The momentous social effect of the price revolution was to open the chasm between the haves and the have-nots—in essential things like diet and housing—wider than it had been for a thousand years.

4. CITY LIFE

At least half the swarming population of London in 1600 had been born and raised in the countryside. Much the same proportion prevailed in other European metropolises during this era of steady urban growth. For though cities of all kinds increased in size, cities in various locations and with different economic concerns, they consistently recorded a larger number of deaths than births. Cities were exceedingly dangerous places, and only the constant influx of country folk kept them growing and maintained them as commercial and industrial centers. So it was that Corsicans made up a significant part of the labor force in Marseilles, as Albanians did in Venice.

The ravages of war and plague might cause a downturn here or there. Fifty thousand Venetians—between one-quarter and one-third of the total—died during the epidemics of 1575-1577,[30] while about 40,000 during the same years perished in Messina and its environs. Antwerp's population declined some 20 percent in the wake of the prodigious Spanish siege of 1584-1585. Yet other towns suffered similar calamities, and still their numbers grew. Eleven thousand died of the plague in London in 1592, and eleven years later upwards of 30,000 more. Such huge figures caused only the slightest flutter on the statistical charts. Perhaps this was because 8 percent of London's population was transient, and a full 90 percent—including 30,000 unemployed—was classified as among the lower orders, who could be, and swiftly were, replaced by immigration.

City governments did what they could to fight off the recurrent plagues.[31] Pestiferous areas were burned down; people and merchandise were quarantined (a practice that started at Venice). Squads of physicians were mobilized to treat the sick. Tickets of health were

---

30. See Ernst Rodenwaldt, "Pest in Venedig 1575–1577 . . . ," *Sitzungsberichte der Heidelberger Akademil d. Wissenschaften* (Heidelberg, 1953), pp. 119 ff.

31. See Paul Geisendorf, *Theodore de Bèze* (Geneva, 1949), pp. 252 ff., for an account of the measures taken against the plague of 1564 by the Genevan magistracy.

issued and made a condition for appearance in the streets. But in an age of primitive medicine and even more primitive sanitation conditions city people learned to be fatalistic about the epidemics of typhus, whooping cough, and the mysterious sweating sickness which cut great swaths through the towns (though smallpox, as yet, was not a large-scale killer). Between 1603 and 1605, more than 3,000 people died in Bristol, along with similar numbers in York and Norwich. In 1581 Marseilles counted 5,000 deaths due to some infectious disease, and six years later a visitor noted that a new pestilence had practically shut the city down. All the inhabitants who could afford it had fled to the country; the poor had stayed behind and died.

In towns where the first crude industries developed, polluted air made lung and throat ailments commonplace: "pestilent smoke which corrodes the very iron and spoils the moveables." The larger towns, thronged by prostitutes and unmarried young men fresh from the country, also had a high incidence of syphilis. A quaint distinction, not without social significance, was drawn between the categories of ladies of pleasure: those who served the rich were called *les courtisanes honnêtes,* while the humbler variety were known as *les courtisanes à la chandelle,* because often as not they practiced their profession in the filthy back room of a candle merchant's shop.

If sickness was a constant peril to city dwellers, hunger was hardly less so. Few widespread famines occurred during the latter part of the sixteenth century, but many local ones did, and even more strictly urban ones. Indeed, some freakish bit of weather could reduce one locality to starvation in the midst of general plenty: in 1575, a sudden spring snow storm in ordinarily grain-rich Rumania left hundreds dead because a transportation system geared to serve in such an emergency simply did not exist.

Cities presented a special problem in this regard. No town of any size could be sustained by its own hinterland. This was as true of the independent imperial cities in Germany—Dortmund, Mülhausen, and scores of others—as it was of Rome, which consumed a million bushels of wheat a year and imported it from as far away as Sicily and Prussia. When the grain-producing areas harvested less than their usual crop, or when some external factor—like a war—threatened the ordinary avenues of transport, city populations were peculiarly vulnerable. Nothing preyed more on the mind of Pope Pius IV than the anxiety over victualing Trent during the last session of the general council, even though the town lay along the route over which Bavarian grain moved through the Brenner Pass into northern Italy.

Every city of importance had a governmental department charged exclusively with maintenance of the wheat supply. In Venice, each day a functionary of this office had to inform the doge what precisely were the stocks in hand. New grain sources were constantly sought, and if a shortage threatened all exports from points of embarkation like Palermo were forbidden until the danger passed. Sometimes, as reserves dwindled, city gates were closed to immigrants or foreign colonies were expelled. At Marseilles, in 1562, the Protestant community was exiled from the city for the duration of the grain shortage. In 1591—a year of universal and particularly severe dearth—the University of Naples closed down and the students were sent back to their homes.

And if perils from disease and hunger were not enough, the peasants who flocked into sixteenth-century cities could always count on the scourges of fire and robbers. Although a citizen's life was governed down to the most trivial details by a glut of statute law, ordinary police protection remained rudimentary. Ramshackle buildings, piled helter-skelter and without reasonable plan against one another, assured that every serious fire was potentially a holocaust. At the English town of Tiverton one market day in 1598, a four-hour blaze killed 50 persons and destroyed 400 houses, 300 pairs of looms, a large inventory of woolen cloth, and a number of horses. Water for drinking was hard enough to come by, to say nothing of sufficient supplies of it to fight fires. But even without disasters on the scale of the Tiverton fire, the demand for new housing was never met, despite the construction boom which marked the last decades of the century. Often enough the immigrant exchanged the mud hut in his native village for a cellar located somewhere within the confines of the city.

If he were lucky enough to have a house, it was a simple place, simply furnished—a table made of planks set upon trestles the most important piece of furniture—with little if any decoration. Outside stairways and balconies jutted into or hung precariously over unpaved streets so narrow that two carts could scarcely pass each other, streets which ended in a maze of paths and alleys and into which were casually dumped human wastes as well as butcher shop refuse of animal heads and entrails. In the empty spaces between the houses, litter and filth of all kinds accumulated, and lean, bright-eyed dogs prowled everywhere.

So bleak was sixteenth-century city life that only the most powerful inducements could have persuaded country folk to go there. In some cases it was simple desperation as peasants were dispossessed of their subsistence plots by enclosure for sheep pasturage or by an efficiency-minded landlord interested in commercial agriculture. But for others the city had a magic, a zest, a raw vitality which fascinated far more than its ugliness depressed. A gaiety prevailed there for a man who was young and strong. He reveled in "the Crowd, and Buz, and Murmurings of this great hive, the City," as Abraham Cowley expressed it.[32] He could jostle with princes, prelates, prostitutes; he could see a real bearded Jew and drink with his friends in a hundred taverns. He could go to a play or a puppet show and be enthralled by the antics of tumblers and minstrels. He could do all this and still be very poor, and perhaps once or twice in his life, even though his ordinary existence squatted amid mud and disease, he could share with thousands like himself the Renaissance splendor of the queen's arrival at Westminster to open parliament, or of the pope coming to hear a Palestrina Mass sung at St. Mary Major.

A few of the refugees who settled in the cities did exceedingly well there, and the rest found the shanty they lived in no worse than the one back on the farm. They were no worse off than the Polish and French peasants who produced fine grain for a luxury market and ate black bread themselves. One alluring thing about the city must have been the great variety of jobs available. Sudbury in Suffolk was a modest-sized town in which 1,600 adults plied forty-five different trades. The German Lutheran engraver Albrecht Dürer (d. 1528) watched admiringly a religious procession in Catholic Antwerp: "This is the order in which they went: the goldsmiths, painters, stone-cutters, silk-broiderers, sculptors, joiners, carpenters, mariners, fishermen, butchers, leather-workers, cloth-weavers, bakers, tailors, shoemakers and all kinds of artisans, also many craftsmen and dealers necessary to the maintenance of life. There were also," he added by way of after-thought, "shopkeepers and merchants."[33] Thomas Stapleton (d. 1598), the English Catholic divine, was in a less tolerant mood when he

32. In a poem called "The Garden." Cowley died in 1667.
33. Quoted in Conrad Huet, *The Land of Rubens* (London, 1888), p. 109.

mocked the Protestant ministry and thus provided an alliterated list of occupations: "And wherein, I pray you, resteth a great part of your new clergy but in butchers, cooks, catch-poles and cobblers, dyers and dawbers, . . . fishermen, gunners, harpers, innkeepers, merchants and mariners, potters, pothecaries, porters, pinners, peddlers, ruffling ruffians, saddlers, sheermen and shepherds, tilers, tinkers, trumpeters, weavers, wherry men et cet."[34] Included among the slightly more than a thousand men admitted to citizenship in Geneva between 1501 and 1536 (the year John Calvin first settled there) were 127 cobblers, 58 tailors, 55 pastry cooks, 26 notaries, 25 barbers, and representatives of more than 20 other professions.[35]

A larger city, or a seaport, would offer many more choices. In Rome the three great categories of employment were food distribution, textile manufacturing, and construction. Wine merchants operated by far the largest number of enterprises, but there were plenty of butchers, fruit sellers, pastry cooks, and fishmongers as well. Tailors and haberdashers abounded, as did carpenters, masons, and ironmongers. All these trades and businesses were small and organized along the restrictive lines developed by the medieval guilds. Their two major concerns remained service of a local market and protection of themselves from the evils of competition. Old habits and regulations survived: apprentices still had to serve a master for up to ten years, and young women, except spinsters, were excluded from the system altogether. Particular tradesmen still had to locate in particular sections of the city; tanners and curriers did so for aesthetic and hygienic reasons, while goldsmiths, chandlers, and others followed suit out of habit and convenience. But in an era of inflation the guilds had lost control of prices, just as they had lost their political independence, in most instances, to the territorial prince. The prince's friend, the entrepreneur, who ignored the guild organization and hired cottage labor with which he supplied tools and raw materials, was already on the scene, and the joint stock company was not far off. It may have been that at least in France the guilds flourished as they never had in medieval times. But they did so under the aegis of royal absolutism; they became a tool by which the crown, and not the guild masters, could fix prices and wages and thus attempt

34. Thomas Stapleton, *A Counterblast to M. Hornes Vayne Blast* . . . (Louvain, 1567), fol. 484.
35. E. William Monter, *Calvin's Geneva* (New York, 1967), p. 5.

to fashion a genuinely national economic policy. So it was that when restless French journeymen went on strike or occasionally rioted they had to account to the king's army.[36]

Most cities either thrived or wilted for predictable economic reasons. Madrid was a notable exception in that it grew after 1560 simply because Philip II established his court and his bureaucratic apparatus there. Barcelona, by contrast, had almost withered away, its once busy docks and shipyards grimly silent and its workers reduced to a diet of coarse bread and garlic. So depleted was Barcelona of artisans that in 1562, when the king determined to build a great naval base there, he had to bring in technicians from Genoa. As the long depression of Catalonian trade eventually emptied Barcelona, so competition from Dutch carriers and English cloth merchants brought about the disintegration of the once rich and powerful Hanseatic League. With their monopoly in the Baltic trade broken, the proud Hanse towns withdrew into the narrower ambit of inland German commerce and watched with dismay the rise of bustling new centers like Hamburg and Danzig.

The key was always the same; commerce meant much, industry meant little. Or rather commercial activity had reached a kind of maturity while industry and finance were still in their infancy. A factory which employed more than a dozen men under one roof was still a rarity. Exchange, and the means of exchange, lay at the root of all. Venice sold in the Levant its own silks and cloths indeed, but also woolens and velvets from Florence, various textiles from Flanders, Milanese fustians and English canvas, and linens, hardware, and copper pots from Germany.

But all these goods moved with tortuous slowness; the ships that carried them were no bigger and traveled no faster than before. No technological breakthrough in transport and communication accompanied the expanding commercial endeavors. This was true of inland trade as well, and as a result many towns flourished or survived because they were a convenient distance from one another. The same old caravans followed the same old routes, and mules still needed rest and muleteers diversion. So, for example, a chain composed of links a leisurely day's journey long bound together Italian cities from Ancona to Milan, by way of Rimini, through Forlì and Bologna to Modena,

36. John U. Nef, *Industry and Government in France and England, 1540–1640* (Ithaca, 1957), pp. 14, 22.

Parma, and Piacenza. A similar axis of mutual dependence could be discerned in northern Spain; it moved through Medina del Campo (site of great market fairs) through Valladolid (capital of Castile until 1560) and Burgos (center of the wool trade) to the sea at Bilbao. These towns thrived or faltered together by a dynamism which had little to do with technology and much with their accessibility to each other.

5. RELIGIOUS REVIVAL

But life is never, after all, only getting and spending. Another powerful dynamism was at work during the latter part of the sixteenth century.[37] A vast religious revival spread among the peoples of Europe and gave a peculiar cast to their social, political, and economic concerns. Religion became an enthusiasm which made the recently fashionable unbelief and neopaganism seem anachronistic. Not that Christian people were less sinners than before or that they shrugged off the heightened sense of individual worth which the Renaissance left as its proud testament. They appear rather to have been struck more forcefully perhaps than ever before by the dread reality of sin and by the unique healing offered to the troubled conscience of every individual by the gospel of Jesus.

Martin Luther contributed more than anyone else to this massive change of heart. Whatever his gaucheries and inconsistencies, however much his vulgarity and philosophical nihilism outraged fastidious people like Erasmus, Luther's basic insight proved to be immensely persuasive. We all stand, he said, naked and helplessly corrupt before the pure white throne of God, but some of us, thanks to God's mercy, will escape the retribution we deserve by wrapping the bloody mantle of Christ's infinite merits around our diseased souls. We do this by a splendid, total act of faith that God's son did indeed die for our sins. This conviction is no mere intellectual apprehension, but a plunging of the whole person into the dark mystery of the cross. It is a grappling of oneself to Christ, as Jacob grappled with the angel; it is the complete giving of myself so that I no longer live but Christ lives in me.

True religion therefore consists in this conversion and, once it has

---

37. Indeed, Hubert Lüthy, *From Calvin to Rousseau* (New York, 1970), would argue that though the Reformation did not foster capitalism, it was a lesser obstacle than the Counter Reformation, which was an outright totalitarian reaction. This is roughly the same position (though advanced on different grounds) of Hugh Trevor-Roper's much printed essay, "Religion, the Reformation and Social Change," *The Crisis of the Seventeenth Century* (New York, 1968).

happened, in nurturing it. Here is what the Scriptures testify to, here is the mystery St. Paul described as hidden since the foundation of the world. The vehicle of conversion is the written word of God, the sharp sword of the spirit which cuts through human evil and pretense and penetrates to the very heart of man. The wound it inflicts is the sweet confidence in God's love through Christ, which wells up into eternal life. This is justification by faith alone.

By 1559, thirteen years after Luther's death, his evangel had passed to second-generation leaders less charismatic than himself and already the sectarian wrangling—Protestantism's permanent curse—was in full swing. But quarrel bitterly as they might among themselves, the ambivalent Melanchthon, the cautious Bullinger, the cold, formal Calvin all held fast to the master's basic tenet, and by 1559 millions of people had committed themselves to Luther's vision of the Christian life. In Germany, Scandinavia, and Switzerland the acceptance was almost universal, and there was reason to think that eventually the rest of Europe would follow their lead. Not all these converts had acted out of unmixed motives, but even so nobody who had pondered the problem of evil, especially as manifested within oneself, could deny the attraction of Luther's idea. For it solved with a blunt peasant simplicity the nagging paradox of the Christian's vocation and, indeed, of human existence. "The good which I will I do not, but the evil which I will not, that I do. Unhappy man that I am, who shall deliver me from the body of this death?"[38] Good works will not deliver you, thundered Luther, neither the Mass nor the sacraments nor the hierarchical priesthood; not by obedience to law nor by regularity in devotions; neither fasts nor vows nor almsgiving; not the cult of the Virgin and not the invocation of the saints; not relics, images, pilgrimages, indulgences, neither theological wisdom nor penitential practices nor mystical prayer, nor indeed any of the complex apparatus of mediation between God and believer which was the mark of late medieval Catholicism. Only the gospel will deliver you, only (as a later generation of evangelicals would express it) the acceptance of Christ as your personal Savior.

The appeal of primitive Protestantism lay in its simplicity; with a stroke it swept away the tangle of theory and practice which over a thousand years had grown up within the Western church, and so it

38. St. Paul to the Romans, VII, 21–24.

freed the believer to seek out the one thing necessary. The Protestant movement was a real revolution because it effected a radical change in the view people had of their relationship to God, and this in turn drastically altered the order of religious practice. Luther's protest was against the Catholic system as such, not merely with the Catholic system shot through with corruption. He called for wholly new priorities, for a new kind of Christian experience, and it mattered little that no amount of later polemic could establish a genuine continuity between his ideas and those of the ancient church. For Lutheran justification was not a reaction to abuses which· had spoiled some imagined state of pristine Christian innocence. It was not a denial but a soaring, joyous assertion.

By the same token, that revival of Catholicism which usually goes by the name Counter Reformation cannot be adequately explained as a frightened response to the Protestant record of success, impressive as that record may have been. To be sure, the rise of a viable alternative shook the old religious order and forced on it a measure of self-criticism which it otherwise might have evaded; competition is always the best antidote for sluggishness and complacency. But, as Professor Evennett has written, "The Counter Reformation could hardly have occurred had it been no more than the hastily improvised defense of the vested interests of an archaic ecclesiastical corporation bereft of contemporary or future spiritual significance." It was rather "a powerful religious movement" which "involved . . . more than the simple reaffirmation of medieval spiritual teachings, and it eventually created a mature spirituality with clear characteristics of its own."[39]

Chronology tells part of the story. Luther was not unique among his contemporaries in pressing for a purified, personal religion, cleansed of late medieval credulity and superstition. Troubled Catholic humanists like Erasmus, More, and Jiménez protested as loudly as Luther did against the mechanistic theory of good works which had gone a long way toward turning the Church into a den of thieves. Cajetan, the learned cardinal legate who confronted Luther at Augsburg in 1518, carried the same fight to the highest councils of the Roman curia.[40]

39. H. Outram Evennett, *The Spirit of the Counter-Reformation* (Cambridge, 1968), p. 24.
40. For documents and commentary on Cajetan's reforming activities see M.-H. Laurent, *Revue Thomiste*, XVII (1934–35), 50–148.

Ignatius Loyola, only a few years younger than Luther, was a reformer too.[41] And as far as Scripture-centered Christianity was concerned, St. John Fisher knew his Bible as well as Luther did and even perhaps as well as Calvin.

The soil which produced Luther and his ideas on justification produced other serious and determined men who still remained unconvinced that scuttling the sacramental system was a necessary prelude to reform. They did not differ from Luther on the urgency of the problem. They too despised the pardoner who sold gullible peasants tickets to heaven like a butcher sold sausage. But the very simplicity which attracted so many to the new gospel put off many more. They could not accept the doctrine of total human depravity; they pointed out that faith, even in the Lutheran sense, need not exclude the salvific value of good works. They argued that the varieties of Protestantism were a hodgepodge of contradictions, inconsistent, iconoclastic, licentious. While university dons devoted learned treatises to such objections, the masses of less sophisticated Catholics raised the same questions in their own way. How can a person be mortally sinful and not mortally sinful at the same time? How can a Protestant quote St. Paul on faith and then refuse to quote St. James on works? What is the worth of this gospel freedom which encourages its adherents to smash saints' statues and to trample underfoot the sacrament of Christ's body?

The quarrel which started on the level of speculative theology ultimately affected the whole quality of life. From royal palaces to mean, back-street cottages the argument raged over the merits of *la messe* as opposed to *le prêche*. The fervor of Luther's generation grew white hot after four decades of rivalry between sacrificing priest and preaching minister. And with the struggle came, on both sides, firmer convictions, which every day made the possibility of reunion or accommodation a little more remote.

Yet Catholics and Protestants shared more perhaps than they knew. The same reckless courage inspired the martyrs on both sides, the same fanaticism drove Spanish infantrymen and Dutch sea beggars to heroic feats, even as they invoked in different accents the same God. Jesuits considered Puritans offsprings of the devil, and Puritans returned the

41. Though more of an age with Luther, Ignatius might be more conveniently compared to Calvin, as in André Favre-Dorsaz, *Calvin et Loyola* (Paris, 1951).

compliment; but Jesuits and Puritans were as one in their willingness to suffer privation and even death for the sake of a single convert. The mystic rapture of direct experience with the divine was common to the Carmelite nun in Castile and to the Moravian Anabaptist who burned his Bible lest letter triumph over spirit and intervene between him and his creator.[42] Catholics and Protestants alike were gripped by a sense of religious excitement which could lead to great holiness and also to ideological war and persecution.[43] In an atmosphere of fundamentalist revival little room was left for toleration. It was no coincidence that this era witnessed savage and irrational witch hunts.[44] It was only simple prudence for skeptics like Queen Catherine de' Medici to keep their doubts to themselves.

The most remarkable physical expression of this fierce new Christian earnestness was the revitalization of Rome: *Roma rediviva*—Rome reborn out of the whirlwind of the Reformation and the wreckage of the imperial sack of 1527. In 1550 a huddle of unkempt ruins, half-deserted and still justifying the medieval jibe that every Roman was a cowherd, a jungle of weeds and broken pillars where bandits prowled at will, Rome by 1600 was described by an awed German tourist as "this very beautiful city which deserves to be called the capital of the world." It had become again at any rate a religious capital in a way that Wittenberg and Geneva could never be. Sacramental Catholicism, which for a moment had seemed destined to disappear, was once more visibly enshrined in the splendid churches and palaces and fountains of Rome. Here was an outward sign of an inner reality: the vibrancy which had survived the persecutions of the Caesars and the vanity of the Borgias had asserted itself once more, ready to give character and direction to a new age.

42. J. W. Allen, *A History of Political Thought in the Sixteenth Century* (London, 1957), p. 39.

43. The comparison between sixteenth-century religious conflict and twentieth-century ideological conflict is interestingly made by Sir John Neale, "The Elizabethan Age," The Creighton Lecture, University of London, 1950, in *Essays in Elizabethan History* (New York, 1958), pp. 21 ff. A more recent discussion is Michael Walzer, *The Revolution of the Saints* (Cambridge, Mass., 1966).

44. There has been a great deal of scholarly interest recently in sixteenth- and seventeenth-century witchcraft. See, e.g., Alan Macfarlane, *Witchcraft in Tudor and Stuart England* (London, 1970), and E. William Monter, ed., *European Witchcraft* (New York, 1969). Much of this work is by way of revision of Hugh Trevor-Roper's "The European Witch-craze of the Sixteenth and Seventeenth Century," many times reprinted since 1956.

Chapter Two

THE CATHOLIC PEACE

THE two churchmen who eyed one another warily across the table had come together to discuss informally terms for ending a war which, by the time they met in May, 1558, had been going on for more than sixty years. Charles of Guise, the Cardinal of Lorraine, represented the Most Christian King of France, while Antoine Perrenot, Bishop of Arras—soon to be known to all of Europe as Cardinal Granvelle—spoke for his Catholic majesty of Castile, Aragon, Naples, Burgundy, and all the Indies. Granvelle himself was a Burgundian, born not a hundred miles from the Guise estates around Joinville, but, as he once wryly observed, service to the Hapsburg world empire had deprived him of a real homeland: "I am from everywhere, *Je suis de partout,*" he said.[1]

Lorraine at thirty-four was seven years younger and far less experienced than Granvelle, who had literally grown up in the diplomatic service of the Emperor Charles V. But in native guile and toughness the two were admirably matched, and under other circumstances they might have engaged in a fascinating personal duel. Sober reality, however, decreed otherwise. The fact was that the long Hapsburg-Valois conflict had to stop because neither side was strong enough to continue it. The fact further was that though both royal combatants had testified to exhaustion by declaring public bankruptcy, France's position was the more precarious and so Lorraine's hand was the weaker—this despite some recent French victories won by Lorraine's brother, the Duke of Guise. On the desperate and mutual need for peace the two ambassadors had little to argue about.

In the course of their conversations Granvelle warned Lorraine that two noblemen, high in the councils of the French king and at the moment Spanish prisoners of war, were in communication with the Calvinist heretics in Geneva. This bit of information underscored another reason why the sovereigns were anxious to end a war which

1. Henri Hauser and Augustin Renaudet, *Les Débuts de l'Âge Moderne,* 4th ed. (Paris, 1956), p. 603.

had begun before either of them was born. The spread of Protestantism within their own dominions had frightened them both with the specter of the kind of sectarian strife which had ravaged Germany for the past generation. Geneva threatened throne as well as altar, Granvelle reminded Lorraine, who needed no persuasion on the point; he and his royal master had already pledged themselves to the eradication of French Protestantism. Heresy and internal subversion, the ambassadors agreed as they parted, could be thwarted only if the Catholic powers came to a peaceful settlement.

More formal negotiations followed in October, 1558, but a month later they were in suspension again when the childless Queen Mary of England died and left the succession to her half-sister, the Princess Elizabeth. The English as Spain's allies in the war had to be party to any peace treaty, but no one could be certain what would happen to that frail alliance now that Philip II's devoted Catholic wife was dead. The King of Spain for his part was eager to maintain it, eager enough to let it be known that he would consider marrying the new English queen, provided she remained true to the Catholic religion and, more important, provided she kept her island kingdom securely within the Hapsburg orbit. During the first months of her reign Elizabeth smiled a virginal smile and said nothing.

So the negotiations lapsed while Philip waited to see what the winds from England would blow. He was not, however, prepared to wait forever. Elizabeth meanwhile found herself in a dilemma. She wanted to initiate a policy independent of Spain, but, like all Englishmen high and low, she also wanted Calais back. That channel port, the vestige of England's once vast French possessions, had fallen to the Duke of Guise in January, 1558, and its restoration—a matter more of national pride than of utility—was the queen's sole interest in the peace arrangements. Without Philip II's support, however, Calais could not be regained, and therefore Elizabeth had to choose. The "first and principal point," one of her advisers told her, "is to think upon the peace"; it would be idle "to stick upon Calais as though we had the Frenchmen at commandment." We are not likely to achieve "such agreement as we desire," so we must take "such as we can get."[2] It was good advice;

2. Wallace MacCaffrey, *The Shaping of the Elizabethan Regime* (Princeton, 1968), p. 46.

England needed peace and disentanglement from Spain more than she needed Calais.

By February, 1559, Philip was satisfied that Elizabeth meant to embark on a policy of her own, even though he could not have known yet how distasteful to him that policy would eventually be. From that moment Calais ceased to interest him and ceased to pose an obstacle to the settlement which he and the King of France were determined at all costs to reach. The Spanish plenipotentiaries arrived at Cateau-Cambrésis on February 5, their French counterparts came the next day, and the disgruntled English trailed in a few days later. Cateau-Cambrésis was neutral territory, an independent enclave on the French-Netherlands frontier, ruled by the Bishop of Cambrai, who (as the name suggests) had a castle there. It was a cold, drab, half-ruined barn of a place, the very discomfort of which perhaps hastened the deliberations.[3]

The glittering Spanish and French delegations were headed formally by the dukes of Alba and Montmorency, both great magnates and veteran field commanders, though Alba—a curious mixture of Renaissance cultivation and feudal hauteur—had by far the better military record. As the long-time Constable of France, Montmorency had led the French armies to a remarkable number of defeats, the latest at St. Quentin in 1557, which had resulted in his own capture by the Spaniards. But the substantive discussions at Cateau-Cambrésis went on mostly between Lorraine and Granvelle, and not only because they spoke fluent Latin: they also enjoyed a higher measure of their respective sovereigns' confidence than the soldiers did. Alba accepted this latter circumstance with a cynical shrug: "Kings use men like oranges," he said; "they squeeze out the juice and then throw them away." The old constable, by contrast, took with ill grace the ascendancy of the Cardinal of Lorraine; he hated the upstart Guises and their brilliance and ambition, and in the young cardinal's smooth, confident manner he detected the eclipse of the house of Montmorency.

The small and lackluster English delegation—a bishop and two second-rank privy councillors—was a sign that Queen Elizabeth did not expect much at Cateau-Cambrésis. Nor did she, after six weeks of haggling, get much more than a dubious face-saving device. By a protocol of April 2 the French promised to restore Calais to England

3. See J. H. Elliott, *Europe Divided, 1559–1598* (New York, 1968), pp. 13 ff.

within eight years or pay an adequate indemnity. No one for a moment believed they would do either.

The Treaty of Cateau-Cambrésis between France and Spain was signed the following day, April 3, 1559.[4] To the extent that control of Italy was what the war had been about, the Spaniards were clearly the victors. Except for a temporary garrison in Turin and one or two other places, the treaty definitively expelled the French from the Italian peninsula. They had to renounce their claims on Milan and to evacuate Savoy and Piedmont, which they had occupied since 1536. Corsica they returned to Spain's ally, the Republic of Genoa. Not only did the Spanish keep Naples and Milan; they also tightened their hold elsewhere. France now formally recognized Spanish-dominated regimes in Florence and Savoy-Piedmont. Indeed, hardly an independent state remained in Italy except the papacy and Venice, and even they had to regard the Spanish colossus in a somber new light. After three generations the day had gone when wily popes and doges could tinker with the balance of power by summoning France into Italy to fight against Spain.

France was compensated somewhat by adjustments on her northern and eastern frontiers. She recovered Calais of course and also the territory along the Somme which had been lost during the St. Quentin campaign. She kept as well the three imperial cities of Metz, Toul, and Verdun, seized some years earlier, despite the complaints of the Emperor Ferdinand, Philip II's uncle, who had not been invited to Cateau-Cambrésis. But if the French had worried about encirclement before the treaty their cause for concern was no less afterward. On the south the Spaniards stood at the Pyrenees, on the north in the Netherlands, on the east in Burgundy. Savoy, to the southeast, was now in the hands of the ablest of Philip II's allies, Duke Emmanuel Philbert. The bitter observation about the treaty by one highly placed Frenchman—"By a stroke of the pen we have surrendered all our conquests of thirty years"—was understandable if hardly justified by the overall performance of French arms. Yet this much was certain: the provisions of Cateau-Cambrésis guaranteed that France and Spain would confront each other again.

Meanwhile, however, the Catholic peace gave time and breath for

4. For text and analysis see Alphonse de Ruble, *Le Traité du Cateau-Cambrésis* (Paris, 1889).

other business, chiefly, as things turned out, for the internal consolidation of the emerging nation-states. This was a momentous task, and
everywhere the dynastic politicians who tackled it met the same three
obstacles: chronic insolvency, an unruly aristocracy, and fierce religious
divisions. Of these the third was the most obvious to the signatories at
Cateau-Cambrésis, who pledged to support the summoning of a
general council and to suppress heresy at home. But in fact all three
factors intertwined, differently indeed in different places, and yet
somehow always the same. The way the kings dealt with this perplexing tangle is the story of the next sixty years.

I. THE PECULIAR POLITICS OF DYNASTY

One who lives in the era of mass democracy finds it difficult to
appreciate that the modern nation-states were midwifed by a gaggle of
kings and queens. Yet so it happened: dynasty was the mechanism by
which peoples were organized into linguistic and geographical groups,
the instrument whereby governmental programs and policies became
genuinely national. The royal family of the late sixteenth century—
Hapsburg, Valois, Tudor, and a dozen others of lesser fame—was the
link between Europe's feudal, fragmented past and her bureaucratic,
bourgeois future.

This evolutionary process was in midterm during the years immediately after Cateau-Cambrésis. None of the kings yet dared say, "L'état,
c'est moi," but neither did any of their subjects dare say that their
primacy was merely one of honor. Their power was real, even if it was
ill-defined, often uncertain, and never as great as they claimed—one
thinks of the imperial sovereignty boasted of in 1534 by Henry VIII,
who was almost toppled from his throne a few years later by a ragtag
band of rebellious monks and farmers.[5] But more important than his
overblown pretensions was the success Henry scored in surviving that
crisis. Out of such triumphs the strength of kingship was forged.

The process of royal aggrandizement was rough and uneven; it
jerked forward two steps only to fall back one. The theoretical justifi-

5. The first of the succession acts (25 Henry VIII, c. 22) speaks of "the imperial
crown" and "the lawful kings and emperors of this realm." See Henry Gee and William
Hardy, eds., *Documents Illustrative of English Church History* (London, 1896), pp.
232 ff. The rebellion called the Pilgrimage of Grace occurred in 1536.

cation for it remained unclear. Some people thought a king ruled by the will of God, others thought by the will of the community, and still others, reflecting an older tradition, wondered why a king should not live within the revenues of his own lands the way other barons did, why a king should function out of the reach of the estates of the realm. But by the time the Age of the Baroque began, certain matters, for good or ill, had been settled: feudalism as a political force was finished and as an economic system largely modified; customary law had gone into eclipse behind the bright sun of the king's statutes and the king's courts; and the right of coercion—government's ultimate high trump—was snatched from baron, bishop, and independent town and placed securely in the hand of the king.

Everywhere the king, the dynastic dictator (who in some places might be titled duke or count rather than king), came into his own during the years after Cateau-Cambrésis. What the mind boggles at after four centuries is the very idea of dynasty, the notion that political power, like original sin, should pass by the seed of one generation to the next. But so it was universally agreed, and the exceptions—a celibate pope or a Polish king elected by the lords whose creature he was[6] —only proved the rule. There attached to the king's person a supremacy and even, sometimes, a sanctity which had nothing to do with his mental or moral gifts or his physical prowess. What mattered was that his blood and marrow had grown out of the seed sprung legitimately from the loins of his father, the old king.

Everywhere the king led the way toward the effective centralization of political function, toward the achievement of the unitary state, with its ideals of ethnic and linguistic uniformity and its obsession about natural boundaries, so that by 1610 virtually every bureaucracy in Europe was stronger than it had been two generations earlier. The intellectual community—theologians, littérateurs, Roman lawyers—advanced involved arguments to prove why providence or nature had determined a king's eminence. But one suspects that much of the theorizing came after the fact, resulted, that is, less from philosophical conviction than from the concrete needs of increasingly sophisticated societies for more efficient methods of government. The king could keep the peace, sustain the economy, build the roads, punish the male-

6. See P. Skwarczynski in *The New Cambridge Modern History*, III (Cambridge, 1968), pp. 381 ff.

factors better than the conglomeration of disparate authorities which had dominated Europe for nearly a thousand years. And so the great mass of men said to one another,

> "Upon the king! let us our lives, our souls,
> Our debts, our careful wives,
> Our children and our sins lay on the king."[7]

A politics set within a dynastic framework was bound to have some distinct peculiarities. Fundamental to them all was the overriding importance of individual personality. The kind of man the king was, his particular strengths and weaknesses, his habits, his preferences—in short, the accidents associated with his character—were factors of the highest political significance. That Elizabeth I was penurious while Henry III was extravagant profoundly affected the course of events in England and France respectively. And how different the history of the late sixteenth century would have been had Philip II caroused more and prayed less.

Impersonal forces were of course always powerfully at work. Inflation, for example, never ceased during these years to shape the lives of men and the destiny of nations. But economic policy, like all political decisions in the dynastic system, depended almost whimsically upon the person who formulated it. It reflected the king's own temperament and experience to a degree that strikes later generations as capricious. What he decided to do about wages and prices, or indeed about anything else, stemmed not only from his intelligence but also from the state of his digestive tract or of his love life. Foreign affairs, no less than domestic concerns, gave evidence of this condition. Diplomacy amounted to personal persuasion among royal fraternity brothers. Ambassadors traveled from court to court not so much representing nations as bearing confidences, gifts, and sometimes ultimatums from one dynasty to another.[8]

Those courts glittered with calculated magnificence. "In pompous ceremonies a secret of government doth much consist," said one shrewd observer of the Elizabethan scene, in which "the splendors of ritual, banished from the churches, were lavished on the sovereign."[9]

7. *Henry V*, Act IV, Scene 1.

8. Garrett Mattingly, *Renaissance Diplomacy* (Penguin ed., Baltimore, 1964), pp. 181 ff.

9. MacCaffrey, *Elizabethan Regime*, p. 179.

No one who saw the French king "reclining in an ocean of cushions" and surrounded by bowing and scraping noblemen could doubt the awesome finality of royal power.[10] Court ritual was a sacrament designed not only to signify the monarch's unique eminence but also to effect it. However short of money he might be, a king could not forgo gorgeous robes and decorations, sumptuous entertainments, and a whole array of elaborate and conspicuous consumption, because these formed the outward sign linked indissolubly to the inner reality of power.

In theory he was accountable to no one, though in practice this was seldom so. He could not ignore the organs of public opinion, and if he was wise he did not try to. Occasionally he had to bow to the manifest will of the masses, as Henry IV did spectacularly in 1594 when he became a Catholic. The masses, however, were by and large inarticulate, and the opinion with which a king had to deal was usually that of the upper classes in their parliaments and estates general. It is wrong to suppose that their interests were consistently at variance with his. But when a clash between them did come, sometimes he could force them to do what he wanted, sometimes he could circumvent them. More often he had to cajole and even compromise with them. A permanent tension existed in this regard within the royal office itself: though like every putative dictator the sixteenth-century king was basically a popular leader who protected the people against the aristocracy of wealth and talent, yet, given the realities of communication and transportation at the time, no monarchy could function without the cooperation of the local magnates.

The intensely personal nature of dynastic government heightened the importance of those who had ready access to the king. This was especially apparent if he were a child or an imbecile, in which case a formal regency had to be set up to rule in his name. It was scarcely less so when the king was in poor health or of a vacillating turn of mind or simply lazy. Then inevitably would come a parade of favorites competing with one another, more or less indecorously, for a place at the king's right hand and for the authority that went with it. In terms of influence the members of the royal family were at an obvious advantage, though a kind of sibling rivalry seemed often to reduce a king's brothers to positions of decorative insignificance. Similarly, while a

10. Philippe Erlanger, *The Age of Courts and Kings* (New York, 1967), p. 16.

wife might enjoy considerable influence, a mistress was likely to enjoy more, because the king's father had chosen the former for him and he had chosen the latter for himself. Diane of Poitiers, Henry II's mistress, was a force to be reckoned with in French politics for a decade, and, among other things, she saw to it that her lover performed his conjugal duties with his wife in order to assure the continuance of the Valois line.

Marriage and childbirth were enormously important in a political scheme of things based upon blood relationship. A king needed many children, and especially many sons, to feel secure in his office, because he was but one linked in a family chain whose overall strength guarded his country from the hazards of an uncertain succession and civil war. The more fertile the queen the better, because the high incidence of infant and childhood mortality made no exception for royal nurseries.

International alliances and peace treaties were also agreements between dynasties, so it seemed natural that they should be sealed by royal couplings. Little attention was paid to the inclinations of those most directly involved, since marriage for a prince was a matter of *Realpolitik,* not an affair of the heart. Mary Queen of Scots was betrothed to the French dauphin when she was five years old. After Cateau-Cambrésis, Philip II, twice a widower, married a French princess half his age whom he had never seen; but every system has its happy accidents, and the King of Spain came to love the beautiful Elizabeth of Valois as he loved no one else in his long life, and so did the Spanish people, who called her Isabel de la Paz, because she was the living sign that the wars with France at last had ended.[11]

Every king had his privy council, which usually included various factions and a limited amount of party spirit. From these nobles and lawyers the king could hear divergent opinions on policy questions, though the ultimate decision remained with him and councillors as councillors were never anything but his creatures. The same was the case with that other ideal instrument of personal rule, the secretary of state. Throughout the sixteenth century this officer of the royal household took on ever increasing responsibilities, as the careers of William Cecil and Antonio Pérez, to mention only the two most famous, amply demonstrate. The reason is not hard to see: in the workaday routine no

11. Braudel, *La Méditerranée et le monde méditerranéen à l'époque de Philippe II* (Paris, 1966), II, 327.

one saw the king more frequently than the secretary, no one stood in a more advantageous position to offer advice, no one was more powerful in the burgeoning bureaucracy than he who supervised the royal correspondence. He had to be a man of some learning, particularly in languages. For this reason, as well as because of the chronic tension between the monarchy and the high aristocracy, he came not from the nobility but from the bourgeoisie or the gentry.[12] Noble status was often his reward, by way of judicial office or the purchase of land. His powers, seldom defined, were varied and flexible, because they depended on the whim of his master.[13]

For even if one can discern in council and secretariat the seeds of the modern cabinet system, the realities of dynastic politics did not yet admit any executive initiative outside the ambit of the monarch's personal will. The maxim of the Roman law—"Quod placet principi habet vigorem legis"[14]—may have been many times breached but not by those in the king's immediate entourage. In 1560, when he had to leave the court for a diplomatic mission in Scotland, Cecil was terrified lest his rivals take advantage of his absence and undermine his influence with the young queen. Elizabeth, however, recognized from the beginning her secretary's incomparable abilities and never dreamed of doing without him. But for any reason or for no reason she might have crushed him and cast him aside, as Philip II did Pérez—such was the relationship between them.[15]

The half-century after Cateau-Cambrésis was the crucial testing time of monarchy. Given the limitations that all flesh is heir to, as well as the magnitude of the problems they faced, the wonder is not that the kings did not do better; the wonder is that they survived at all. But survive they did, and more, they put together the essentials of a regime that would last down to the great democratic revolutions. They deserve perhaps more sympathy than historians customarily offer them, for, as

12. The education of the nobles was such that few posts which demanded technical knowledge were open to them. "The non-nobles did not take the judicial posts from us," said Tavennes, "it is ignorance that keeps them from us." See Davis Bitton, *The French Nobility in Crisis, 1560–1640* (Stanford, 1969), p. 47.

13. See Nicola Sutherland, *The French Secretaries of State in the Age of Catherine de' Medici* (London, 1962).

14. "What the prince wills has the force of law."

15. Conyers Read, *Mr. Secretary Cecil and Queen Elizabeth* (London, 1956), pp. 166 ff.

Francis Bacon observed, "it is a miserable state of mind to have few things to desire and many things to fear, and yet that commonly is the case with kings."

2. THE MERCHANT'S DAUGHTER

Henry II, a man of dark moods and occasional bursts of enthusiasm, wanted to celebrate the Catholic peace of Cateau-Cambrésis by launching a Franco-Spanish crusade against the heresy nest in Geneva or, perhaps, against England. Philip II, his erstwhile enemy and, by virtue of the same treaty, future son-in-law, patiently explained to him that the bankruptcy and internal disarray of their respective dominions, which had made it impossible for them to keep fighting each other, also ruled out military adventures against a third party. Henry reluctantly acquiesced and contented himself by sending several prominent French Protestants to the Bastille and by planning the elaborate festivals to be held in connection with the wedding of Philip to his daughter Elizabeth. In the midst of these revels Henry was cruelly injured—a lance splinter pierced his eye—and on July 10, 1559, he died.[16]

In accord with the iron laws of dynasty he was succeeded by his eldest son, a dull, sickly boy of fifteen. Francis II was legally of age to rule without a regency, but his physical and emotional immaturity guaranteed that the court factions, which a robust and fully grown king had trouble enough controlling, would enter into savage rivalry to capture him and the royal power. It is well to remember that these factions were composed not of effete hangers-on but of barons powerful in their own right, who with their vast estates and men-at-arms represented competing reservoirs of feudal strength across the country. Henry II's hand on them had been firm if sometimes dilatory. Such firmness would not exert itself in France again for thirty years. Meantime eight discernible civil wars would be fought, and disorder, often amounting to anarchy, would prevail in between. These struggles are usually called the Wars of Religion, but they could just as well be called the wars of the factions.

Of the three groups prominent at the court of Francis II the bloc led by Francis, Duke of Guise, and his brother Charles, the Cardinal of

16. Hauser and Renaudet, *L'Âge Moderne,* pp. 545 f.

Lorraine, was the strongest.[17] Both these superbly gifted and ruthlessly ambitious men had enjoyed high favor during the late king's reign, and they had earned it. In the recent wars, otherwise marked by unrelieved disaster to French arms, the duke had scored impressive victories at Metz and Calais. The cardinal meanwhile had proved himself a capable administrator and financier and even something of a states-man. The Guise cut an impressive figure with their rugged, blond good looks, their energy and charm. And they made an excellent team: the duke followed the cardinal's lead most of the time, out of respect for his younger brother's subtle intelligence, while the cardinal, more astute than the duke but not nearly so brave or popular, always revered his brother as head of the family.[18]

More than talent and past service, however, led the young king to place himself in the hands of the Guise faction. His child-wife, the legendary Mary Queen of Scots, was a niece of the duke and the cardinal. The king had for her a doglike devotion, as though her graceful beauty compensated somehow for his own addled wits and stunted body, and he gladly left the work and trouble of governing the realm to Mary's able uncles. They seized the mandate with an alacrity which soon provoked the murmur around court that the arrogant cardinal thought himself pope and king in one. For a little span of time he was, and not till his brother was murdered did he doubt that he and his family could solve the problems of the nation and, if need be, of the universe.[19]

A flatterer once explained that the family emblem—the double-barred cross of Lorraine—meant that the Guise were destined to die twice for Christ, once in France and again as crusaders in the Holy Land. The clan's legion of enemies retorted that the device really meant that Christ was crucified twice, by the Jews and then by the

17. For a sympathetic though superficial treatment, see Henry Sedgwick, *The House of Guise* (New York, 1938).

18. Though restricted in ambit, still by far the best study of Lorraine is H. O. Evennett, *The Cardinal of Lorraine and the Council of Trent* (London, 1930).

19. Professor Trevor-Roper in his much debated essay "The General Crisis of the Seventeenth Century" alleges that the Guise provide an example of "the empires of per-sonal patronage" which subverted the monarchy. This typically hasty judgment over-looks the position of magnates like the Guise as survivals of feudal power anxious to accommodate themselves (and profit politically thereby) to the new centralization. See Hugh Trevor-Roper, *The European Witch Craze . . . and Other Essays* (New York, 1969), pp. 65 ff.

Guise. Ultimately the duke and the cardinal were judged largely on the basis of sectarian allegiance. To French Catholics they were champions of the true faith threatened by heretical malevolence; to Protestants they were diabolical persecutors, and Duke Francis, according to one Calvinist spokesman, stood as the worst enemy the gospel ever had.

A consideration of the French religious wars raises the large question as to the degree that leaders on both sides exploited popular fervor as a means of advancing their factional objectives. A precise answer is difficult and perhaps impossible, since it presumes a distinction between politics and religion which most sixteenth-century men were not prepared to make. The opportunism of Anthony of Navarre may have been clear enough and also the lofty, unselfish zeal of Coligny. As for the Guise, for whom heresy and rebellion coalesced into a single enemy, the measure of calculation in their religious policy is hard to measure. In any case, they were not fanatics. The Gallican Church for which the duke cheerfully spilled heretical blood involved commitment as much to a cultural heritage as to a supernatural idea, and he never lost the grand seigneur's contempt for Catholic mobs bent on pillage and murder. The cardinal, for all his credentials as a Counter Reformation churchman, remained an exceedingly supple theologian, more ready to discuss doctrine with Protestants than with popes and councils.

The ascendancy of the Guise over Francis II left the other two great factions seething with frustration and envy.[20] This was particularly the case with the princes of the blood to whom tradition gave a special place in the councils of the French monarchy. These Bourbon cousins of the king, descended as he was from St. Louis, stood next in line for the throne should the Valois family die out. In 1559, however, such an eventuality appeared unlikely, since Francis II had three younger brothers who among them could be expected to produce a satisfactory number of heirs. Of the three Bourbon brothers, one was a cardinal, another a king, the third a prince, and none of them had the talent to match his title. The eldest, "the first prince of the blood," was Anthony, who had married the queen of the tiny Pyrenees principality of Navarre and was thus a king, though not one of much intrinsic consequence. Indeed, the resources of the Bourbon lands in central and southern France counted for more than Navarre, especially since the

---

20. See Jean Mariéjol, *La Réforme et la Ligue* (Paris, 1911). This is Vol. VI, Part I, of Ernest Lavisse, *Histoire de France depuis les origines jusquà la Révolution*.

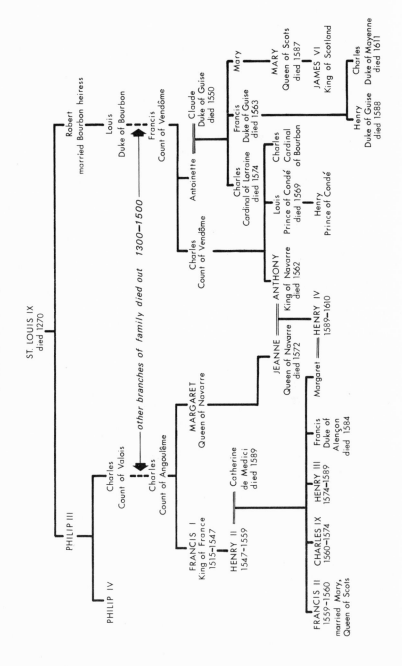

VALOIS, BOURBON and GUISE

ST. LOUIS IX
died 1270

PHILIP III

PHILIP IV

Charles
Count of Valois

Charles
Count of Angoulême

other branches of family died out 1300—1500

Robert
married Bourbon heiress

Louis
Duke of Bourbon

Francis
Count of Vendôme

Charles
Count of Vendôme

Antoinette

Claude
Duke of Guise
died 1550

Mary

MARY
Queen of Scots
died 1587

JAMES VI
King of Scotland

Charles
Cardinal of Lorraine
died 1574

Francis
Duke of Guise
died 1563

Charles
Cardinal
of Bourbon

Charles
Duke of Mayenne
died 1611

Henry
Duke of Guise
died 1588

Louis
Prince of Condé
died 1569

Henry
Prince of Condé

MARGARET
Queen of Navarre

FRANCIS I
King of France
1515—1547

HENRY II
1547—1559

Catherine
de Medici
died 1589

JEANNE
Queen of Navarre
died 1572

ANTHONY
King of Navarre
died 1562

HENRY IV
1589—1610

Margaret

FRANCIS II
1559—1560
married Mary,
Queen of Scots

CHARLES IX
1560—1574

HENRY III
1574—1589

Francis
Duke of
Alençon
died 1584

Spaniards had seized the greater part of the kingdom years before. Anthony was conniving, inconstant, mendacious, and, above all, weak —totally dedicated, as Calvin acidly put it, to the delights of Venus.[21] His brother Louis, Prince of Condé, did not neglect those pleasures, but his reckless courage and infectious gaiety gave him a charm that Anthony never had. Yet "this dainty little man," as the poet Brantôme described him, had more the gifts of a boon companion than of a party leader in a time of crisis. As for Cardinal Bourbon, he was, when compared to his colleague of Lorraine, an ecclesiastical cipher.

It cannot be said with certainty when Navarre and Condé became Calvinists, nor to what degree they were motivated by the success of the Guise in identifying the Catholic cause with themselves. Neither conversion went very deep, and in Anthony's case it was patently insincere. Religion was the ideology of the sixteenth century, the mechanism for rallying popular support, and if the Guise had staked out a claim to the Catholic ground the Calvinist ground remained. The Huguenots[22] were a small minority, but they were expanding rapidly. Condé estimated that 2,500 churches would have to be built to house Calvinist worship properly, and it was said that 50,000 Huguenots lived in Normandy alone. These numbers were tantalizing indeed to the frustrated princes of the blood. More than that, the Calvinist congregations were highly organized and disciplined. They were composed no longer just of artisans and petty shopkeepers, but they also included an increasing proportion of gentry—*les hobereaux*—to whom Calvinism appealed not only as a religion but as the cause of an embattled minority in need of secular leadership. The Bourbons did not fail to grasp the significance of this dramatic transformation of a movement which had for so long borne persecution without a thought of resistance.[23] *Les hobereaux* were gentlemen and as such had the right, denied to the general populace, to carry arms. As Huguenots they did not suffer

21. See Nancy Roelker, *Queen of Navarre, Jeanne d'Albret, 1528–1572* (Cambridge, Mass., 1968), p. 161.

22. For origin of the word "Huguenot" see Émile Léonard, *A History of Protestantism* (London, 1967), p. 113 n.

23. Calvin, like most of the reformers, imposed upon his followers the duty of passive resistance to magistrates. Rebellion against Catholic rulers was forbidden unless the princes of the blood and the estates should act to secure their just rights. This made the conversion of the Bourbons especially significant. See J. W. Allen, *A History of Political Thought in the Sixteenth Century* (London, 1928 and 1960), pp. 57 ff.

discrimination gladly, and it was no coincidence that by 1559, with so many of them, unpaid and unemployed, home from the wars, French Calvinism had taken a distinctly militant turn.

The Duke of Montmorency was also aware, painfully, of this new development. For a long time the constable had been a dominant figure at court and a power bloc had formed around him. In recent years he had leaned heavily upon his three gifted nephews, the Châtillon brothers: Odet, who was Bishop of Beauvais and a cardinal; Francis d'Andelot, a crack army commander; and Gaspard de Coligny, who, thanks to his uncle's influence, held the office of Admiral of France. The constable despised the Guise as half-foreign upstarts, and he particularly envied the duke, whose victories contrasted so sharply with his own dismal military career. At the same time he deeply suspected that the ambitions of the Bourbons were scarcely less dangerous than those of the Guise. But the religious situation infinitely complicated matters for him. "Une foi, une loi, un roi" had been the creed of the constable's honest life and the staple of his limited intelligence. To subvert the old faith in order to control the young king—as it appeared to him the Bourbons were planning—was to try to square the circle. More distressing still, and more destructive to the collection of certainties on which the Montmorency had based a generation of service to the Valois, was the fact that his nephews were not, like Navarre and Condé, toying with Calvinism but were zealous converts to it. That one of them, Coligny, was a man of rare genius, destined to be the savior of French Protestantism, did not ease the cruel dilemma in which the bluff old constable found himself.

At the eye of this hurricane of conflicting ambitions, blood feuds, and religious passions was the placid maternal figure of a forty-year-old woman. Despite nine pregnancies, despite a ripe age and a certain plumpness, Catherine de' Medici remained very alert, a great horsewoman, a great walker, a great eater. She had lovely smooth skin, and her large eyes and bulging forehead reminded people of her late kinsman, Pope Leo X.[24] But in 1559, when her eldest son came to the throne, this wife of one French king and mother of three others was still an unknown quantity. The ascendancy of the Guise seemed to

24. See Jean Mariéjol, *Catherine de Médicis* (Paris, 1920), still the standard biography. See also Lucien Romier, *Le Royaume de Catherine de Médicis* (Paris, 1922), and the popular treatment, John Neale, *The Age of Catherine de' Medici* (London, 1957).

assure that she would continue in her familiar round of domestic preoccupation.

With an arrogance typical of the Guise, Catherine's daughter-in-law once reduced her to tears by calling her "this merchant's daughter." The Florentine banking family, though perhaps parvenu by Joinville standards (the Guise liked to claim direct descent from Charlemagne), was hardly an ignoble race to have sprung from, and in any case Catherine de' Medici was related by blood to some of Europe's first families, including, ironically, the Guise. A further irony was that Mary Queen of Scots's father had not married a Guise woman until he had been rejected by Catherine.

The duke and the cardinal showed more discretion than their niece in dealing with the queen mother. The succession was never far from the mind of these dynastic politicians, and they knew well that unless Francis II fathered a son—it was by no means certain that he would or could—the crown would pass eventually to another of Catherine's large brood of children. And if Francis died young the influence of a new child-king's mother could be crucial.

So Catherine de' Medici, even while the Guise were riding at their highest, began her political career. She proved surprisingly adept at it, considering that before her husband's death the court had known her chiefly as a tasteful art patroness and a commendably fertile princess. The Cardinal of Lorraine consulted her regularly, and if he did not always follow her advice neither did he ignore it. Indeed, it might be argued that the Guise provided Catherine with a hurried course in the art of government.

Scarcely a year after his coronation Francis II was dead, Mary Queen of Scots put on widow's weeds, the Guise ascendancy was over, and Catherine de' Medici assumed the pivotal position which was to be hers until she died nearly thirty years later. In December, 1560, her second son, aged ten, became King Charles IX with his mother as regent; power, unexpected and unsought, belonged now to the merchant's daughter. And now began the spinning of a "black legend" about Catherine de' Medici which has tarnished her name no less than a similar one has tarnished that of Philip II.[25] Since Catherine managed the considerable feat of outraging all factions and both religions,

25. For a discussion of the "black legend" see Nicola Sutherland, "Catherine de Medici and the Ancien Régime" (London, 1966), a Historical Association pamphlet.

contemporary disapproval of her was almost unanimous, and hostile pamphlets have evolved into respectable history. They accused her of cruelty, atheism, deviousness, and unbridled ambition; they blamed her for the weakness and perversity of her sons; they laid at her door the blood guilt for a million Frenchmen who died in the religious wars.

The truth about Catherine, however, seems to be something else. First of all, she was a woman in politics at a time when politics possessed an intensely personal character. To Catherine service of France meant service of the dynasty, and the Valois dynasty was no abstraction: it was her children, the continuation of her flesh and spirit and of the flesh and spirit of that strange, moody man she had loved. All her life the ghost of Henry II hovered over Catherine; the courtiers sensed his presence when his widow wore black or when she retired to the mourning room carefully set aside in her Paris house. Whatever she did she needed to believe that Henry would have done the same. She saw herself as a tigress who stood alone between her cubs and the jungle of factional and religious violence. Even the worst blot on her memory—responsibility for the St. Bartholomew Massacre—testifies more to a mother's fear than to a sectarian's villainy.

To admit this, however, is not to deny that Catherine de' Medici's flaws of character and intellect intensified the troubles of the times. Instinct is not a substitute for principle, not even the noble instinct of motherhood. Catherine was shrewd rather than wise, adroit rather than thoughtful. Over and over she sacrificed the long-term gain for the short-term advantage, not out of wickedness indeed but out of an inability to grasp the difference. She was too reluctant to relax her hold on her sons, perhaps because she knew better than others of what frail stuff they were made. How dismal was the result of her protectiveness: after the retarded Francis II came the hollow and wet-eyed Charles IX, the pathetic half-man Henry III, the crooked, trivial intriguer Alençon.

Catherine had lived so long at the French court—since her marriage at fourteen—that she understood the nature of the noble factions and the need for the monarchy to balance Guise with Bourbon and Bourbon with Montmorency. She had the lesson underscored when in 1560 a plot connived at by the Bourbons (the so-called Tumult of Amboise[26]) almost succeeded in kidnapping Francis II and again a few years later when the Guise took her and Charles IX into protective custody.

26. See L.-R. Lefèvre, *Le Tumulte d'Amboise* (Paris, 1949).

But she failed to see that the religious question infinitely complicated the old game of factional equation. To counter Guise with Bourbon now involved arousing confessional strife, since the Guise captained the Catholics and the Bourbons the Protestants. At first she wildly exaggerated the numbers and power of the Huguenots, and later she estimated that they could be wiped out at one bloody blow. Catherine's own lack of religious enthusiasm lay at the root of these misjudgments. The Venetian ambassador no doubt said too much when he said the queen mother "was in no way troubled by the mysteries of the life to come." Yet it was true that without religious passion of her own Catherine remained dangerously out of touch with her generation. She never really accepted the fact that millions of her sons' subjects, Catholics and Protestants alike, were enthusiasts enough to die for their religion and to kill for it. Catherine de' Medici naïvely relied on maneuver and court intrigue in her admirably constant quest for peace, but the furies of the age and her own limitations were too much for her.

Too much for her too may have been the rickety governmental structure which she or anyone in her position had at hand to keep the peace. In the long run "the political trend was toward centralized, authoritarian state power. . . . The turbulent insurrections and revolutions of the period compelled peace-loving people to support strong rulers who could restore order."[27] But in France before a ruler could impose peace upon truculent barons and religious fanatics he had first to subdue the overgrown jungle of competing jurisdictions and to reduce the fiscal chaos to predictable order. "The kingdom of France in the sixteenth century," writes M. Doucet in a monument of understatement, "was far from forming a homogeneous whole, all the parts of which were subject to the same laws and to a consistent method of administration."[28]

It was not just the diversity of legal traditions—Roman law in the south, customary law in the north—or the different juridical prerogatives enjoyed by the various provinces, or the vast inequities in the tax structure. More difficult still for a king who aimed toward an efficient unitary state was the virtual absence of tested administrative techniques and trained personnel. Moreover, the kingly office itself suffered from a kind of identity crisis. It combined in itself, theoretically at least, func-

27. Richard Dunn, *The Age of Religious Wars, 1559–1689* (New York, 1970), p. x.
28. R. Doucet, *Les Institutions de la France au XVIe siècle* (Paris, 1948), I, 35.

tions which were at cross-purposes with each other: the king was high priest of the Gallican Church, feudal chieftain, and absolutist emperor all in one. He could in theory rule by divine-right edict, but he could not put an army in the field without his vassals; he was the anointed religious leader with special links to the clergy, but he could not, if he chose, become a Protestant.

The king governed through his officers and councils. His administrative chief of staff was the chancellor, usually a lawyer, who presided over a corps of clerks and notaries and who dispatched edicts under the royal seal.[29] At the rare meetings of the estates general he spoke for the king. Because of this and similar vicarious activities he was often the scapegoat for unpopular policy and, as such, highly expendable. A bellwether of a particular regime, he incarnated its moods as much as its policies. An instructive instance of this was Michael l'Hôpital, Catherine de' Medici's chancellor, a good man but, as M. Mariéjol observed, "cet honnête homme était un habile homme."[30]

The constable was commander in chief of the royal armies, an ambiguous post in that the royal armies still depended upon feudal levies. Montmorency, constable from 1538 until his death in 1567, outranked even princes of the blood in military matters, but the king might always create independent commands, as Henry II did for Francis of Guise. The constable's naval opposite number was the admiral who had originally been an active sailor. By the mid-sixteenth century, however, administrative and judicial duties having to do with maritime matters had converted the admiralty into a desk job, so that Coligny, an infantry colonel innocent of the sea, filled it until he died in St. Bartholomew.

More important in the long run than these gaudy officials of the royal household were the masters of requests, a cadre of between forty-five and sixty professional executives and judges—civil lawyers mostly and a few bishops—who weaved their way throughout the texture of the king's administration. Theoretically subject to the chancellor, they nevertheless acted with unprecedented independence; they were like royal commissars who brought the king's bureaucracy to remote *gouvernements* all over France. The very vagueness of their charge—

29. See Hélène Michaud, *Le Grand Chancellerie et les Ecritures Royales au seizième siècle* (Paris, 1967).

30. Mariéjol, *La Réforme,* p. 20.

circuit justices, tax assessors, troubleshooters—made them ideal instruments for breaking down the formalities of feudalism. Mobile, astute, servants of no interest but the king's, they were the shadowy ancestors of the intendants and prefects of later times.

The masters of requests had seats on various of the royal councils. These bodies, however, were in such rapid transition during the late sixteenth century that even knowledgeable contemporaries had difficulty in delimiting them precisely or in discerning exactly their particular functions. The basic conciliar institution—called variously *conseil du roi, conseil privé, conseil étroit, conseil d'état*—ranged in size between thirty and sixty members, always including the great lords and prelates (thus all six French cardinals in 1559 were councillors). Its composition attempted to reflect and so in some measure control national antagonisms. "The conflict between Montmorency and Guise, between Catholics and Protestants, . . . was fought out in the council chamber at the same time as on the battlefield."[31] This large council was subdivided by specialized function into groups like the *conseil des parties* (judicial) and the *conseil des finances*. Ultimately there emerged a compact committee to attend to general policy, foreign relations, and indeed anything of interest to the king; this was the *conseil des affaires,* and it was the genuinely powerful, the real privy, council.

Though the king might expect subservience and even servility from his various councils, the same could not be said of those other organs of royal jurisdiction, the parlements of the realm. These eight sovereign courts—not "parliaments" in the sense of legislative bodies—guarded the shadowy Gallican constitution and its *lois fondamentales,* and though their power was theoretically only an extension of that of the crown, the parlements saw themselves as charged to maintain the ancient laws of the kingdom even, if need be, against the king. Indeed, the oldest and most prestigious of them, the Parlement of Paris,[32] enjoyed a kind of negative veto, in that no edict or statute could take effect until "registered"—formally accepted—by the parlement. This gave the 180-odd Paris *parlementaires* enormous power when they chose to use it, and no king dared leave the president of the parlement

31. Doucet, *Les Institutions,* I, 137.

32. For a recent analysis see J. H. Sherman, *The Parlement of Paris* (London, 1969). More useful on this subject is Nancy Roelker, *The Paris of Henry of Navarre* (Cambridge, Mass., 1958), a translation of and commentary on the work of a distinguished *parlementaire.*

off the royal council. It would be wrong, however, to suppose that king and parlements were constantly at odds; in fact, the *parlementaires* were consistently royalist in their sympathies, and Paris's veto, though at times a nuisance, could also serve the king's purpose. Thus, since no papal documents could be promulgated in France without parlement's registration, the king had at hand a mechanism to exclude his only possible rival for control of the Gallican church.

At Orléans, in December, 1560, the estates general met for the first time in seventy-six years. That the king (or rather the Guise and the queen mother) summoned the representatives of the clergy, nobility, and bourgeoisie after so long an interval was a sign of how desperate the financial crisis had become. For the theory of an estates—the king in conference with the great men of the land—was too medieval to mesh very well with the notion of an absolutist monarchy. Francis II's immediate predecessors had relied instead on an occasional assembly of notables, which had no constitutional foundation but which, as an ad hoc enlargement of the royal council, was presumably much easier to manipulate. Nothing came of the estates of 1560 or of several other convocations which followed it; in 1614 the estates general adjourned for the last time till the Revolution.

The estates general did not emulate the English parliament and evolve from its feudal origins into a modern legislature, because, quite simply, the estates had no control over the national purse. But the easy assumption that this resulted from the dark machinations of the crown does not tell the whole story. French kings were chronically short of money and sometimes desperate for it, as witness l'Hôpital's pleas at Orléans in 1560. On that occasion the estates took the medieval line that the king must live within the income derived from the crown lands and that universal taxes could be levied only to meet temporary emergencies. Such complacency belied the realities of the times, when bureaucracy was expanding and inflation was pushing up the cost of government services. Necessity is the mother of invention. Since the estates would not or could not help alleviate the fiscal crisis, the kings found other means, like frightening the clergy into a huge grant in 1561. More important, they converted little by little temporary sources of revenue into permanent ones, into various sales taxes (*aides*), a tax on salt (*gabelle*), export-import duties (*traites*), and, above all, a land tax, the *taille*.

To collect this money involved plunging into a nightmare of personal and class exemptions, provincial privileges, practically nonexistent collection and accounting procedures, graft, inefficiency, and peasant guile. Yet the kings did collect it—not all of it, to be sure, and not equitably, and not without resorting to bluff and force. They were driven to other expedients as well, particularly to the sale of offices— what Professor Hurstfield calls taxing the economy by subterfuge[33]— and even to the invention of offices in order to sell them. That this opened the door to corruption and to the dangers of a hereditary bureaucracy seemed less important than finding enough money to allow the state to function. The kings did so, and here was their great and lasting victory: the acceptance by the nation of their right to tax without reference to a parliament. Here was what rendered the estates general irrelevant and caused it to disappear.

Perhaps the key to that victory was the exemption from the *taille* enjoyed by the first two estates (as well as by some of the more affluent bourgeoisie). As onerous and capricious a tax as was ever conceived, the *taille* fell upon peasants and peasant land; priests and nobles—the praying caste and the fighting caste—were exempt from it. The kings indeed found other ways to fleece the other classes: the forced loan never repaid, the *don gratuit,* the *contrat.* But to be free of the *taille* was an inestimable boon, a status symbol no less than a financial advantage. The privilege may also have doomed meaningful parliamentary government in France, since society's natural leaders, unlike the inarticulate rural masses, saw no personal advantage in restraining the king's power to tax. One wonders what might have happened if the estates of 1560 had been lavish instead of niggardly in its help to the embattled monarchy. Would French kings have learned, as their English cousins did, to go crown-in-hand to the nation's representatives for the money they needed? It is only speculation of course, and anyway by 1560 it was probably too late.

3. EL REY PRUDENTE

"I will gain nothing by staying here," Philip II observed in June, 1559, "except lose myself and these states. . . . The best thing [is] to seek the remedy, . . . and if the remedy is not here I will go to seek it in Spain." Two months later he sailed from Flushing and left the Netherlands, where he had resided since 1555 and where he had been

33. In *The New Cambridge Modern History,* III, 126 ff.

tutored in his final lessons in kingship by his father, the Emperor Charles V. The royal fleet encountered heavy seas at the end of the voyage, and not before several ships had sunk did the king manage to scramble ashore near Laredo. This inauspicious homecoming was followed by swift disillusionment about the availability of a "remedy" for the crown's financial troubles. "I give you my word," Philip wrote to Granvelle in Brussels, "I have found here a situation worse than that there. . . . I confess that when I was in the Low Countries I never thought that things could be like this."

This kind of revelation was not common with Philip II, a man who had steeled himself and his emotions to a degree worthy of a Stoic philosopher. Already by 1559, when he was thirty-two years old, this process had converted his face into a mask and rendered his manner unfailingly courteous and invariably noncommittal.[34] But crisis in his Spanish dominions moved him at least this once to a *cri de coeur,* because he recognized that here lay the center of his empire, that part upon which all the other parts depended. For Philip II was more an emperor than his uncle Ferdinand or later his cousin Maximilian, who off in Vienna bore that august title. Even the designation by which he is remembered, King of Spain, is something of a misnomer. Actually, in the time of Philip there was no Spain. There was the crown of Aragon, which looked toward Italy and the Mediterranean and which included Catalonia and Valencia as distinct but integral parts; and there was the crown of Castile and León, which took in Granada in the south and the Basque provinces and Spanish Navarre in the north. Over all these, with their cultural, constitutional, and even linguistic differences, Philip II presided because, quite simply, he was the dynastic heir of his great-grandparents, Ferdinand of Aragon and Isabella of Castile.

But Philip was more than this. Through his paternal grandfather he was a Hapsburg and so linked to the ancient line of archdukes of Austria, and from the same source he was Count of Flanders and Duke of Burgundy,[35] which meant he ruled by dynastic right the Nether-

34. "Nearly all standard accounts are written from the viewpoint of enemies." See R. B. Merriman, *The Rise of the Spanish Empire* (New York, 1934), IV, 321, still one of the best and most objective studies. For a modern Spanish view see M. Fernández Álvarez, *Felipe II: Semblana del Rey Prudente* (Madrid, 1956).

35. The word "Burgundy" involves some terminological as well as geographical confusion. During the fourteenth century the duchy of Burgundy grew out of a welter of

lands and Franche Comté, an enclave on the east central frontier of France. His right to be Duke of Milan and King of Naples may have been more shadowy from a dynastic point of view, but his title, tested by two generations of warfare, was no less secure for that. Finally, Philip was Lord of the Indies and all their treasure, because he wore the crown of Castile, from whence the great explorers, beginning with Columbus, had been commissioned.

This accumulation of duchies and kingdoms was Philip's inheritance from Charles V, who, if he had had his way, would have left his son the Hapsburg possessions in central Europe and the imperial title as well. But events forced upon Charles a division of his vast estate, and when he abdicated in 1555–1556, there emerged in succession two royal branches of the family: the Austrian Hapsburgs, sprung from Charles's brother Ferdinand, and the Spanish Hapsburgs, Philip II and his descendants.[36]

Philip was a small man, with fair hair and blue eyes, who even as a youth had an air of gravity which discouraged intimacy. Yet he could be easy and relaxed, and the servants who were in daily attendance upon him adored him. Always, in that century of fops, he dressed simply, just as he shunned pretentiousness of any other kind. Apparently as a young man he had indulged in some amorous escapades, but once the scepter was in his hand he had no more time for frivolity. He allowed himself hardly any private life at all.

The King of Spain was rigorously pious. He was genuinely committed, in his personal as in his public life, to the practice of his faith in a manner and to a degree unmatched by any of his royal contemporaries. He felt directly accountable to God for the well-being of his peoples no less than for the salvation of his own soul. But piety never made of Philip a clericalist. No monarch held the Church in his dominions in so tight a grip as did Philip; nowhere more than in Spain were ecclesiastics so completely the creatures of the state. No ruler, Catholic or Protestant, quarreled more violently and more often with

---

principalities to independent status. It combined noncontiguous territories in the Low Countries with the Free County of Burgundy—Franche Comté—which lay between the Rhine and Saône rivers, just to the north and west of Lake Geneva. The province of Burgundy, which remained subject to the French crown, lay directly west of the Free County.

36. Henry Hauser, *La prépondérance espagnole* (Paris, 1948), pp. 7 ff.

the Roman See than Philip; indeed, he was, once he made up his mind, as heedless of the popes as William of Orange would be heedless— when he dared—of the Calvinist preachers. Philip might consult with his confessor and the court theologians about the moral implications of this or that decision, but the decision was his, not theirs. About one matter the king had not the slightest doubt: as he dispatched viceroys to act for him in Milan or Sicily, so God had sent him, Philip, to be viceroy, and not only to his own dominions but to Christendom at large.

It is difficult to argue with a man convinced that he speaks with the authority of God. Shy and intense as Philip was, those who knew him best loved him most. But few broke through his icy reserve and stiff manner, few realized that he was a man who wrote poetry, who loved music and books and the singing of nightingales, who played the guitar with loving skill, who had a deep interest in mathematics and architecture. As he grew older his frail body suffered agonies from gout and asthma and probably from the lack of physical exercise for which he never found time. But emotionally he did not falter; not for a moment did he lose his poise or his sublime sense of kingship as a sacred vocation.

Whatever unconscious motivation may have lain behind this conviction, it was supported by the fact that the only principle of unity Philip could discern in the cluster of principalities over which he ruled was himself. So one finds in Philip II the notion of dynast carried to its purest abstract form and, by that token, in some degree to its most absurd form. No decision was too trivial for the king because only he had responsibility for Calvinist burghers in Antwerp, spirited Milanese nobles, and naked savages in America. When everything is important, nothing is important. Philip's regime became characterized by the heaps of paper—reports of ambassadors, minutes of council meetings, written critiques—which littered the Escorial, the palace-monastery complex Philip built about 20 miles outside Madrid. The king, so Philip's working theory went, must know all before he could decide anything. But no man, not even God's viceroy, can know all.

A sort of paralysis gradually crept over his administration as Philip tried manfully to achieve the impossible task of seeing to everything himself. Though he worked with a furious dedication beyond the imagining of a modern bureaucrat, yet every day he fell a bit further behind. Today's decisions were put off till tomorrow, and tomorrow's till next week or next month or next year. At least once the king's confessor rebuked him on the grounds that justice delayed is justice denied. Such a charge was particularly bitter to Philip, because he saw his function as primarily a judicial one. His peoples shared this view with him; for them, behind the cold and formal apparatus of the state was the person of the Prudent King—*el Rey Prudente*—dispensing justice. And so Philip remained compulsively chained to his desk and to the mountain of papers on top of it.

His jealousy of power, his reluctance to delegate, saved Philip's dominions from the rule of favorite or faction. Indeed, one of the king's most common maneuvers was to play off faction against faction, personality against personality. But the advantage of disinterested independence brought with it many drawbacks besides the famous procrastination. Philip increasingly distrusted strength of character in others; he preferred the affable, courteous Portuguese expatriate Ruy Gómez de Silva, Prince of Eboli, to the Duke of Alba, because Alba was a Castilian grandee, a man of enormous wealth and influence who could afford to be his own man and speak his own mind. In fact a pattern emerged by which Philip studiously excluded nobles like Alba from posts in the central administration, while still consulting them in matters of broad policy and compensating them by leaving their economic advantages intact and reserving for them vice-royalties and high military commands. Around the king gathered a squad of technicians from the middling and even lower classes of society—a "horde of mediocrities," in Professor Lynch's telling phrase.[37] So did the machinery of state grind on.

The fundamental problem was always money. Though revenues increased significantly during the course of Philip's reign, they never kept pace with expenditures. War on two fronts, and sometimes on three, was responsible for this. Imperial pretensions brought endless consumption of blood and treasure, and had it not been for the increasing flood of American silver, Philip's government could hardly have survived without a radical reversal of policy. And even the silver, as we have seen, brought overall economic damage in its wake, for it inflated the price of goods and services for which the regime had to pay. So even with the silver, Philip could not avoid a humiliating round of bankruptcies.

37. Lynch, *Spain*, I, 189.

The proportion of total revenues from silver importation rose to about 20 percent by the end of the reign (1598). The remaining four-fifths had to be raised in Spain, or, more specifically, in Castile. The crown of Aragon was too poor to contribute significantly, and as the years passed, Milan, the Netherlands, and the rest tended more to consume tax income than to produce it. The result was a staggering burden of sales and property taxes imposed upon the frail Castilian economy. One very important source of income—roughly equivalent to the American windfall—was the Church. The *cruzada,* for example, or crusade subsidy, had begun as a kind of money indulgence granted by the papacy to help finance the fifteenth-century wars against the Moors. By Philip II's time it was converted into a permanent tax, vaguely related to the maintenance of Spanish—and hence Christian—interests in the Mediterranean. The *cruzada* fell on the laity, and there was another tax on the income of clerics. In 1567, a new tax called the *excusado* was imposed upon the property of all parishes. It is little wonder that Philip II promoted the extension of ecclesiastical holdings and saw no advantage in confiscating any of them.

Nobody in Castile, not even the grandees, escaped the impositions of the ravenous regime. Yet it proved one thing to impose taxes, and another to collect them. With no central agency of his own, Philip had to turn to the farming of taxes by international banking houses, few of which were Spanish. So by the cash they advanced to the government and by the concessions—mineral rights, for example—which had to be granted them, foreigners held the Spanish economy by the throat even during the era of Spain's national greatness. But this sacrifice of pride and maneuverability was not enough. The government borrowed against future *cruzada,* invented offices in order to sell them, and still there was not enough money. Toward the end of the reign Philip was driven to the expedient of contracting *asientos,* or direct loans, of huge sums to keep the war in the Netherlands going on a month-to-month basis.

In holding this rickety structure together it was Castile that mattered. Here the king settled in 1559, and here he stayed. As time passed, Philip's empire took on an ever deeper Castilian color. This much is clear, even though it may be difficult to summarize the methods Philip II employed in ruling his various principalities, since they possessed no common constitutional principle except himself. And as a genuine dynast he went to some pains to preserve the formalities of each of his dominions. Thus, for example, the cortes (parliament) of Castile was traditionally weak with no power of the purse or indeed power of any other kind. Philip used it for no more than a sounding board of public opinion. Under the crown of Aragon, however, the case was far otherwise, for here, along the Mediterranean coast, were three cortes to deal with (Aragon, Catalonia, Valencia), each with a lively and independent tradition behind it. Philip walked warily among them—no less the authoritarian, to be sure, but content to follow the pattern established by time and custom.

From day to day Philip operated within a system of conciliar government based on a distinction between groups which advised him about general policy and those concerned with particular dominions.[38] In the former category were the councils of state, war, finance, and the Inquisition. There was considerable overlapping on these bodies; the inquisitor general, for instance, usually served also as president of the council of state. Within the broad areas of military and foreign policy Philip was apparently interested in the views of the Spanish magnates. A sample of forty members of the council of state in the later years of the reign reveals twenty-eight grandees, nine high ecclesiastics, and three country gentlemen (hidalgos).

In sharp contrast was the methodical way Philip excluded such people from the councils which regulated the affairs of his various states. The councils of Castile, of Aragon, of Italy, later of Portugal, and the abortive Council of Flanders were recruited largely from among jurists (*letrados*) who came from the urban middle class and who were imbued with Renaissance ideas of centralized absolutism. All the councils were in attendance upon the king, and what was noted and resented about them at the time was their Castilian character. Barcelona was much displeased when Castilians were introduced into the Aragonese council. The Council of Italy, which dealt with the affairs of Milan, Sicily, and Naples, included three Italians and three Castilians. The same preference could be discerned in the viceroys whom Philip dispatched to exercise executive authority in his stead: six of nine viceroys in Sicily were Castilians and ten of thirteen in Milan. Granvelle was the only northerner to hold high office south of the

38. For an excellent summary, see J. M. Batista i Roca's introduction to Helmut Koenigsberger, *The Government of Sicily under Philip II of Spain: A Study in the Practice of Empire* (London, 1951), pp. 9–35.

Alps, and he for one saw how this insistence upon Castilian hegemony weakened the Hapsburg system. He pleaded with the king to appoint William of Orange to a responsible position in the Mediterranean area and thus bind that unruly prince more closely to the throne.[39] But Philip never grasped the need for a wider choice in key personnel, which has led later critics[40] to wonder whether the king, confined within the fastness of the Escorial, ever really understood the imperial character of his regime.

Over all that regime's machinery brooded the shadow of Castile. With four or five times the population of the crown of Aragon, and with relatively vast amounts of taxable property—including merino sheep and American silver—Castile was uniquely that part of his realms upon which Philip had to depend for men and money. And it was Castile, with its political timidity, its almost nonexistent constitution, that the king ruled most forcefully and directly. Had the Castilian cortes exhibited the robust and independent spirit of its Catalan counterpart, Philip would have had to crush it. He could afford to indulge the constitutional prerogatives of his Aragonese subjects, so few were they and so poor.

Thus Castile dominated the monarchy, empire, and Spanish nation which emerged under Philip II. This happened more out of economic necessity than out of conscious design, and yet it displayed itself in other ways. Burned deep into the Castilian psyche was the notion of *reconquista*. For centuries Castile had borne the major burden of the crusade against the Moors. There came with this struggle a heightened racial and religious consciousness which continued long beyond the fall of the last Moorish stronghold, Granada, in 1492. The "reconquest" at that moment was formally accomplished, but troublesome problems remained. Succeeding governments, as well as Christian Spaniards at large, were particularly concerned about absorbing into the new and fragile nation-state the two significant minorities, the Jews and the conquered Moors. A generally repressive policy reached its climax when the minorities were confronted with the alternatives of conversion to Catholicism or expulsion from Spain.

In this manner had come into Spanish—and especially Castilian—society the two groups called conversos ("new Christians" of Jewish

39. Charles Petrie, *Philip II of Spain* (New York, 1963), p. 217.
40. Notably Koenigsberger, *The New Cambridge Modern History*, III, 238–41.

origin) and moriscos (Moorish Christians). And along with them came the Spanish Inquisition.[41] This fabled institution—a distant cousin to the Roman Inquisition with which it had no real connection—functioned from the last years of the fifteenth century as an agency to promote religious uniformity and, later, racial purity—*limpieza de sangre*. It was organized as a council of state, very much an arm of the government which sometimes used it in patently nonreligious matters—to counter, for example, horse smuggling on the French frontier. Such uses were a tribute to the efficiency of the Inquisition whose secretiveness, its regular forays into every corner of the countryside, and its auto-da-fé[42] became commonplaces of Spanish life by the time Philip II succeeded to the throne.

By that time too the Inquisition had formalized and moderated much of its earlier terrorism. It had never been of course the simple machinery of mindless cruelty which Anglo-Saxons like to think is part of the "Latin character." Like all tribunals of the time, it used torture, but infrequently and with considerable safeguards. Yet, even though this was the case and even though the ultimate penalty of death by burning was exacted rarely, the Inquisition had a doleful effect upon Spanish life. Among other things, it opened another avenue to greedy officialdom, for confiscation of property was an ordinary form of punishment. Moreover, it represented a serious subversion of healthy legal practice in that the defendant, though he had counsel, remained in ignorance of the nature and source of evidence against him, and suffered besides the disadvantage that prosecutor and judge were in effect one person, the inquisitor. But the most elemental damage of all may have been the universal atmosphere of suspicion engendered by the Inquisition; perhaps not since the times of the Roman Emperor Trajan was the populace of a civilized state put so much at the mercy of spies, informers, and the neurotically vindictive.[43]

Though Spaniards were terrified of the Inquisition, they never doubted the need for it. They never doubted the need to keep a wary eye on those enemies of God and the people, crypto-Jews, crypto-Moors, and, later, occasional pockets of Protestants. Religious and

41. For a recent bibliographical analysis of this still highly controversial subject see Paul Hauben, ed., *The Spanish Inquisition* (New York, 1969).

42. An auto-da-fé was a public exhibition of those convicted of heresy. Sometimes an execution was part of this.

43. Elliott, *Imperial Spain*, pp. 215 f.

racial pluralism never occurred to them as a viable solution; such a view would have run counter to the whole psychology of the *reconquista*. The continuing struggle with the Moslem Turks and the religious wars of other European nations provided some justification for their attitude, if not for the racist Castilian hauteur which reflected it.

Professor Braudel describes the "empire" of Philip II as "more vast, more coherent, more solid than that of Charles V, less engaged in Europe, more exclusively centered in Spain and turned again toward the ocean."[44] All the more an anomaly was it then that so much of Spain's scanty resources should have been spent in maintaining Philip's dynastic hold in the far-off Netherlands. Undoubtedly Philip subscribed to Lord Bryce's analysis of Charles V's power: "its sources were the infantry of Spain, the looms of Flanders, the barbaric treasures of Mexico and Peru";[45] he could not do without the looms of Flanders.

Yet the Netherlands formed a world which had psychologically little in common with the no less tempestuous local life in Spain. The seventeen provinces stretched along the shore of the North Sea from Denmark to France had been for generations a thickly populated congeries of manufacturing districts. In the south three of the greatest rivers in Europe—the Scheldt, the Meuse, and the Rhine—found entrance to the open sea and made the country the terminus of a vast trade, the market and entrepôt for northern France and for western Germany as far south as Switzerland. Here, in a land of traders and businessmen, cultural and social life had a burgher quality practically unknown in Spain.

Armies, military glory, *reconquista*—the Low Countries honored no such tradition as this. And the religious life of the Netherlands had a quality hardly intelligible to the average Castilian. The people were still mostly Catholics, but they displayed none of the stern crusading temperament so prominent in a country that had only recently overcome the last of its Moorish kingdoms. So much deeper is the irony, therefore, that here was the cockpit for the bloodiest religious battles of all.

Still, though Calvinist militancy and Catholic persecution triggered it and lent it an intense savagery, the revolt of the Netherlands was not essentially a religious war. It grew rather out of a tangle of political,

44. Braudel, *La Méditerranée*, II, 23 f.
45. James Bryce, *The Holy Roman Empire* (New York, 1961, reprint), p. 372.

economic, and social factors, in which religion indeed did play an increasingly important part. The root trouble was that Philip II's sovereignty was a dynastic accident which forged an unnatural bond between Spain and the Low Countries. Charles V's empire, which included both, had made some theoretical sense because it had also included so much more. But when the son succeeded to only part of the patrimony, the practical difficulties in maintaining the connection were immediately apparent. At least they were to the wily Charles, who arranged the marriage in 1554 between Philip and Queen Mary Tudor of England in hopes that a geographically and economically rational triangle of states—Spain, England, the Netherlands—might emerge for his dynasty. This scheme, however, came to nothing when Mary died childless four years later, and Philip was left with his checkered inheritance: a Spanish dog that wagged a Dutch tail.

The political bond among the provinces was extremely fragile. Each of them had its own estates, which jealously guarded its local liberties and prerogatives. As the dukes who immediately preceded Philip attempted to foster a sense of national unity (and thus provide one instead of seventeen sources of general tax revenue) the overriding question became the fate of local autonomy—a revered political tradition in the Netherlands and one more easily honored by dukes of Burgundy when they were just dukes of Burgundy. Even the national assembly, the States-General, reflected this bias. Clergy, lords, and burghers, chosen in a manner each province preferred, met in Brussels at the duke's summons (as frequently as fifty-eight times in the sixty years before Philip's accession) to hear his plea for money. The different delegations then separately discussed the amount they proposed to offer, and if the offer was insufficient, the duke's officers brought to bear what pressure they could. Clearly, the States-General was a far cry from a genuine parliamentary body.

Much has been made of the contrast between the popular Charles V—who was born in Flanders and often resided there—and his dour son, who never visited his Netherlands subjects after 1559 and who never learned to speak French, much less Dutch. Yet in fact the disaffection which exploded into rebellion in the mid-1560s had been brewing for a long time. Philip did not depart significantly from the policies established by his father. Neither religious persecution nor severe financial exactions began with Philip, who, for all his narrowness and inflexibility, simply carried on. He was no less—but no more—anxious than Charles had been to reduce the seventeen provinces to a single, prosperous fief. The basic difficulty was, as Professor Geyl has pointed out, that "the national forces living in the people found it difficult to cooperate with the state-building forces directed by the monarchy."[46] Charles, unlike his son, was lucky enough to depart the scene before these forces collided.

When Philip left the Netherlands for Spain in 1559, he appointed as governess his half-sister Margaret, Duchess of Parma. Practical power, however, was denied her because Philip set up within the executive organ of the Netherlands government a cabal headed by Granvelle. The purpose in this of the Duke of Burgundy was identical with that of the King of Castile: to reserve to himself every significant decision. Also excluded were the great Netherlands lords—like the Count of Egmont, the Count of Hoorne, and William of Orange, Count of Nassau—who all belonged to the honorific Order of the Golden Fleece and many of whom were the crown's provincial governors or stadholders. They soon discovered, through the obstructive tactics of Granvelle, that Philip intended them to enjoy no more political initiative than he allowed the tame nobility of Castile.

The endless delays of decisions from Madrid could not hide for long Philip's intent to rule without nobility, States-General, or any meaningful local participation. The result was at first a sullen withdrawal from public life by the Knights of the Golden Fleece, the nation's natural leaders, and then a growing crystallization among them of hostility toward the monarchy. As time passed, one man emerged as the chief of the opposition. William of Orange,[47] handsome, accomplished, radiating charm, "le plus séduisant des hommes," was twenty-six years old in 1559. He followed in a lesser way the pattern of Philip II as a multiple dynast. Thanks to his County of Nassau (east of the Rhine and just north of Frankfurt) and the tiny enclave of Orange, he was an independent Prince of the Holy Roman Empire—he had, in other words, a power base and connections outside the Low Countries, a circumstance which in the impending struggle would be of considerable importance. Added to these were vast estates in Brabant which he inherited as a

46. Pieter Geyl, *The Revolt of the Netherlands* (London, 1958), p. 61.
47. Henri Pirenne, *Histoire de Belgique* (Brussels, 1923), III, 404 ff. See also C. V. Wedgwood, *William the Silent* (London, 1945), a laudatory biography.

child and which placed him in the middle of the Netherlands
maelstrom.

In the matter of religious belief, William was tolerant as no other
public man of his time. Himself born a Lutheran, raised a Catholic, a
Lutheran again, and finally a Calvinist, he tested most contemporary
religious currents without being much affected by any of them, except
insofar as they had political significance. Neither Lutheranism nor the
Anabaptist sects—which reflected social unrest as well as theological
peculiarity—had made much progress in the Netherlands due to the
brutal persecution by Charles V. Calvinism came later and came to
stay. As in France, though it never approached majority status, it
nevertheless attracted some of the more vital and productive elements
of the population—artisans, burghers, and the gentry. And of course as
everywhere it was organized, tough, militant. This was the movement
which came to be inextricably tangled with the cause of Dutch
nationalism and with the personal fortunes of the Prince of Orange.

Perhaps that is why Philip's troubles in the Netherlands can be said
to have begun with the affair of the bishoprics.[48] Almost since Roman
times the ecclesiastical organization in the Low Countries had remained the same: three small dioceses in the south and one immense
diocese in the north. In 1550 Philip determined to systematize the
Church structure in a more rational way and at the same time give
himself firmer control over these choice domains. By papal brief, fourteen new dioceses, grouped into three archbishoprics, replaced the old
ones.

The basic good sense of this reform was obscured by the patently
political objectives which Philip included in it. The new bishops would
all be crown appointments and agents of the crown around the country, would be supported by the income from monastic foundations,
would be chosen from among those likely to be useful civil servants
and not from the younger sons of the nobility, would insist upon a
wholesome level of morals among the clergy, and would enforce no less
than a Castilian orthodoxy. To add insult to these injuries to local
vested interests, Granvelle was named Archbishop of Mechlin, primate,
and cardinal.

"The red dragon of Spain," the pamphleteers began to call him, and

48. See Michel Dierickx, "La Reorganisation de la hiérarchie ecclésiastique des Paysbas
par la Bulle de 1559," *Revue d'Histoire Ecclésiastique*, LIX, 2 (1964), 489–499.

Orange and the other nobles took the same line: not yet ready to attack the sovereign (and not yet aware that they ever would), they followed the ancient device of attacking the minister instead. Granvelle's hair went white under the pressure, even as laconic edicts demanding money and religious conformity continued to come regularly from the king far off in the woods of Segovia. The new bishops were installed not with thurifers and plainsong but with pike and cannon. Then in January, 1561, the last Spanish troops were withdrawn, an act which, while it quieted one local complaint, revealed the vulnerability of Philip, who had to let the soldiers go because he had no money for them. It was an admission of weakness for which the Prudent King would pay all the rest of his life.

4. THE VIRGIN QUEEN

The brilliant achievements of Elizabethan England tend to dazzle the eye of the later observer and to obscure the shaky beginnings of Elizabeth's reign.[49] In 1559, after twelve years of internal disorder and a ruinous foreign war, nobody had an inkling of the glory to be revealed. Nor did the accession of a twenty-five-year-old queen in itself produce any particular euphoria;[50] from experience Englishmen were disinclined to expect stability from a female ruler.

It was well for the regime that momentous victories came early. On the domestic scene the queen and parliament reached a religious settlement which, while it satisfied no one completely, proved generally acceptable to the country and so defused the most dangerous ideological issue of the time. Not till twenty years later was it seriously challenged, and by then it was more than strong enough to survive. In 1560, by the Treaty of Edinburgh, Elizabeth—or rather Cecil, whose coup the treaty was—ended forever the "auld alliance" between France and Scotland, and so, with Scotland a satellite, England enjoyed a measure of security on the northern borders for the first time in centuries.

Elizabeth's internal problems were much less than those of her Hapsburg and Valois contemporaries, just as her place in the sun was more modest than theirs. Compared to the dominions of Philip II, England was a tiny place, and its population was hardly a sixth that of

49. J. B. Black, *The Reign of Elizabeth* (Oxford, 1959), pp. 5 ff.
50. John Neale, *Essays in Elizabethan History* (New York, 1958), pp. 9–20, examines the growth of November 17 (Accession Day) festivals and myths.

France. Feudalism in England had never attained the level of independent strength it had elsewhere. There was a tradition of strong monarchy and even a bureaucracy and civil service of sorts which reached to every town and county.[51] The parliamentary tradition was also strong, but thanks to her shrewd employment of the crown's normal resources, Elizabeth seldom had to bargain for grants from the purse-conscious House of Commons. Parliament met nine times—each sat a couple of months—in forty-five years, and though sharp disagreement arose between it and the queen on such matters as religion and the succession,[52] she always dominated the partnership, at least until the gloomy end of the reign when she was old and sick and the country plunged into an expensive war.

The reign of Elizabeth was marked by no momentous economic changes. The same inflation operative elsewhere afflicted England too, though perhaps in not so severe a form. One reason for the somewhat happier price picture was the government's obsessive concern for solvency—the queen's own shrewd, almost niggardly sense of economy, supported by Cecil—and its restoration of the debased coinage. Relatively speaking England, until 1588, was at peace: the northern rebellion, the Scottish adventures, and the various interventions in the Low Countries were only skirmishes when compared to the religious strife in France or the endless wars of Philip II. A sign of this was Elizabeth's enviable credit rating in the international money market at Antwerp.[53]

The most significant social event was the emergence of the gentry to a dominant position and the relative eclipse of the nobility. Here was a process which had been at work through the whole of the Tudor period; it had begun even earlier indeed, during the Wars of the Roses (1455-1485). It should not be overstated; the great lords did not disappear by any means. But by 1603 the Commons, controlled by the landed gentry, had become for the first time the more important of the two parliamentary houses. No magnate like Condé or Guise or William of Orange threatened the English throne, unless one counts the

51. See, for an analysis of the relationship between county elites and the central government, J. H. Gleason, *The Justices of the Peace in England, 1558–1640* (New York, 1969).

52. The first decade of the reign was crucial. See Mortimer Levine, *The Early Elizabethan Succession Question, 1558–1568* (Stanford, 1966).

53. Braudel and Spooner, *Cambridge Economic History*, IV, 383.

inept and feckless plottings of the Duke of Norfolk, who in 1572 paid for his indiscretions with his head.

The yeoman class—free farmers but a cut below the gentlemen—also flourished as their landholdings expanded. City merchants got rich, and many of them invested in land and merged by wedlock and common interests with the gentry. Elizabethan England was also a place where litigation thrived in an unprecedented fashion, and so there was marked growth in the legal profession's numbers and influence. Though the masses remained as ever the masses, subject to poor diet, bad housing, inadequate sanitation, and all the other ills the common people of the sixteenth century were heir to, there existed nevertheless a good deal of mobility within the class structure as individuals and families moved up and sometimes down. Elizabeth's era was in this sense an adventurous time when fortunes could be made and one's status altered dramatically. Present, however, at the same time was the stabilizing factor of primogeniture, which, in this small, land-hungry world, preserved estates and landed families and hence guaranteed, amid a considerable amount of social fluidity, a measure of conservatism.[54]

Ostentation was the order of the day—in dress, speech, architecture, food and drink, entertainment. Noblemen spent fortunes on the maintenance of wasteful households, and it was not unknown for a two- or three-day visit by the queen to cost her host thousands of pounds. At a time of religious revival and of stern calls to ethical probity, there still went on an enormous amount of getting and spending and sheer hedonistic exercise. Englishmen, commented a disgruntled bishop, pursue pleasure as though they would die tomorrow and build buildings as though they would live forever.

In religion the country bore the scars of thirty years of turmoil. The important fact as Elizabeth came to the throne was not the revulsion over the persecution of Protestants by her Catholic predecessor (though there was some) but the by now established principle that the government would decide what the nation's religion would be. Henry VIII, Edward VI, Mary I: each of them, in different ways, had put to work the adage "cujus regio, ejus religio," and everyone knew that Elizabeth would do the same.

54. Rowse, *The England of Elizabeth*, pp. 221 ff.

Little doubt could have existed that Elizabeth aimed at a radical departure from the religious policy of her sister. Her Lutheran upbringing, the Protestant character of her intimates, to say nothing of the fact that passion for her mother had led Henry VIII to break with Rome in the first place: all signs pointed in a new direction. At a deeper level lay the queen's conviction that the kind of religious settlement she had in mind could bind together a sorely divided people; in this she stubbornly maintained the medieval ideal of a commonwealth whose outward sign was baptism. Her intent was to comprehend as much of the nation as possible and to avoid the ravages of sectarian war which tormented her neighbors.

Elizabeth was more Protestant than her father, less so than her brother, and though she was probably more theologically learned than either of them, her emotional commitment was considerably less. Her interests remained essentially secular, as Puritans as well as Catholics discovered to their cost. She wanted to identify the Church of England with the English nation, and in this project she was largely successful. The genuinely Protestant character of her settlement, however, should not be overlooked because of the queen's political preoccupations or because of the retention in the Anglican system of such things as vestments, episcopal structure, and the like. Insofar as "Protestant" had a precise theological meaning applicable to the sixteenth century, it meant that philosophy of life based on the doctrine of justification by faith alone, as opposed to the "Catholic" view of the Christian life as a conjunction of faith and good works, especially sacramental good works. By this distinction the Elizabethan settlement was never anything but Protestant, so that the term "via media" sometimes used to describe it—as though it were a unique middle way between Catholicism and Protestantism—does not really apply.[55]

Yet Elizabeth never went along with the more radical of her Protestant subjects, who were as troublesome to her notions of unity as the most errant papist. These people, whom convention lumps together under the name Puritans, were heavily represented in the original Elizabethan hierarchy, primarily because the queen could persuade none of the Catholic bishops, in possession in 1559, to endorse her

55. The nineteenth-century Oxford Movement attempted to chart a via media between Romanism and Elizabethan Protestantism. See Marvin R. O'Connell, *The Oxford Conspirators* (New York, 1969), pp. 253 ff.

settlement. The House of Commons also had a good-sized Puritan contingent which constantly pressed the queen to purge the Church of its popish dregs.[56] Elizabeth stoutly resisted the Puritans' evangel, not only out of distaste for their fanaticism or because she sensed they were a noisy minority without widespread support, but most importantly because she knew that the lessons they had learned in Geneva and Zurich left them basically hostile to her prerogative to rule the Church. The Puritans, for their part, needed Elizabeth as much as she needed them. She was their Deborah, their embattled prophetess, without whom there could have been no English Protestantism at all. They had little choice but to accede to her policy of comprehension, of muffling the cries of internal enthusiasm under the mantle of external conformity. Their greatest victory came probably early in the game, in 1559, when the queen had to accept the outlawing of both the papal supremacy and the Mass when she had preferred a more gradual program.

With the Catholics—probably the majority of the nation in 1559—Elizabeth's problem was different. It was not enthusiasm with which she had to contend—especially not enthusiasm for the pope—but a massive, inert kind of resistance which might have ruined her religious arrangements. Here the queen's diplomatic gifts, her willingness to let events and time unfold at their own pace, served her well. Except for the fiasco of the northern rebellion (1569) the Catholics never stirred.[57] The poor and middling went to church Sunday after Sunday and listened to homilies drawn up to indoctrinate them in a new faith, while the rich stayed home and paid increasingly stiff recusancy fines and found themselves frozen out of the public life of the nation. The result, after twenty years and more of this, after a generation grew up who remembered no prince but Elizabeth, no religious order but that of the Book of Common Prayer, was a gradual withering away of the old allegiance. By the time the secular priests and Jesuits came from the continental seminaries in any numbers, they had to confront the hard reality that the policy of slow attrition had weaned away most of the old Catholics and had prevented a new group from developing.

Queen Elizabeth's highly pragmatic mind did not underestimate the

56. John Neale, *Elizabeth I and Her Parliaments* (London, 1958), pp. 51 ff.
57. See William Trimble, *The Catholic Laity in Elizabethan England* (Cambridge, Mass., 1964), pp. 9 ff.

character and location of the various confessional groups with which she had to deal. The most fervent Catholics were concentrated in the semifeudal north. The Protestants, on the other hand, although few in numbers at the beginning of the reign, included in their ranks heavy representation from the artisan class, from merchants, small employers and the intelligentsia. And so they tended to locate in towns and especially in London. Indeed, London was a Protestant city as Paris was a Catholic one, with similar results in each case. If Paris were worth a Mass for the Huguenot Henry IV, London, with its large percentage of hot gospelers, was not a whit less important for Elizabeth and played no less an important role in determining what her religious policy would be.

Elizabeth, however, had little patience with ideology, and her basic tenets remained basically simple, however much she might have indulged in Reformation rhetoric. First, at home, the clerical estate would be treated essentially as it had been by her father. She desired comprehension, pacification; but priests must be kept in their place, subject to hard-eyed lay statesmen, and if she let them wear surplice and miter despite strenuous Puritan objections, she left no doubt that she would enforce what she and her parliament had wrought in 1559. For upon this settlement depended the internal harmony of the nation.

Religion—the political ideology of the late sixteenth century—also had impact upon foreign policy. When she began her reign (and through most of its forty-five years), Elizabeth was the only Protestant ruler of any consequence in Europe. Many of her closest advisers would have had her mount a Protestant crusade, or at least give aid and comfort to true believers who languished under Catholic monarchs. But the queen took a decidedly worldly view of the dangerous world she lived in. She saw as well as anyone the advantage of France and Spain suffering chronic problems with religious minorities, but to her the advantage to be pressed was English not Protestant. She followed a venerable pattern: play off the French and Spanish giants against each other—now allying with one, then with the other—and so protect her smaller, weaker kingdom. An instructive instance of this was her shifting policy in the Netherlands.[58] Here, just over the narrow seas in Flanders, squatted the Spanish Leviathan, troubled and

58. See Charles Wilson, *Queen Elizabeth and the Revolt of the Netherlands* (London, 1970), especially pp. 23 ff.

harassed indeed by rebels but still terrible as an army in array. Yet the queen never gave a full commitment to William of Orange, lest Spanish collapse lead to French expansion. Instead she engaged in one long, complex, incredibly skillful maneuver until, late in her reign, with France in the throes of the last crucial phase of the religious wars and almost completely distracted, she finally went to war with Spain. Religion, insofar as religion means some sort of commitment to a supernatural order, had nothing to do with all this.

This was why such fiery men of God as the Scottish reformer John Knox wondered whether Elizabeth or indeed any royal female possessed the credentials of a ruler such as the Bible could approve. This was why her closest advisers—Cecil, the Earl of Leicester, Walsingham, Nicholas Bacon—all of whom, even the disreputable Leicester, could have been called fervent when compared to their queen, despaired of her more than once. Yet they served her with remarkable constancy and vigor, and one of them—Cecil—with real genius. It was not always easy, for Elizabeth treated them much as she treated foreign sovereigns, caressing them one moment and lashing out at them the next. But she brought out the best that was in them for the service of the state, and despite their weariness at dealing with a headstrong woman and their impatience at her lack of sectarian commitment, in the end they threw themselves and all they had at her feet. Still, in private, they grumbled. "Well," said Cecil on one trying occasion, "God send our mistress a husband, and by time a son, that we may hope our posterity shall have a masculine succession."

It was not to be. Her dynasty died with Elizabeth Tudor, for though she was in love once and perhaps twice, she never married. Instead she carried on a long affair with the English people and became enshrined in their consciousness as the virgin queen. She was a handsome woman, attractive, vivacious, beguiling when she chose, but perhaps too much her father's daughter to submit to a husband's will, as even queens regnant had to do in the sixteenth century, as her sister Mary had so pathetically and tragically done. Elizabeth, one of her contemporaries observed, was more than a man and less than a woman. If this meant that her passion to rule was greater than her desire for love and children, then it appears accurate enough. To marry a subject meant that she would lead a faction and not a nation; to marry a foreign prince would draw her into the whirlpool of continental politics and hostilities as Mary had been. Her suitors were legion, including a hot-blooded prince from Sweden, an Austrian archduke, and even Philip II himself. In her youth she would gladly have married Leicester, and in middle age Catherine de' Medici's youngest son, the Duke of Alençon. But she held back in the end, and so without issue of her own she left as her heir apparent that other woman, so unlike herself, her cousin, the mercurial Mary Queen of Scots.

The death of Francis II in December, 1560, ended not only the political ascendancy of the Guise in France but also the dazzling French career of the Guise woman, who up till then had been the pampered child of fortune. The following August Mary bade farewell to her uncle and mentor, the Cardinal of Lorraine, and took a ship for the Scotland she had not seen since she was six years old. Now a widow of eighteen, schooled in the graces of the Valois court and already a tantalizing beauty—tall, slender, oval-faced, and hazel-eyed, with long fluttering hands and amber hair and a delicately sensuous look[59]—Mary Queen of Scots was, even so, very much a young girl caught in the swirling currents of dynastic politics. She was by nature bright and quick but not nearly so intelligent or so well educated as her cousin Elizabeth. Abounding in energy and vitality, Mary was never-theless frail, never in her life free from nagging ailments. Thanks to the cardinal's tutelage she was not entirely innocent of statecraft, but nothing—not even the turmoil and uncertainties she had experienced at St. Germain and Amboise—could have prepared her to meet her tumultuous subjects and the bleak, wild land they lived in.

Scotland stood on the far edge of Christendom—"the arse of the world," as a papal nuncio called it in 1529. Of six or seven hundred thousand Scots, only a few lived in towns: Edinburgh, the biggest by far, had a population of 15,000. The rest were mostly peasants strung out from the northern highlands to the English border who worked their rocky soil with primitive tools and uncertain tenure. What agri-cultural prosperity there was lay with the fertile land in the south—in such places as Lothian and the dales of the Tweed and Clyde—where English raiders and freebooters routinely ravaged it. So broken was the countryside and so few and ill-maintained the roads that only hap-hazard contact existed between north and south, as when, for example,

59. Antonia Fraser, *Mary Queen of Scots* (New York, 1969), p. 78.

Gaelic-speaking highland drovers brought their cattle down to lowland markets.

Natural conditions like these left little chance for the development of a centralized Renaissance monarchy. Occasionally a man of remarkable talent like Mary's grandfather, James IV, could create a temporary illusion that Scotland was a kingdom in fact as well as in name. But James, with 10,000 of his subjects, had died on Flodden field (1513) in a battle which proved that even a second-rate English army was too much for the courageous, disorganized Scots, armed with spears eighteen feet long and with huge Flemish cannon they did not know how to aim. The question was not whether Scotland would be a satellite state but whose.

The decision lay with the barons, and no more ignorant, rapacious, brave, venal, superstitious band of men ever lived than the Scottish nobility of the sixteenth century. Most of them were barely literate, and to Mary they must have seemed barely civilized. Despite lip service paid to the crown, they recognized no loyalty save to their clan. They engaged in endless feuds among themselves. They were violent and cruel enough to shock an era when violence and cruelty were taken for granted. Their castles were not the palaces of sunny France but crude fortresses presided over by noble viragoes who, like Lady Macbeth, appear to have been unsexed at least with regard to the gentler characteristics of femininity.

These magnates were very wealthy in terms of the lands they possessed either in their own right or through their almost complete control of church patronage, but, chronically short of cash, they were open to the bribes offered by French and English politicians who competed for their favor. Before Mary came home the issue had been settled by the Treaty of Edinburgh. Cecil had persuaded the reluctant Elizabeth to support the Scottish lords who were in revolt against the regent queen mother, Mary of Guise, and her French troops. The fighting prior to June, 1561, when the regent died, had been typical of Scottish wars, desultory and savage. What set it off from ordinary clannish feuds was the religious factor.

Protestantism won early and widespread popular support, due in large measure to the monumental disarray of the Scottish Church.[60]

60. See Matthew Mahoney, Gordon Donaldson, et al. in David McRoberts, ed., *Essays on the Scottish Reformation, 1513–1625* (Glasgow, 1962).

No people in the Catholic world were worse served religiously than the Scots. The crown and nobility viewed the vast church lands as a source for pillage, and the Roman Curia, out of blindness or rapacity, cooperated by providing, for a fee, the necessary dispensations. Thus James IV appointed his illegitimate eleven-year-old son Archbishop of St. Andrews and Primate of Scotland, and James V secured for three of his bastards, all less than five years old, the richest monasteries in the country. Meanwhile churches crumbled to the ground and Mass ceased to be offered; of the thousand parishes in Scotland hardly a hundred had a resident pastor, even though the country swarmed with as many as 3,000 vagabond priests who could not find a living. Among these was a short, stocky, black-bearded, swarthy-complexioned man named John Knox.[61] Ordained in 1536, Knox passed through the economic and moral perils endemic in an underemployed clerical proletariat until he discovered Christ in the Bible and in the writings of the divines of Geneva. Many of his confreres did likewise, and the common people followed suit. The result was persecution and reaction to persecution with a peculiarly Scottish savagery. Typical was the judicial strangling and burning in 1546 of the Scottish protomartyr George Wishart. David Cardinal Beaton, who had condemned Wishart, watched the execution from a comfortable seat on the wall of St. Andrew's Castle. A few months later the cardinal, while resting after a night with his concubine, was stabbed to death by sixteen assassins who then proceeded to urinate in the dead prelate's mouth.

The religious struggle in succeeding years was marked by a phenomenal growth of Protestantism among the masses. Then, in 1558, when they were satisfied that they could find a means of keeping the revenues from their bishoprics and priories even if they repudiated Catholicism, the barons turned a movement into a revolution by solemnly proclaiming themselves Lords of the Congregation and protectors of the Protestant Kirk. Knox, who returned from exile the following year, knew well enough that the lords were more interested in overthrowing the Guise-dominated regency, with its centralizing pretensions, than in accepting Christ as their personal Savior. But he knew also that the difference between keeping and losing the nobility's

---

61. Jasper Ridley, *John Knox* (Oxford, 1968), supersedes all earlier studies. Still interesting is Albert Bushnell Hart, "John Knox as a Man of the World," *The American Historical Review*, XIII (1908), 259–280.

allegiance was the difference between success and failure for the reform of Scotland. During the next crucial two years Knox displayed exactly the right combination of gifts: a fiery, disinterested zeal for the gospel, a fierce personality, and the practical cunning of the born revolutionary. With Cecil's help—paid for by reducing Scotland to an English fief—he won a smashing victory. The pope and his minions were banished from Scotland, and to celebrate Mass was, by the time Mary arrived in Edinburgh, a crime punishable by death.

But Knox feared that all might be undone by the Guise woman, and he recalled later the day of Mary's coming in a sullen, heavy rain and thick fog: "The very face of heaven, the time of her arrival, did manifestly speak what comfort was brought into this country with her, to wit, sorrow, dolor, darkness and all impiety." Mary, for her part, from that first day determined to be agreeable at all costs, and for a while the brightness of her charm cast a shadow over John Knox. The half-savage noblemen were enthralled by her beauty and her French manner, and what chivalry they had was aroused by her helplessness. Their Calvinist fervor was not so hot that they objected to the queen's having private Mass in her own chapel, as long as she did not interfere with the religious settlement of the country or, above all, with their ecclesiastical revenues. And she did not. She scrupulously supported the Protestant Kirk, even to the point of enraging the pope by demanding papal subsidies while she denied papal nuncios entry into Scotland. Perhaps she remembered the Cardinal of Lorraine's parting advice, that she should keep all options open, including, if it should prove expedient, conversion to Protestantism herself.[62] More likely, she hoped simply to survive in the wilds of Scotland long enough to pass in triumph someday south of the border. For by one of those strange quirks of dynasticism Mary Queen of Scots, as great-granddaughter of a sister of Henry VIII, was heiress to the virgin queen of England. Should Elizabeth die without issue—and death could strike with lightning speed in the sixteenth century—Mary would pass from Holyrood to Windsor, a consummation devoutly to be wished.

But it was a dangerous game for an untried young woman, alone in a primitively masculine world, far from her real home and from family and disinterested friends, a young woman fond of pretty clothes and

62. Gordon Donaldson, *The First Trial of Mary Queen of Scots* (New York, 1969), p. 91.

pretty compliments, of dancing and of tall, handsome men. Even had the self-righteous malevolence of John Knox not been pitilessly turned against her, one wonders if she would have succeeded. For there proved to be a tragic flaw in her character: if prudence is the virtue proper to princes, then Mary Queen of Scots was a lady of easy virtue.

5. THE ERASMIAN EMPEROR

Through nearly forty years before his brother Charles finally passed on to him the crown of the Holy Roman Emperor, Ferdinand of Hapsburg had labored in behalf of the dynasty's interests in the hereditary archduchy of Austria and in Germany at large. From the time he arrived at Vienna in 1521—a courteous, modest young prince with a taste for French poetry—Ferdinand had cheerfully taken second place and had been Charles's loyal and skillful vicar even though from his vantage point on the spot he was not always convinced that his vagabond brother really understood the true state of German affairs. Some bitterness emerged between them at the end when Charles considered endowing his son Philip with the imperial dignity as well as the throne of Spain. This plan, however, did not materialize; Ferdinand I and his descendants, under one title or another, ruled Austria and vast stretches of central Europe from 1558 to 1919.[63]

The division of the Hapsburg patrimony with Charles V's abdication left the Austrian branch of the family a mixed inheritance. Deprived of the support of the other dominions and especially of the revenues from the Netherlands—from "the looms of Flanders"—Ferdinand was immeasurably weaker in Germany than Charles had been. But by the same token Vienna remained unentangled in those politico-religious adventures which emanated from Madrid. During the years their Spanish cousin bled himself white in battles with Moslem corsairs, Dutch rebels, and red Indians, to say nothing of Elizabeth I and Henry IV, the Austrian Hapsburgs, poor as churchmice, lived in peace.

It was a precarious peace indeed, imperiled by enemies without and fierce tensions within. Immediately to the east stood the mighty Turks, constantly probing from their Hungarian outposts toward Vienna and the heart of Europe. The fear which their presence inspired and its effect upon the internal life of Germany cannot be exaggerated. Ferdi-

---

63. Friedrich Heer, *The Holy Roman Empire* (New York, 1968), pp. 176 ff. This is a book more admirable for its illustrations than for the accuracy of its text.

nand, with the family knack for picking up crowns, intensified the problem when, in 1526, he was elected King of Bohemia and Hungary. Bohemia, with its independent nobility and its tradition of religious dissension dating back to the Hussite wars of the fifteenth century, was scarcely governable, while the kingship of Hungary put the Hapsburgs face to face with the Turks who had conquered most of the country. Ultimately these non-German lands would form the nucleus of Austrian greatness. Meanwhile the Hapsburgs, more through bluff, bribery, and guile than military strength, managed to put off the definitive confrontation with the Turks to a time (the 1680s and 1690s) when they could win.[64]

Like the Abbé Siéyès, the Austrian Hapsburgs could take satisfaction in having survived. The Holy Roman Empire of the German nation over which they presided survived too, but this most venerable European monarchy did not, like monarchies elsewhere, provide the mechanism for building a unitary state. Instead Charlemagne's empire evolved into a more or less gentlemanly confederation of princes, knights, and towns—300 distinct sovereignties altogether, ranging in size from Bavaria with a population larger than Scotland's to tiny *Ritterschaften,* each composed of a crumbling castle and a few cottages.[65] The imperial diet (*Reichstag*) did meet now and then, but its deliberations took on an increasingly dreamlike character as the notion of a pan-German Reich grew dimmer and each scheme to breathe life into it, each gesture of *Reichsreform,* came to nothing. Neither the principle of empire-wide taxation nor a standing army nor even an imperial customs union (*Reichsgrenzzol*) was acceptable to the princes,[66] who were busy constructing little dynastic dictatorships of their own. An inverse proportion can be discerned in the political development of sixteenth-century Germany: as the empire became weaker the individual states became stronger, became indeed miniatures of the French and Spanish royal courts. Saxon dukes and margraves of Brandenburg had their privy councils too, their cadres of

64. Johannes Janssen, *History of the German People at the Close of the Middle Ages* (London, 1905), VIII, 97 ff. This is a translation from Vol. IV of the 16th German edition.

65. See E. C. Hellbling, *Osterreichische Verfassungs und Verwaltungsgeschichte* (Vienna, 1956).

66. Geoffrey Barraclough, *The Origins of Modern Germany* (New York, 1963, reprint of 2d rev. ed., 1947), pp. 368 ff., has a useful summary.

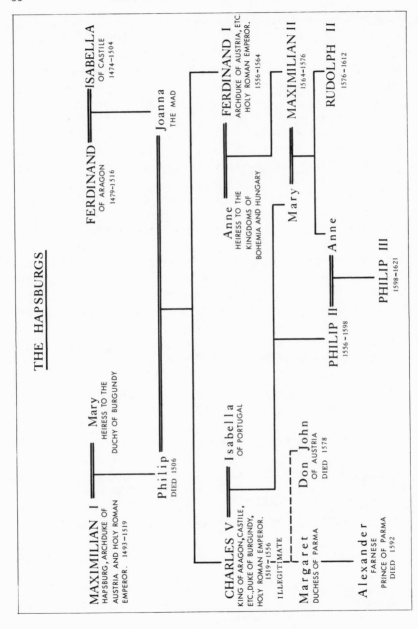

THE HAPSBURGS

MAXIMILIAN I
HAPSBURG, ARCHDUKE OF
AUSTRIA AND HOLY ROMAN
EMPEROR. 1493–1519

Mary
HEIRESS TO THE
DUCHY OF BURGUNDY

FERDINAND
OF ARAGON
1479–1516

ISABELLA
OF CASTILE
1474–1504

Philip
DIED 1506

Joanna
THE MAD

CHARLES V
KING OF ARAGON, CASTILE,
ETC., DUKE OF BURGUNDY,
HOLY ROMAN EMPEROR.
1519–1556

Isabella
OF PORTUGAL

Anne
HEIRESS TO THE
KINGDOMS OF
BOHEMIA AND HUNGARY

FERDINAND I
ARCHDUKE OF AUSTRIA, ETC.
HOLY ROMAN EMPEROR.
1556–1564

ILLEGITIMATE

Don John
OF AUSTRIA
DIED 1578

Mary

MAXIMILIAN II
1564–1576

Margaret
DUCHESS OF PARMA

PHILIP II
1556–1598

Anne

RUDOLPH II
1576–1612

Alexander
FARNESE
PRINCE OF PARMA
DIED 1592

PHILIP III
1598–1621

professional civil servants, their campaigns to convert extraordinary revenues, traditionally granted by estates, into permanent, predictable taxes. This arrangement worked better in north and east Germany, where the governmental units were relatively large and self-sufficient, than it did farther west among the welter of little princedoms in the valleys of the Rhine and the Main. But everywhere in Germany the prestige and power of the empire withered away.

The religious settlement of 1555, the so-called Peace of Augsburg, hastened the imperial decline, because it immeasurably strengthened the hands of the particular princes. Augsburg's famous slogan, "Wessen das Land, dessen auch die Religion," expressed the repudiation not only of the medieval "holy" empire but also of the pan-German nuances of Luther's appeal against an Italian pope. The formal agreement at Augsburg, to allow each ruler to determine whether his state would be Catholic or Lutheran, merely ratified what had long existed in fact. But it was an important political formality because it guaranteed that religion, which elsewhere served as an ideological tool to promote national unity, would in Germany confirm territorial uniformity instead. So long as religion remained a burning issue, the Germans would not have a unitary state.

The settlement of 1555 did not take account of the possibility that a notable prince might become a Calvinist. When the Count Palatine did so in the early 1560s and began to expel from his Rhenish dominions Lutherans and Catholics with zealous indifference, nothing could be done about such illegal activities, save to grieve at the further fragmentation of the German *Volk*. What was called the "ecclesiastical reservation" caused another kind of trouble.[67] This provision of the Peace of Augsburg decreed that the prince-bishoprics—about fifty independent enclaves within the empire, mostly in the west, and a few, like Cologne, of some significance—had to stay in Catholic hands and that if an incumbent converted to Lutheranism, he had to resign. The Lutherans found such an arrangement intolerable, and conflict over it was not long in coming.

Finally, the settlement of 1555 had overall a stultifying effect upon German religiosity, though less upon Catholicism—less because a Catholic prince like the Duke of Bavaria, however forcefully he

67. G. D. Ramsay, *The New Cambridge Modern History,* III, 336 ff.

defined orthodoxy for his subjects, still had to deal with an international ecclesiastical system of which he confessed himself to be a part. No such check acted upon Protestant rulers, who disposed of religious matters pretty much as they saw fit and who increasingly locked the Lutheran churches into an outward juridical conformity which mocked the dynamism of their founder's original protest. Geneva did not repeat Wittenberg's mistake and allow its evangel to be determined by the interests of confessional states; perhaps that was why Geneva led an international movement and Wittenberg did not.

Yet, for all its shortcomings, the Peace of Augsburg did in fact bring religious peace to Germany for sixty years, no mean accomplishment in an era of general sectarian conflict. It was, moreover, the kind of pragmatic solution which the supple intelligence of Ferdinand I could appreciate. The emperor considered himself a disciple of the Dutch humanist Erasmus, who would have applauded the forbearance with which Ferdinand treated heretics in his own archduchy. His conciliatory attitude was no sign of any personal heterodoxy, for Ferdinand was always a regular and indeed a pious Catholic. When in 1561 he learned that his son and heir was flirting with the idea of turning Protestant—young Maximilian had been heard to refer to the pope as "the impudent bishop of Rome"—he demanded and received a sworn submission to the Catholic Church as a condition for succession to the thrones of archduchy and empire.[68] But forty years of riding the whirlwind of German politics had taught Ferdinand to accept facts he could not alter, to eschew extreme religious positions and to accommodate himself to reasonable demands for reform—to adopt, in short, a sensible, not necessarily consistent, program worthy of Erasmus, without, hopefully, sacrificing the essentials of the old faith. This was more easily said than done, and to strive for it took a measure of patience and compromise which looked like pusillanimity to the hotheads on both sides. In any case, though he was unrepresented at Cateau-Cambrésis, the Emperor Ferdinand contributed according to his lights to the Catholic peace.

---

68. For a summary of Maximilian's religious position at this time see Bodhan Chudoba, *Spain and the Empire, 1519–1643* (Chicago, 1952), pp. 105 ff.

Chapter Three

REFORM OF HEAD AND MEMBERS

THE death of Pope Paul IV on August 18, 1559, was the signal for frenzied rioting all over Rome, as though the populace thought that the memory of the hated old man could be effaced by disfiguring the monuments on which his coat of arms appeared and by emptying and then razing the prisons of the Roman Inquisition. Giampietro Carafa had been a widely admired apostle of ecclesiastical reform before his election in 1555. Once he became pope, however, his austerity changed into a fanaticism which at times verged on madness.[1] Surrounded by a gang of greedy, disreputable relatives who looted the patrimony of St. Peter, Paul IV blundered from crisis to crisis until, when he died, the condition of the Papal States and the prestige of the Holy See had sunk to their lowest point in a generation.

The three-month conclave chose a successor cut out of different cloth. Cardinal Gian Angelo de' Medici,[2] a sixty-year-old Milanese (and no kin to the queen of France), had the habits and temperament of a careful lawyer and administrator. A vigorous man of middle height, his basic geniality sparkled in his gray-blue eyes. He was devoted to physical exercise ("Exercise maintains good health, and we do not wish to die in bed," was one of his pontifical maxims), and, disdaining the haughty reserve of his predecessor, he often appeared afoot or on horseback unattended in the streets of the city. Many sophisticates were put off by his coarse manners and garrulousness, but the pope went cheerfully along his own way, shrewd and not always predictable, pleased and sometimes a little astonished that he had managed to climb to the top of the greasy pole.[3]

Pius IV (as Medici styled himself) had a horde of nephews who hurried to Rome to take advantage of their uncle's windfall. Unlike

---

1. For an eloquent evocation of Paul IV's severity, see Owen Chadwick, *The Reformation* (London, 1964), pp. 270 ff.
2. Ludwig Pastor, *History of the Popes* (London, 1952), XV, 66 ff.
3. Leopold von Ranke, *History of the Popes* (New York, 1901), I, 218 ff.

Paul IV, however, the new pope kept a tight rein on his relatives, and he was lucky in their quality: several of them were men of high caliber who served the papacy well. One of them, Charles Borromeo, possessed an extraordinary combination of moral and intellectual gifts. Yet it remains testimony to the deep roots of papal nepotism that within the space of a few weeks Pius IV conferred upon this untried youngster of twenty-one the archbishopric of Milan, the legation of Bologna, the secretariat of state, and a cardinal's red hat. Borromeo needed more than ordinary virtue if he were not to be smothered at the beginning of his career in the lap of plenty.

Such heedless favoritism with its happy outcome was typical of the ironic good fortune which was to pervade the new pontificate—ironic, because, in contrast to his predecessor, Gian Angelo de' Medici did not come to the papal throne with the credentials of a reformer. A keen-witted, amiable, ambitious man, whose past life was not without its scandals,[4] he was a churchman of the old school, a citizen of that lush Renaissance world which had fallen to ruin under the shock of the Reformation and the imperial sack of Rome in 1527. He knew nothing about theology. Reform was not a concept congenial or even readily intelligible to him; indeed, it rubbed against the grain of his whole career. And yet to him, and not to the rigorous, respectable Carafa, was due the initiative which reversed the disintegration of the Roman Church and saved it from the doom predicted on all sides. In a word, to have brought the Council of Trent to a more or less successful conclusion, and thus to have set the course of the Counter Reformation, was no mean accomplishment for any man; for Pius IV it was a prodigy.

I. TRIDENTINE INHERITANCE

During the conclave of 1559, Medici had sworn that if elected he would make it his first business to convene a general council. He was good as his word. On the last day of the year the new pope told the imperial ambassador that he proposed to summon a council, and on January 4, 1560, he formally announced this intention to the consistory of cardinals. During the months following he lost no opportunity to

4. He acknowledged three illegitimate children, and similar moral lapses, even after he became pope, are not beyond question. See Pastor, *Popes*, XV, 74–75.

reiterate his conviction that only a general council could cure the manifold ills of Christendom.

A council already existed in suspension. Though it had not met since 1552, the Council of Trent, its decrees as yet unconfirmed and unpromulgated, was technically still in session, adjourned but not dissolved. As Pius IV attempted to rally support for a new conciliar adventure, his greatest problem was what to do about his Tridentine inheritance.

The cry for reform of the Church was an old one, heard through the anguished voices of humanists and Protestants and, more remotely, of the conciliarists of the fifteenth century.[5] The abuses in clerical life and the low, almost pagan preoccupations of many laity set in motion the original mandate for reform. The administrative machinery of the Church was seen increasingly as a factor contributing to the overall malaise, and so there came into common parlance the pointed slogan, "Reform of Head and Members!"

Connected to such laudable concerns was a theoretical problem, with serious practical ramifications, that went back at least as far as the fourteenth century. Who was to correct ecclesiastical abuses? Did the pope have the ultimate authority to decide matters of faith, morals, and discipline, or did a general council? And indeed what was a council? The apostolic college of pope and bishops? Or these plus the princes, the feudal estates, the universities, the canonists, the theologians? Or perhaps whomever the Holy Roman Emperor, as spokesman for Christendom, should designate?

These questions became relevant only as the papal monarchy in fact foundered from 1300 onward. The Great Western Schism (1378–1415), when two and then three claimants competed for the pope's crown, brought them to a head: the Council of Constance (1414–1418) not only settled the schism but attempted to establish permanent conciliar authority over the papacy by the decrees *Sacrosancta* (which stated that superiority) and *Frequens* (which required the pope to summon a general council every five years).[6]

---

5. For the background to Trent and its early sessions, see Hubert Jedin, *A History of the Council of Trent*, Vol. I (St. Louis, 1957) and Vol. II (London, 1961).

6. For the texts see Joseph Alberigo et al., eds., *Conciliorum oecumenicorum decreta* (Rome, 1962), pp. 415 ff.

Neither the pope elected at Constance nor any of his successors ever confirmed *Sacrosancta* or *Frequens,* and by the last decades of the fifteenth century the "conciliar movement," based on those decrees, no longer posed a threat to the practical hegemony of the papacy. But the "conciliar theory," as a view of the Church's constitution, did survive, notably in the universities, among some canon lawyers, and, more surprisingly, even in the college of cardinals, which pined to establish its theoretical independence. Could not, for example, the cardinals qua cardinals summon a council by defining a state of emergency due to a pope's intransigence?

Learned conversation notwithstanding, the popes had beaten the conciliarists, and at the very moment of their victory they had plunged with gusto into the delights of the Renaissance. They became lavish patrons of the arts, conspicuous in every kind of consumption and ever more deeply involved in the dynastic politics of Italy and Europe. All this meant the expenditure of vast sums of money, with the accompanying growth, to an unprecedented degree, of financial exactions, the nature of which intensified the old problem of reform. For they were not so much legitimate taxes as charges for unwarranted exceptions to the law. Thus Rome used its sovereign authority, so recently challenged by *Sacrosancta,* to interfere in the ecclesiastical affairs of various localities by way of granting dispensations from its own laws. So a bishop could purchase—for all practical purposes this is the correct word—permission to reside outside his diocese, or a monk outside his monastery; priest or layman could buy a dispensation to hold multiple benefices. The Roman Curia, without whose formal approval a candidate could not receive a high ecclesiastical post, cooperated in the appointment of mediocre and even notoriously wicked people by granting, for a fee, dispensations whereby a child could be an archbishop and a king's mistress the superior of a convent of contemplative nuns. With these aberrations went a thousand variants which conspired to undermine any movement of reform anywhere. Members cannot be reformed, it was widely said, until the head is reformed. And who shall reform the head but a council?

The emergence of Luther turned a problem into a crisis. Rising out of what Professor Jedin calls "the spontaneous reform of the members,"[7] the Protestant movement fed upon the gravamina, the com-

7. Jedin, *Trent,* I, 139.

plaints raised by all sectors of German society against the financial chicanery of the Curia. But also at issue was the basic confusion about authority in the Church, especially now that "reform" had an ambiguous connotation. The earlier need for reform was as pressing as ever, but the new sense of the word—reform of doctrine rather than simply reform of practice in accordance with doctrine which was presumed to be immutable and itself unsullied—made the call for a council more compelling and at the same time more hazardous. The hope that Protestantism would go the way of so many medieval heterodoxies and disappear, or at least close itself off into a small enclave of eccentrics, was not realized. Instead it acted, like the schism a century and a half before, as a trigger setting off the process which led inevitably to a council.

The secular powers who held the churches in their kingdoms in so tight a grip took up the cry for a reforming council. But it soon was apparent that they judged the enterprise in the light of their particular circumstances. The pious Charles V, for example, wanted a council less for religious reasons than because he saw it as the only way of restoring the internal peace and strength of Germany. The impious Francis I, reflecting the permanent concern of French policy, did not want a council for precisely the same reason. And so the conciliar project became a ploy in the Hapsburg-Valois conflict, a circumstance calculated to overawe a timid, devious, irresolute man like Pope Clement VII (d. 1534), who evaded with about equal dexterity demands for a council and demands for curial reform.

His successor, the Farnese Pope Paul III (d. 1549), confronted the crisis more forthrightly and decided that, despite the hazards, a council had to be called. His task was infinitely complicated because its success depended upon the good will of monarchs who hated each other and distrusted him. Moreover, the demand for a reforming council, at least in the parts of Europe disaffected by the Lutheran movement, had assumed a more specific form: a "general, free, Christian council in German lands." Harmless and indeed sensible as the formula may have sounded, it expressed a serious threat to Paul III, to the papacy, and to any hope of a restored Christian unity. "Free" meant a council entirely independent of the pope; "general" involved the old conciliar notion of a meeting with a lay as well as an episcopal character; "Christian" was another way of saying that conciliar decisions had to rest exclusively on the Scriptures—that is, on the Scriptures as Martin Luther interpreted them.

So other religious and political factors, besides the papacy's calculated hesitancy, played their parts in working against a council. Yet Paul III displayed a stubborn integrity by convoking a council to Mantua and then to Vicenza in the spring of 1537. Nothing came of this attempt, however, as a fresh war simultaneously broke out between the emperor and the French. The pope then agreed, albeit reluctantly, to send a representative to treat directly with the Lutherans, but this Colloquy of Ratisbon (1541), which Charles V hoped would heal the German schism, achieved nothing either.

The next year saw the first convocation of a council to Trent. Largely Italian in population and of relatively easy access from Italy, Trent was nevertheless a free imperial city, ruled by its prince-bishop, and far enough away from Rome—perhaps 200 miles to the northeast—to satisfy the Germans that a meeting there might avoid undue papal influence. Paul III was not overly happy with the site for that very reason, but he issued the bull of convocation anyway (May 22, 1542). Two weeks later Francis I declared war on the emperor, and once more papal legates were dispatched to a council only to find no one else there. The pope had no choice but to suspend the council until the Peace of Crépy (September, 1544), in which the victorious emperor extorted from the French an agreement to support a council and to be represented at it. The pope accordingly reconvened the council, which finally opened at Trent on December 13, 1545.

Enormous obstacles—described here only in the sketchiest of outlines—had to be overcome in order to have a council at all. The fact that it had at last met, however, did not guarantee a happy termination. The two matters which the bull of convocation had specifically defined as conciliar business were the definition of dogma and internal reform. This somewhat obvious mandate immediately embroiled the assembled fathers[8] in the procedural problem as to what subject was to take precedence. A compromise eventually emerged whereby the two were discussed simultaneously: that is, a doctrinal question took first place on the agenda, then a reform measure, then a doctrinal one again, and so on. Such an arrangement, which worked well enough, proved

8. By "fathers" is meant those who enjoyed a vote—bishops mostly and a few abbots and generals of religious orders.

to be necessary, because there existed an honest difference of opinion with regard to which kind of issue was the more pressing. The lay princes, and particularly the emperor, feared that premature doctrinal definition would harden the divisions which were troubling their domains; what they wanted from the council was structural reform of the Church and strong measures against clerical abuses. At the same time, they were not prepared to surrender any of their princely prerogatives which had contributed so largely to those abuses. The clerics, for their part, insisted on the need for clear-cut doctrinal definitions so that the Catholic people would not be seduced from their faith in the midst of growing intellectual confusion.

The Council of Trent settled on an internal constitution significantly different from what had prevailed at the councils of the fifteenth century, the heyday of the conciliar movement.[9] At Trent only the bishops (the disappointingly small number of thirty-one were on hand for the opening session in 1545), the four or five generals of religious orders, and the handful of representatives of monastic congregations enjoyed the franchise. Moreover, they voted not, as at Constance (1414–1418), by nations but as individuals, which gave rise to the complaint that the Italians (and by implication the pope) possessed an automatic majority. The papal legates who presided also controlled the agenda, though anyone—including the princes' ambassadors—could offer proposals for consideration through the legates.

The format adopted at Trent quickly settled into a consistent pattern. The first stage was the "particular congregation," composed of theological and canonical experts, who debated a proposed decree with the bishops as an audience. Then, once these technicians had explored the doctrinal or reform problem at hand, the bishops met in a "general congregation," during which they formally went over the same ground and hammered out a final text. The last step was the public meeting called a "session," at which an open vote was taken and the decree read out as the council's definitive decision. (Some "sessions" were devoted to liturgical and procedural formalities.)

The work done by the technical experts and the fathers was exhaustive and of a very high caliber. To cite one instance: it took seven months, forty-four particular congregations, and sixty-one general con-

9. For a summary of procedure see Philip Hughes, *The Church in Crisis* (New York, 1960), pp. 310 ff.

gregations before the crucial decree on justification was ready to be voted on at the council's sixth session (January 13, 1547).[10] Give and take was constant, debate lively and free. In all, nine dogmatic decrees—covering such matters as Scripture and tradition, original sin, the sacraments, and of course justification—were issued by the first two meetings at Trent (1545–1547 and 1551–1552). Progress, though less spectacular, was also achieved on the thornier question of internal reform. Episcopal pluralism was condemned and new regulations passed to enhance the efficiency of the pastoral ministry. The fathers of the council, however, found putting their house in order a harder and more frustrating task than barring the doors against Protestant innovations.

The outbreak of still another war ended the first Tridentine meeting in 1547, and there was a lapse until May 1, 1551, when the council took up its burden again. Paul III had died meanwhile. His successor Julius III (d. 1555) faced much the same practical difficulty in securing support for a reconvening at Trent, and his success was only qualified. The French refused to have anything to do with the new convocation. This unhappy circumstance was compensated for to some degree by the appearance in 1552 of Protestant representatives who had spurned invitations to the earlier meeting.[11] A flicker of hope went up that at last a council of reunion had been achieved, but in fact little came out of the discussions, since the Protestants refused to accept the validity of a council presided over by papal legates and the council fathers would not abandon the dogmatic decrees already approved. By the time of adjournment (April 28, 1552), the council could boast of some further progress in the doctrinal area—notably on the sacraments—but of mournfully little in reform. Indeed, the touchy issue of reform of the Roman Curia almost ended the meeting before it started.

10. Henry Denzinger and Clement Bannwart, *Enchiridion Symbolorum Definitionum et Declarationum de rebus Fidei et Morum,* ed. by Karl Rahner (Freiburg, 1952), pp. 284 ff. This is the classic collection of doctrinal as distinct from disciplinary decrees.

11. See for example, Theodore Casteel, "Calvin and Trent: Calvin's Reaction to the Council of Trent in the Context of His Conciliar Thought," *Harvard Theological Review,* 63 (1970), 91–117, which leans heavily on Robert Kingdon, "Some French Reactions to the Council of Trent," *Church History,* XXXIII (June, 1964), 149–155. Calvin called the council "a diseased whore," and the fathers "horned beasts with stinking muzzles."

The election of Paul IV seemed to close the door on the possibility of continuing the Council of Trent, since among Carafa's illusions was the conviction that he could reform the Church by himself. The disasters of his reign, however, as well as the curious phenomenon of a suspended ecumenical council with its decrees unpromulgated and unapplied—even though the troubles were as deep and dark as they had been in 1545—led all concerned, including Pius IV, to think of one more attempt.

It took two years of tortuous diplomacy before the Council of Trent convened for the third and last time.[12] The ultimate success of the negotiations was due to the skill and, even more, to the persistence of Pius IV. The obstacles confronting him were formidable; they included the adamant hostility of the Protestant world, his own curia's instinctive suspicion of any conciliar program, and the general reluctance among the bishops to take on the trouble and expense involved in a journey to and probably long residence at some remote conciliar site.

But the most serious and delicate task the pope faced was to reconcile the divergent views of the three chief Catholic sovereigns, without whose cooperation the council could not succeed. The pope had to deal with a tangle of conflicting plans and purposes, since each of the monarchs in question judged conciliar proposals in terms of his own domestic and foreign policies.

Of the three the position of the Emperor Ferdinand I was the most precarious. Since 1555 an uneasy peace had prevailed among the Lutheran and Catholic princes of Germany, and Ferdinand, as the officer who presided over the rickety confederation of German states which, in effect, the empire was, dreaded above all anything that might disturb the settlement of Augsburg. In the Hapsburg crown lands Ferdinand's Catholic orthodoxy and genuine concern for ecclesiastical reform were beyond question. Even so, he opposed a council unless it were held somewhere else than at Trent and unless it were an entirely new meeting, with no commitment to the decisions reached in 1547 and 1552. What the emperor desperately wanted was religious peace; in this desire, of course, he was not unique, but he knew better than most

12. The best summary is still H. Outram Evennett, *The Cardinal of Lorraine and the Council of Trent* (Cambridge, 1930).

how hated the very name of Trent was to the Protestant princes and how suspicious they were that a papal council would only be a prelude to aggressive action against themselves. A continuation therefore of the former council was to the emperor unthinkable. No Protestant would appear at a meeting whose earlier sessions had already condemned the fundamental Protestant positions. If there had to be a council, said Ferdinand, let it be an entirely new beginning, at a new site, with all questions—including justification—explicitly declared open. And in the meantime, to stall the galloping progress of Protestantism across central Europe, let the pope grant priests permission to marry and laity to receive the cup as well as the host in the Eucharist.

Philip II was not anxious for a council either. The younger Hapsburg still hoped that Elizabeth of England might yet be brought round to the true Church and a Spanish alliance, thereby checkmating French intrusion into Scottish affairs and French ambitions in the Netherlands. A council, especially one that might hurl anathemas at the English heretics, could well upset that design, and so Philip was in no hurry to endorse the pope's plans. On the other hand, he also acknowledged, with a disinterestedness rare among sixteenth-century monarchs, that genuine religious renewal was the overriding need of the times, and once convinced that a council was the necessary instrument of that renewal, he was prepared to support it.

He remained, however, at odds with his uncle on one crucial point. If there were to be a council, it must meet at Trent and it must be a continuation of the earlier sessions. Philip would not abide reopening questions like justification, the nature of the sacraments, and other doctrinal matters which he considered settled and for denying which subjects of his had been burned at the stake. Reunion was one thing, he said; appeasement was something else. Nor did he want further discussion of certain disciplinary canons framed at Trent fifteen years earlier; chief among these was the restriction of the power of that feudal institution the cathedral chapter, a restriction much to the liking of the Spanish crown, which in the interests of centralization was eager to bring to heel any and every independent estate.[13] As pledged in one of the articles of the Treaty of Cateau-Cambrésis, Philip would, as a dutiful son of the Church, support a council; but only a certain kind of council.

13. See Alberigo, *Decreta*, pp. 663 ff.

In France the Guise responded without enthusiasm to Pius IV's call for a council. They pointed out that the kind of religious dissension which was unknown in Spain and which appeared to be pretty well over in Germany now threatened to wreak its havoc in France. They did not oppose the conciliar idea in itself, but they feared that the hard doctrinal definitions which a council might be expected to endorse would render impossible a reconciliation between the armed camps of French Catholics and Protestants. Like Ferdinand they wanted to establish the climate of reunion, and therefore like him they resisted Trent as a conciliar site as well as any suggestion of continuation. The Cardinal of Lorraine, supremely confident in his own powers of persuasion, was certain that in the venerable Gallican tradition of independence from Rome he could himself settle what was amiss in French religious life and ultimately heal the national schism. A general council, yes, he said airily to the papal nuncio, but not now, not at Trent, and, above all, not a continuation.

Here then was the uneasy troika that Pius IV had somehow to harness to his conciliar chariot. Yet he was by nature a cheerful man, and early signs appeared to confirm his optimistic outlook. France and Spain were bound by treaty to support a council, and the emperor was thought to be receptive to the idea. For his part, the pope, as a token to the princes of his good will and of his resolve to treat realistically the ills of the Church, appointed (January, 1560) a commission of cardinals who were to undertake an internal reform of the Curia itself. When the council met, he kept repeating to the various ambassadors, every subject would be open for discussion, every ecclesiastical institution would be scrutinized.[14]

Through the spring of 1560 Pius IV remained expansive and sanguine about his conciliar project. By April gossip in Rome had it that the council would soon reopen at Trent and that funds were being quietly allocated for that purpose. But then in mid-May the pope learned to his astonishment that the King of France had convoked a national council, scheduled to meet in December.[15] This maneuver revealed the fine hand of the Cardinal of Lorraine, for whom such an exclusive French conference could serve a double purpose; it could give him an opportunity to try his considerable powers of persuasion on the

14. Pastor, *Popes*, XV, 179 ff.
15. L. Cristiani, *L'Eglise à l'époque du concile de Trente* (Paris, 1948), pp. 180 ff.

Huguenot leaders in one grand confrontation; or, if circumstances should dictate, the threat of it could be used to force the pope to convene the kind of general council—a new one and not at Trent— acceptable to the Guise.

To the pope the idea sounded like schism, and privately he railed against the arrogance of the Cardinal of Lorraine. In fact, however, the French ploy turned out to be the mechanism by which the deadlock among the powers was broken. Envoys scurried out of Rome—to Vienna, to Madrid, to Venice—all with the same urgent message: the general council must meet soon or France may be lost to the Church. Philip II, as much alarmed as the pope at the thought of a French national council (and the bad example it might be to his own subjects), immediately moved from his reserved position and endorsed the pope's summons. Even Ferdinand, opposed as he was to Trent and continuation, disliked Lorraine's plan even more.

There followed months of diplomacy almost comic in its twists and turns. The emperor said first he would support no council until clerical celibacy and the eucharistic liturgy had been modified,[16] and then he said he would come to Trent if the pope did. Under the impression that Ferdinand had agreed to Trent as a site in return for Pius IV's abandonment of continuation (an incredible miscalculation on the part of Lorraine, for Trent had significance solely because of continuation), the French called off their national council. With that Philip II's conciliar enthusiasm suddenly cooled, only to heat up again early in 1561 when Lorraine's plan was revived; then the King of Spain abruptly ordered his bishops to prepare to leave for Trent.

Through all of this the pope moved warily. As Pastor delicately expressed it, "he was careful not to give offense to the princes, upon whom everything depended, by any definite decision or by too great plainness of speech."[17] Operating as he did with the immense advantage of a single-minded policy, he always kept one step ahead of his unruly royal sons, who had to worry not only about him but also about

16. There was nothing new or particularly imperial or German about these suggestions. The distinguished Cardinal Cajetan had proposed them as early as 1531. See W. Friedensberg, ed., *Quellen und Forschungen aus Italienischen Archiven und Bibliotheken*, III (Rome, 1900), 17 ff. For Cajetan's stature as theologian and protoreformer see the double number of *Revue Thomiste* (Nov., 1934–Feb., 1935), *passim*.

17. Pastor, *Popes*, XV, 194.

each other. On the crucial matter of continuation, Pius IV, though he never doubted that new sessions at Trent must continue the earlier work done there, flatly refused to use the word, and the bull *Ad Ecclesiae Regimen* (November 29, 1560) which formally convoked the council was, at the pope's personal insistence, ambiguous on the point. Meanwhile he privately assured all parties that their conflicting wishes would be satisfied if only the council were allowed to meet. In this manner, little by little and step by step, Catholic Europe was nudged along the road that led back to Trent.

In hopes that the council could open at Easter, 1561, Pius IV named in March a presidium of five cardinal-legates. But when a month later the first two of these passed under the decorative arches set up at Trent's main gate, they found only a handful of bishops present, most of whom had been dragooned from the neighboring districts to put a decent face on the legates' arrival. The opening had to be postponed. One at a time the Italian bishops drifted in. On May 18 the worried legates were cheered when the Archbishop of Braga arrived, after a long and exhausting journey from Portugal. His example was cited by an increasingly impatient pope who could not seem to hurry the departure of the reluctant bishops resident in his own states. On September 26 the first of the Spanish delegation appeared. At about the same time French prelates were assembling at Poissy for Lorraine's national council (though they didn't call it that and claimed they met to select delegates to go to Trent—which they did not do). Papal diplomats dispatched to Germany reported that the Catholic bishops refused to attend the council either in person or by proxy, and the Protestant princes curtly did likewise—indeed, the latter returned the ornate written invitations unopened. The nuncio sent to England was not even allowed to land in the country.[18]

On December 9 the last of the legates arrived at Trent with the pope's order that the council should open at once. The emperor pleaded for a few weeks' delay, and finally, on January 18, 1562, 113 voting fathers began with liturgical splendor the last fateful sitting of the Council of Trent.

18. Wallace MacCaffrey, *The Shaping of the Elizabethan Regime* (Princeton, 1968), p. 109.

2. TRIDENTINE FINALE

It lasted just less than two years,[19] and often in the course of that time it teetered on the brink of collapse. Inside the cathedral where public meetings were held, and in the private committee rooms, hardly a day passed without some bishop or ambassador laying an ultimatum on the conciliar table. During one ten-month period formal business had to be suspended, because the fathers were so closely and so bitterly divided. The wrangling spread to the streets of Trent, where the retainers of bishops of different nationalities drew their swords and railed at each other with cries of "Italia" and "España." Yet, when the day of adjournment finally came, men who had been at such deep odds were seen to embrace as tears of joy streamed down their faces. Out of fury and reconciliation was the Council of Trent fashioned, and so it passed into the lifeblood and the folklore of the Roman Church.

It was not a council of reunion. Though safe-conducts were offered to the Protestants, no one really thought they would be accepted; no one dared hope that the council could heal a schism now nearly a half-century old. Trent turned instead to the task of reinforcing and invigorating what had not been lost. To do so meant to define Catholic doctrine as precisely as possible and to correct as far as was practical the abuses which disfigured the Church.

To omit the qualifications imposed by possibility and practicality from an analysis of Trent leads to conclusions about it no less inaccurate than uncritical adulation does.[20] The fathers of the council lived in a real world and contended with forces not always ready to yield to abstract argument. In fact they operated within an area of broad agreement: they agreed, for example, on the sacrificial character of the Mass and on the primacy of the pope. But their debates revealed fierce differences of opinion as to how the Mass is a sacrifice offered for the quick and the dead, and how the pope's preeminence in the Church ought to be understood. They realized that the money indulgence,

19. A useful summary is Hubert Jedin, *Krisis und Abschluss des Trienter Konzils* (Freiburg, 1964).

20. Contrast the often sardonic comments of Ranke with the euphoric ones of H. Daniel-Rops, *Un Ère de Renouvenu: La Réforme Catholique* (Paris, 1955), and of Pierre Janelle, *The Catholic Reformation* (Milwaukee, 1949).

whatever its theoretical justification, had to be eliminated, but they also realized that Philip II would never surrender the *cruzada* which, though technically still a money indulgence, was now a cornerstone of Spanish fiscal stability. The conciliar decree had somehow to reflect both realities.

By its nature the council was dominated by compromise and by the kind of partisan maneuvers that result in compromise. This does not mean, as has sometimes been alleged, that it evaded the major issues for the sake of a jerry-built uniformity. It does mean, however, that the basic rule of any conciliar venture prevailed also at Trent: no decision could be reached without moral unanimity. A simple majority could not express the mind of the council, because, as the fathers firmly believed, the Holy Spirit did not manifest his will in that fashion. If debate and argument did not produce a clear mandate on a particular issue, the council as council had to remain silent about it or, at best, say no more formally than what the fathers could agree to. A general council is a species of high politics, and as such its art is the art of the possible.

Some honest differences were resolved at Trent, others were not. In January, 1562, a great many options still remained open, a great many divergent traditions clamored for a hearing. The panel of distinguished cardinal-legates whom Pius IV had the good sense to appoint gave evidence of the variety of attitudes which abounded at the council. The princely Cardinal Gonzaga, senior legate and the council's presiding officer, brought to Trent, along with the prestige of his great name and reputation, the credentials of that learned, pious, but somewhat effete Christian humanism which had become as fashionable in noble Italian families as pagan humanism once had been.[21] More roughly hewn was Cardinal Hosius, a Pole who had already done direct battle with the Protestants and was itching to do so again. The Augustinian Cardinal Seripando was the theologian on the legatine bench; he understood to an extent rare among Catholics the thrust of the Protestant doctrinal position and sympathized with what he considered the positive aspects of it. Like most intellectuals he found the routine of governing irksome and painful.[22] Cardinal Simonetta, by contrast, was in his element as legate; a practical man, a lawyer, a curial careerist, he may not have understood why the ecclesiastical system was as it was, but he knew down to the smallest detail how it worked.

The legates guided the proceedings of a body which ultimately totaled 255 voting members, many of whom, like the fiery Peter Guerrero, Archbishop of Granada and leader of the Spanish delegation, were men of considerable stature. Only two of the fathers were German, only one was English (and he an exile), and one Dutch. Thirty-one came from Spain with about as many from the Spanish-ruled parts of Italy, twenty-six from Venice, and the same number, including eventually the Cardinal of Lorraine, from France. The largest single bloc of bishops, forty-five, was from the Papal States, and they helped give Pius IV a large voice in the conciliar hall, if not the automatic majority he was often accused of having. The corps of canonists and theologians, the sixteen ambassadors accredited to the council by various princes, the servants attached to all these personages (Gonzaga's suite alone numbered 160), composed an army which severely strained the resources of a town whose normal population was only 6,000. High-priced bread and inadequate housing were permanent features of the Council of Trent.

Just as constant was the less mundane, still unresolved constitutional question of the relationship between the body of bishops and the pope. It appeared at the council under various guises. For instance, was the council really free if its agenda was controlled by the papal legates who received regular instructions from Cardinal Borromeo in Rome? The fathers certainly did not envisage a council free in the sense of separate from the pope or entirely independent of his direction, but they differed strongly over the degree of that direction; what some called leadership others called unwarranted interference.[23]

A related problem had to do with the Roman Curia. No one, including the pope, denied the urgent need to reform the Curia, but who was to do it? The pope claimed that his administration was his unique

---

22. Hubert Jedin, *Papal Legate at the Council of Trent* (London, 1947), contains much background information besides a biography of Seripando.

23. A. Vacant et al., eds., "Pie IV," *Dictionnaire de Théologie Catholique* (Paris, 1903–50), XI, cols. 1635 ff.

concern, that conciliar action in this field would encroach upon his prerogative. The bishops did not want to challenge the primacy as such, and they had to admit the pope's argument was not unreasonable. But, when they pondered the papacy's recent record, they were skeptical about the pope's promises to put his own house in order. The non-Italians in particular despaired of a conciliar program which legislated local and universal reform without at the same time curbing the Church's central bureaucracy's power to dispense with such legislation. And Pius IV did not help his cause much when news reached Trent that he had promoted to cardinal one boy of eighteen and another of eleven.

Yet despite such lapses, which showed he had still some nostalgia for the good old days, the pope handled these dangerous topics adroitly enough. He by no means lacked support among the fathers, some of whom indeed were more papalist than he was. As an experienced diplomat he knew when to bend and when to stand firm. But in the spring of 1563 even he and the saintly Borromeo could not have saved the council from the combined attack of the emperor, the Cardinal of Lorraine, and the Archbishop of Granada; it took John Morone to do that.[24]

The issue appears at first glance harmlessly academic. Was a bishop required to reside in his diocese by a law of God or a law of the Church? Everybody agreed that in practice a bishop had a moral obligation to live among and care for his people and that the widespread failure to do so was probably the single greatest cause of the Church's troubles. The pope was as anxious as any council father to effect this crucial reform and thus be rid of the hundred and more nonresident bishops who regularly lived in Rome. But if the council proclaimed that such episcopal residence was required by divine law it would be tantamount to saying that the pope's primacy was merely of honor; it would be conciliarism come to life again. It would mean that a bishop assumed his powers and jurisdiction directly from God and without the mediation of the pope.

Involved then in this debate, which ultimately monopolized the council's deliberations, was a tangle of doctrinal and practical considerations, interwoven with less exalted matters like individual ambition and political expediency. The Spanish delegation, led by Guerrero,

24. Henri Hauser, *La prépondérance espagnole* (Paris, 1948), pp. 23 ff.

pressed vigorously for a divine-law definition, and though it never reached majority status it was a steady bloc and enjoyed the prestige which the unquestionable ability of the Spaniards and the ambivalent support of the Cardinal of Lorraine earned for it. If tragedy is the conflict between right and right, the seeds of tragedy for the Council of Trent were here, because except for Lorraine, who kept shifting from side to side, the antagonists confronted each other strong in argument, character, and conviction. The attempt at compromise by the Jesuit general Laynez, who argued that a bishop's sacramental powers came directly from God and his jurisdictional ones through the pope, did not persuade his fellow Spaniards. The reformation of the Church demands a corps of bishops sanctioned by God and their king, said Guerrero. To define residence as divinely ordained means the end of the papacy and the destruction of the Church's unity, replied the papalists. The legates parried one Spanish thrust after another until by March, 1563, the council ground to a standstill, deadlocked and threatened by premature closure. Then an act of God intervened.[25]

On March 2 Gonzaga died, and a few weeks later so did Seripando. Pius IV, immediately and instinctively (he consulted no one about the decision), appointed Cardinal Morone president of the council. Milanese by birth and a cardinal since 1542, Morone was at the height of his powers as a diplomat and man of affairs. He was firm yet supple; his speculative intelligence was keen enough to penetrate the subtlest theological issue and yet not so prepossessing as to immobilize him from action. Pius IV trusted him without reserve, and so did the emperor, who had known and respected him for thirty years. That Morone had been imprisoned for alleged heresy by the half-mad and wildly anti-Spanish Paul IV was appreciated by Philip II and Guerrero. Above all, he had the courage and singleness of purpose which could preserve the council in its most difficult hour. He was, as Ranke said, the indispensable man.[26]

Through a whirlwind of personal diplomacy—his first official act as senior legate was a three-week conference with Emperor Ferdinand at Innsbruck—Morone got the council going again. He played upon Lorraine's vanity and succeeded first in isolating and then in convert-

25. For detailed account, see C-J. Hefele, H. Leclercq, and P. Richard, *Histoire des Conciles* (Paris, 1931), IX, 837 ff.

26. Ranke, *Popes*, I, 235.

ing that fickle Frenchman to his own side. He reminded the emperor how important it was for the Hapsburg dynasty that the pope should confirm the election of Maximilian as his father's successor on the imperial throne. He defused the residence issue by suggesting a formula which guaranteed episcopal dignity within the framework of the papal primacy. In so doing he convinced the stubborn Guerrero that, since divine-law residence lacked any semblance of moral unanimity among the fathers, to insist upon it could only wreck the council and preclude the possibility of any meaningful reform, and that in any case King Philip, who needed the pope's cooperation in his Mediterranean policy, was not likely to thank his bishops if their intransigence weakened the papacy without any concomitant gain.

But Morone was not content merely with skillful maneuver. He silenced Laynez and the other extreme papalists. He persuaded the pope to allow the council to take up certain measures of reform affecting the Curia and the college of cardinals. When the pope, under pressure from Spain, suggested procedural changes in the conduct of the council, Morone threatened to resign, and the suggestion was withdrawn. He presented during the summer of 1563 a sweeping program of clerical reform which incorporated views acceptable to the pope, the secular rulers, and all the factions within the council. He even submitted a long schema for the reform of Christian princes who, as he said wryly, were so anxious to reform everybody else though it was due largely to their rapacity and scandalous private lives that so many curses had fallen upon the Christian commonwealth. The clamor of the ambassadors forced the eventual substitution of a bland exhortation to rulers to respect the rights of the Church, but Morone (and Pius IV) had scored a point, and he may have foreseen that the withdrawal of his original proposal could serve a turn when the time came to promulgate the Tridentine decrees in the various European capitals.

Thanks to Morone, the Council of Trent in its final phase accomplished an enormous amount. In the area of doctrine it completed the work on the sacraments begun at the earlier sessions (and thus, as Pius IV had hoped, settled without adverting to it the much debated continuation question). The essentially peripheral matters of purgatory, indulgences, veneration of the saints, and the like, which had loomed so large in the early Reformation controversies, received brief but definitive statement in a form destined to shape Catholic piety for the next four centuries.[27] The council in effect established a thoughtful theological alternative to Protestantism.

In bulk the reform legislation of the council's last two years far exceeded what had been approved at Trent before. It was, however, narrow in scope in that it aimed almost exclusively at restoring the tattered state of the clergy. Except for the celebrated *Tametsi,* which outlawed clandestine marriages and hence affected the laity, the reform decrees concentrated on cutting away the tangle of abuses which, at the eve of the Reformation, had almost smothered the effectiveness of the Catholic priesthood. Simony, pluralities, nonresidence, ignorance, racketeering: these the council fathers attacked ruthlessly and, if one bears in mind that they were themselves personally involved, courageously. And to the extent that the passage of laws could cure ills that went so deep, their radical surgery must be judged a success. Nothing the council did was of more enduring practical importance to the future of Catholicism than the delineation of the Tridentine ideal of the priest. He was to be well if narrowly educated, decently but not extravagantly supported, wedded to his parish, subject to his bishop, sober, unworldly, sustained in his vocation by the regular prayer of the breviary. He was still a member of a distinct caste—a world away in this regard from the Protestant preacher—but he must see his caste's raison d'être in sacramental service to the less spiritually endowed inhabitants of the Lord's vineyard. The Council of Trent elevated the ministerial priesthood to the skies by eliminating the vagabond priest of the Middle Ages, the chantry priest, the illiterate and promiscuous priest, the absentee parson, the pardoner, the relic-peddling friar. Nor were the fathers content with pious exhortation: so that bad priests would never again be commonplaces of Catholic life, they set out in detail the regulations of residence, the financial arrangements, the type of training—in new institutions called seminaries—out of which was to emerge this dominant father figure of post-Tridentine Catholicism.

On December 4, 1563, the Council of Trent came at last to an end, almost eighteen years from the day it began. Its decisions were to affect the day-to-day life of a religious body to which three-quarters of the population between the Atlantic and the Russian frontier belonged. At Trent a great variety of interests met; the council was a microcosm

27. Alberigo, *Decreta*, pp. 772 f., for the brief decree on indulgences.

wherein could be seen actually at work the conflicting forces that would shape much of Europe's destiny down to the Treaties of Westphalia. How much of this was sensed by those gathered that December day for the solemn closing cannot be said. But afterward they recalled how the cathedral's walls shook at the wave upon wave of cheering, led by the Cardinal of Lorraine, a magnificent figure in his scarlet robes of office.[28]

3. THE NEW LEAVEN

The Council of Trent provides a striking example of a valid distinction between the conservative and the reactionary. On both the doctrinal and practical levels the solutions reached at Trent had their roots deep in the past, and yet took into account the specifically contemporary questions Protestantism had raised. With regard to the crucial decrees on justification and the sacraments, the fathers, to put it briefly and no doubt oversimply, reasserted the traditional explanation that righteousness was an internal quality of the human spirit and not merely, as Luther had maintained, an external decree by which guilt was not imputed to the sinner. The life of grace, produced by God's inscrutable mercy in conjunction with man's good works, was in fact a divine friendship which elevated human capacities to a supernatural plane of activity where sustenance was to be found most appropriately in these supreme signs of God's favor, the mystic works called sacraments. The fathers of Trent, far from being satisfied with mere assertion in this regard, argued their view of Christian revelation point by point, employing the most sophisticated theological tools available to them and addressing themselves to those matters which the religious tumults of the sixteenth century had made particularly relevant.

Similarly, the reform decrees, though precise and in many cases minutely detailed, represented no radical departure from the Church's accepted institutional framework. They took for granted that the basic structure of curia, diocese, and parish, as well as of monastic and conventual foundations, was sound, and that shortcomings in the organization were due to human wickedness. Instead of entertaining an overhaul of ecclesiastical finances, the fathers reaffirmed and even strengthened the benefice system with its essential feudal rationale of real estate income attached inalienably to a particular office. They

28. *Dictionnaire de Théologie Catholique,* XV, col. 1484.

aimed not to alter but to correct, to strip away abuses encrusted on the structure, to tighten it and render the exploitation of it by greedy individuals and corporations more difficult.[29] As Europe was in 1563, and would be for a long time, such a program, though conservative, could not be labeled anachronistic.

Trent and the Counter Reformation movement to which Trent gave direction were conservative also in the sense that they expressed a prior religious awakening that went back at least a hundred years. Informal, often inarticulate, this spirit of reform was hard to delineate, scattered as it was in sources so disparate as Thomas à Kempis's *Imitation of Christ* and the fierce sermons of Savonarola. Luther had no corner on the adventure of inner conversion; Ignatius Loyola, founder of the Jesuits, passed through a similar experience six years after Luther, and Gaspar Contarini, the Venetian nobleman whose luminous piety helped transform the college of cardinals, six years earlier. This longing for a renewal of Christian life manifested itself in a hundred different ways and different places, and ultimately it came to Trent, to the papal court, to the new seminaries, and to the old religious orders.

It came dramatically to the city of Rome in the person of St. Philip Neri (d. 1595), whose career showed that the Catholic revival was a phenomenon which preceded, sustained, and finally survived the formalities of the council.[30] Born at Florence in 1515, Philip by mid-century was leading a nomadic, hand-to-mouth existence in Rome, where he had organized an informal confraternity to care for the poor and sick. A few years later he was ordained priest, but instead of changing his mode of life he merely added sacramental good works to those he was already performing. Before long his confessional at San Girolamo attracted a large and varied group of penitents who sought Philip's advice as much as sacramental absolution. Little by little his confraternity evolved into an oratory, a kind of study club with its accent, as the name suggests, on prayerful, almost pentecostal action. And as men of fashion and men of power—curial officials, scholars, aristocrats—joined the oratory, Philip Neri's peculiarly personal apostolate gradually permeated to every stratum of Roman society.

29. See especially the reform decree of July 15, 1562 (Session XXIII), in Alberigo, *Decreta*, pp. 720 ff.

30. A classic study is L. Ponnelle and L. Bordet, *Saint Philippe Neri et la Société Romaine de son Temps* (Paris, 1928). See also Meriol Trevor, *Apostle of Rome: Philip Neri, 1515–1595* (London, 1967).

Philip possessed a contagious sense of humor, a wit, and an eccentricity which helped make him for forty years a familiar and immensely popular figure on the streets of Rome. Other factors no doubt were at work in transforming the world's most cynical city into a capital of religious revival, but none of them mattered as much as St. Philip Neri. God's jester, he called himself, a "mystic in motley";[31] behind the buffoon's mask was a man on fire with zeal and conviction. But the reform spirit alive in him was of the old-fashioned variety, conservative as Trent had been conservative, with no thought of altering the Church's structure or trying to live outside it.

St. Philip and the oratory nevertheless met considerable official resistance. Paul IV, always suspicious, contemplated suppressing the movement, but when the cardinal he had put in charge of investigating it suddenly died, he desisted, apparently because he shared to some extent the general Roman view that God had directly intervened to save his jester. Everywhere the reform spirit encountered opposition, sometimes in high places, more often from the masses of men who understandably hesitated to endorse the ardor of the saints. Spain, for example, had a long familiarity with mysticism, especially among the clergy which was famous for its fervor and its ignorance. But when St. Teresa of Avila (d. 1582) tried to combine this tradition with theological learning and the internal reform of the Carmelite order, she aroused widespread hostility as well as the somber suspicions of the Inquisition.[32]

Teresa was exactly the same age as Philip Neri, and though, like him, she was totally untouched by Protestant ideas, she too represented the same religious awakening that under other circumstances had produced Luther and Calvin. As a young woman she entered the Carmelite community in Avila and followed a respectable if unexacting religious routine until, at forty, she experienced her conversion and began those flights of mystical prayer which eventually led her to the ecstasy of the "spiritual marriage." Such divine favor, however, brought with it no relief from illness, frustration, and a prodigious amount of physical exertion, as Teresa took upon herself the task of restoring in Spain the primitive rule and austerity of Carmel. In 1562 she started

31. The title of a popular biography by Theodore Maynard.
32. Cristiani, *Concile de Trente,* pp. 442 ff., has a good summary and helpful bibliography.

with a few like-minded companions in a new convent located in an Avila back street. Its pristine rigidity was symbolized by the bare feet of the nuns, the "discalced" Carmelites who abandoned all things to seek communion with Christ, the bridegroom. Through the rest of her life St. Teresa was poised between the necessarily private life of the contemplative and the relentlessly public activity of the reformer. She crisscrossed the bleak and dangerous countryside of old Castile, overcoming apathy and outright opposition to set up her foundations of reformed sisters and friars; and yet she never left that mysterious, silent land of contemplation, where heart speaks to heart and words are unnecessary.

Her profoundly interior spirituality left her little patience with formalism; "I am not," she once said, "one of your sign of the cross mongers." Yet she never dreamed of departing from the doctrine of the sacraments as proclaimed at Trent; indeed, she viewed the contemplative vocation as rooted in that doctrine. Similarly, though to win her way she had to battle some of her superiors, she did so always confident of the basic soundness of the ecclesiastical structure. This formidable woman, in an age which frowned upon assertive females, had the drive and shrewdness of a political organizer. No fanciful designs for her; true religion, she liked to say, begins with common sense. But she possessed as well an acute speculative intellect and a flair for literary expression which combined to make her a great Spanish stylist. The books she wrote at the command of her confessors not only recounted but explained her adventures in the higher reaches of prayer. These treatises, along with those of her poet-disciple, St. John of the Cross (d. 1591),[33] have formed the staple of mystical theology ever since and, as used by spiritual directors all over the Catholic world, have had, it is not extravagant to say, a continuing effect upon millions of people.

St. Teresa's success in joining the active to the contemplative vocation was matched, though perhaps less attractively, in the work of St. Charles Borromeo (d. 1584) in Milan.[34] Pius IV's nephew, the first resident archbishop in a century, wore himself into an early grave converting Milan into the ideal of the Tridentine diocese. He person-

33. The standard biography is Crisógno de Jesús, *Vida de San Juan de la Cruz* (Madrid, 1955).
34. See Paul Broutin, *L'Évêque dans la Tradition Pastorale du XVI*e *siècle* (Brussels, 1953), especially pp. 97 ff., and Paolo Prodi, "Charles Borromée Achévêque de Milan, et la Papaute," *Revue d'Histoire Ecclésiastique*, LXII (1967), 379–411.

ally oversaw every facet of the reform activity: parochial visitations, regular synods with his suffragans, preaching (which he found very difficult), exhorting, disciplining in season and out of season. Despite a certain grimness in private demeanor which spilled over into some of his administrative acts—he decreed, for instance, that men and women must worship in separate buildings—Borromeo demonstrated what a bishop who simply tended to business could accomplish and, conversely, how calamitous episcopal absenteeism had been. He founded a new seminary and a new religious order; hospitals, hospices, schools, sprang up under his hand. Nothing was too insignificant, nobody in his vast jurisdiction was too unimportant, for the cardinal's personal attention. Heedless of his own comfort, his body emaciated by horrendous fasts and long vigils of prayer, he drove rather than led his flock into the postconciliar era. When the Spanish rulers of Milan tried to interfere in his projects, he cited the precedent of his fourth-century predecessor, the great Ambrose, and called down on their heads the thunder of excommunication. He died at forty-six, and ordinary Milanese, always a little afraid of him, remembered how this prince had given all his possessions away and how, when the dreadful plague of 1576 had struck the city, he had ministered to his people with his own hands.

St. Charles, unique in the measure of his gifts, in his personal sanctity, and in the extent of his influence, was nevertheless only one among a legion of episcopal reformers. To be sure, he had learned much from the handful of devoted, pastoral bishops of the previous generation, and so he too was a product of that reform spirit which preceded and outlasted the Council of Trent. But he and others of like age were able to carry the reform much further, because the council had greatly strengthened their authority within their dioceses. This was an important instance of the way Trent channeled, formalized, and thus made more effective the spasmodic instincts for reform. The low quality of the pre-Tridentine episcopate reflected the weakness to which the venal policies of the Curia had reduced it. So many frustrations were built into the office that a man could not do a decent job even if he wanted to, and therefore fewer and fewer decent men wanted the job. The council, by clipping the wings of the Curia, assured a bishop of control over his subjects who could no longer evade his jurisdiction by purchasing a Roman dispensation. He enjoyed

firmer authority too over the exempt religious orders, so called because
as international organizations they were independent of a bishop's territorial supervision. Trent saw to it that in practice Franciscans or
Dominicans at work in a particular diocese had to account to the
bishop almost as much as the secular clergy did.

The tension between the episcopate and the orders was never entirely
eliminated, nor could it have been. But as both became imbued with
Tridentine ideals, they learned to cooperate effectively, as St. Charles
and the newest of the orders, the Society of Jesus, did most of the time.
Already by the 1560s the Jesuits considered themselves, and were
widely considered by others, the elite of the reform movement, the
shock troops of a revived Catholicism. No group within the Church
gave more consistent testimony to the Tridentine doctrine of the value
of good works, and indeed the scope and variety of Jesuit avocations
soon became the wonder of the world.[35]

From the original seven University of Paris students who at Montmartre in 1534 had bound themselves together by religious vow,[36] the
Society twenty-five years later counted more than a thousand members,
organized into provinces which stretched as far from Europe as Brazil
and India. By 1610 their numbers would multiply twelve times again.
None of this prodigious growth could have been foreseen by the unlettered young Basque soldier who had wrestled with God in lonely,
mystic rapture in a cave near the Spanish town of Manresa. But St.
Ignatius Loyola (d. 1556) proved himself a supple as well as a holy
man, an organizational genius indeed.[37] By the time he died he had
molded his order's tone and spirit and its constitutional structure as
well. The latter emphasized mobility and flexibility within a framework of iron discipline. Jesuits had to be prepared to go anywhere, do
anything, and adapt to any circumstances in the service of religion.
They had therefore to be well and variously educated,[38] seasoned by
experience before being admitted to final vows, ready to adjust their

35. See James Brodrick, *The Origin of the Jesuits* (London, 1940), for a readable and
scholarly account.

36. Michael Foss, *The Founding of the Jesuits* (New York, 1969), is a detailed account.

37. A short biography out of an immense literature is Alain Guillermou, *La Vie de
Saint Ignace de Loyola* (Paris, 1956).

38. Something of the primitive Jesuit notions about education for a post-Tridentine
Catholic can be seen in F. de Dainville, *Les Jesuites et l'Education de la Société Française: la Naissance de l'Humanisme Moderne* (Paris, 1940), I, especially 166 ff.

apostolate to the needs of those they met. They wore no distinctive garb, and their freedom from the obligation of chanting the divine office in choir gave them two or three hours a day more than the average monk to preach, to catechize, to administer hospitals, orphanages, and colleges, to teach in diocesan seminaries, to write books, to shrive kings and tutor royal children, to travel to Ingolstadt and Posen and London and, as St. Francis Xavier did, across the mysterious East to the very gates of Cathay.

Xavier and his companions at Montmartre had sworn to bring Christ to the Moslems in the Levant; in the end they accomplished almost everything except that vaguely romantic scheme. The genius of the Society lay in its readiness to turn realistically to the tasks at hand, or, as its enemies put it, to trim sails and seize the expedient opportunity for its own advancement. The struggle against Protestantism did not figure in the plans of the first Jesuits, but events, and the Jesuit capacity to adjust to events, determined that the Society's greatest labors would be done in Europe itself, where the old religion had fallen prey to corruption and heresy. So James Laynez, instead of going to Palestine, first taught theology in Rome, then was a missioner in several Italian cities, then accompanied a Spanish expedition to Africa, and finally went to Trent and assumed a leading role in all three sessions of the council.[39]

St. Ignatius saw the Jesuit as a man who developed his particular talents as much as possible and then joined with others similarly ripened in a cooperative venture of Christian service. To recruit and keep together gifted individuals, who tended, because they were gifted, to be buoyant, restive spirits, involved strong direction from the top. To effect this St. Ignatius established a constitution which was in tune with the political currents of the time and made the Society a microcosm of those centralized dictatorships which everywhere were replacing the medieval system of checks and balances with efficient bureaucracies.[40] Jesuits were ruled by a general who held office for life and governed through a hierarchy of assistants, provincials, and rectors appointed by himself. The Society's sole legislative body met to elect a new general and otherwise only at his discretion. The general soon

39. A popular treatment is Joseph Fichter, *James Laynez, Jesuit* (St. Louis, 1944).

40. A good summary is Alain Guillermou, *St. Ignace de Loyola et la Compagnie de Jésus* (Paris, 1960), pp. 113 ff.

received the nickname "the black pope," and not inappropriately, for as the order thrived and expanded he controlled an ever increasingly sophisticated and powerful human machine.

The smooth running of that machine was due in large part to the caliber of the early generals.[41] Laynez (d. 1565), after a brief internal struggle, succeeded St. Ignatius and was succeeded in turn by St. Francis Borgia (d. 1572), once a duke and grandee of Castile and the complete antithesis of his disreputable great-grandfather, Pope Alexander VI. The extraordinarily able Claud Aquaviva (d. 1615), another Spaniard, guided the fortunes of the Society into the seventeenth century. But equally necessary to success was the willingness of individual Jesuits to see their cooperative endeavors as dependent upon obedience to the will of their superiors. This was one, though by no means the only, reason for the importance of *The Spiritual Exercises*.[42] The members of the Society used this little book, the genesis of which went back to St. Ignatius's experiences at Manresa and Paris, as the instrument of their conversion and perseverance. The *Exercises* "were in a sense the systematised, de-mysticised quintessence of the process of Ignatuis' own conversion and purposeful change of life, and they were intended to work a similar change in others."[43] With their carefully planned states of inner purification and organic growth in mental prayer, they formed a spiritual manual which, however, was to be lived rather than read. They may seem at this distance a slender thread with which to bind a man, embattled perhaps by heretics or savages, to judgments decided upon by his general far away, but, like the Jesuit vocation itself, the *Exercises* were infinitely variable, and as applied by a skillful director—often by way of a thirty-day retreat—they could appeal to people of very different temperaments and levels of religious discernment.

Except possibly for Calvin's *Institutes,* no sixteenth-century book had the far-reaching effect of *The Spiritual Exercises*.[44] The Jesuits used their method and content to sustain an *esprit de corps* and, no less, to

41. See Guenther Lewy, "The Struggle for Constitutional Government in the Early Years of the Society of Jesus," *Church History*, XXIX (June, 1960), 141–160.

42. The classic commentary is Joseph de Guibert, *La Spiritualité de le Compagnie de Jésus* (Rome, 1953). See especially pp. 525 ff.

43. H. Outram Evennett, *The Spirit of the Counter Reformation* (Cambridge, 1968), p. 45.

44. See comparison in André Favre-Dorsaz, *Calvin et Loyola* (Paris, 1951), pp. 143 ff.

vitalize the host of apostolates they engaged in. As their influence spread so did the Ignatian idea of the Christian's vocation as analogous to that of the soldier who joins his own skills to those of his comrades and moves with them and under his captain's lead to battle the enemy. Courage, discipline, perseverance, and a kind of Renaissance optimism about the human condition and the value of human endeavor were the hallmarks of the Jesuit message and, indeed, of the whole mentality of the Counter Reformation.[45]

As that *Weltanschauung* took gradual hold, a subtle but momentous change could be discerned in Catholic societies all over Europe: reform became fashionable. There is no need to interpret this development cynically. How much of life, religious and otherwise, turned then, as it does now, on convention and social acceptability. How important it was that the Catholic community should begin to assume that bishops ought to be at work in their dioceses and pastors in their parishes. Priests increasingly were expected to know something about theology, to be able to explain the Scriptures to their people and to give counsel as well as absolution in the confessional. It was not new to consider a priest who kept a mistress a sinner; but now he was judged to be gauche as well, and respectable people were no longer prepared to indulge him. Once it ceased to be extraordinary, the reform movement had won its victory.

4. ROMA REDIVIVA

Besides the traditional religious vows of poverty, chastity, and obedience, the professed Jesuit also swore to submit himself directly to the will of the pope. This was the famous "fourth vow," which brought the Jesuits so much hostility from secular rulers and independent-minded bishops (to say nothing of understandably suspicious Protestants). Indeed some of the popes themselves, despite the almost embarrassing pledge of loyalty, had reservations about the Society's novel approach to the religious life. Sixtus V never much liked or trusted the Jesuits, while Paul IV considered their sainted founder a fraud and a tyrant. But by and large the ministry of the fourth vow, carried on by the Society's superbly organized, disciplined, and talented

45. Robert McNally, "The Council of Trent, the *Spiritual Exercises* and the Catholic Reform," *Church History*, XXXV (March, 1965), 36–49.

men, provided the papacy with its most effective single instrument of reform.

That the popes should have so completely taken charge of the Counter Reformation was something of an irony. For generations the corruption of the Roman court and its resistance to any meaningful program of amelioration had been the scandal of Christendom. Yet the revolutionary character of Protestantism had convinced those who believed in sacramental Christianity that only the papacy could hold the traditional system together, just as the persistence of Pius IV proved that only a pope could bring a reform council to a relatively happy termination. This latter achievement gave the papacy immense prestige and helped people forget how stubbornly Pius IV's predecessors had, to put the kindest face on it, evaded the call for internal reformation.

Moreover, Trent, by leaving so much of its unfinished business to the pope, helped guarantee the emergence of a papal monarchy stronger than ever. "I sent bishops to Trent," observed Philip II, "and they came back parish priests." The King of Spain no doubt exaggerated the pope's victory, because in many ways the council had enhanced episcopal power and certainly had not diminished his own. He allowed the promulgation of the Tridentine decrees only after a typical delay and then with the proviso that they were binding only to the degree that they did not infringe any royal prerogative. And when one of his own bishops fell foul of the Spanish Inquisition, the best Rome could do was save the poor man's life, with no hope of rehabilitating him.[46]

Even so, Philip was correct in that by entrusting to the pope, for example, the preparation of an index of heretical books, the council endorsed the principle that Rome should in fact decide who was orthodox and who was not. And such a fleshing out of the skeleton of the theoretical papal primacy took effect wherever Trent was even implicitly accepted (as in France, where the decrees were never formally promulgated), unlike the recently revived (1542) Roman Inquisition, which had force only in the Papal States or in those jurisdictions whose princes could be persuaded to introduce it.[47]

46. This was the unfortunate Bartolomé de Carranza, Archbishop of Toledo. See John Lynch, *Spain Under the Habsburgs* (New York, 1964), I, 260 f.

47. The medieval Roman Inquisition, juridically separate from its Spanish cousin, was reinstituted by Paul III.

The fathers of Trent also charged the pope to edit a popular catechism and a standard missal and breviary. These three tasks, all completed by the end of the 1560s, assured the long-term Roman character of Catholicism because they gave to the pope an unprecedented control over the liturgical worship of the Church, the prayer life of the priests, and the instruction of the faithful. The result was a measure of conformity in these crucial areas of Catholic life undreamed of before. It may have seemed at the time more important that the council had left it to Pius IV to negotiate with the emperor the latter's cherished proposals for a married clergy and a Utraquist Eucharist.[48] As it turned out, these hotly disputed matters amounted to little: celibacy proved to be quite feasible for a properly trained and motivated body of German priests, while the eucharistic chalice, conceded ultimately by the pope to Bavaria and the Hapsburg crown lands, was repudiated by the Catholic people themselves, who viewed it as some sort of Protestant trick. In the long run the imperial and papal diplomacy involved was a triviality when compared to the establishment of a Roman missal, a Roman breviary, and a Roman catechism. And when the new Vatican press published the definitive Vulgate text of the Bible; when the various new Roman seminaries and colleges, often staffed by Jesuits, began sending their graduates to every corner of Europe; and when the popes assumed the patronage of the revived Thomastic theology and of the critical study of the Church fathers—when all of this took place within a decade of the final session at Trent, it signaled a Roman hegemony wider and deeper than ever before.

Yet it would have meant little had the popes not kept their promise to put their house in order. They did; though the process was long and difficult, in the end they purged the Curia of the blatant abuses which had so deeply entrenched themselves.[49] Perhaps the most remarkable feature of that process was that it came about without altering the essential structure of the Curia. Once more the conservative character of the Counter Reformation revealed itself. The papacy indeed assumed new initiatives and developed new techniques in governing the Church and thus by direct action finally put to rest any theoretical doubts as to its supremacy. The parallel here between the popes and the secular kings is unmistakable, with the significant difference that

48. See Holborn, *Modern Germany,* pp. 281 f.
49. A good summary is in Evennett, *Spirit of Counter Reformaton,* pp. 89 ff.

the popes already possessed a central administration of long standing. They needed only to build upon and adapt an ancient apparatus of departments, bureaus, and tribunals, not to create one in order to effect the efficient centralization which was the object of all sixteenth-century rulers.

This is why reform of the Curia really meant the reassertion of the pope's right to control his own administration. For almost a century before the election of Pius IV the Curia had grown like a wild jungle plant, its tentacles reaching out toward any possible source of revenue. Desperate for money, the Renaissance popes had sold thousands of offices and then allowed their incumbents to profit from their investments by charging fees for every conceivable papal service and, indeed, by inventing new services in order to charge new fees.[50] The Curia became increasingly Italian and almost exclusively clerical—the once large lay civil service practically disappeared—as bright and often unscrupulous men hastened to Rome to make their fortunes. By the multiplication of charges and the accumulation of benefices, by acting as the agents by which the pope's supreme judicial power was exercised, and paid for by taxes, throughout the Catholic world, they carved out lucrative careers for themselves and formed eventually a bureaucratic caste, the most successful members of which were crowned with a cardinal's red hat and put within reach of the tiara itself.

The popes beginning with Paul III who wanted to remedy this situation had not only to contend with the usual tactics of an entrenched vested interest but also to deal with the danger that, with abuses so entangled with legitimate papal prerogatives, to correct one might involve destroying the other. So at any rate the curialists argued, and their argument had enough truth in it to assure that reform, when it came, would be slow, cautious, and jealously kept in the pope's own hands. By the nature of the case and the temper of the institution, revolution was from the first ruled out. Thousands of superfluous functionaries were indeed ultimately dismissed, 400 of them by Pius IV from his own household. But not even the most suspect curial offices were abolished, and whatever the practical adjustments, not one iota

50. For summary list of curial offices and exhaustive bibliography, see Léopold Willaert, *La Restauration Catholique* (Paris, 1960), pp. 54 ff.

of papal preeminence was surrendered. The datary,[51] to cite the most notorious example, did not disappear from the Roman scene; instead he behaved himself better, and by 1588 he had become the respectable head of a full-fledged department.

The datary provides a typical if somewhat flamboyant instance of the kind of complexity involved in curial reform. As an agent who administered the personal favor, as contrasted to the juridical power, of the pope, he granted dispensations, privileges, exemptions, and honors with a certain measure of capriciousness. Complaints were widespread at the illegality or at least extralegality of such arbitrary interference, but they were nothing compared to the protests over the datary's apparently insatiable appetite for money. Yet to reform his activity, even the simoniacal excesses of it, was more easily said than done. The suppression of the datary's office might have seemed the simplest course, but would not that be the same as admitting that the pope's sovereignty did not include the right to intervene directly in the affairs of the universal Church? Neither the pope nor the generality of Catholics was prepared to go so far. Moreover, the monies collected by the datary amounted by 1550 to a substantial proportion of papal revenue; to repudiate them without replacing them—particularly in a time of constantly rising prices—would have been to invite bankruptcy.

Two factors combined to resolve the perplexing problem posed by the datary and by the Curia as a whole. The first was the reform spirit itself which formally at Trent and less formally elsewhere demanded the purging of curial procedures whatever the cost. The second factor—more mundane but just as important—was the gradual reduction of the chaotic papal administration to an acceptable measure of control, and this, in turn, depended upon a realistic organization of papal finances. To the extent that the popes could regain direction over their own organs of government, the key problem of personnel would solve itself and reform could be effected without the radical structural alterations which might have raised troublesome questions of sovereignty.

Contributing to this long-term solution were many blessings in

---

51. The basic work is still L. Célier, *Les Dataires du XVIe siècle et les origines de la Daterie Apostolique* (Paris, 1910). See also *Dictionnaire de Théologie Catholique*, Vol. IV, cols. 2461 ff.

disguise. The Treaty of Cateau-Cambrésis, by establishing Spanish power in Italy and reducing the papacy to political insignificance, relieved the popes of imperialist illusions and freed them from expensive military adventures and from the intrigue within the Curia so often initiated in Paris, Madrid, or Vienna. The alienation of vast portions of Europe from the Catholic faith—however tragic from the strictly religious point of view—meant that ecclesiastical speculators had a much narrower field to exploit, and therefore fewer of them appeared on the scene. Finally, the Council of Trent, with its decrees on pluralism and absenteeism, took away the chief reason why a racketeer, with no interest in religion, wanted a job in the Curia; if he could not accumulate benefices and their revenues himself or sell others a license to do so, he might as well seek his fortune in some other line of work. Eventually the whole character of the curial personnel reflected these altered conditions.[52]

The absolute purity of the Curia after Trent is a myth, just as absolute purity in human affairs is always a myth. Yet once papal finances were reorganized, the difference was real. Bad men had formerly earned a good living, and sometimes enormous wealth, by taking personal advantage of a papal fiscal policy based on taxes and fees levied on the whole Catholic world. After Trent this haphazard and incredibly wasteful system was gradually replaced by one more narrowly based and more efficiently and honestly administered. Charges for spiritual services did not cease, but they were reduced to an acceptable level. By skillfully exploiting commercial enterprise (the papacy had practically a corner on the European alum market), and by pioneering in the field of public credit (the famous monti[53] were government bonds which, among other benefits, delivered the papacy from moneylenders' ruinous interest rates), the popes found the income which they had received before from the sinister activities of the datary. Above all, they organized the Papal States, much as their fellow sovereigns were doing elsewhere, as a source of regular and predictable income from taxation and the sale of offices. Indeed, the datary, no longer allowed to traffic in dispensations, took charge of this latter activity, which brought considerable sums into the papal treasury and

52. Jedin, Trent, I, 349 f., tells of one Spanish curial official who held 130 benefices.
53. See Jean Delumeau, Vie Économique et Sociale de Rome dans la seconde moitié du XVIᵉ siècle (Paris, 1957), II, 783 ff.

guaranteed a modest return to the officeholder. The overall result was not lessened expenditures—inflation and a mammoth building program saw to that—but a new financial climate in which there was less room for waste, fraud, and personal extravagance.

In the end the popes overstrained the limited resources of the Papal States, and by the middle of the seventeenth century the papacy found itself in another economic crisis. But during the crucial early years of the Counter Reformation the refurbished fiscal system worked well enough to give the popes credibility when they claimed leadership in the reform movement. This claim, however, might have come to nothing had those popes not been men of courage and integrity. Pius IV, even though observers noted some slackness in his behavior once the pressures of the council were over,[54] set the tone and the pace. His successor, Michael Ghislieri, who took the name Pius V (d. 1572) and who was elected largely through the efforts of Charles Borromeo,[55] proved to be a relentless reformer. A grim and narrow man in many ways, neither singularly intelligent nor free from impulsiveness, Pius V was so transparently holy, so totally dedicated and disinterested, that an awestruck Roman populace called him appropriately *il Papa Santo*. Such a man had to be listened to when he insisted that curial officials must cultivate above all the simplicity and purity of Christ; such a man could be expected to appoint a new kind of cardinal who in a papal election tended to vote for a new kind of candidate.

Indeed, the twenty cardinals created during the pontificate of St. Pius V marked the culmination of the sacred college's moral transformation which had begun with Contarini thirty years before. The next two popes, Gregory XIII (d. 1585) and Sixtus V (d. 1590), completed its administrative transformation. By the end of the century the cardinals no longer formed an unruly baronage, competing with the sovereign (and sometimes intriguing against him) for power; they had become instead a corps of tame civil servants who carried in the pope's name the Tridentine program of reform to every part of Europe or else toiled in one or another of the Curia's efficient new bureaus. In either case, they were much like aristocracies elsewhere which had given up pretensions of independence and had adapted themselves to the position of a court nobility.

54. So Ranke, *Popes*, I, 240 f.
55. See Pastor, *Popes*, XVII, 19 ff.

The overall difference to Catholicism was startling. Rome had re-gained its self-respect and identity, and the monarchical papacy was stronger than it had ever been. Its religious leadership was taken for granted by friend and foe alike. In short, by their patronage of the genuine revival of piety and ecclesiastical learning, in their reasonably honest and efficient administration, perhaps most of all by their belief in themselves and in the divine institution of their office, the popes had kept faith with the fathers of Trent.

Chapter Four

RELIGION AND REBELLION

DOWNSTREAM from Paris the Seine follows a looping, erratic course so that to travel by water from the capital to St. Germain where the peripatetic court of Catherine de' Medici often resided involved a journey rather longer than the twenty miles or so which actually separated the two places. Not far from St. Germain, an hour's walk across woodland and meadow, lay the royal borough of Poissy, where the Carolingians had once lived and where, more recently, St. Louis had been baptized. In a castle given them early in the fourteenth century by King Philip the Fair the Dominican nuns had established at Poissy the most fashionable convent in France; in Charles IX's time twenty-six sisters, all of noble family, occupied these spacious premises and had their spiritual needs ministered to by no fewer than six chaplains. Here, at one o'clock in the afternoon on September 9, 1561, the Protestant Reformation reached its high-water mark.[1]

The scene was the convent's capitular hall, a vast, Gothic room, shaped like a square, which rose out of the middle of the cloister. At one end, the boy-king Charles IX, his mother, and the high functionaries of the court had just taken their places. At right angles to the royal benches and facing each other ran the tiers of seats reserved for the bishops and theologians who since mid-morning had been fussing over the precedence of their seating arrangements. Slightly ahead of them, in a space otherwise empty save for a secretary's table, sat the six French cardinals in attendance and the chancellor of the realm. Directly across from the courtiers the square was closed by a temporary balustrade with the area immediately behind it vacant, though by this hour the rest of the room was crowded.

A hush fell as Chancellor l'Hôpital rose to speak. He uttered the expected platitudes about the king's gracious and amiable purpose in summoning a national council to deal with the religious crisis. He

1. H. O. Evennett, *The Cardinal of Lorraine and the Council of Trent* (Cambridge, 1930), pp. 283–393, provides an excellent treatment of the Colloquy of Poissy.

expressed the royal hope that by a mutually respectful exchange of views between Catholic and Huguenot spokesmen peace might be preserved within the Gallican Church. His voice hardened perceptibly as he reminded the audience that in no way was this colloquy to be construed as a tribunal; the only judge present, he said sharply, was the king himself.

Immediately Cardinal Tournon, Archbishop of Lyons and Primate of France, was on his feet to protest in the name of the clergy that the procedure outlined by the chancellor should itself be submitted in writing and formally discussed by the assembly. There was an awkward pause until the twelve-year-old monarch, prompted by his mother, shook his head. A murmur spread across the episcopal benches as the primate, his face as red as his robes, sat down again. Except for a handful of liberals, the bishops were, like Tournon, prelates of the old school who, for all their Gallicanism, did not look kindly on a government-refereed debate between themselves and heretics. If the heretics wanted a hearing, let them come to the bishops, not for debate but for judgment.

This precisely was what Catherine de' Medici had determined to avoid. Accommodation was her watchword, accommodation at almost any price, and above all no ultimatums or anathemas. She raised her hand and the doors of the hall swung open to admit the Huguenot delegation, led forward with full ceremony by the Duke of Guise. About thirty of them took their places behind the balustrade—eleven ministers in their black Geneva gowns and twenty lay representatives of the various Calvinist congregations in France. They had awaited their summons outside under Guise's supervision, and that Catholic champion, whatever his inner feelings, had treated them with exquisite courtesy. Now, as they stood looking down at the brilliant company, the tense, smoldering silence was broken by Tournon's stage whisper, "Voici ces chiens genevois!"[2]

All eyes fixed on Théodore de Bèze.[3] Calvin's confidant and heir apparent was still a convicted felon under French law, and it had taken a special safe conduct, secured by Condé and Coligny, to bring him to

2. "There they are, those Genevan dogs!" See Jean Mariéjol, *La Réforme et la Ligue* (Paris, 1904), p. 48.

3. The standard biography is Paul Geisendorf, *Théodore de Bèze* (Geneva, 1949), thorough but hagiographical. His treatment of Poissy, pp. 125–166, curiously makes no use of Evennett's much superior account, written nineteen years earlier.

Poissy from his thirteen-year exile in Switzerland. Bareheaded and standing, he faced his clerical enemies who sat motionless, their purple birettas firmly on their heads. Despite l'Hôpital's assurances and the warm support of the Bourbons and Châtillons, he looked more like a prisoner in the dock than a participant in a conference. But Beza (as the name is usually spelled in English), a Burgundian gentleman born to wealth and position, had grown up with men like these and all his life had moved easily among the elite of society. Now, at forty-two and at the height of his powers, they held no terrors for him, particularly since he could count on the eager sympathy of the queen regent. Besides, he possessed that indefinable quality Frenchmen call élan, a boldness and shrewd insight into the circumstances of the moment which enabled him to seize the psychological advantage. His first words, barely audible, were a request that the king permit him to preface his remarks with a prayer. Then, to the astonishment of the seated and hatted throng, the ministers at the balustrade fell to their knees, and the rich, vibrant voice of Theodore Beza echoed through the great hall: "Lord God, Father eternal and all-powerful, we confess before your majesty that we are poor and miserable sinners."

The speech was a virtuoso performance, worthy of the superb gesture with which it began. The audience, mostly hostile to him and his cause, was yet fascinated by Beza's eloquence. For an hour he moved learnedly and elegantly from those matters about which there was no controversy—the Trinity, for instance, and the Incarnation—to controverted issues like authority and the nature of the sacraments. But he said everything in a tone so sweetly reasonable that the queen regent flushed with appreciation and the bishops, while still suspicious, were not unmoved. Only as he neared his peroration did the fateful simile come: as far, said Beza, as heaven is from earth, so far is the Body of Christ from the bread and wine in the popish Mass. Instantly the cry "Blasphemavit!" went up all around the hall, sharp and harsh as the crackle of pistol shots. Beza was visibly shaken, and only with difficulty did he recover his composure enough to end with a rhetorical flourish. But the spell had been broken, and as Beza stepped away from the balustrade Catherine de' Medici gave him a sour, fretful look.[4]

Though the Colloquy of Poissy lasted another month, the cross-

4. On September 14 Catherine called Beza's simile "absurd and offensive." See *ibid.*, p. 149.

purposes revealed in that first dramatic session predetermined its course. On September 16 the Cardinal of Lorraine delivered the formal Catholic position paper with his usual high style. Condé and Coligny thought it conciliatory, but Beza predictably dismissed it as "impudent and inept." Peter Martyr Vermigli, the much traveled ex-Augustinian friar who came to Poissy as the representative of the Reformed Church of Zurich, explained to the ever hopeful Catherine, as one Italian to another, that the cardinal had sounded irenic because he had omitted any reference to the Eucharist. What had wrecked Beza's speech as an instrument of reconciliation had been his repudiation of the Mass. Here, prophesied Martyr, the scarred veteran of years of eucharistic controversies, would be the sticking point, the rock upon which all attempts at compromise would break.[5]

He was right. When late in September the colloquy shifted from grandiose oratory to bargaining sessions between teams of theologians, the eucharistic impasse haunted every meeting. Accommodation, real or imagined, appeared attainable on other controverted doctrines, but no Catholic could deny the Real Presence or the sacrificial character of the Mass, and no Calvinist could accept them. At this distance in time it may seem strange that so many of the furies let loose by the Reformation had to do with a wafer of sacramental bread. But the fact was that the Eucharist provided the basic quarrel over justification between Catholic and Reformed with its simplest, most provocative expression: either the Mass was the Christian community's supreme good work in which the corporeal Christ was offered and received, or else it was the supreme folly and idolatry, a blasphemous charade, a wicked device to hoodwink and rob believers and deprive them of true gospel righteousness.

Such stark alternatives left little room for maneuver, even for an expert like Catherine de' Medici. The two eucharistic doctrines were the outward manifestations of two distinct, fully elaborated, and mutually exclusive ideologies. The Catholic Mass presumed a priesthood to confect it, and the priesthood in turn presumed an ordaining bishop and a hierarchy headed by St. Peter's successor, and so a whole

5. For Peter Martyr's early career see Philip McNair, *Peter Martyr in Italy* (Oxford, 1967). For Poissy see André Bouvier, *Henri Bullinger* (Zurich, 1940), pp. 279 ff., and Benjamin Paist, "Peter Martyr and the Colloquy of Poissy," *Princeton Theological Review*, XX (1922), 212 ff., 418 ff., 616 ff. Also see Marvin Anderson, "Word and Spirit in Exile (1524–61)," *Journal of Ecclesiastical History*, XXI (1970), 193 ff.

clerical caste with special powers and prerogatives. Intimately connected to the Eucharist were the other Catholic sacraments, devotions, practices, and attitudes, all of them designed to render Christ in some way present to the Christian people. This view of God immanent within an ecclesiastical structure profoundly shocked the Calvinist (and indeed any serious Protestant), whose much simpler system began with God's dread transcendence and incommunicability.[6] He knew, moreover, that the Catholic Eucharist was the visible part of the iceberg, the palpable summing up of the whole hateful apparatus. And not only palpable but vulnerable: it was no accident that whenever Protestants attained political power they immediately suppressed the Mass, that Protestant iconoclasts exposed the consecrated hosts—what Catholics called the Blessed Sacrament—to every form of indignity, that the usually gentle Thomas Cranmer, once a priest himself, was moved to a paroxysm of rage at the memory of Massgoers "tooting and gazing at that thing the priest held in his hands."[7] Luther had understood from the beginning that once the people were weaned from the Mass the rest of Catholicism would crumble away.

Catholics knew this too. The Eucharist embodied their values and priorities, it expressed their *Weltanschauung*. It also provided a simple rule of thumb: those who would not bend the knee during a Corpus Christi procession or who insisted on receiving communion under both species were easy to discern, to fear, and ultimately to hate. A Spanish soldier needed no theological lore to convince him that Calvinism was inherently wicked and a direct threat to all he held dear; the sight of a church gutted by iconoclasts and of consecrated hosts strewn about trampled and urinated on was evidence enough. Later generations, which have not hesitated to kill and die for a bit of colored bunting or some egalitarian slogans, profess to be surprised at the ferocity of the sixteenth- and seventeenth-century religious wars. Yet the difference is less one of violence and cruelty than of the values for which men were willing to be violent and cruel.

Hardly anybody was left in Poissy on October 18, 1561, when the

6. The controversy over the interpretation of the Reformation provoked by Guy Swanson, *Religion and Regime* (Ann Arbor, 1967) covers many areas. See the symposium in *Journal of Interdisciplinary History*, I (1971), 381 ff. In any case Professor Swanson is surely right (*Religion and Regime*, pp. 8 ff.) in seeing the fundamental contrast between Catholic notions of immanence and Protestant ones of transcendence.

7. Cranmer, *Writings and Disputations* (Cambridge, 1844), I, 229.

colloquy was formally dissolved. The disgruntled bishops had one by one drifted away, but not before the government had extracted from them a heavy new tax.[8] Beza and the other ministers continued their "politique de la présence"—preaching, marrying, baptizing, setting up, in effect, a congregation in the villas of the Protestant chieftains at St. Germain. Ominously the great Catholic lords, pleading business on their estates back home, withdrew from court; Guise and Lorraine departed on October 19, and the constable—after a violent scene with Catherine de' Medici—four days later.[9] The national council had changed no minds, even though all the positions had been explored, all the expedients had been tried. A Gallican Church with a doctrinal ambit wide enough to embrace Catholic and Huguenot was as far from realization as ever. The only argument left was the argument of blood.

1. "THE MOST PERFECT SCHOOL OF CHRIST"

In Geneva the account of Beza's great speech at Poissy was received with rapture. "God has marvelously directed your spirit and your words," John Calvin wrote exultantly to his lieutenant. Not that Calvin put much stock in theological conferences as such; he had learned in his youth[10] that they seldom if ever achieved anything, and he watched with indifference the collapse of the Colloquy of Poissy. What mattered was that Beza had gained entry to the court and continued to operate freely and familiarly within it. Already the princes of the blood, and the incomparable Coligny as well, had accepted the true gospel. Might not Catherine de' Medici prove to be one of those upper-class women who seemed to find the reform so attractive?[11] Calvin pondered the report that she had attended a Huguenot *prêche* accompanied by the royal children and—of all people—by the papal legate. Though he was no respecter of persons, Calvin appreciated the political and

8. See Mariéjol, *La Réforme*, p. 47, for this levy, the so-called Contract of Poissy.

9. Lucien Romier, *Catholiques et Huguenots à la cour de Charles IX* (Paris, 1924), pp. 242 f., 261 f.

10. The huge biography of Emil Doumergue, 7 vols. (Lausanne, 1899–1927), remains indispensable. Among many other classics worthy of attention see the biographical works of Abel Lefranc, P. Imbart de la Tour, and Jacques Pannier.

11. For the prominent part played by women in the Huguenot movement, see Émile Léonard, *A History of Protestantism* (London, 1966), II, 111–113. John Bossy, "The

social realities which placed a premium on the conversion of the mighty. More significant than the debates between divines, he told the Geneva city council with unwonted gaiety, was the amusement of the court nobility at Admiral Coligny's parrot which chattered, "Vie, vie, la messe est abolie!"

In the wake of Poissy it appeared just possible that the Mass might indeed be abolished from France, and Calvin, though he was dying, pressed on with all the energy he could muster toward that goal: "Until the end he maintained his correspondence with the powerful French aristocrats who were his main hope for the conversion of the entire kingdom."[12] Beza remained his agent on the spot until the spring of 1563. When Calvin died a year later, the issue was still in doubt.

By that time, however, there was little doubt about the overall success of Calvin's work. The dominant Protestant orthodoxy was his. As the Lutherans, squabbling among themselves, withdrew to the protection of the courts of north Germany and Scandinavia, the Calvinist evangel spread undeterred from Scotland to Bohemia. In England, Hungary, the Netherlands, even in western Germany—in all the places in which Lutheranism had sprung up like an exotic flower only to wither and dry up under persecution—Calvinism came and stayed. Tough and resolute as their founder, Calvinist congregations, largely recruited from the most productive and best-educated elements in society, stubbornly dug in, grew and prospered. The Zwinglians came to terms with Geneva, and the Anabaptists hovered as ever on the eccentric edge of Protestantism. So when a reformed Catholic Church finally aroused itself, the enemy it encountered everywhere wore the face of John Calvin. His followers were to be as simple as doves, as befitted the remnant of Israel, the little band of the elect which must expect to suffer for the truth. But the master had also taught them to be as wise as serpents and, if circumstances called for it, as deadly. France provided precisely these circumstances.

Calvin's triumphs did not stem from originality. His genius was

---

Character of Elizabethan Catholicism," in Trevor Aston, ed., *Crisis in Europe* (New York, 1967), p. 247, argues the same point in a different context: a persecuted religion tends to have its institutional center in homes where women's influence is paramount.

12. Robert Kingdon, *Geneva and the Consolidation of the French Protestant Movement, 1564–1572* (Madison, 1967), p. 14.

rather for organization, speculative and practical.[13] He was not a creative thinker as Luther had been, and he borrowed freely from the reformers who had gone before him, most of all probably from Martin Bucer[14] and least from Zwingli. His basic tenets depended ultimately (as did all varieties of Protestantism) on Luther's insights, the total depravity of man, the free gift of justification through a trusting faith in Christ's imputed merits, the discoverability of these paramount truths in the Bible. Even predestination, the doctrine most closely associated with Calvin's name, was no more than a logical consequence of Luther's fundamentalism; if in fact the depraved human will had no freedom and human works had no intrinsic value, then it followed that some people have been created in order to be damned and so satisfy God's justice.

Calvin did not fear logical consequences, nor, for that matter, did he fear anything else. Inside a body ravaged by chronic insomnia, migraine, hemorrhoids, kidney stones, malaria, and tuberculosis dwelt an indomitable spirit.[15] "A poor timid scholar I am and always have been," he protested on his deathbed.[16] Indeed, he was a scholar, a skilled humanist, an able student of law, language, and dialectics. He had been superbly educated, and it was said he knew the whole Bible from memory. But his real strength lay in his heart rather than in his finely honed intelligence. This timid scholar possessed an iron will that no obstacle could intimidate. Once convinced that God's truth was discernible in the Scriptures and that he, John Calvin, had discerned it there, he never faltered.

The consistent application of relatively few principles was the dominant motif of Calvin's career. His aim was to bring biblical order into thought and action. His prodigious literary output—fifty-nine volumes in the modern critical edition—displayed the speculative side of what

13. A good survey is John McNeill, *The History and Character of Calvinism* (New York, 1954).

14. The debt to Bucer is a constant theme in the superb study, François Wendel, *Calvin: The Origins and Development of His Religious Thought* (London, 1965). The French original was published in 1950.

15. Calvin suffered as much from primitive medicine as from his wretched health. Toward the end of his life his doctors prescribed as treatment for kidney stones a horseback ride across broken country.

16. Much of the two famous deathbed speeches—one to the magistrates, the other to the ministers of Geneva—is printed in E. William Monter, *Calvin's Geneva* (New York, 1967), pp. 93 ff.

was essentially an organizational talent. Typical was his celebrated *Institutes of the Christian Religion*, a handbook of Reformed teaching, an "orderly arrangement of all branches of religion," as he described it himself, "a comprehensive summary . . . that [used] with proper attention no person will find any difficulty in determining what ought to be the principal objects of his research in the Scripture and to what end he ought to refer anything it contains."[17] This Protestant *Summa*, which offered a sure guide through the tangles of biblical interpretation, was perhaps necessary for the survival of a religion for which the Bible, that most difficult of books, was the exclusive authority. In any case, the *Institutes* had the most profound and widespread influence and went a long way toward establishing the intellectual conformity of scattered Calvinist congregations. And what the *Institutes* did for the more theologically sophisticated, Calvin's *Catechism*[18] did for the masses of believers. This clear and charming manual was used in one form or another all over Europe to drill children in the same tenets of faith which were being expounded to their parents in several long sermons a week.

These two books revealed not only Calvin's clarity and consistency or his firm belief in the uses of indoctrination. They also testified to that quality which made Calvin at once the least appealing and the most successful of the great reformers. His mind did not soar like Luther's or Zwingli's; it moved rather along the horizontal plane where systems are fashioned. Compared to Luther and Zwingli, Calvin was a tiresome pedant. But the system carefully and patiently put together lasts long after the heroic figures have run their brief course. Calvin's mind was closed not to new arguments but to new ideas, because for him the evangelical vision was already final and complete. More conservative than any pope, he was totally committed and absolutely convinced. The *Institutes* grew from a pocket-sized pamphlet in 1536 to a huge octavo volume of eighty chapters in the definitive edition of 1559. Yet, as M. Benoît has observed, this enlargement represented not the breaking of new ground but "the maturing and expansion of thought within the framework which already existed."[19] Calvin turned his fierce

17. From the preface to the 1559 edition (John Allen's translation).
18. Calvin wrote two catechisms, the definitive one in 1542.
19. Jean-Daniel Benoît, "The Institutes," in G. E. Duffield, ed., *John Calvin* (Grand Rapids, 1966), pp. 102 ff.

genius to explaining and preserving intact what he had learned in his original conversion. More than that, he imposed upon Protestantism an intellectual discipline which its more colorful leaders neglected or disdained.[20] When the direct charisma of Luther and Zwingli was removed from the scene, their respective churches fell into bickering, schism, compromise, and isolation. By contrast the death in 1564 of the "timid scholar" of Geneva did not halt Calvinism's forward march.

Other signs pointed to the care with which Calvin planned. In 1559 he founded the Academy of Geneva, which was at once a preparatory school and a university and which when he died had under instruction 1,500 students from all over Europe. Formal education in the gospel, carefully supported by the finest humanistic training, guaranteed that the Calvinist version of Protestantism would have skilled and zealous missionaries for generations to come.[21] Then, too, through the enormous correspondence he carried on, Calvin kept in touch with the fortunes of the movement everywhere, directing, admonishing, or advising as the occasion demanded. But perhaps most significant for the continuity of the cause was his choice of successor.

Theodore Beza—clever, famous, experienced in diplomacy and literary controversy—stood head and shoulders above his colleagues. His quality, however, would have meant little if Calvin himself had not recognized it. On first acquaintance Calvin had been put off, perhaps by stories of Beza's riotous youth or by his urbanity and charm, which the dour Calvin tended to suspect as a species of weakness. But the master soon came to a genuine appreciation for the disciple's many gifts, including his absolute loyalty to Calvin's religious principles. He named Beza the first rector of the Academy, sent him on numerous diplomatic missions, and, as his own health deteriorated, leaned on him more and more in the routine tasks of governing the church in Geneva. In the last year or so of Calvin's life, all the world saw upon whom the prophetic mantle had been bestowed when Calvin's letters began to be signed by Beza as well.

Beza was the first to admit that Calvin was unique and irreplaceable,

20. As the radical Caspar Schwenckenfeld (d. 1561) put it: "Luther has brought us up out of the land of Egypt and left us to perish in the wilderness." Quoted by J. W. Allen, *A History of Political Thought in the Sixteenth Century* (London, 1957), p. 16.

21. The classic study is Charles Borgeaud, *Histoire de l'Université de Genève: L'Académie de Calvin, 1559–1798* (Geneva, 1900). See especially pp. 79–83, 313–330.

and so when in June, 1564, he was elected Moderator of the Company of Genevan Pastors—the post Calvin had held for life—he insisted that he could accept the mandate for one year only.[22] As it turned out he was duly reelected every year till 1580, when he voluntarily retired. Into his robust old age, however (he lived till 1605), he continued to exert even outside office the brand of conservative leadership Calvin had counted on him to provide. Decisionmaking became more collegial than it had been prior to 1564, and Beza sometimes had to bend in ways that the imperious Calvin would have found intolerable. But by and large Beza kept a firm if supple hand on the tiller. Thanks in no small measure to him the Church of Geneva through the forty years of his ascendancy was not disturbed by a single serious doctrinal quarrel. Or perhaps credit was due rather to Calvin himself, who had fought the crucial battles earlier and had won so completely the adherence of a man of Beza's caliber. In any case, the Calvinist witness remained sturdily what its founder had made it, "an ensemble of theological, ecclesiastical, and moral conceptions and preoccupations which were born of the knowledge and experience of the sovereignty of God over the soul and over society."[23]

But man does not live by theological conceptions alone, however lofty they may be. Man lives in community with other men, and his religious no less than his civil existence must be acted out within an institutional framework. Doctrine as revealed in God's Word always took primacy in Calvin's scheme of things, but doctrine remained, so to speak, at the mercy of the church which proclaimed it. Popes, councils, bishops, canon law, and the rest of the Roman paraphernalia had to be rejected precisely because they taught falsehood and connived at idolatry. They had to be replaced by a godly government which would preach the true gospel, dispense the sacraments properly, and enforce the moral law.

Calvin approached the problem of church polity with the same confidence which inspired the *Institutes* and the *Catechism*. The godly government revealed in the New Testament, he said, was a presbyterian system with a fourfold ministry of pastors, teachers, elders, and

22. Eugene Choisy, *L'État Chrétien calviniste à Genève au temps de Théodore de Bèze* (Geneva, 1902), pp. 169 ff.
23. *Ibid.,* pp. 475 f.

deacons who administered the church for the sake of and with the consent of the community.[24] The test of pastors was the purity of their doctrine and of their liturgical practice, and this in turn could be measured only by the conformity of their views to Scripture. The pastors, though not theoretically a caste based on Holy Orders like the Roman priesthood, were nevertheless a self-perpetuating body which claimed in practice an independent status based upon their spiritual mission.[25] Calvin opposed a sacrificing priesthood without being anti-clerical.

Teachers were judged by their competence in biblical and related studies, and deacons by their skill in overseeing the church's material fabric and its charitable activities. The key to the system, however, was the consistory of elders. Composed of ministers and distinguished lay-men, this board was charged with maintaining discipline within the local church, a function upon which Calvin placed the highest impor-tance. The elders or presbyters in effect supervised the moral lives of the people, investigated aberrations, and, when necessary, punished the guilty. The ultimate sanction they could impose was excommunication.

From the perspective of a pluralistic society it may be difficult to appreciate the impact of such a penalty. In the sixteenth century a man expelled from the Church was for all practical purposes drummed out of the community; excommunication sent him to Coventry, literally cut him off from ordinary associations with his fellows. Once excom-municated he had, ideologically speaking, nowhere to go. Moreover, since civil governments insisted on religious uniformity as a political duty, he invariably suffered punishment—imprisonment, loss of prop-erty, sometimes death—from the secular arm as well. Medieval Cathol-icism had established its juridic right to this much control over its membership, and Calvin, so unabashedly conservative in this as in other matters, demanded no less. Not that he viewed excommunication primarily in its penal aspect; rather he considered it part of the cure of souls, because it guaranteed that ecclesiastical authority could define the norms of acceptable moral conduct and enforce them.[26]

24. See Wendel, *Calvin*, pp. 69 ff.
25. A thorough examination is in Alexander Ganoczy, *Calvin, Théologien de l'Église et du Ministère* (Paris, 1964), especially pp. 300 ff.
26. The word itself gives a clue to the important consequences. To "excommunicate" means to cut one off (1) from Holy Communion or the Lord's Supper, the believer's

But here Calvin did not get his way, not even in Geneva, at least not until 1555 when his allies—mostly French refugees like himself—won control of the city government. And even then the principle that a consistory could put a believer, who was also a citizen, under a ban independently of the civil power was not admitted. The tension which had marked the relationship between church courts and kings' courts during the Middle Ages was renewed in Geneva and indeed everywhere that the Calvinist polity was proposed. It was a tension as old as organized society, *sacerdotium* versus *imperium*, and it was unavoidable in the conditions which prevailed in the sixteenth century. Will the priest rule or will the magistrate rule? Were ministers to dictate to the congregation even when the congregation included lords, financiers, philosophers, and kings? Was a man to be driven from the Church when such an expulsion automatically imposed on him serious economic and political disabilities? If so, by whom? Calvin's presbyterian center successfully steered between democratic congregationalism to the left and sacramental hierarchy to the right. By stubbornly asserting the independence of the clerical estate it also escaped the smothering embrace of ambitious governments like those which reduced Scandinavian and German Lutheranism to an appendage of the state. But the complex and sensitive questions raised by the excommunication issue showed that it could not by itself solve the old church-state problem. In matters as diverse as sexual ethics, interest rates, and wills and testaments—indeed, in that whole gray area commonly called public morality—both God and Caesar claimed ultimate jurisdiction. Except in Geneva and Scotland, compromise and modification of the consistorial system indicated that eager converts to Calvin's doctrine did not necessarily endorse his polity.

Even Geneva—"the most perfect school of Christ that ever was in earth since the days of the apostles," as John Knox glowingly described it—was never the theocracy which later legend has invented. Calvin never intended the spiritual to supersede the civil jurisdiction, nor did it in his or Beza's time. His victory was to convince the Genevan ruling classes that to accept his notions of godly government served their best

---

most significant public act, and (2) from communion or association with the faithful who, given nonpluralist circumstances, were all one's compatriots, business associates, relatives, etc.

interests, religious and secular. Geneva, after all, was a small town, ruled through a set of interlocking councils by an exclusive commercial oligarchy.[27] There were not really very many people to convince, and anyway, after 1541, Calvin controlled the pulpit, which was the sole vehicle of mass propaganda. Moreover, in Geneva reformation went hand in hand with revolution. Only a few years before Calvin's arrival the city had expelled its Savoyard prince-bishop and begun its precarious course as a republic. The danger remained that that prelate might come back again with a Catholic army at his back. Or possibly the Swiss Confederation, dominated by Zwinglian Berne, might decide to swallow up little Geneva. During an epoch when city-states practically disappeared from Europe, the religious solidarity promoted by Calvin's presbyterianism had its political uses, too.

Long association did not endear the Genevans to Calvin: "a perverse and unhappy people," he called them at the end of his life. Their affection for him was likewise restrained, but they believed him and followed him, and he put steel into their backbones. Calvinist Geneva was a notoriously harsh place, and much of the harshness was due to Calvin himself.[28] Discipline was his watchword, constant, vigilant, minute discipline. The consistory, supported by the city government, engaged in the meanest inquisitorial practices. Censorship, search and seizure, spying, torture—in short, the whole apparatus of the police state—operated in the city. At first the objective was to stamp out any flickering remains of Catholicism. A hidden crucifix or statue could be, if discovered, cause for prosecution; a barber was once arrested because he had tonsured a priest. But soon the activity spread to maintaining true religion through forced attendance at sermons and the Lord's Supper, and through direct assaults upon wickedness and frivolity. The consistory often appeared obsessed with trivialities, and it expended a good part of its energies in campaigns against games of chance, cosmetics, dancing, and vain fashions. The direst penalties, however, were reserved for idolators, usurers, and adulterers. And in a city where informing on one's neighbor became a way of life, no powerful connection could guarantee safety: Calvin's sister-in-law and Beza's niece were

27. See E. William Monter, *Studies in Genevan Government (1536–1605)* (Geneva, 1964), especially pp. 85 ff., and W. Fred Graham, *Calvin and His City: A Study of Human Seizure of Control* (Richmond, 1970).

28. But see Richard Stauffer, *L'Humanité de Calvin* (Neuchâtel, 1964), for a brief appreciation of Calvin's warmer side.

both imprisoned for sexual irregularity. It may be instructive that in the latter case the woman was more severely punished than her lover, because while in prison she had been overheard uttering blasphemy— she had said that she did not want anyone to pray for her since God would not listen anyway.[29]

Yet this tale of tyranny in an Alpine town must not be told as though it were Calvin's responsibility alone. True enough, he had something of an Old Testament prophet's fiery intolerance of sin and sinners, and he had no doubt that pain and trial, to which he was no stranger himself, were the price men paid for their perversity. But he did not act without support or without precedent. The overwhelming majority of Genevans agreed with Calvin and upheld his consistory, just as the masses of Spaniards supported the Inquisition. And Geneva was far from unique in claiming the right to regulate citizens' behavior down to the smallest detail. Every state, big and little, had sumptuary laws on its books, dealing minutely with things like diet, apparel, and entertainment, and designed to curb wastefulness or to maintain class distinctions. In Nuremberg it was against the law to hold a christening party until at least two months after the event; in France only the wives of noblemen were allowed to wear a certain type of hat.[30] Calvin's Geneva differed from the rest of Europe in the strict way it enforced such legislation and added to it out of religious conviction.

The result was a quality of life which moved Knox to his rhapsodic testimony. Other places he had visited had the true gospel preached, but only in Geneva were "manners and religion so sincerely reformed." In the Church of Zurich, for example, where Zwingli's disciple Henry Bullinger (d. 1575) still held sway, doctrine was sound but practice did not live up to doctrine. Bullinger was essentially a peaceful man, almost an ecumenist,[31] whose considerable influence in Switzerland and elsewhere could not match the organized apostolate of Calvin and, later, of Beza. Formal peace indeed existed between Zurich and Geneva,[32] and except for some liturgical practices there was little to

29. Choisy, *L'État Chrétien*, pp. 41 ff., and Geisendorf, *Bèze*, pp. 256 ff.

30. Gerald Strauss, *Nuremberg in the 16th Century* (New York, 1966), p. 109, and Davis Bitton, *The French Nobility in Crisis* (Stanford, 1969), p. 98.

31. "Réformateur et conseiller oecuménique," his biographer Bouvier calls him. But see also John McNeill, "Calvin as an Ecumenical Churchman," *Church History*, XXXII (1963), 379–391.

32. For the text of this famous Consensus Tigurinus (May, 1549), see Beresford Kidd, *Documents of the Continental Reformation* (Oxford, 1911), pp. 652 ff.

choose between them from a doctrinal point of view. But Calvin's discipline was in a class by itself, and so Geneva was the holy city for Knox and countless others. It remained as long as Beza lived the moral and intellectual center of an international movement.

It is difficult to overestimate Calvin's impact upon the course of Christianity. He appeared at a moment when the Protestant reform was wavering perhaps on the brink of anarchy. He breathed life back into it, even into those branches of it, like Lutheranism, which were more or less hostile to himself. No doubt his dynamic leadership had much to do with forcing the Roman Church to cleanse itself of ancient abuses, but by the same token it also checked Catholicism's development, hardened its contours, made it more defensive, more Latin, centralized, papal, curial. Ironically Calvin fought the hated externals of Rome by externalizing Protestantism: excommunication, clericalism, and legalism were the hallmarks of his system. But certainly that spirit of reverence and seriousness—so often and so wrongly disdained as "Puritanism"—was Calvin's gift to the whole Church.[33]

2. THE ARGUMENT OF BLOOD

Nicodemus was the Pharisee who visited Jesus only at night because had he come openly in the daytime and been seen he might have suffered some disability as a result. Nicodemism was a term to describe a similar attitude common among sixteenth-century Protestants who practiced their religion secretly while out of fear they outwardly conformed to Catholicism. From his house on the Rue des Chanoines in Geneva, Calvin (and later Beza, who lived there after Calvin died) proclaimed that Nicodemism was a grave sin. Believers who trifle with the "manifest idolatries" of the Mass in order to avoid persecution, said Calvin, resemble Nicodemus only "in that they now bury Jesus as he once did."[34] As usual, Calvin was no respecter of persons. When the Bishop of Troyes let it be known that he hesitated to announce his conversion because he did not want to lose his benefices, Calvin replied sternly that loss of income was little enough to sacrifice for the true faith. (His lordship, however, preferred a classic Nicodemistic solution wherein on Sunday morning he first sang pontifical Mass and then immediately afterward presided over the Huguenot *prêche*.)

33. See André Favre-Dorsaz, *Calvin et Loyola* (Paris, 1951), pp. 431–438.
34. Léonard, *Protestantism*, II, 81 and 102 ff.

Calvin's condemnation of Nicodemism placed his non-Genevan followers in a painful predicament. One reason was that certain Catholic ritual acts—like baptism and marriage—had direct civil as well as religious consequences. Moreover, Calvin condemned armed resistance to persecution just as severely as he did subterfuge in religious practice. Though this stance may have reflected the spirit of the Sermon on the Mount, it produced an almost unbearable tension within the French Calvinist congregations. By the time of Poissy, with the numbers and belligerency of the Huguenots growing swiftly, Calvin had had to moderate his earlier position. By what M. Mariéjol called "the casuistry of insurrection,"[35] Calvin had reluctantly conceded that if the estates general or the princes of the blood or the parlements were to rise against the crown, Huguenot participation in such a case would not be rebellion but a holy war. Nevertheless, Calvin continued to shrink from organized violence, and most of the Huguenot ministers supported him.

This was why Beza's ascendancy at court appeared so crucial as 1561 drew to a close. If the Valois could be converted, the problem would solve itself, because then Catholics, if they took to arms, would be the rebels. The situation seemed rich in promise. "The queen regent, I don't know why," Beza reported modestly, "looks on me with a favorable eye; this she has repeated to many people, and I have experienced the fact myself." And the little king told Jeanne d'Albret, the fervently Calvinist Queen of Navarre, "I assure you, aunt, that if I were my own master, I would be through with the Mass."[36] But as they exulted at such omens as these, the Huguenots learned to their distress that Jeanne's husband, Anthony, the first prince of the blood, was publicly going to Mass again. Clearly the final wagers were being placed.

Catherine de' Medici had arrived at her decision. Though Paris, whipped to anti-Protestant frenzy by the popular preachers, remained stubbornly Catholic—Paris, Beza said bitterly, "la ville sanguinaire et meurtrière entre toutes celles du monde"[37]—the queen mother was convinced that the nation as a whole was rapidly going Calvinist. If she was right, the dynasty's survival demanded immediate concessions to the Huguenots. "The disorders which every day disrupt this kingdom,"

35. Mariéjol, *La Réforme*, p. 13.
36. Geisendorf, *Bèze*, pp. 169 f. and 181 f.
37. "The most bloody and deadly city in the world." Mariéjol, *La Réforme*, p. 43.

she told an assembly of notables on January 3, 1562, point not only to the seriousness of the crisis but to the need for a radical solution.[38] Two weeks later that solution came, the famous Edict of January, which granted the Huguenots freedom of worship to go along with the freedom of conscience they had enjoyed de facto since March of 1560. The edict did include a stricture—the *prêche* could not be held in public places within walled cities. But it went substantially further than the "minimal degree of liberty" Beza had hoped for, and it implied the promise of still more. D'Andelot swaggeringly remarked that soon the temples of idolatry—the Catholic churches—would be handed over to God's elect. The Edict of January represented an almost miraculous reversal of fortunes since Cateau-Cambrésis only three years before.

It also meant war. The queen had dispatched reassurances to the pope, who received them quietly and, while issuing a *pro forma* protest, bided his time. But the danger did not come from Rome. It came from within the nation, whose temper Catherine and l'Hôpital had badly misjudged and whose powerful factions had been drastically realigned. Nearly a year before, Constable Montmorency and another magnate of the old school, Marshal St. André, had buried their differences with the Duke of Guise and had entered with him into an informal alliance which court wits quickly dubbed the Triumvirate. The triumvirs wasted no time in letting the world know of their intention to resist the Calvinist influences around the throne. More discreetly, they opened secret negotiations with Spain about an international crusade against Calvinism. Philip II had neither the taste nor the means to undertake such romantic ventures, but he made encouraging noises and even suggested the possibility that he might allow Spanish Navarre to be reunited with its French-speaking counterpart. (This latter circumstance was why Anthony of Navarre returned so suddenly and enthusiastically to his Catholic duties.) In any event, a France weakened by civil strife was not a prospect to sadden the King of Spain.

Now, in disgust at the Edict of January, the constable, repeating his performance of the previous October, got on his horse and galloped off to Chantilly. Guise meanwhile and his brother the cardinal were engaged in secret diplomacy of their own. For several days in mid-

38. Romier, *Catholiques et Huguenots*, p. 285.

February they met near Strasbourg with Duke Christopher of Würt-temberg, a pious German Lutheran prince whose relatively conserva-tive views, especially about the Eucharist, made him appear in some ways closer to the Catholic than to the Calvinist position. Lorraine was still pursuing in his devious and yet idealistic fashion that overall ecclesiastical bargain which, if it could not include the Calvinists, could then effectively isolate them. The meeting was cordial enough but inconclusive. Guise returned to his estates, and by the end of the month, anxious to consult his fellow triumvirs about the Edict of January, he was ready to depart for Paris.

On Sunday, March 1, the duke, with a large cortege including his pregnant wife, paused in their journey at the town of Vassy to hear Mass. Most of the inhabitants were his feudal subjects, and among them was a large and notoriously ardent group of Huguenots. As he was about to enter the church, word reached him that about five hun-dred Calvinists were assembling in a nearby barn to celebrate their *prêche*. Since Vassy was a walled town, such a service defied even a liberal interpretation of the Edict of January. Annoyed perhaps more by the bravado of his own subjects than by the activity itself, Guise ordered the assembly to disperse. The answer was a shower of rocks, one of which hit the duke himself. His retainers fired their harquebuses into the barn. When the shooting and confusion were over, at least twenty-three Huguenots lay dead and more than a hundred wounded.[39]

The Massacre of Vassy did not trouble Francis of Guise's conscience, but it alerted his prudence. As he moved his caravan toward Paris, he avoided Huguenot strongholds such as Vitry and Châlons. His mis-givings vanished, however, when he met the triumvirs at the gates of Paris and rode with them into the city to a hero's welcome. The news had traveled ahead of him, and the parlement, the municipal govern-ment, and the populace generally hailed Vassy as a victory for God and king.

The court was at Fontainebleau, where Beza and Condé came on March 13 to protest Vassy and the triumvirs' seizure of Paris. Cath-erine received them graciously, but Anthony of Navarre, who stood next to her during the audience, observed that the trouble stemmed

---

39. Twenty-three is Mariéjol's estimate, *La Réforme*, p. 59. Romier, *Catholiques et Huguenots*, p. 321, says thirty; Geisendorf, *Bèze*, p. 191, says about sixty; J. H. Elliott, *Europe Divided, 1559–1598* (New York, 1968), p. 103, says seventy-four.

from the Protestants coming armed to their services. "Arms in the hands of wise men bring peace," Beza retorted, "and Vassy proves how necessary such precautions are." But Navarre was beyond argument. The Huguenots at Vassy threw rocks at a prince, he said, "and princes do not have to endure such things." Then holding up his hand in a dramatic gesture, he concluded, "Who touches the tip of Guise's finger wounds my whole body."[40] His brother Condé listened in brooding silence.

For her part Catherine decided on a desperate gamble. During the last week in March she sent a series of anguished letters to Condé pleading with him and the rapidly arming Calvinist congregations to rescue her son from Guise. Condé, however, hesitated, while the triumvirs acted swiftly and decisively. On March 27 they appeared at Fontainebleau with a thousand men and informed Catherine that for safety's sake she and the king must return with them to Paris. Guise's courteous demeanor did not hide the fact that he was leaving the queen mother no choice.

Though Condé had missed his chance to seize the king, he was nevertheless ready to fight. On April 8 he issued a manifesto from Orléans in which he announced his intention to take the field in order to deliver the royal prisoners from the Guise. Thus France drifted into the first of the Wars of Religion. At first only skirmishes occurred, and Catherine, to her everlasting credit, worked mightily for a negotiated settlement. But her efforts were fruitless. The Huguenots, strong in the Bourbon lands around Montpensier, south and west of the Loire, and (so Coligny claimed) in Normandy, quickly secured control of Angers, Blois, and Lyons, along with Orléans. Both sides sent out calls for help to prospectively friendly foreign powers.

But before an army worthy of the name could be mobilized on either side, a vast convulsion of violence shook the nation. The Catholic populace fell with fury upon the Huguenots at Sens (April 12) and later at Tours, Moulins, and elsewhere. A barbarous frenzy spread across France, and hundreds of Huguenots were murdered by mobs which the Duke of Guise himself called "detestable." On July 13, the Parlement of Paris lent formal blessing to these outrages by a decree legalizing armed Catholic attacks upon any Huguenot gathering. In

40. Geisendorf, *Bèze*, pp. 193 f.

effect, the parlement's action loosed the lowest criminal elements upon the whole of society.

The Huguenots, no longer timid, replied in kind. Their special targets were priests and monks, and though the murders committed by them were fewer in number (there were fewer of them to do the killing), they contributed to the savagery by their wild iconoclasm. Everywhere they went the tale was the same: wanton destruction and senseless sacrilege. Not even the dead were safe: tombs were opened and bones were scattered about in an orgy of desecration. All of these excesses, on both sides, were only intensified when the armies began to march.[41]

The Huguenot host, though smaller than the Catholic, was of a higher caliber in training and weaponry. It was ably led by the likes of Condé, d'Andelot, and Coligny. But its enthusiasm reflected its feudal character; the great lords upon whom its manpower depended grew restless under centralized command, and Condé, in order to avoid desertions, had to dispatch segments of the army to operations in their home provinces. Thus the fighting spread in a fitful way across Languedoc, Poitou, and the southwest.

In Normandy an English expeditionary force occupied Le Havre in fulfillment of a treaty (September 20, 1562) whereby Queen Elizabeth agreed to aid the Huguenots with 6,000 men and 100,000 crowns in return for Calais. The royalists reacted quickly by besieging the Huguenot Norman stronghold of Rouen. The city fell at the end of October. The most notable casualty of the operation was Anthony of Navarre, who died on November 17 and left as heir a boy named Henry, aged eight.

Meanwhile, Condé at Orléans, heavily reinforced by German mercenaries, determined to march upon Paris, but a series of delays and checks enabled Francis of Guise to block the road to the capital. The Huguenots accordingly turned west into Normandy in hopes of effecting a juncture with the English. Guise followed and joined Constable Montmorency at Dreux, where, on December 19, 1562, the only significant pitched battle of the war was fought. Early in the day Condé's vigorous attacks seemed to have gained victory for the Huguenots; the constable was captured and the royal army was in full retreat. But

41. See Henri Hauser, *La prépondérance espagnole* (Paris, 1948), p. 60.

Guise and St. André committed their reserves at precisely the right moment. Their counterattack turned the tide and the Huguenots were driven from the field, but not before they had captured and killed St. André. They left Condé behind, wounded and a prisoner. What was left of their army retreated under the skillful direction of Coligny, who sent his brother d'Andelot to command at Orléans while he himself fled deeper into Normandy.

With two triumvirs out of action, leadership on the royalist side fell to Francis of Guise. Instead of pursuing Coligny, he determined to loosen the Huguenot grip on the Loire by reducing Orléans. The siege began early in February, 1563. On February 18, the duke was shot from ambush and six days later he died. The assassin, under torture, claimed that he acted by inspiration and commission of Beza and Coligny. The latter admitted cheerfully that he rejoiced that God had struck down an implacable foe of the gospel, even though he denied having ordered the murder. Guise's heir, young Henry, swore that only the admiral's blood could avenge his father. Nine years later he made good that oath.

The death of Guise, Anthony of Navarre, and St. André, and the capture of Condé and Montmorency, provided Catherine de' Medici with a chance to seize the initiative and open peace negotiations. She did so, however, without the sympathy she had shown the year before for the Calvinist cause. The leadership of the factions had been wiped out, and so had any lingering thought in the queen mother's mind that the Protestants would ever be able to win. "She judged it necessary to tolerate them but impossible to give them equal rights with the majority."[42]

The Peace of Amboise (March 19, 1563) reflected this conviction. The direct negotiations were carried on by the two imprisoned leaders, Condé and Montmorency, who were understandably eager to reach a settlement and secure their freedom. The end result was a retreat from the Edict of January. Liberty of worship was allowed in their homes to Protestant nobles. City folk could attend the *prêche* in only one town designated for each district. No Huguenot worship was allowed in Paris, and no provision was made for country dwellers who were not gentlemen.

Condé's acceptance of this arrangement brought upon him the fury

42. Mariéjol, *La Réforme,* p. 73.

of Calvin, who said that the prince "out of vanity has betrayed God." Coligny was no less bitter; Condé, he said, with a stroke of the pen had done the Huguenot cause more damage than ten years of Catholic persecution.[43] These judgments were hardly too harsh; the Peace of Amboise did isolate the Huguenots, and it rendered remote any chance of swaying the French masses. Condé had saved himself and his caste, for they could continue to enjoy their ancient privileges and their new religion, but he made it impossible that Calvinism would ever be a popular cause.

For most of the next four years the queen mother, with all the factional chiefs (save Coligny) dead or discredited, kept the reins of power more or less securely in her own hands. She scored a diplomatic victory early by arranging the bloodless withdrawal of the English expeditionary force, still at Le Havre. Internally, the regent was less successful. It was one thing to sign a pacification treaty; it was another to execute it. Both Catholics and Huguenots remained restive and belligerent. In mid-July (1563), the Princess of Condé was set upon by a Parisian mob and one of the gentlemen attending her was killed. Across the country provocations multiplied on both sides, and often the queen mother's attempts at moderation, condemned with equal vehemence by Calvin and the pope, seemed futile. But though disorder continued rampant, the worst evils of civil war were for the time being avoided.

Meanwhile, Catherine achieved some success in asserting the crown's national prerogatives. Steering skillfully among the nobles, the municipalities, and the learned lawyers of the parlements, she built up the power of the central government (or tried to) by a series of royal edicts. One, in 1563, ordering a general disarmament of the population—at one swoop an attempt to diffuse the religious hatreds and to concentrate the means of coercion in the king's hands—and another (1564) reserving to the crown the final appointment of municipal officers were followed, in 1566, by the Ordinance of Moulins which aimed to strengthen the royal supremacy in judicial matters over local tribunals and even over the parlements.

On a different level, Catherine promoted the crown's prestige by the

43. In a public speech in Geneva shortly after his return from service with Coligny's army (as a kind of chaplain and propagandist), Beza accused Condé of being more concerned with his amours than with the fate of his coreligionists.

magnificence of court life, into whose gay, frivolous, sometimes vicious ambit were drawn the nobles of all factions and both religions. Old hostilities seemed to diminish under the softening influence of tournaments, masques, and gallant love affairs. Thus Condé, "this little prince, so handsome and always laughing and singing,"[44] walked arm in arm with the young Duke of Guise, all the dour warnings of the Calvinist ministers apparently forgotten.

Most important of all, in Catherine's mind, was to draw together Charles IX—now technically of age—and the people of whom he was the natural and the consecrated leader. To effect this she put the king and his court on a grand tour of the realm. For two years (1564–1566) she led them from one end of France to the other in order that as many as possible might have palpable contact with the dynasty. It was a shrewd enough idea, and it might have led to a considerable success had the little king possessed a charisma capable of stirring the imagination of the masses. Whatever else it accomplished, the leisurely progress saved the government a good deal of money, as the court enjoyed for weeks at a time the hospitality of provincial lords and cities.

The most notable event of the tour was the interview at Bayonne between the Duke of Alba and the queen mother.[45] Catherine had hoped to meet her son-in-law, the King of Spain himself, but Philip pleaded the heavy press of business and sent instead his wife, Catherine's daughter Elizabeth, and Alba. From June 14 to July 2, 1565, the Spanish and French held court together. The negotiations that went on at the same time were of little consequence. Alba hinted that his master would appreciate Catherine's help in containing the Netherlands Calvinists, while the queen regent, promising everything and nothing, pressed for matters closer to her heart, namely, for marriage alliances between the Spanish royal family and several of her own children.

The Huguenots, who did not know of the trivial character of the Bayonne conversations, were alarmed that they had taken place at all. Besides, it was widely suspected that the Cardinal of Lorraine, fresh from his exploits at Trent, and General Montluc had replaced the

44. A contemporary description, quoted by Mariéjol, *La Réforme,* p. 88. For Brantôme's equally charming picture of Condé, see Henry Sedgewick, *The House of Guise* (New York, 1938), p. 149.

45. See John Potter, "The Conference at Bayonne, 1565," *American Historical Review,* XXXV (1930), 798–803.

1. Peasants at work. Copper engraving after Breughel, 1568

Note: All illustrations in this section are from The Bettmann Archive except those numbered 19, 27, 29, 35, 37.

2. Philip II (Collection of Her Majesty the Queen, at Windsor)

3. Mary, Queen of Scots.
Drawing by Clouet

4. Catherine de'Medici.
Drawing by Clouet

5. The Vatican, 1570

6. The Escorial Royal Palace near Madrid. From a contemporary woodcut

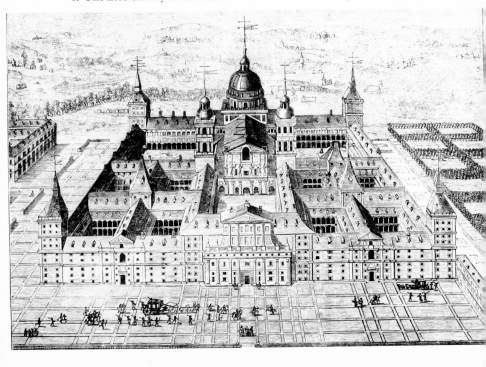

7. Last session of the Council of Trent. Copper engraving, 1565

8. Pius IV

9. St. Philip Neri. Copper engraving

Calvinisch Gasthauß zur Narrenkap-
sen genant/
Darinnen die Calvinisten so wol
offentlich als heimlich in jrer Thorheit erwischt/die Lar-
va vermeinter vnschuldt/vnd heiligkeit jhnen abgezogen/vnnd
sambt dem Hause vnd Thorheit vmbgestürtzt werden.
Wie beygefügte Figuren anzeigen.
Von dem krefftigen Posaunen Hall Göttliches Worts:
Beschrieben vnd mit Gottes Wort klar vberweiset
Durch
M. Johannem Prætoriun Saxo Hallensem Dienern
am Wort des Creutzes im Pilgramsthal.

QVICQVID EGO GAPIO MECVM PERIT

Leasse mit mir zum verderben zue.

Was ich Gricht Sathan/sahen thue.

Quod Monstri cernis, Calvini dogma, figurat: Principium terret, mediu sern, ultima mordent.
Was lengst zuvor der Bösewicht   Durch viel Ketzer hat ausgericht/
Mit falscher Lehr/vii Menschen tand/   Zurstört manch Volckreich Kirch vnnd
Diß alles er itzt scherffet sehr/ (schreckt/ Durch der schal Calviniste Lehr/ (Laud/
Ach fleuch dis Thier/welchs forn er.   Mitten dich ritzt/hinden ersteckt.

Im Jahr Christi/ 1598.

10. Title-page of an anti-Calvinist lampoon, 1598

11. The aged Calvin at Geneva. From a woodcut

12. Gaspard de Coligny, Admiral of France. Portrait by Ravesteyn

13. William, Prince of Orange. Painting by Thomaskey

14. Protestant propagandist's view of "The Council of Blood." Alba sits on the throne, and Granvelle, bellows in hand, stands at his right

15. Anne du Bourg defends himself and fellow-Protestants before the king and the Parlement of Paris, June, 1559. *Insert upper left:* du Bourg arrested and imprisoned

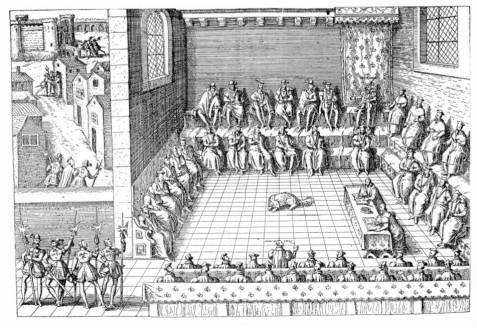

16. Death of Coligny. St. Bartholomew's Day, 1572

17. The Massacre of St. Bartholomew. Painting by d'Amiens, 1584

18. Constantinople in 1576

19. Justice. Statue by Vittoria decorating the Doge's palace. Venice, 1579

20. Don John of Austria

HENRI de LORRAINE
Duc de Guise né le 31.
Decembre, 1550. et Assassiné
a Blois en 1588.

21. Henry, Duke of Guise
Le Balafré

22. Lepanto. After a painting by Van Artevelt

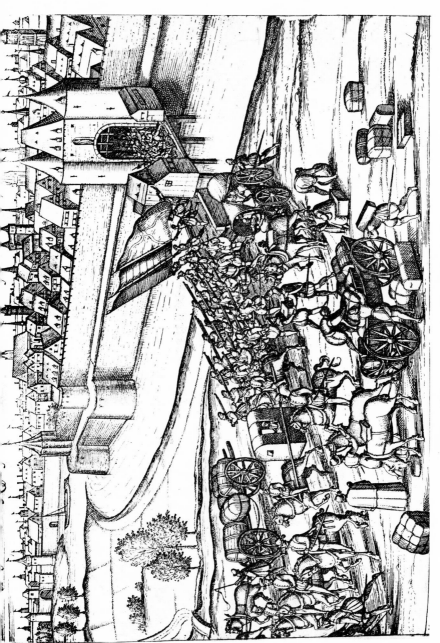

23. Spanish troops evacuating Maestricht, April, 1577

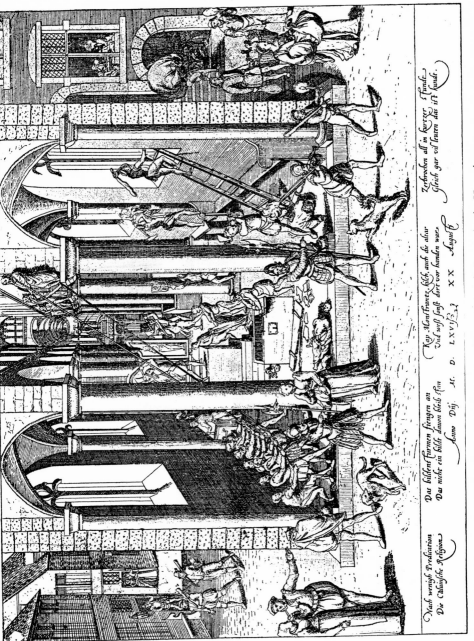

Calvinist Iconoclasts in a Flemish church. Engraving by Hogenberg, 1570.

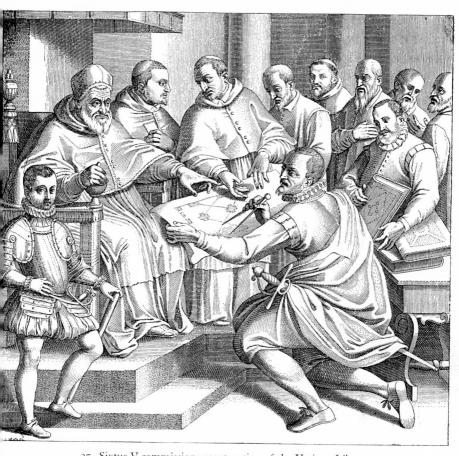

25. Sixtus V commissions construction of the Vatican Library

26. Erection of the Obelisk in Vatican Square, 1586. From a woodcut, 1590

27. Stephen Batory, King of Poland. Monastery of the Missionaries, Cracow, 1583

28. Cardinal Hosius debating with Protestants. Drawing by Treterus, from *Theatrum virtutum d. Stanislai Hosii* (Peplin, 1928)

29. Ivan the Terrible. Woodcut

31. John Knox

30. Henry of Navarre
King Henry IV
Medallion by Dupré

32. Henry III

33: The Court of Henry III

34. Execution of Mary, Queen of Scots. 1587

35. Spanish soldier. Anonymous drawing, from Pidal's *Historia de España* (Madrid, 1958)

36. A Janissary

37. Alexander Farnese, Prince of Parma. Portrait by van Veen, Musées Royaux des Beaux-Arts, Brussels

38. William Cecil, Lord Burghley, in old age

39. The Invincible Armada

40. Elizabeth I Gloriana Triumphant, 1589

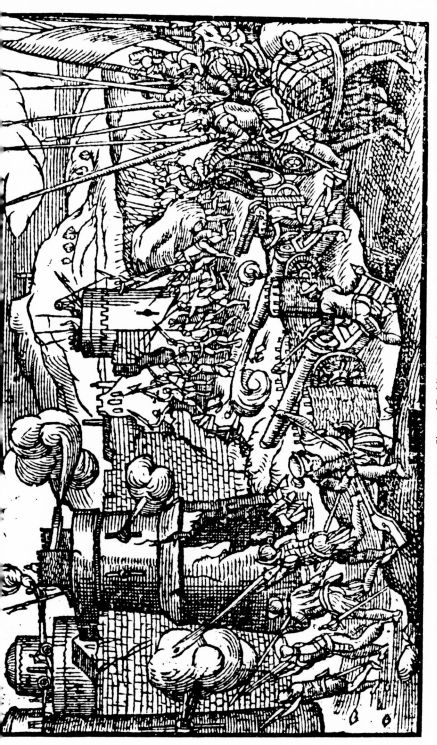

41. Siege of Dublin. Woodcut, 1577

42. St. John the Baptist in the Desert. Painting by Caravaggio

43. The Burial of Count Orgaz. Painting by El Greco. The head of the aged Philip II can be seen in the upper right corner, third figure to the left of the man holding the carpenter's square. Toledo, Spain

45. Montaigne

EL INGENIOSO
HIDALGO DON QVI-
XOTE DE LA MANCHA,

*Compuefto por Miguel de Ceruantes
Saauedra.*

DIRIGIDO AL DVQVE DE BEIAR,
Marques de Gibraleon, Conde de Benalcaçar, y Baña-
res, Vizconde de la Puebla de Alcozer, Señor de
las villas de Capilla, Curiel, y
Burguilios.

Año,   1605.

CON PRIVILEGIO,
EN MADRID, Por Iuan de la Cuefta.

Véndefe en cafa de Francifco de Robles, librero del Rey nfo feñor.

Titel der ersten Auflage des ,,Don Quijote'' von Miguel de
Cervantes Saavedra, Madrid 1605

Title Page of the First Edition of ,,Don Quixote'', Madrid 1605

44. Title-page of the first edition of *Don
Quixote*, 1605

46. Shakespeare. Engraving
by Droeshout

defunct Triumvirate in seeking Spanish aid for a grandiose Catholic crusade. If the queen mother intended a wider dynastic connection with Spain, the danger to the Huguenots seemed obvious. In fact, Catherine's policy had not altered, but the rumors multiplied, and by the summer of 1566 the religio-factional rivalries were clearly heating up again. Encouraged by the outbreak of Calvinist iconoclasm in Flanders, the Huguenots began again to arm and organize themselves. Terror ran through their ranks and indeed through the whole nation when, a year later, Alba led a crack Spanish army overland from Milan along the French border to Brussels (August, 1567). As a precaution Catherine hired 6,000 Swiss mercenaries, though with typical ambivalence she also sent supplies as a gesture of good will to Alba's army as it passed along the frontier.

For the Protestant chieftains, the trouble in the Low Countries was a signal, and savage outbursts across France punctuated their alarm. Huguenot bands seized Montereau and Orléans, and at Nîmes (September 30) there was a general slaughter of Catholic notables, with dead and dying buried together in the same pit.

A few days before this, Condé and Coligny attempted to kidnap the king at Meaux. They might have succeeded but for the pluck of the Swiss mercenaries who marched the court to the safety of Paris. The fury of Catherine de' Medici knew no limit after this humiliation. Perhaps nothing contributed more to that hardness of her heart responsible ultimately for the Massacre of St. Bartholomew than the sorry sight of her son being conducted to his capital by foreign pikemen.

So came the Second War of Religion.[46] Once again sectarian and factional motives were mixed together. Condé and Coligny commanded the rebels; Constable Montmorency, backed by his sons and the young Henry of Guise, led the royalists. On November 10, 1567, the two armies met at St. Denis, just outside Paris, where they fought to a bloody draw. Though the constable was killed, the Huguenots, too few in numbers to hold their positions, retreated from the field and made juncture with 10,000 German mercenaries. This help, however, was not enough. Though Condé, early in the new year, could count 30,000 effectives, he could neither pay them nor feed them. On March 23, 1568,

46. A thorough account in James Thompson, *The Wars of Religion in France, 1559–1576* (New York, n.d. [1909]), pp. 318 ff.

he signed the Peace of Longjumeau, which simply restated the terms of five years before and left the bitterness and fanaticism of both sides intact.

Formal peace this time lasted only a matter of months. The Huguenots did not even bother to evacuate their strongholds at Orléans and La Rochelle, and the Catholics, for their part, were busy forming local leagues or brotherhoods whose object was to keep watch on Huguenot notables. The contemporary Calvinist d'Aubigné[47] claimed that 10,000 leading Huguenots were murdered during the spring and summer of 1568. In July Montluc hanged seven gentlemen in the suite of Queen Jeanne of Navarre.

But the genuinely new factor which now began to dominate the situation was the decision of the Huguenot leadership to link the cause in France with the growing forces of revolt in the Netherlands. Once more, it was not an entirely religious matter, since the brutalities of the Alba regime and, more generally, the unnatural political connection with Spain created rebels in the seventeen provinces without reference to confessional allegiance. Their leader indeed, William, Prince of Orange, was still, nominally at least, a Catholic. Even so, Condé and Coligny on one side, and Orange and his brother Louis of Nassau on the other, recognized their common need of Calvinist shock troops inspired by a sense of crusade, and they believed that their common enemy was Philip II and the power of Spain.

It was Catherine's anxiety lest France be sucked into the Spanish king's hostilities in the Netherlands that sparked the Third War of Religion. Aware by late summer of Orange's negotiations with Condé and Coligny, the court determined to arrest the two Huguenot leaders, but, forewarned, the prince and the admiral fled to La Rochelle. Their arrival there (September 19, 1568) was the signal for Calvinist risings all over the west and southwest. The government swiftly revoked all previous toleration edicts, sacked the moderate chancellor l'Hôpital, and, with the pope's concurrence, raised money by a stiff tax upon all ecclesiastical property. Orange meantime at the head of a ragtag force of 25,000 mercenaries invaded the Spanish Netherlands.

A juncture between the two insurgents proved impossible. By the end of the year, Orange's army had melted away. In France, however,

47. "Qui toujours exagère," says Jean Mariéjol, *Catherine de Médicis* (Paris, 1920), p. 167.

the war dragged on for two miserable years of carnage and destruction. Through the autumn of 1568 the royalist and rebel hosts groped for one another in the mud. They did not meet until March 13, 1569, at Jarnac, a hundred miles northwest of Bordeaux, where the Huguenots were badly defeated and Condé captured and promptly murdered. When news of the prince's death reached Paris, a Te Deum was sung at Notre Dame.

3. CONFESSIO BELGICA

The revolt of the Netherlands against Spain must be counted among history's irrepressible conflicts. Rooted in a political union which neither geography nor economics nor mutual interest of any kind could justify, it would have happened even had there never been a phenomenon called Calvinism. Yet the passions aroused by competing religious systems brought the struggle out into the open, shaped it, and lent it a peculiar savagery. What dynastic accident had joined together, ideology put asunder.

The earliest records of Netherlands Calvinism tell of Flemish refugees in Germany and in the London of Edward VI. When the peace of 1559 reopened the southern frontier, a steady movement of French-speaking Calvinists began into the Walloon provinces, into Artois and south Flanders especially. The leading figure here was Guy de Bray,[48] an itinerant preacher who organized a congregation along Genevan lines at Tournai in 1560 (and a little later at Lille and Valenciennes). His *Confessio Belgica* (1561) received Calvin's blessing and, according to de Bray, represented the views of 100,000 of Philip II's Netherlands subjects. Even if this claim was an exaggeration, the parades and outdoor rallies at which huge crowds sang the psalms in Clement Marot's lilting translation[49] gave evidence that Calvinism was attracting a larger constituency than Lutheranism and Anabaptism had.[50] And not only in the French-speaking south: in Holland and Zeeland prosperous

48. For a modern estimate see the works of E. M. Braekman, especially *Guy de Brès* (Brussels, 1960).

49. Clement Marot (d. 1544), an early but relapsed Calvinist, published 49 psalms in French. In 1562 Beza translated the other 101, thus compiling the first vernacular psalter in verse for Protestant use.

50. The usual factors of Calvinist organization and propaganda are advanced to explain this. But see also Peter de Jong, "Can Political Factors Account for the Fact That Calvinism Rather Than Anabaptism Came to Dominate the Dutch Reformation?" *Church History*, XXXIII (1964), 392–417.

burghers studied the *Institutes* intently, while the Flemish artisan class tended to identify the aggressive new religion with their aspirations for social reform. Antwerp was said to contain more Calvinists than Geneva itself.

The king's government in Brussels reacted by invoking the harsh antiheresy laws of Charles V,[51] which were laconically reinforced by directives from Madrid. Between 1561 and 1563 fifteen Calvinists were burned at the stake in Tournai, and by 1567 more than a hundred in Antwerp. This policy, however, became increasingly difficult to implement in the face of massive public resistance to it. The population of the Low Countries, if unattracted by the Calvinist creed, nevertheless shrank from the persecution, and as time went on, fewer judges and officials were prepared to enforce the full rigor of the law. Since the government had no coercive means of its own,[52] it could do little but plead with local estates, municipalities, and stadholders to do the king's will.

The governor general was Philip II's large, swarthy, mannish half-sister Margaret, Duchess of Parma, a woman of character and intelligence who compensated for an unhappy marriage to an Italian princeling she despised by dedicating herself totally to the service of the Hapsburg dynasty.[53] Philip had no qualms about placing his illegitimate relatives in high and sensitive positions, as he showed in Margaret's case and, more spectacularly, in that of another of his father's bastards, Don John of Austria. But the king never fully trusted anybody, and Margaret's lot in Brussels was not a happy one with Cardinal Granvelle in direct communication with Madrid. Even after Granvelle's recall in 1564—Philip admitted no more than that the cardinal was granted leave to visit his ailing mother in Franche Comté, but in fact he never returned to the Netherlands—Margaret was left with an unpopular policy and without the means to carry it out.

Pressure on the government to relax the persecution was intense. The great lords—Orange, Egmont, Hoorne—took the lead now that with

51. Henri Pirenne, *Histoire de Belgique* (Brussels, 1910), III, 360 ff.

52. See above, p. 66.

53. See Leopold von Ranke, *History of the Popes* (New York, 1901), I, p. 179, and Hubert Jedin, *A History of the Council of Trent* (St. Louis, 1957), I, 494. Margaret's husband, Ottavio Farnese, was the grandson of Pope Paul III. Their son, the great Alexander Farnese, who will figure later in these pages, sprang therefore from illegitimate eminence on both sides.

Granvelle gone they had returned to the council of state. On December 31, 1564, in the midst of a council debate, William of Orange offered a defense of freedom of conscience which, from a personage of his rank and generation, was unique: "However strongly I am attached to the Catholic religion, I cannot approve of princes attempting to rule the consciences of their subjects and wanting to rob them of the liberty of belief."[54] That in fact Orange was not particularly attached to any religion did not detract from the landmark quality of this statement.

Early in the new year the council sent Egmont to Madrid to discuss the religious situation face to face with the king. Their conversations were easy, even genial, and the count came home (April, 1565) convinced that his case had made a real impression at the Spanish court. But the sealed documents he presented to the Duchess of Parma at Brussels told another story, or rather the same old story. Philip declared that he would prefer to lose 100,000 lives than to alter his religious policy. Six months later, in the famous "Letters from the Woods of Segovia,"[55] he repeated his conviction and added that what the Netherlands needed was its own version of the holy Inquisition.[56] It demanded all of Margaret's loyalty to sustain her as she realized what others had known for some time—that the king could not distinguish between Castile and the Netherlands.[57] Again, Orange, Egmont, and Hoorne withdrew from the council, and, as one witness reported at the end of 1565, "Madame de Parma no longer brings her sewing to the council. She takes note of all that is said, her head resting on her left hand, and talks of resigning since nothing she says makes any difference to the king."

Meanwhile, a league of four or five hundred lesser nobility and

54. Pieter Geyl, *The Revolt of the Netherlands* (London, 1962), p. 78.
55. L. P. Gachard, ed., *Correspondance de Philippe II sur les affaires des Pays-Bas* (Brussels, 1848), I, cxxix, 373 f. The Segovia Letters (October 17, 1565) came in the midst of controversy about how or whether to promulgate the disciplinary decrees of Trent. See F. Claeys Bourraert, "A propos de l'intervention de l'Université de Louvain dans la Publication des décrets du Concile de Trente," *Revue d'Histoire Ecclésiastique,* LV (1960), 508–512.
56. See Michel Dierickx, "La Politique religieuse de Philippe II dans les anciens Pays-Bas," *Hispania,* XVI (1956), 130–143. A papal inquisition already existed in the Netherlands from Charles V's time, and so technically it was true that Philip never intended to introduce the Spanish Inquisition there. What he wanted was enforcement.
57. Pirenne's somber judgment (quoted by Hauser, *La prépondérance espagnole,* p. 8) of Philip II: "his mediocre intelligence, his hesitations, his incurable slowness, his taste for petty expediencies and petty intrigues."

gentry under Calvinist leadership had been organized. It was called the Compromise, and its avowed purpose was to resist the establishment of the Inquisition. The bond of brotherhood which all members of the Compromise signed was carefully worded to give no offense to Catholics, and Orange was offered formal command. But William was wary, for he knew that beneath the bland words of the bond was the threat of armed rebellion, and until the great lords could be persuaded to join such a venture and foreign powers to support it, he considered it folly. Moreover, he feared (as it turned out with reason) that Calvinist fanaticism might frighten the Catholic masses. So he proposed that the Compromise sponsor a monster anti-Inquisition petition, the gathering of which would itself constitute a kind of grass-roots organization.

This was a shrewd idea, and the result a smashing success. On April 5, 1566, the governess received the petition, and the Compromise turned the affair into a massive nativist demonstration. Margaret agreed to present the king the petition and to suspend the execution of the heresy laws until his reply. That night, at a banquet, one of Granvelle's old friends on the council snorted in disgust that the duchess had demeaned herself in giving audience to such scum, to mere beggar men—*gueux* in the Brussels vernacular. In the years to come, many a glass would be raised in toast to "Les Gueux!" The Beggars became a watchword destined to be immortal.

The first result of the duchess's decision was the return in great crowds, from May on, of the émigrés who had fled the persecution. The bold emergence of the consistories, the preachers with their fiery denunciations of Roman idolatry and the Spanish Antichrist, terrified Margaret, who had practically no troops of her own and had to depend upon the magnates to preserve public order. Active in the agitation was Orange's younger brother, Louis of Nassau, a fervent Calvinist. William himself, however, kept aloof, for though he hoped money might be raised for the anti-Spanish cause through the consistories, he still feared sectarian enthusiasm, and he warned his brother that by whipping up the Calvinists he risked ruining the whole affair.

But the warning came too late. Quite suddenly, on August 10, 1566, a new phenomenon appeared.[58] Armed mobs in two small towns of west Flanders sacked and looted the local churches. From there it spread rapidly. Methodically, gangs well provided with wrecking

58. See E. de Moreau, *Histoire de l'Église en Belgique* (Brussels, 1952), V, 122 ff.

apparatus broke statuary, smashed stained glass, burned pictures and tapestries and stole the communion plate, and set fire to what remained. The destructive cyclone moved in an orderly fashion northeast until some four hundred towns and villages had seen their churches sacked. Nor did the violence occur only in the small towns. Ghent, Antwerp,[59] Amsterdam, Leyden, Delft, and Utrecht also knew this visitation. And it all happened in little more than six weeks (August 10–September 25), whereupon the mobs disappeared as suddenly and as unexpectedly as they had come.

To this day it remains unclear whether these iconoclastic riots were spontaneous or, what is rather more likely, premeditated.[60] But in either case, the general rising some had thought they signaled never got beyond the level of tavern gossip. Indeed, William of Orange's gloomy predictions about the backlash effect Calvinist fanaticism might have upon the national cause proved in the main correct. The Catholic rank and file began to pull out of the Compromise, and when the governess, with money sent from Madrid, hurriedly hired troops to restore order, not a finger of resistance was raised against them. Apparently Margaret caught the public pulse as accurately as Orange, even though her pious observation that religious revolution was worse than sedition drew from Egmont the acid retort, "Not a man with anything to lose would agree." For their part, the great lords found themselves facing a dilemma. They could hardly afford to oppose the one active anti-Spanish force and yet neither dared they antagonize the nation at large by conniving at anarchy. Margaret shrewdly enlisted their aid in the work of hanging and shooting looters in their several provinces, while her mercenaries chopped up the patchwork armies the Calvinists managed to mobilize.

The lords tried not to let their right hand know what their left was doing. Orange secretly encouraged Calvinist activity in Holland and Zealand while he suppressed it in Antwerp, where he was stadholder. Egmont testified to their common vacillation by going to Mass at Ghent but keeping his hat on during the service. When at the begin-

59. For an eyewitness account of the Calvinist fury in Antwerp, see Marvin R. O'Connell, *Thomas Stapleton and the Counter Reformation* (New Haven, 1964), pp. 31 ff.

60. The debate has raged since at least 1951. See Léonard, *Protestantism*, II, 89, for some references. Professor Koenigsberger (*New Cambridge Modern History*, III, 270) thinks "there is some evidence that it was an organized movement but it is not conclusive."

ning of 1567 Margaret demanded of them a new oath of unconditional
loyalty to the king, Egmont swore it, Orange and Hoorne refused. A
few months later (March 13, 1567) the agony of decision for William
of Orange reached its cruelest pitch. As the last little Calvinist army,
pursued by victorious royalists, fell back from Flushing toward Antwerp, Orange closed the gates of the city. He would neither allow the
rebels in nor allow their supporters inside the city to assist them. From
the walls he watched impassively while the governess's troops cut them
to pieces. For this exercise in *Realpolitik* Guy de Bray called down upon
the prince the curses of heaven. But within weeks Guy de Bray was
burned at the stake, and Orange, with a farewell manifesto (April 11),
left the Netherlands for his County of Nassau. The disaster had convinced him that the national cause could succeed only with foreign aid;
not yet was he ready to identify that cause with militant Calvinism.

Margaret of Parma was now in control as she had never been before,
as the Calvinist movement went underground, shattered and discredited. The governess was also wiser now than before, and she proposed a convocation of the States-General and a mild interpretation of
the religious penal laws. Of the many afflictions the country had
suffered, one in particular made her anxious, the emigration of so
many skilled workers and "the consequent impoverishment of this
country whose whole being is manufactures, navigation and trade." So
she wrote to Philip II, saying also how pleased he must be at "this most
glorious victory won for him, the punishment of the leaders and the
humiliation of the rebels, and all this with so little shedding of blood."

But Philip did not think so. Freed for the moment from his military
preoccupations in the Mediterranean, he decided to impose the harsh
strictures of martial law upon his recalcitrant Netherlands subjects—a
policy long recommended by the hard-liners around the king. Prominent among these councillors was the Duke of Alba, who in the
summer of 1567 marched overland from Italy at the head of a superb
Spanish army and assumed the reins of government from Margaret
of Parma, who, unwilling to be a figurehead a second time, resigned
the governorship. During the next five years the tyranny of Alba
breathed new life into the nationalist cause which had died in 1567
beneath the walls of Antwerp. The duke's political philosophy was
simplicity itself: "Kings are born to give orders, subjects to obey them."
Setting aside all local organs of government, he formed the famous

Council of the Troubles or the Council of Blood (as it came to be called), which proceeded to implement "his program of political repression and pursuit of heresy with a ruthlessness that has earned him universal condemnation."[61]

More than 12,000 men and women were condemned by Alba's Council of Blood, of whom one in twelve suffered execution or banishment and the rest heavy fines and forfeiture of property.[62] The most celebrated victims were Egmont and Hoorne, beheaded in the Brussels main square on June 5, 1568. The people of the Netherlands bowed to this reign of terror with hardly a murmur, except for the so-called Wild Beggars, who were as much bandits as patriots and who now and then disturbed the remote sections of west Flanders. Farther north the smaller and more scattered Spanish garrisons invited a few attempts at resistance. Louis of Nassau, Orange's impulsive brother, raided into Groningen and enjoyed some success until Alba himself marched in pursuit. Then Louis barely got away with his skin (April–August, 1568).

Orange meanwhile scoured Germany for men and money; he found more of the former than of the latter. By October he had hired a huge force of mercenaries whom he could pay for two or three months. On October 6 he led them across the Meuse and deep into Brabant, as Alba's much smaller army retreated before him. Manifestoes proclaiming the day of liberation preceded him, but they had little effect on a populace as fearful of the liberators as of the oppressors. Alba refused battle and let the invasion destroy itself. Orange's rapacious, undisciplined horde looted, burned, and raped its way over the countryside. By the new year Alba had maneuvered the remnant over the border into France, and there, one dark night, the penniless Prince of Orange deserted it. The fiasco was complete, the disillusionment total.

The moment was ripe for reconciliation, but the Spaniards, cursed by their peculiar political blindness, let it slip. Instead Alba proclaimed (March 1569) a new fiscal program bound to alienate those many natives whom nationalist and Calvinist propaganda had left unmoved. It featured a permanent 10 percent sales tax, the famous *Tiende Penning*. Philip II was determined not only that the seventeen prov-

61. John Lynch, *Spain Under the Habsburgs* (New York, 1964), I, 281.

62. See J. Scheerder, "Les Condamnés du Conseil des Troubles," *Revue d'Histoire Ecclésiastique*, LIX (1964), 90–100.

inces should conform politically and religiously but also that they should contribute to the solvency of his larger empire. That the "tenth penny" represented no more onerous a burden than the *alcabala* did in Castile did not impress the mercantile classes—proportionately so much larger in the Netherlands than in Spain—upon whom it chiefly fell. They predicted that it would spell the ruin of commerce and industry, and indeed so violent were their protests that Alba put off imposing the tenth penny until 1571, and then only in a modified form. He professed to be amused at these burghers who cared nothing about God or country but who reacted so strongly when their pocketbooks were involved. Such a sentiment was a measure of the iron duke's failure to understand the character of the land he had turned into an impregnable fortress.

4. "THE MONSTROUS REGIMENT OF WOMEN"

"If the queen herself would but banish [the Mass] from her private chapel, the whole thing might easily be got rid of. Of such importance among us are the examples of princes. For whatever is done after the example of the sovereign, the people, as you know, suppose to be done rightly." An English divine named John Jewel wrote these words to Peter Martyr at Zurich in April, 1559.[63] A few weeks later the parliament passed the Act of Uniformity which banished the Mass not only from the chapel royal but from the whole kingdom. Jewel shortly afterward was named Bishop of Salisbury and went on to become the premier apologist for the Elizabethan settlement of religion.[64] But in his new eminence he did not forget his mentors: "As to matters of doctrine," he told Martyr in 1562, "we have pared everything away to the very quick, and do not differ from your doctrine by a nails-breadth."

Popish teaching may have been "pared away to the very quick," but in the eyes of Geneva and Zurich the reform in England was far from complete. Beza, after studying it for some years, saw one overriding reason: "The papacy was never abolished in that country," he said to

---

63. H. Robinson, ed., *The Zurich Letters* (Cambridge, 1846), pp. 28–29.

64. Jewel's *Apologia Ecclesiae Anglicanae* appeared in 1562 and the translation by Lady Bacon (Francis's mother) two years later. It occasioned a tremendous literary controversy which lasted for years. See A. C. Southern, *English Recusant Prose* (London, n.d. [1950]), pp. 60 ff.

Bullinger, "but transferred to the sovereign."[65] This was not an unfair description of what had happened in England, or indeed what had happened in the Low Countries, where Alba, *mutatis mutandis,* was a kind of pope. For statesmen of the late sixteenth century were unanimous that religion, both in itself and in its cultural and political ramifications, was too important to be left to the clergy.

Elizabeth I, it cannot be said too often, came to the throne at a moment when England's fortunes had reached a particularly low ebb. Defeated in war, threatened by powerful foreign enemies, distracted by grave social and economic difficulties, the nation desperately needed a period of peace and stability, and therefore it needed a solution to its bitter religious divisions. Because this was undoubtedly so, and because the character of Elizabeth's personal religion remains open to question, one might be tempted to presume that the Elizabethan regime sought religious peace simply for the sake of its secular objectives. Such a view might seem to be confirmed by the admittedly comprehensive nature of the settlement of 1559 and by its calculated ambiguities. But the truth appears somewhat more complicated, perhaps too complicated for a post-Christian era to appreciate. Formal religion in sixteenth-century Europe was not the compartmentalized, entirely private, and peripheral matter it has since become; it touched then every facet of life and in the atmosphere of revival which had begun with Luther it did so at almost a fever pitch. Religion informed, explained, rebuked, consoled, justified; it was the glue that kept a people stuck together when there were as yet no effective bureaucracies or armies to do so. Elizabeth and her counselors did not say, "Let us settle the religious question and then we can get at the really important issues"; rather they said, "Let us settle the religious question because, mixed up as it is so intimately with every other concern, foreign and domestic, it is the most important issue."

Out of this conviction came the Anglican Church, at once Protestant, Episcopal, and Erastian. Faithful to England's long tradition, it came not through edict but through two key statutes passed by Elizabeth's first parliament in 1559.[66] The Act of Supremacy abolished the pope's

---

65. *The Zurich Letters,* p. 246 (July, 1566).
66. For the texts of the Acts of Supremacy and Uniformity, see Gee and Hardy, *Documents,* pp. 442 ff. and 458 ff. Neale, *Elizabeth I and Her Parliaments, 1559–1581,* pp. 51 ff., describes their passage through both houses.

spiritual jurisdiction within the queen's dominions and annexed to the crown forever any jurisdiction ever exercised or claimed by the pope. It imposed upon certain classes of people an oath, to refuse which was to disqualify oneself from all public offices. To maintain or defend the proposition that the pope enjoyed any spiritual authority in England was punishable on a first conviction by the loss of all one's goods and chattels or, for a poor man, the same together with a year in prison; on a second conviction the penalty was loss of all property and life imprisonment; and on a third death in hideous fashion prescribed for traitors who were hanged, drawn, castrated, quartered, and beheaded. The severity of this legislation was intensified in 1563 by inflicting the death penalty on those who twice refused the oath or twice defended, even verbally, the pope's pretensions, and it was extended by increasing the numbers of those who had to swear the oath.

The Act of Uniformity imposed the rites and prayers of the Book of Common Prayer of 1552 as the only lawful form of worship, and it too possessed penal provisions. The clergyman who refused to use this restored Protestant prayer book, or who criticized it, was subject for a first offense to the comparatively lenient sentence of loss of a year's income and six months in jail. But if he were stubborn and were convicted a third time, he could be imprisoned for life. The layman was shrewdly hit in his pocketbook: every absence from his parish church on Sunday or other appointed days was punishable by a fine.

So the queen, with her lords and faithful commons, abolished the Mass as John Jewel hoped she would. But she kept other things, like bishops and vestments and candles and a kneeling posture for reception of the Lord's Supper. Some of these "dregs of popery," so bitterly denounced by continental Protestants, were preserved because they helped to soften the transition and thus hopefully appeased that vast majority of Englishmen unenthusiastic for the reform. Jewel and his colleagues on the episcopal bench, most of whom had spent Queen Mary's reign breathing the pure evangelical air of Switzerland, could only swallow their embarrassment over bells, caps, and incense and protest that compared to the soundness of Anglican doctrine these were mere trifles, mere matters of ceremony. But this argument did not meet Beza's fundamental objection, which was that decisions in ceremonial as in all other affairs of the Church came from the government or, more specifically, from a headstrong woman.

So Jewel wore his miter and cope and consoled himself in the Calvinist orthodoxy of the Thirty-nine Articles,[67] the formal Anglican confession of faith drawn up by the convocation of clergy in 1563 and given parliamentary sanction eight years later.[68] The queen, for her part, let no one doubt that the Church belonged to her, body and soul. In 1565 several of the most prominent clergymen in England were suspended for failure to wear the prescribed vestments, and the next year a host of lesser lights joined them.[69] "We hear," Bullinger wrote sadly, "that many other things are obtruded upon the godly ministers which were fabricated in the school of anti-Christ, new filth and the restored relics of wretched popery." Such protests, however, were whistling in the wind. The queen and her advisers had decided that the settlement of 1559 was final, and zealous English Protestants could do little more than plead to their confreres abroad that the Bible did not enjoin a presbyterian form of church government as clearly as it revealed justification by faith alone.

During the decade after Cateau-Cambrésis, during "these ten grim, unlovely years," as H. A. L. Fisher called them, "the reformation was unalterably riveted upon the English people."[70] The settlement met with hardly any public resistance, except from the Protestant radicals. The Catholics for the most part obeyed the laws and were at any rate physically present at the new Sunday service. The Massing priests became officiating ministers with practically no fuss. "They were not all happy with what they saw around them in the shape of reform," as Professor Chadwick says, "but they preferred the vernacular to Latin, and a wife to a concubine, and knew that their parishioners had souls which must be baptized and fed and married and buried."[71] Ordinary men sensed that somehow the Church like the land in which it was rooted would outlast the threats and alarums of a contentious generation. Meanwhile, if "grim and unlovely" abuses did not cease, if the parochial clergy remained in appalling ignorance, if even the best of

67. "Calvinist in doctrine," says Léonard, *Protestantism*, II, 68. Perhaps "susceptible of Calvinist interpretation" would be a better way to put it.

68. See William Haugaard, *Elizabeth and the English Reformation* (Cambridge, 1968), pp. 52 ff., for an account of the convocation.

69. See Patrick Collinson, "The 'nott conformytye' of the young John Whitgift," *Journal of Ecclesiastical History*, XV (1964), 192–200.

70. Quoted by Philip Hughes, *The Reformation in England* (New York, 1954), III, 50.

71. Chadwick, *Reformation*, p. 135.

the new Protestant bishops, Matthew Parker of Canterbury (d. 1575), showed all the pedantic remoteness, the zest for personal profit, the indifference to corruption in his diocese, of the most arrogant medieval prelate,[72] at least things were no worse than they had been, at least a man could seek his God in peace.

That peace, however, depended upon the strength of one slender woman. And so inevitably the religious settlement of 1559, especially during its first fragile decade, was bound up in the vagaries of dynastic politics. Specifically, the problem was the succession. Elizabeth refused to marry, indeed refused to discuss the possibility of marriage. Nor would she, as the last member of the Tudor family, designate a successor, because, as she told a parliamentary delegation in 1566, she knew that the rising was more attractive than the setting sun; "I have been a 'second person' and have tasted of the practices against my sister, who, I would God, were alive again."[73] There was therefore to be no "second person," no heir presumptive, no competitor for the virgin queen.

Still, men had to consider the future. Though other shadowy claimants hovered on the periphery, by the dynastic law of blood relationship the next ruler of England would be Mary Queen of Scots. And Mary was a Catholic. Not a fanatical Catholic, to be sure; she appeared to live comfortably with John Knox's Scottish Kirk, which hewed as closely to the Genevan ideal as was possible in this imperfect universe.[74] But Mary was also a Guise with powerful connections in the Catholic world outside Britain, and she was a young, beautiful, royal widow. What if she married Don Carlos, Philip II's son and heir? Or her one-time brother-in-law, Charles IX of France? Or an Austrian archduke? That she would marry somebody soon was a certainty, and then presumably children would follow to solidify her dynastic position in Scotland and in England as well.

Not a few Englishmen may have privately subscribed to Knox's antifeminist thesis as put forth in his 1558 pamphlet "The First Blast of the Trumpet against the Monstrous Regiment of Women,"[75] which

---

72. See J. J. Daeley, "Pluralism in the Diocese of Canterbury during the Administration of Matthew Parker," *Journal of Ecclesiastical History,* XVIII (1967), 33–49.

73. Black, *Reign of Elizabeth,* p. 3.

74. Professor Parker (*New Cambridge Modern History,* III, 116 f.) describes its polity as a cross between Presbyterianism and Congregationalism.

75. Published in Geneva, but without Calvin's knowledge or approval.

argued that female rulers were an absurd violation of nature's own laws. But the "regiment of women" was a present fact, and as long as Elizabeth remained her inscrutable self, saying neither yea nor nay about the succession, it promised to stretch far into the future. Increasingly, those opposed for whatever reason to the Elizabethan regime looked to Mary as a symbol, a rallying point, a token of dynastic respectability. For the inner circle of that regime—Cecil, Leicester, Walsingham, Bacon, and the rest—she came to represent all the dark forces of reaction.

Mary's impact upon England was not unrelated to her strength in Scotland. By 1565 her home base appeared relatively secure.[76] She had succeeded at least momentarily in curbing the turbulent Scots nobles and in winning their loyalty. By cultivating moderate Protestant elements she had practically isolated Knox, who was reduced to ranting about the High Mass sung at Holyrood palace very early in the morning and the dance music played there late at night. In all this, and in her dealings with her "sweet cousin" of England, she let herself be guided by the two ablest statesmen in the realm, her bastard half-brother, the Earl of Moray, and her secretary, William Maitland of Lethington. Not that Scotland moved out of the English orbit; but Mary did feel strong enough to refuse to ratify the Treaty of Edinburgh[77] because it did not specify her right to the English succession. And when her hopes for a foreign marriage were disappointed, she scoffed at Elizabeth's tasteless suggestion that she marry Leicester, widely reputed to be the virgin queen's own lover.

But Mary left to herself chose an even worse husband and in the process brought down upon herself personal and political disaster. Henry Stuart, Lord Darnley, a tall, handsome youth—"yon long lad," Elizabeth called him—was a scion of one of Scotland's first families and, like Mary, was a grandchild of Margaret Tudor (but by her second marriage) and so himself in line for the English succession. Queen Elizabeth bitterly resented the match which joined two of the claimants to her throne, and the faction-ridden Scottish nobility did too, on the grounds that it elevated one clan above the others. Moray was so incensed that he left the court, and a few weeks after the

---

76. See J. H. Burns in David McRoberts, ed., *Essays on the Scottish Reformation* (Glasgow, 1962), pp. 19 f.
77. See above, pp. 67, 77.

nuptials (July 29, 1565) he was in open rebellion. The "Chaseabout Raid," as this ludicrous rising was aptly called, quickly sputtered out, and Moray fled over the English border into exile. But Pandora's box had been opened and a sign had been given of how fragile Mary's hold on Scotland really was.

Even had Darnley been a better man than he was, the marriage involved serious risks for Mary, because it threatened to alienate the people she was most anxious to appease. But Darnley soon proved himself worse than bad. Drunken, abusive, syphilitic, utterly without talent and without scruple, he was scarcely in the royal marriage bed before he was intriguing against his wife. Like many weak men, he fancied himself put upon and listened to the seductive voices which told him he should be king in fact as well as in name. Instead of the strong arm Mary thought he would be for her when she convinced herself that she loved him, Darnley by the beginning of 1566 had become the pawn of her enemies, chief among whom were now her former advisers Moray and Maitland.

By this time Mary was pregnant, ill, and depressed. She took some consolation in the sprightly talk and musical talents of one David Rizzio, a Savoyard drifter who had attached himself to the Scottish court and who perhaps reminded Mary of her sunny days in France. The relationship was harmless, but Darnley was persuaded by Moray's confederates that his wife's affections, so visibly removed from himself, had been transferred to the little Italian.[78] On the evening of March 9, 1566, Darnley and four or five armed men suddenly burst into the queen's apartment and murdered Rizzio before her eyes. This crime, in which Rizzio's body was pierced by more than fifty stab wounds, was the prelude to an attempted coup whereby Moray, Knox, and the lords allied to them intended to seize power. But then the treacherous Darnley lost his nerve, changed sides again, and helped Mary slip out of Holyrood and Edinburgh. Together they galloped furiously off to Dunbar, a twenty-seven-mile ride in five hours for a woman six months pregnant. Within days 8,000 men had rallied to her, and on March 18 the Queen of Scots returned to her capital in triumph.

"Darnley," writes Lady Antonia Fraser, "rode beside her like a sulky

78. The queen's relationship with Rizzio occasioned many snickers. "Woe is me for you when Davy's son shall be a king of England," wrote the English ambassador in Edinburgh to Leicester. Many years later Henry IV of France jokingly referred to James VI as "Solomon, son of David."

page," and the cunning Moray, who had carefully kept his hands clean of Rizzio's blood, greeted her at Holyrood.[79] As the other conspirators, including Knox, scattered to await another opportunity, the principals made a show of reconciliation and Mary withdrew behind the battlements of Edinburgh castle, where, after a long and painful labor, she had her baby on June 19.

The birth of Prince James left his father in an exposed and dangerous position. For now into this improbable tale of treachery and passion strode the burly figure of James Hepburn, Earl of Bothwell. About thirty years old, well traveled and well educated for a Scots noble, Bothwell owned large estates in the southern lowlands. Already famous as a womanizer and soldier of fortune, he had been Mary's sturdiest support during the Rizzio crisis, and his unabashed masculinity must have attracted a woman whose love life had had to find satisfaction with the likes of Francis Valois and Darnley. By the autumn of 1566 the queen was once more openly at odds with her husband and certainly not sleeping with him. Sometime during those months Moray suggested divorce and Bothwell suggested murder.

An analysis of the wildly conflicting evidence pretty well absolves Mary from any direct part in Darnley's death. But complicity is a wide term, and to the extent that its meaning includes general knowledge and approval the Queen of Scots cannot be entirely exonerated. Though she was probably not Bothwell's mistress during Darnley's lifetime, it is likely that she gave him some kind of personal commitment. She was genuinely shocked and even horrified at the brutal assassination (February 10, 1567), but her expressions of sorrow were strictly conventional, and Knox thought her strangely composed for a woman who wept so easily. By May she was married to Bothwell (in a Protestant ceremony after his obscenely hurried divorce), and by June Moray and his friends—most of whom had connived at Darnley's murder and urged the queen to marry Bothwell—had taken the field. The two little armies met at Carberry Hill, Mary was captured, and Bothwell escaped to Dunbar and ultimately to Denmark, prison, madness, and death. On July 29, thirteen-month-old James VI was crowned king at Stirling, with Moray as regent. A few days before, the

79. The assessments of Moray have varied down to our own time. Contrast, e.g., the favorable judgments of Wallace MacCaffrey, *The Shaping of the Elizabethan Regime* (Princeton, 1968), pp. 251, 258 and 272, with those of Gordon Donaldson, *The First Trial of Mary Queen of Scots* (New York, 1969), pp. 56, 92, and 129.

deposed Queen of Scots, imprisoned on an island in the middle of a lake, miscarried Bothwell's twins.

A less hardy spirit might at this point have given up. But Mary's blood was Stuart and Guise, and what she lacked in prudence she compensated for in courage. On May 2, 1568, she escaped from her waterbound prison and rode west into territory dominated by the Hamilton clan, which was notoriously hostile to Moray. The regent's troops caught up with her on May 13 at Langside, a village near Glasgow, and routed the Hamiltons. But Mary got away again and vanished into the primitive border country. "I have endured injuries, calumnies, imprisonment, famine, cold, heat," she later wrote her uncle, the Cardinal of Lorraine, "flight not knowing whither, ninety-two miles across the country without stopping or alighting, and then I have had to sleep upon the ground, and drink sour milk, and eat oatmeal without bread, and have been three nights like the owls, without a female in this country."[80] At three o'clock in the afternoon of May 16 she stepped into a fishing boat which carried her over Solway Firth and deposited her four hours later on English soil, a few miles from Carlisle. Less than three years had passed since the Darnley marriage.

The royal fugitive, so beautiful and so forlorn, captivated every Englishman in sight. Her very helplessness lent fascination to her appeal for help against the wicked men who had stolen her crown and her child. In the shiver of enthusiasm that ran through the northern counties during the early summer it seemed that the Queen of Scots's luck might indeed have changed for the better. In London, however, far from direct exposure to the lady's charms, policy prevailed over chivalry. Mary's impulsive flight to England was viewed there as an embarrassment bristling with potential dangers. While Elizabeth preferred a Scotland ruled by a baby king and a venal regent, she still could not suffer gladly the deposition of a fellow monarch whose anointed person was de jure and de facto sacred. One of her courtiers put it this way: "She who has a crown can hardly persuade another to leave her crown because her subjects will not obey. It may be a new doctrine in Scotland but is not good to be taught in England." For the same reason Mary's case could not be tried in the ordinary sense of the word, nor could she be dispatched unceremoniously back across the

80. Quoted by J. B. Black, *The Reign of Elizabeth* (Oxford, 1959), pp. 109 f.

border. But neither was it in the English interest to restore her to her throne by force, or, finally, to allow her to pass to France or Spain, where she might revive some version of the "auld alliance."

Yet despite the quandary a solution of sorts lay ready at hand. Mary stood convicted in Scotland of her husband's murder, and Darnley's person too had been sacred. Until that cloud was removed, Elizabeth decreed that her sweet cousin should live under royal but strict confinement and that the circumstances of Darnley's death should be investigated by a special commission whose findings would determine the English government's posture. Accordingly, Mary, over her tearful protests, was placed under comfortable house arrest at Bolton Castle, and in October, 1568, a quasi-judicial hearing began at York. Moray came in person, and in the course of the interminable proceedings—they dragged on into the new year and were eventually transferred to Elizabeth's presence at Westminster—he produced the infamous "casket letters," allegedly Mary's love letters to Bothwell, and other equally dubious evidence. The Queen of Scots was represented at the conference, but her emissaries were not allowed to know the existence of Moray's documents, much less to examine or answer them. Indeed, from the point of view of objective justice, the conference was a farce.[81] But it gave Elizabeth a chance to render the sort of decision she liked best. On January 10, 1569, she formally adjourned the commission and declared that since neither side had proved its case, the *status quo ante* would for the time being prevail. Moray, with a loan of 5,000 pounds in his pocket, went back to Edinburgh not unaware that he must behave well toward the English, who, with Mary still their prisoner, could reverse the decision when they chose.

Elizabeth probably thought Mary guilty of Darnley's murder; there was documentary evidence enough, and Elizabeth could not have guessed how much of it was forged. But in all likelihood the question of guilt or innocence was not a compelling factor in her decision to let things stand. The problems of Scotland and the succession came together in Mary's person, and so to hold her for a while—and to hold the suspicion of murder over her head—seemed the most advantageous course to follow. Delay and equivocation were diplomatic tools that Elizabeth used with great skill and, most of the time, with great success. In this case, however, her calculated ambiguity brought her more

81. Donaldson, *First Trial,* treats of the evidence definitively.

trouble than she had bargained for. The duel between the two queens had just begun.

Meanwhile, the Duke of Alba had imposed the tenth penny upon the burghers of the Low Countries, and Louis, Prince of Condé, had fallen on Jarnac field.

5. THE ADMIRAL COMES TO COURT

The kingdoms of England, France, and Spain moved along strangely parallel paths toward the climactic summer of 1572. Each of them endured the danger of internal subversion and survived it, though not completely or decisively. Often it seemed as though they must eventually come into direct conflict, but they did not; instead each fished in the other's troubled waters. The increasing importance of the quarrel of religion revealed itself in that the rebels who looked to foreign courts for aid against their own monarchs were in each case members of a proscribed and persecuted religious minority. Yet, as always, intertwined with ideological commitments were the intense personal rivalries inherent in dynastic politics, as well as mundane concerns measured in pounds and florins.

The key figure was Gaspard de Coligny, the Admiral of France. Once he had led the shattered Huguenot host from Jarnac, the whole weight of the Calvinist-Bourbon cause fell upon his shoulders. He was more than equal to it. During the next eighteen months he achieved an incredible victory.[82] The Huguenots were beaten often—most notably at Poitiers (August, 1569) by the young Henry, Duke of Guise, and at Montcontour (October, 1569) by Marshal Tavennes—but the admiral, now no longer harnessed to the enigmatic Condé, never admitted defeat. The intensity of his sense of godly mission set this austere, grave, careful man apart. His single frivolity was the toothpick that dangled from his mouth every waking hour. There was nothing gentle about his stern Calvinist dedication to duty or about the men he commanded. They were mostly mercenaries whom he could pay only with pillage and rapine, and they left a trail of smoking ruins behind them. But somehow Coligny remained unsullied by the miseries he inflicted. His strength of will and undeviating purpose gave him an immense

---

82. For Coligny and the Third War of Religion and St. Bartholomew, the classic study is the third volume of Jules Delaborde, *Gaspard de Coligny, Amiral de France* (Paris, 1882).

moral superiority over his enemies. He was no tactician, as his dismal battlefield record showed, but he had the winning strategy for this third of the Religious Wars: to preserve Huguenot control in the south and west, to keep his army intact, and to wait until the royalists, riddled by jealousies and conflicting ambitions, collapsed. For nothing essentially had changed at the Valois court: a weak and listless king tied to his mother's apron strings, a new generation of Guise at the throat of a new generation of Montmorency, an aging Cardinal of Lorraine deep in ineffectual intrigue with Spain and Rome, no money, no plan, no conviction.

The Peace of St. Germain (August, 1570) formalized Coligny's triumph. It provided the Huguenots with a wider measure of freedom than ever before, and more than that, it allowed them to maintain a separate military establishment centered in the fortified cities of La Rochelle, Cognac, Montauban, and La Charité. Thus from the Atlantic coast east to the Loire and south to the valley of the Garonne a huge, jagged triangle was carved out and secured for those who had been lately rebels against their king. In vain did Tavennes protest that the government had created a state within the state; in vain did Pope Pius V descry "this shameful peace which had been dictated to the French king by the conquered enemies of God."[83]

For two prominent refugees the admiral had won more than a local victory. Among the provisions of the Edict of St. Germain[84] was Charles IX's formal recognition of the Prince of Orange and the Count of Nassau as his kinsmen and friends. The brothers had stayed in constant touch with Coligny, and Louis indeed had fought in the Huguenot ranks during the last year of the war. Orange, never the enthusiast his brother was, made his restless way from one petty German court to the next, still seeking means to raise an army and invade the Netherlands again. His fortunes had sunk to a new low, his mood was desolate; the summer of 1569 had afflicted him, along with everything else, with the divorce action against his faithless, drunken wife. Out of a kind of desperation he had meanwhile issued in his capacity as a sovereign prince of the empire letters of marque to the Dutch sailors already known as the Sea Beggars—*les Gueux de Mer*—thus lending respectability to men of whom he had disapproved as pirates

83. Ludwig Pastor, *History of the Popes* (London, 1932), XVIII, 131.
84. See Delaborde, *Coligny*, III, 569–578.

and Calvinist fanatics. But while he still placed most of his hopes on foreign (and especially French) intervention, Orange was beginning to understand that of all the Netherlands population only the Calvinists were organized enough and bold enough to offer Alba any significant resistance, as the Beggars assuredly did by preying on Spanish ships. One of the beneficial side effects of the Huguenot connection had been La Rochelle as a haven for Beggar vessels, the tricolor of Orange flying from their tattered mastheads; now, after St. Germain, La Rochelle was still a Huguenot port, and Louis of Nassau, the King of France's friend and kinsman, was there in person.

Elizabeth of England too had granted sanctuary to the Beggars, just as she had connived more or less openly at aid for the French Protestants. To help keep the Catholic monarchies preoccupied with internal dissidents was shrewd but, as the queen learned in 1569, dangerous policy. The series of crises that began that year was triggered by a particularly daring English initiative. A small fleet carrying 800,000 ducats, borrowed by Philip II from Genoese bankers and bound for Alba at Antwerp, took refuge in Plymouth and Southampton to avoid the Beggars and other privateers lurking in the Channel. The cargo was being transported overland to Dover when suddenly the English government seized it on the grounds that the queen desired to borrow it herself.[85] Alba, desperate for the money to pay his troops, retaliated by placing an embargo on English goods in the Netherlands and confiscating the property of English merchants resident there. Elizabeth countered with similar sanctions against Flemish interests in England. And at this tense moment, when the ancient English-Burgundian commercial relationship hung in the balance, France delivered an ultimatum which threatened war unless England desist from aiding the Huguenots (March, 1569).

So within a few weeks of the ambiguous sentence delivered at Westminster in the case of Mary Queen of Scots the delicate balance upon which English external security rested had been upset. Moreover, during the months following, Elizabeth discovered that she herself was not immune from those internal troubles she so cheerfully encouraged elsewhere. For ten or fifteen powerful barons, under the leadership of the

---

85. "Our precise knowledge of the treasure fleet crisis is very slight indeed," says MacCaffrey, *Elizabethan Regime*, p. 289.

Duke of Norfolk, chose this perilous moment, with foreign policy in disarray, to bring down Cecil. Their plan—insofar as they had a plan—was to seek a rapprochement with Spain (or rather with the Spanish Netherlands, whose trade was essential for England's prosperity), a marriage between Norfolk and Mary Queen of Scots, the restoration of Mary to her throne, the unequivocal declaration of her rights as Elizabeth's successor, and above all, the political destruction of Secretary Cecil, the parvenu commoner whose evil ascendancy over the queen had brought—they said—so much trouble to England. A few of these lords were Catholics, and the rest probably would not have minded a reversal of the religious settlement of 1559, which, after all, had been largely Cecil's work. Because he thought it would help him in Brussels and Madrid, Norfolk emphasized this aspect of the scheme when he approached the Spanish ambassador in London.

That diplomat was a fiery Catholic, blessed more with imagination than practical sense. The appearance at his door of the first noble of the realm moved him to draw fanciful parallels with Orange and the Bourbon princes in France and to dream of 40,000 Catholic Englishmen ready to spring out of the ground and overthrow the heretical regime. But Alba, to whom he reported Norfolk's overtures, entertained no such fantasies, and he warned the ambassador to act with extreme caution lest an indiscretion cost the Queen of Scots her life.

The cabal drifted aimlessly into the summer, by which time Cecil himself had got wind of it. Meanwhile, the diplomatic crisis had eased; indeed the French ultimatum had been quite forgotten, as stern resolutions were wont to be at the court of Charles IX. As for Alba, his attempts to impose the "tenth penny" were meeting unexpected opposition, his unpaid troops were restive, and his naval resources were nonexistent. Philip II agreed with him that the time was not ripe for an English adventure and approved his initiation of formal talks with the government of England on the subject of the Genoese treasure.

Then suddenly, in early October, Norfolk was sent to the Tower of London. Elizabeth had discovered the intrigue, and with a fury reminiscent of her father she fell upon the lords of the council who had conspired at the removal of her chief minister and, far worse, at the aggrandizement of the Queen of Scots. "Four months of that marriage," she said to Leicester, referring to the projected alliance between Mary and Norfolk, "and I should find myself in the Tower." Norfolk, a decent but not an overly brave or intelligent man,[86] collapsed in the face of Elizabeth's anger. North of the Trent, however, two of his erstwhile allies were not ready yet to throw in their hands. When the Earls of Northumberland and Westmorland, heads respectively of the clans of Percy and Neville, received the peremptory order to proceed at once to the court, they refused to go (November 4, 1569). Ten days later, with a feudal host 8,000 strong at their backs, they rode into Durham.

The Rising of the North was many things. It reflected the sectional antagonisms between the populous, capitalist south of England and the backward and conservative north. It expressed dying feudalism's reaction against the centralizing tendencies of a Renaissance monarchy. But most of all it was a call to crusade for the old religion which in the south was fast withering away. In Durham the rebels lit a huge bonfire of Geneva Bibles and Books of Common Prayer, and of the wooden communion tables that had replaced the Catholic altars. High Mass was sung in Durham cathedral before a vast, weeping crowd, and the earls' proclamation of intent, while it insisted that evil councillors, not the queen herself, were the targets of their action, also pledged without qualification to suppress the "new found religion and heresy contrary to God's word by the space of twelve years now past set up and maintained."

Throughout her long career Queen Elizabeth was at her best at moments of danger. Now she acted with dispatch and determination in mobilizing her forces to meet the rebellion. The earls, by contrast, had no clear strategic objective, except the liberation of the Queen of Scots. They marched their half-armed levies to a point 75 miles south of York, and then, on the news that Mary had been moved out of their reach to Coventry, they marched back again without firing a shot. By the end of November the Rising of the North for all practical purposes was over. The earls and the other gentlemen, still squabbling among themselves, escaped into Scotland and left the rank and file to face Elizabeth Tudor's wrath. She hanged more than eight hundred of them, ninety in Durham alone and at least one in every village in the disaffected area. The north never forgot this savage retribution and never stirred again.

86. Donaldson, *First Trial*, pp. 96 f.

One factor contributing to the ineffective leadership of the Rising of the North had been the widespread doubt about the morality of rebellion of any sort. Northumberland, an older, more cautious man than Westmorland, had felt this scruple especially keenly, but neither his nor others' inquiries produced anything like a unanimous opinion from the Catholic theologians available. To settle this vexing theoretical question, and all its dire practical implications, Pope Pius V produced one of the most extraordinary documents in the long history of the papacy.[87] On February 25, 1570, while the queen was still busy hanging her rebels, he signed the bull *Regnans in Excelsis,* by which he excommunicated Elizabeth, declared "her people forever released from obedience" to her, deprived "the said Elizabeth of her alleged right to the throne," and ordered "her people not to obey her commands and laws." The pope did not say that English Catholics must rise against their queen, nor that other Christian princes must cooperate in her deposition. Indeed, the pope did not consult with or even inform other Christian princes of his sentence, and they, when they learned of it, were as angry as Elizabeth herself. For a public document copies of *Regnans in Excelsis* were exceedingly difficult to obtain (though one turned up in May, nailed to the door of the Bishop of London's house), as if some curial official belatedly recognized what a blunder it was and tried to suppress its circulation. In any event, the simple-minded Pius V, by trying to solve the earls' *casus conscientiae* after the fact—the sole reason, he told the Spanish ambassador in Rome, why he had issued the bull—landed the English Catholics in an impossible dilemma. What answer could they have now to the charge that their religion was tantamount to treason, when the pope himself had decreed that if convenient they might in good conscience rebel against lawful authority? In the hands of those who wanted to decatholicize England, *Regnans in Excelsis* was worth more than all the penal laws combined.

The lesson, however, was lost on Pius V himself and on one Robert Ridolfi, a Florentine businessman resident in London, who wrote the pope in September, 1570—when the hostile reaction to the bull was still at its height—of another scheme to overthrow Elizabeth. The letter was "a tissue of absurdities"[88] about nobles and Catholic masses eager

87. For text and analysis of the bull, see Philip Hughes, *The Reformation in England* (New York, 1954), III, 272 ff., 418 ff.

88. Francis Edwards, *The Dangerous Queen* (London, 1964), p. 217.

to rise (as the earls had done so catastrophically less than a year before), if only Alba could be persuaded to supply them with arms. Norfolk and Mary Queen of Scots—both, it should be noted, under house arrest and separated from each other by hundreds of miles—were described by Ridolfi as the leaders and ultimate beneficiaries of this new rebellion. During the months of tortuous intrigue that followed, the pope once more demonstrated his utter naïveté by endorsing Ridolfi's harebrained plot and warmly advising Philip II to do the same. From April to July, 1571, Ridolfi traveled from Brussels to Rome to Madrid seeking support for a revolution which was the creature of his own imagination. Alba saw through him at once and urged Philip to repudiate this "foolish chatterbox." The King of Spain, after the usual procrastination, did so. By that time Cecil's agents had intercepted Ridolfi's correspondence and were spinning the web in which to entangle more important personages. Mary had imprudently committed herself in writing and thus further darkened her prospects. As for Norfolk, the evidence, much of it contradictory, much of it forged or obtained by torture, was less clear, and he denied all. But he was condemned to death for high treason anyway, on January 28, 1572.

The season was rife with plots, one of them as far-fetched and even more grandiose than Ridolfi's. Coligny, in whom the Calvinist ideologue wrestled endlessly with the practical man of affairs, had hit upon the idea of a Protestant crusade against Spain. He pressed his case in the highest councils of France, for the admiral, with the victory of St. Germain in his pocket, had returned to court after an absence of nine years. He did not originate the plan to conquer and partition the Netherlands by the joint action of France, England, and the native Protestants; and since it ignored certain pertinent facts—Orange, for instance, would never consent to partition, and Elizabeth would never permit a French presence in the Low Countries—the admiral had to play variations on his borrowed theme. But to the young king his message was consistent: war with Spain would heal the divisions among Frenchmen who, fighting the national enemy, would forget their recent hatred of one another; it would extend the French frontier into the heart of the wealthy Netherlands; and it would bring Charles IX himself some of the military glory he so much desired.

The king was susceptible to Coligny's mature and masculine charm. For the first time in his life he escaped his mother's direction, much to that lady's growing displeasure. As ever Catherine de' Medici was searching for internal peace by way of factional balance which the ascendancy of the admiral clearly threatened. Catherine had succeeded, after long negotiations with the Huguenot battle-queen, Jeanne d'Albret, in arranging a marriage contract between her daughter Margaret and Jeanne's son Henry of Navarre, first prince of the blood and titular head of the Protestant party. Charles IX meanwhile was listening avidly as the real head of that party plied him with stories of Alba's vulnerability to such a potentially great warrior as himself. He told his mother only snatches of this, but eventually she learned what was afoot. One terrible scene between them followed another, and each time Charles abjectly promised to commit himself to nothing without his mother's counsel. Gradually the conviction grew in Catherine's mind that the admiral was the most dangerous man alive.

But he appeared to be getting his way. On April 1, 1572, the Sea Beggars, under the intrepid Captain van der Marck, seized the fishing village of Brill, located on an island where the lower Rhine runs into the sea, just below Rotterdam. A week later Flushing, which dominated the approaches to Antwerp, fell to them, and during the rest of the spring and summer towns all over Holland welcomed the Beggars and ran up the Orange flag. Thus with ridiculous ease was Alba's fortress breached, as the duke, certain that the major thrust would come from the south and east, ignored the deteriorating situation in the north and concentrated his little army in Flanders. His military instincts proved reliable as ever, for though an Anglo-French mutual assistance pact had been signed at Blois on April 19, the English soon sent an expeditionary force to Flushing, not to help the rebels or to harass the Spaniards, but to keep the French out.[89] On May 24, with a secret commission from Charles IX, Louis of Nassau at the head of a band of Huguenot volunteers struck across the frontier from France and captured Mons and Valenciennes. Alba managed to box Louis into those cities, but a greater danger was looming across the Meuse, where the Prince of Orange, his credit rating suddenly improved, was gathering a large army of mercenaries. They marched into Roermond on July 23 and were poised to attack west across Alba's unprotected flank toward Brussels.

But because Coligny was the pivot around which all these actions

89. Black, *Reign of Elizabeth*, p. 156.

swung, the really crucial event occurred a week to the day before that. A French relief column advancing toward Mons was annihilated by Don Frederick Alvarez, Alba's son. Incriminating papers were discovered, and when the Huguenot general was put to the torture he amplified their content: Louis of Nassau's invasion was in fact an enterprise sponsored and paid for by the government of France. Coligny could now have his war with Spain if Philip II chose to respond to a clear provocation. Instead the prudent king said nothing and waited for events to unfold at their own pace. His habitual caution, which so often exasperated his subordinates, this time served him well.

Catherine de' Medici's fury at her son's secret diplomacy—the fury almost of a woman scorned—bordered on hysteria, and from the moment she knew the truth, Coligny was a dead man. Whatever other judgment might be arrived at about the queen mother's activities during the next month, this much must be said in her behalf: she hated war in a century that seemed to thrive on it. To her war was the supreme evil, and this war, to which the admiral would commit a bitterly divided France allied to a handful of Dutch pirates and the false-hearted Queen of England, was madness. Now began that process of reconciliation between Catherine and the House of Guise that led straight to St. Bartholomew's Day. By mid-August, on the eve of the marriage of Henry of Navarre and the king's sister Margaret, the bargain had been struck: the queen mother would use one set of enemies to rid her of another, and the Guise would finally be avenged for the murder of Duke Francis nine years before.

The summer of 1572 was alive with bloody rumors, some of which came true. The Duke of Norfolk was beheaded on June 6 for his part—whatever it was—in the Ridolfi Plot. The Earl of Northumberland, the reluctant rebel of 1569, suffered the same fate on August 22. That very morning as he walked along a Paris street, Gaspard de Coligny was shot and painfully wounded in his right hand and left arm by a gunman in the employ of the Duke of Guise. The would-be assassin escaped, and an ugly tension settled over the notoriously fanatical Catholic city to which thousands of Huguenot gentry had come for the wedding, celebrated only a few days earlier. Charles IX and his mother visited the admiral in the afternoon, and the king swore in the hearing of many that by God's death he would find and punish the culprits.

August 23 was a Saturday, and sometime in the course of it Charles agreed to a general massacre of the Huguenots in Paris. What arguments were advanced to break down his weak will can never be known with certainty; he told nothing but lies afterward. Probably he was convinced that the implication of his mother in the assassination attempt committed him to the ghastly step she now urged him to take. In any case, very early the next morning, the Feast of Bartholomew the Apostle, the grisly killing began.

Coligny was first. Henry of Guise led a large troop to the admiral's house. When the Huguenot guard was dispersed, three or four Guise retainers broke into Coligny's upstairs bedroom, killed him, and tossed the body down into the courtyard, where the young duke stood astride it in grim satisfaction. The slaughter spread through the city, and Brantôme said that by nightfall 4,000 corpses had been thrown into the Seine.[90] Other similar massacres followed in succeeding days at Rouen, Orléans, Lyons, and elsewhere.

As senseless and cruel as it was, the Massacre of St. Bartholomew amounted really to no more than another chapter—if a more than usually dramatic one—in the tale of terror through which Frenchmen had been living now for thirteen years. The government protested, falsely, that it had acted because of a Huguenot plot against the royal family. In a private letter Charles IX told the pope that the massacre had been the outcome of clashes between the armed retainers of Guise and Coligny. Later, an official communiqué informed the pontiff, also falsely, that the king had acted out of zeal for the Catholic religion and as a sign of his repudiation of the Peace of St. Germain. The Cardinal of Lorraine, in Rome by September 5, confirmed this latter version in a speech delivered with his usual eloquence to the consistory.

On August 27, when he had finally raised enough money to pay his mercenaries, Orange led them across the Meuse, still unaware that Coligny had died and with him had died the hope for massive French aid against Alba. The campaign itself was a repetition of the fiasco of 1568. His ragtag army cared for nothing but loot, and the southern

90. Three thousand is the figure suggested by the dispassionate Hauser, *La prépondérance espagnole*, p. 94.

Netherlands did not stir to help him. When Alba beat off his attempt to relieve his brother on September 9, and when, ten days later, Mons fell to the Spaniards, he had little choice but to herd his rabble out of the Netherlands and disband them. This time, however, unlike 1568, the Prince of Orange did not go with them. Instead, by a circuitous overland route he slipped into Holland and joined the Beggars. Here, north of the rivers and in the shadow of the dikes, he would stand and fight again. "I have come," he said simply, "to make my grave in this land."

Chapter Five

THE SOUTHERN SEA

Two months after the signing of the Treaty of Cateau-Cambrésis Philip II, freed at last from the war with France, instructed his viceroy in Sicily to organize an expeditionary force whose object was to be the capture of Tripoli. Not until December, 1559, had sufficient ships, soldiers, and stores been gathered from the various Spanish dependencies in Italy, and by that time any hope of keeping the venture a secret had vanished. Even so, the joint command—shared by the viceroy and a Genoese admiral, one scarcely less lackluster than the other—determined to put to sea in foolish defiance of the year's worst sailing weather. The fleet left the rendezvous ports of Messina and Syracuse and limped as far as Malta, where it was obliged to take shelter from the fierce winter storms. When the ill-starred voyage was resumed ten weeks later, the immediate objective of the expedition had changed; with no chance of surprising Tripoli, the Spaniards sailed west along the African coast to the island of Jarbah, which they occupied without resistance on March 7, 1560.

They hoped that Jarbah would serve as a base of operations against Tripoli and, if the opportunity presented itself, against other Moslem strongholds on the Barbary coast. The Spaniards had a toehold on the African mainland at Oran and Goletta, but this had proved inadequate to protect their shipping from the constant attacks of Moslem corsairs. Indeed, continental Europe itself was not safe from them, for not only did they raise havoc with the crucial grain traffic between Sicily and Spain, but season after season they raided Naples, Valencia, and even Catalonia, burned crops and villages, and carried off thousands of Christian prisoners to be sold in the slave markets of Algiers.

The pacification of the Mediterranean area was a matter of life and death to Philip II, who recognized that however important his Burgundian provinces might be, the center of his dynastic system rested here on the bright blue waters of the southern sea. But to exert a measure of Spanish control even in the western end of the basin involved more than rooting out a few pirate enclaves. It involved a serious problem of internal stability within Spain, where a large and vital minority, resistant to national assimilation, was related in culture, blood, and religion to those very pirates. More than that, it involved a confrontation between empires, because to the east lay the vast empire of the Ottoman Turks, cousins and coreligionists of the North African Moors, over whom they exercised a kind of loose, protective sovereignty. In 1560 the Turks had in fact reached the limit of their expansion, but no one at the time dared presume this to be the case. They had enjoyed an almost unbroken record of military success and under the leadership of the greatest of their sultans, Suleiman, called the Magnificent,[1] they had turned Belgrade and Budapest into Turkish cities and the eastern Mediterranean into a Turkish lake. If the environs of Tripoli were too far away for permanent Turkish occupation, they were close enough for a lightning intervention, as the Viceroy of Sicily learned to his sorrow.

On the morning of May 12 lookouts atop the Spanish ships anchored off Jarbah sighted a powerful Turkish squadron bearing down on them. The Spaniards had not had the slightest warning of its approach, and indeed the speed with which it had sailed from Constantinople came to be ranked among the most spectacular nautical achievements of the sixteenth century. The Spanish fleet had barely time to scramble into ragged battle line before the Turks smashed into it. Panic compounded with surprise and ferocious fire power, and by sunset half the Spanish vessels had been captured or sunk and the rest were fleeing pell-mell toward the north and west. The Turks then sealed off the island and waited until the 19,000 soldiers there were starved into surrender.[2]

The Jarbah disaster was an immense blow to the prestige of Philip II. But, as so often happened through his long reign, the prudent king learned a lesson in adversity and ultimately profited from it. The policy of flamboyant punitive expeditions with no follow-up—a policy which had already failed in Charles V's time—would never reduce the

1. The standard account in English is Roger Merriman, *Suleiman the Magnificent* (Cambridge, Mass., 1944). Highly readable is Harold Lamb, *Suleiman the Magnificent, Sultan of the East* (New York, 1957).

2. John Lynch, *Spain Under the Habsburgs* (New York, 1964), I, 220 f., and J. H. Elliott, *Imperial Spain* (London, 1963), pp. 228 ff.

western Mediterranean to Spanish control, would never tame the Moslem furies. What was needed rather was the patient accumulation of permanent naval strength and a diplomacy which could unite against the common enemy all the resources of Christendom. On the waters off Jarbah began the long perilous voyage which ended in the Gulf of Lepanto.

I. THE SUBLIME PORTE

A foreign diplomat in Constantinople observed that Suleiman the Magnificent evinced little if any elation over the news from Jarbah: "When I saw him two days later on his way to the mosque, the expression of his countenance was unchanged; his stern features had lost nothing of their habitual gloom. . . . So self-contained was the heart of that grand old man, so schooled to meet each change of fortune however great, that all the applause and triumph of that day wrung from him no sign of satisfaction."[3] It may have been that the sultan's list of victories was so long that one more could not impress him very much; or perhaps his impassivity was due to the weariness of advanced age: he was now nearly seventy and had headed the government of the Ottoman Empire—the Sublime Porte, as it was called—for forty years. Then too he might that day have been contemplating the savage peculiarities of Turkish monarchy which had led him to execute one of his sons a few years before and would induce him within a matter of months to duplicate that grisly deed.

The Turks[4] were among those tribes which emerged out of the social wreckage left in eastern Europe and central and western Asia by the Tartar invasions of the thirteenth century. Their ethnic character defies classification; broadly speaking, their blood was mixed Caucasian and Mongolian, a circumstance which derived from the habit of bringing captive women into the harem and of incorporating captive boys into the ruling circle; by Suleiman's time the Turks had reduced the latter practice to a fine political science. They possessed something of a national structure by the reign of Osman I (d. 1326), their found-

3. Albert Lybyer, *The Government of the Ottoman Empire in the Time of Suleiman the Magnificent* (Cambridge, Mass., 1913), p. 89, quoting the Austrian ambassador.
4. See the first volume of J. von Hammer-Purgstall, *Geschichte des osmanischen Reiches* (Pest, 1827).

ing sultan, who gave his name in a corrupted form to the people, to the state, and to the dynasty of which Suleiman was the latest representative. The Ottoman Turks learned Islam from the Saracens, legal and fiscal technique from the Persians, and from Byzantium "many details of governmental organization both imperial and local, a supplementary system of taxation, a greatly elaborated taste for court ceremonial and splendor, a plan of organizing foreign residents under a special law and a host of lesser usages and customs."[5]

Their civilization grew as others faltered, or, perhaps more accurately, grew because the others faltered. The Turks drove their herds out of the Eurasian steppe and into Anatolia—that pulsing heart of a dozen empires since the days of Cyrus the Great—just at the moment it had become a contested borderland between the tottering Seljuks and Byzantines, neither of whom were strong enough to hold it. From there the matchless Turkish cavalry rode east and west until Suleiman could boast a sovereignty that extended from Algiers to the valley of the Don, from the outskirts of Vienna to Alexandria to Baghdad. There had been momentary checks, to be sure; the fabled Tamerlane (d. 1405) had led the last great eastern horde into Asia Minor and smashed the finest Ottoman armies,[6] while in Europe shrunken Byzantium had resisted the Turks with fatalistic courage which intensified the closer they came to the Golden Horn. But by the time Constantinople fell (1453), Tamerlane was a bad memory, a bogeyman with which Turkish nannies shushed their children, and St. Sophia, for nine centuries the most glorious of Christian churches, was about to become, by supreme irony, the model of a thousand mosques.

Success on such a grand scale, however, did not alter the Turks' *Weltanschauung*. They remained a marcher people, a tribe of soldiers who responded to the tattoo of the sultan's war drum with the same fervor as their pastoral ancestors. They were organized not for commerce or industry or agriculture but for conquest, and the sultan was their chief whose essential function was to lead them in battle. Islam lent a measure of fierceness to their combat with infidel Christians, but they warred against fellow Moslems with almost equal zest and effi-

---

5. Lybyer, *Government*, 24.
6. Rene Grousset, *The Empire of the Steppes* (New Brunswick, N.J., 1970), pp. 448 ff., trans. from the French edition of 1952.

ciency—a sign perhaps that their religion, important as it was, did not itself determine a cultural orientation that was deeper than faith and older than memory.[7]

For a people so constituted victory brought problems in its wake. When the riding and fighting were done, when the natural limits of expansion had been reached, the instincts of the warrior had to give way to those of the governor. In one sense, however, the Turks never admitted their ships and horses could not carry them to the ends of the earth; throughout the sixteenth century, and most of the seventeenth, they continued to probe first west and then east, as though some primeval appetite at work within them obscured their judgment as to what was in fact possible. Their courage was never in question, but they possessed neither the technology nor the physical resources to go much beyond the limits to which Suleiman had brought them. Indeed, it could be argued that by 1560 they had already overreached themselves and were ripe for the reverses that lay just ahead. In any case, retrenchment, when it was finally forced upon them, took some of the vitality out of the Turkish spirit and helped reduce the Ottoman Empire to its low estate as the venal and slovenly sick man of Europe.

But that day was still a long way off. The Sublime Porte meanwhile showed a remarkable skill in administering its vast territories without sacrificing, as yet, its élan. To speak only of its European provinces, it learned to live with certain unalterable realities. The conquest of Greece and the Balkans had been relatively swift and easy, mostly because the social structure of the peninsula, riven by ethnic and religious divisions and economic inequities, was fragile as a house of cards. The Turks had seemed to many natives—particularly to the peasants so long and so systematically pillaged by the aristocrats—almost as liberators. The pattern was everywhere the same: Turkish cavalry spread havoc through a countryside, and the infantry followed at a more leisurely pace to occupy the rich lowlands with hardly any resistance. But the Turks never completely subdued the more remote regions or the mountain fastnesses of Albania and the Morea. A Turkish army, raised ad hoc, could of course crush any of these recalcitrant pockets by a punitive campaign, but then the levies would go

7. V. J. Parry, "The Ottoman Empire," *The New Cambridge Modern History*, III, 347 ff.

away, because the economy would not support them, and the local strongmen, more or less chastened, would assert themselves again.[8]

A sultan, like a Spanish king, had to face the physical impossibility of establishing a totalitarian state in the modern sense of the word. Distance alone was too much for him. The northern Ottoman provinces—Transylvania, Wallachia, Moldavia, the Khanate of the Crimea—paid scant attention to Constantinople, unless they themselves were threatened by Russians or Poles, or unless the sultan decreed a holy war with its glittering promise of loot and glory. Authority went out from the Ottoman center in waves which grew fainter as they approached the outer circumference. Turkish expansion in Europe was essentially colonial in nature, as the British expansion in India was to be later on: it amounted to the imposition of an alien ruling class whose numbers, and therefore whose cultural influence, diminished the farther west and north it went. The contrast was clear, for example, between the cities of Thrace and Bulgaria, with their clusters of minarets, and Dubrovnik on the Adriatic coast, where the population remained stubbornly Christian even if the women went veiled in the Moslem fashion.

Behind the shifting and embattled frontiers, the Turkish nobles had to learn to live with peace. At first their social structure was based upon the *timar,* a life fief very broad in scope—it included rights over villages, water supplies and uncultivated land—but conditional upon supplying troops to the sultan's local representative (*sandjak*). Gradually *timars* became hereditary and a genuinely feudal class of aristocrats, rooted in the land, replaced the Anatolian warlords of an earlier time. By the end of Suleiman's reign, this very numerous nobility—perhaps as many as 200,000 horsemen and 1,000,000 adults altogether—had turned most of its attention to exploitation of the territory it had conquered. The model economic unit little by little became a kind of colonial plantation, harshly managed but highly productive. In appearance and organization it was not unlike a medieval European manor—at the center of the domain the lord's turreted stone castle stood watch over the peasants' clay cabins scattered around in all directions—only it was usually more efficient, with its lavish use of irrigation and draft animals, and more abundant in grain, rice, corn, and later cotton. New

8. Fernand Braudel, *La Méditerranée et le monde méditerranéen à l'époque de Philippe II* (Paris, 1966), II, 11 ff. and 63 ff.

lands meant new private estates of this type, and the plantation system spread ever more widely.

To some degree the warrior ethos gave place to the entrepreneurial, and the sultans found themselves in a situation somewhat akin to that of their fellow monarchs farther west. They needed to maintain and build up a centralized authority which could check the pretensions of an increasingly wealthy and independent aristocracy. One immense advantage the sultan possessed was his status as leader of Islam, the successor of the Arabian caliphs, "executor and interpreter of the sacred law and defender of the faith."[9] The absolute obedience he could demand and usually count upon from his Moslem subjects went a long way toward qualifying the economic power accumulated by the lords. Islam had its heretics, but no sultan ever had to contend with an alliance between religious dissidents and ambitious barons of the sort which so bedeviled the Christian kings.

But the Sublime Porte did not for that reason neglect more mundane techniques to conserve its primacy. It developed a carefully nonhereditary civil and military administration entirely dependent upon the sultan's will. The parade of bureaucrats came and went—viziers, pashas, *beylerbeys,* many of them renegade Christians, most of them without any links to the aristocracy and all of them technically the sultan's slaves (*kullar*), whatever heights of wealth and prestige they might attain. The spahis of the Porte, the sultan's own household cavalry, were also slaves, as were the celebrated janissaries, the crack infantry recruited exclusively from among captive Christian boys who were trained in Islam, the arts of war, and unswerving loyalty to their master. This ingeniously devised establishment, which numbered as many as 80,000 people, was in a constant state of flux; no soldier's son could himself become a soldier, no administrator was allowed to fancy himself indispensable, for only the sultan, Allah's chosen one, was indispensable. The chancellery no less than the harem witnessed a dizzying succession of favorites whose only essential qualification was the sultan's pleasure. Nor was this slave-centered absolutism much modified by a judiciary whose personnel was restricted to Moslem freemen, however much such a circumstance cheered the morale of the generals whom their chief had systematically excluded from executive

9. Lybyer, *Government,* p. 150.

function. But law in the Islamic scheme of things remained inextricably joined to religion—Islam, after all, means total submission—and the sultan, as the prophet's unique spokesman, was the final and universal judge.

Yet despotism in fact seldom matches the claims of despotism in theory. The Sublime Porte could not alter geography or turn back the clock, and its real power was relentlessly eroded by the new feudalism, the withering away of old tribal loyalties, and the centrifugal forces inevitably at work over such extended territory. The sultans could not stabilize the Levant trade, which fluctuated wildly through the century and then declined steadily at the end of it, leaving the imperial exchequer considerably diminished. And they could not preserve their swollen bureaucracy from the ravages of inflation: in the 1580s the Turkish coinage was debased and the janissaries, foundation of the abstractly perfect "slave state," rose in furious rebellion against the sublime paymaster who failed to keep prices in line with their wages.[10]

But a graver weakness than these lay at the heart of the Ottoman system.[11] The sultan had evolved from nomadic warlord and priest into autocrat of the most populous and sophisticated empire in the world. He was expected to know all and to decide all, as though the simplicities of earlier days still prevailed, as though he still rode at the head of his rough but honest horsemen instead of lounging on the royal divan amid chattering crowds of sycophants and concubines. The leadership role he assumed had more a moral and sacral character than political, and yet he attained it only by climbing over the corpses of his brothers—a state of affairs determined by the harem's profusion of offspring and the Ottoman constitution's silence on primogeniture. (One sultan celebrated his accession by murdering his fifteen brothers and the three wives his father had left pregnant.) Nor did the savage contest for power cease even then, for new rivals sprang from the sultan's own loins; Suleiman found it necessary to eliminate two of his scheming sons to clear the way for a third, who turned out to be a weakling and a drunkard. The demands of the office, psychological as well as administrative, were, in short, too much for any man, even a superbly gifted one like Suleiman. And after he, the last of the great

10. F. Braudel and F. Spooner, "Price Levels in Europe from 1450 to 1750," *Cambridge Economic History*, IV, 380.

11. See A.-D. Alderson, *The Structure of the Ottoman Dynasty* (Oxford, 1956).

sultans, died (1566), his successors presented an increasingly distorted caricature of his almost heroic qualities: his genuine piety became their formalism, his ruthlessness their cruelty; and where he had been wise, they were merely cunning.

"The fate of the Ottoman sultanate is perhaps an example of the corruption of absolute power," Steven Runciman has observed; "but the corruption of absolute impotence began to show itself among the Greeks"—among those Europeans generally, Greek and Slavic alike, who had fallen under Turkish rule.[12] At the Greek-speaking center of the empire, close to Constantinople and the sultan's court, the conquered Christians may have had more poignant reminders of the vanished glories of Byzantium—Justinian's St. Sophia, for example, converted into a mosque—but even in the further provinces the ascendancy class of Turkish nobles saw to the reduction of the natives to second- or third-class citizenship.

Once the conquest was complete, however, there was no persecution as such. The Turks apparently preferred to limit massive bloodletting to foreign war or to quarrels among themselves, and in any case they were too intelligent to attempt a pogrom against a large majority. Besides, the conquered peoples performed necessary economic services; they worked the nobles' plantations and managed the Levant trade, for which the Turks, with their ignorance of things maritime and their soldierly contempt for bourgeois endeavor, felt themselves unsuited. But the Christians were never allowed to forget their subject state. They had to wear distinctive garb. They were forbidden to build a church without special permission and could never build one in the vicinity of a Moslem shrine. They could not serve in the armed forces or even ride horseback. Any legal altercation they might have with a Moslem was tried in a Turkish court, by Koranic law, where they could scarcely hope for impartiality. They were very heavily taxed, and—the crowning indignity—their boy-children were never safe from the press gang and forced service in the Porte's equivalent of the praetorian guard.

Yet, despite these disabilities, the Christian population of the Ottoman Empire did not fare as badly as it might have. Some of the sultans, though by no means all, were pleased to see themselves as

12. Steven Runciman, *The Great Church in Captivity* (Cambridge, 1968), pp. 187 ff.

successors not only of Mohammed but also of Caesar and Constantine, and were prepared to treat their infidel subjects with a measure of benevolence. The *Pax Turcica,* imposed from without and paid for by their own sweat, was nevertheless a boon to the masses, as peace always is. As for the administration of their internal affairs, the sultans considered them a *milet* or a separate nation which was allowed to govern itself according to its own laws, so long as it remained submissive to its Ottoman overlord. At the head of the Christian *milet* stood the officer whom the Greeks and, in varying degrees, other Eastern Christians recognized as the personage of greatest importance now that the emperor was gone, the Orthodox Patriarch of Constantinople.[13]

The patriarch had never been an Eastern version of the pope, nor did he become one now. Indeed, much of the quarrel between the Latin and the Greek churches had turned on the issue of the universal sovereignty claimed by the Bishop of Rome, whom the ancient sees of Alexandria, Antioch, Jerusalem, and Constantinople were willing to acknowledge as Patriarch of the West and even as *primus inter pares,* but no more than that. The split between the two branches of Christendom had been definitive since the eleventh century, and though the intervening years had witnessed many overtures for reunion and several formal agreements—most recently at Florence in 1439—the schism was by the time the Turks came if anything wider. Apart from the question of papal primacy, and some rather abstract trinitarian theology, the alienation was traceable less to doctrinal than to psychological and cultural factors. Thus the Greek emphasis upon the mystical tradition tended to run at cross-purposes with the Latins' more pragmatic interpretation of the Christian vision; the Greek reluctance to endorse precise dogmatic formulations and ecclesiastical structures seemed to the Latin a kind of calculated vagueness. And so the two liturgies, while they expressed essentially the same commitment to a sacrament-centered worship, developed along lines increasingly unfamiliar and antipathetic to each other.

The Turkish conquest radically upset the ancient constitution of Orthodoxy, which had looked to the Byzantine emperor as the real head of the Church. The Patriarch of Constantinople, who had been in

effect the emperor's chief priest, now had new and anomalous eminence thrust upon him as leader of the Christian *milet* and liaison
between the Porte and the European community. It was an infinitely
delicate position, balancing as it did the demands of a hostile ruling
class with the aspirations of a disfranchised populace. The patriarch
took on a host of secular activities with the result that his bureaucracy
was considerably expanded and laicized. He became in one sense a
much more important man under the sultan than he had been under
the emperor—more important perhaps than any ecclesiastic had ever
been in the eastern Mediterranean world. But through the change in
regime one circumstance remained the same: the patriarch's genuine
authority lay within the area directly controlled by the central government, the specifically Greek territories around Constantinople. Farther
away, in the Balkans, whose Christian princes were more or less independent vassals of the Porte, his name was revered while his dicta were
observed only to the extent that the sultan chose to or was able to
enforce them. The same held roughly true for the patriarch's relations
with his brothers of Alexandria, Antioch, and Jerusalem, who, under
Turkish rule themselves, remained as jealous of their prerogatives as
ever.

The burden imposed upon Orthodoxy by the Turks involved terrible
tensions, and as the years went by the "corruption of absolute impotence," in Mr. Runciman's telling phrase, became more glaringly
apparent. The people grew poorer, their priests more ignorant, their
masters more contemptuous and whimsical. The habit of servility
gradually replaced the glowing hope that some day the Christian
empire would reemerge. The patriarchal office—the only significant
post open to a population reduced to a state of political and social
inferiority—was increasingly the object of competition between ambitious and often disreputable men who tried to outbribe each other for
the sultan's favor. Laboring under such disadvantages, some Orthodox
looked longingly toward the free churches of the West, to revivified
Catholicism especially, as a means of deliverance from religious servitude.[14] But in the end the vigor of the Eastern Church and the deep

14. For Latin influences on Orthodoxy, see Owen Chadwick, *The Reformation* (Harmondsworth, 1964), pp. 356 f. See also S. A. Fischer-Galati, *Ottoman Imperialism and
German Protestantism* (Cambridge, Mass., 1959).

faith of its people proved enough to sustain it through its long captivity which was in many ways crueler and more destructive than a blood bath would have been.

2. THE HOLY LEAGUE

The Turkish sultan was defined by the tribal constitution as the supreme and unique chieftain without whose presence the nation could not go to war. As a result—and no doubt also out of elemental prudence—Ottoman military adventures were confined to one front at a time. The sultan or his vicar could ride at the head of armies directed against revived Persia to the east or against the Christian kingdoms to the west, but not both at once.

The King of Spain found himself in a similar position, for although no such theoretical consideration limited his activities, the economic facts of life did. The overall European depression of the 1550s, and particularly the low receipts of American bullion during that decade, had forced Philip II to terminate the long war with France. And during the years that followed, the hostilities in which Spain was almost constantly engaged reflected in their duration and intensity the irregular course of the Castilian economy. But never, not even in the heyday of silver imports in the 1580s, could the king afford a two-front campaign. Throughout his reign he gave the appearance of a boxer who challenged one opponent one round and another the next; only when the Dutch, English, and French were relatively subdued could he turn his back on them and face the Turk.

This need to husband resources and fight one battle at a time might almost be reduced to a function on a graph. As Philip's involvement in the Netherlands waxed, that in the Mediterranean waned, and vice versa. It was no coincidence that the Lepanto campaign succeeded at a moment when the Low Countries lay quiet under Alba's repressive administration, nor that a few years later, with the situation in the north deteriorating once more, Philip reached an accommodation with the Ottoman Empire.

The twists and turns of Spanish policy in the Mediterranean also revealed that by himself Philip could not begin to cope with Turkish and Barbary power. This was particularly the case during the early years of his reign. The Jarbah disaster simply reiterated that the king's naval strength was insufficient to protect normal shipping lanes west of

Malta or even Spanish coastal waters, much less to sustain serious operations farther east. The crash program in the construction of war galleys, begun shortly afterward in Catalonia under competent Genoese supervision, would eventually make a difference, but meanwhile the Spaniards had to endure a round of humiliating defeats in which even the elements seemed to conspire against them. The winter after Jarbah, unusually mild, witnessed an unprecedented number of corsair raids along the Italian and Spanish coasts. In July, 1561, the redoubtable Dragut, the sultan's chief Barbary vassal, captured the entire Sicilian squadron. The following year a Spanish fleet bound for Oran was destroyed by a storm; twenty-five ships and 3,000 men went to the bottom of the sea. Some six months after that the Spaniards managed to repulse a Moslem attack on Oran, but their own attempt on Algiers ended in disheartening failure.[15]

These reverses did not smother the fires of *reconquista* which still burned brightly in Spanish hearts and still gave special intensity to the national consciousness. The attitude and ambition, moreover, of the conquistador in America—"to serve God and his Majesty, to give light to those in darkness and to grow rich as all men desire to do," as Bernal Diaz put it—continued to dominate the Castilian nobility as a whole. Since time immemorial caballeros had ridden out to fight the Moslem for the glory of God and their own glory. Now, with the battle having shifted to the sea, the Renaissance cult of the individual still found scope in them, in their pride and touchiness no less than in their daring and in their indifference to pain, danger, or fatigue. They saw themselves "not as imitators but as rivals of the heroes of antiquity and of romance."[16] It was not a lack of such men as these that hampered Philip II in his struggle for the Mediterranean, but the society from which they sprang—rigid and pastoral, not particularly blessed with nautical skills, economically vulnerable to German bankers.

So Philip looked to Italy for the stuff of a grand anti-Moslem alliance, and in theory at least his prospects there were bright. He ruled Sicily, Naples, and Milan outright, while Genoa was his satellite and Piedmont and Tuscany were scarcely less so. But the realities of empire

15. Roger Merriman, *The Rise of the Spanish Empire* (New York, 1918), IV, pp. 100 ff.

16. J. H. Parry, *The Age of Reconnaissance* (New York, 1963), pp. 33, 46.

in the sixteenth century had to be measured as much by the King of Spain as by the sultan in terms of distance, communication and transport, technology, and available resources; in short, how many ships, guns, and men could the king count on and of what quality were they? None of Philip's own Italian dominions or his allies possessed a naval tradition formidable enough to impress the Turk, and, besides, ship construction all over the peninsula was in decline due to the scarcity and high price of timber. The dukes of Piedmont-Savoy were almost entirely preoccupied in fashioning an absolutist inland state, while the cadet branch of the Medici—now ruling Florence as grand dukes of Tuscany—managed the maritime industry with the family's customary disregard for the distinction between its own and the public purse.

The popes after Paul IV were relatively friendly to Spain and of course ideologically hostile to the Ottoman Empire, against which they periodically invoked the weary rhetoric of the crusade. But they were also suspicious of Philip's ecclesiastical policies and constantly at loggerheads with him over jurisdictional and financial matters. In Naples the dispute turned on the so-called *monarchia sicula,* the king's alleged right to govern the Church in southern Italy as permanent apostolic delegate and without reference to the Curia. In Milan the clash arose largely out of the reforming zeal and prickly personality of Cardinal Borromeo, who laconically excommunicated one Spanish viceroy after another.[17] Yet, despite these irritants, basic sympathy and mutual need—for example, Philip needed the regular renewal of the pope's license to impose lucrative taxes on the Spanish clergy—bound Rome and Madrid together. The same could hardly be said about Madrid and Venice.

The Republic of St. Mark, that cluster of sandbanks at the head of the Adriatic, was the only Italian state strong enough to be taken seriously by the Porte and to be genuinely independent of Spain. That strength depended upon the vitality of Venetian commercial enterprise which, during the 1560s, reached its highest level of prosperity. The business of Venice was business, and the haughty Venetian oligarchs, who defied conventional wisdom by looking down their noses even at the ancient Romans, formed the only nobility in Europe given over exclusively to commerce. More specifically, they were carriers who

17. Léopold Willaert, *La Restauration Catholique* (Paris, 1960), pp. 417 ff.

carted goods back and forth across northern Italy, through the eastern passes of the Alps into Austria, and over the sea to the Levant. At the heart of their enterprise was the profitable traffic called the "spice trade"—a term which meant not only flavorings like ginger and pepper but all manner of products which found their way by caravan from the far east to Venetian depots in Damascus and Aleppo, and from there to the marketplaces of Europe.

Since the days of Justinian, through all the ups and downs of Byzantium, in the wake of Arabs, Saracens, crusaders, Turks, and Tartars, Venice had maintained its crucial maritime connection with the eastern Mediterranean. In the course of time it accumulated a string of Levantine trading posts, some of which, like Cyprus and Crete, of considerable importance, to go with its land "empire" in northeast Italy (the *terraferma*) and along the Dalmatian coast. During the first third of the century the Portuguese had jolted the Venetian economy by penetrating the spice trade through direct passage to India around the Cape of Good Hope, but by 1550 Venice had recovered its preeminence and "was again the leading purveyor of spices to the rest of Europe."[18] Yet even then, at the moment when they had survived the novel hazards of competition and were approaching the recorded peak in their population and business volume, the Venetians were already nervously shifting their economy away from commerce to industry and agriculture. This trend toward capital investment in woolen mills and, even more, in landed estates on the *terraferma* quickened through the rest of the century and was reflected by, among other signs, the drastic decline—as much as 50 percent—in registered Venetian shipping between 1560 and 1600.[19] Eventually this process destroyed imperial Venice and, when what was left of the Levant trade became the preserve of Dutch, French and English merchants, reduced it to a backwater catering to tourists. So much did the Republic depend for its very being upon the fruits of commerce.

As far as anyone could see in 1570 Venice was as bustling as ever and as serenely confident as ever in the essential superiority of its institutions. Moreover, with Florence in eclipse and Rome distracted by

18. William Bouwsma, *Venice and the Defense of Republican Liberty* (Berkeley, 1968), p. 104.
19. D. S. Chambers, *The Imperial Age of Venice* (New York, 1971), p. 189.

religious revivalism,[20] the Republic had assumed the unaccustomed role of chief Italian patron to the arts: Titian, the doyen of European painters, now nearing his hundredth birthday, headed a Venetian school which included such notables as Tintoretto (d. 1594) and Veronese (d. 1588). From the earlier and richer outburst of Renaissance creativity Venice had cautiously shied away, too much occupied, the city's critics said, with making money. Conservatism, stolidity, and caution were in fact the ancient hallmarks of the Venetian ruling class, and not less now that the Republic stood virtually alone as a free Italian state.

The power of that class operated through a constitution of mystifying complexity.[21] The nobles or patricians, between 2,000 and 2,500 of them during the sixteenth century, formed the basis of it in a closed corporation called the greater council. Between them and the totally disfranchised 90 percent of the population were the "citizens" whom long residence, nonmanual occupations, or financial means could qualify for lesser state jobs—as notaries, secretaries, and the like—but who were excluded from the policymaking functions of the greater council. The patricians dispensed major patronage among themselves—perhaps 800 positions altogether, two-thirds of them in Venice itself and the rest scattered across the *terraferma* and the overseas possessions. A smaller body, a senate of about 200 members elected annually by the greater council, worked through various colleges or permanent committees which handled specific areas of business; the most famous of them was the council of ten charged with security matters. The executive—the *serenissima signoria*—consisted of six elected ministers and three judges together with the doge; they composed a cabinet known as the lesser council. The doge was chosen for life by an electoral college of forty-one patricians. He presided rather than ruled over all this apparatus, for his constitutional powers were not wide and much of his time was spent in ceremonial activities. But his moral influence was considerable. Almost always an elderly man who had already enjoyed a distinguished career, the doge was conscious of his dignity as spokesman for Europe's oldest and proudest state, even if

20. See H. J. Koenigsberger, "Decadence or Shift? Changes in the Civilization of Italy and Europe in the Sixteenth and Seventeenth Centuries," *Transactions of the Royal Historical Society*, X (1960), 1–18.

21. A good summary is in Chambers, *Imperial Venice*, pp. 73 ff.

under his horned biretta of office he looked rather like an Inca prince.

To provide as Venice did the only counterpoise to Ottoman and Spanish power in the Mediterranean involved the Republic in some painful choices. The Venetians had to get along with whoever dominated the Levant. But the Turks, always bellicose and often capricious, were exceedingly difficult to deal with. At various times Venice had gone to war with them only to decide on each occasion that paying tribute to the Porte—as the Holy Roman Emperor had to do for his lands in Hungary—was the better way to preserve the profits of the spice trade. Nor was the Republic interested in bearding the sultan to the advantage of Spain, for if the Turks raided the coasts of Italy and threatened Venetian territory in the East, the Spaniards were, so to speak, at the very door. The popes often tried to play honest broker between Spain and Venice, but to little purpose, since Philip II's constant bickering with the Curia was mild compared to Venice's long anticlerical tradition.

This distrust of ecclesiastics may have been intensified by rivalry along the frontier Venice shared with the Papal States. Certainly the popes for their part had come to consider the Venetian church an unruly daughter and the Venetian state an unfriendly neighbor. In any event the oligarchy kept a firm hand on its clergy and a wary eye on Rome. No priest was allowed to serve Venice in any official capacity whatever. Any citizen or patrician who received income from a benefice was ipso facto excluded from office. The Republic saw to its own Catholic orthodoxy by an inquisition explicitly distinct from the Roman version, and no appeal to the Curia from it or from any other ecclesiastical court was permitted. Church construction could commence only with a special government license, and stated policy (though never completely implemented, due to the resistance of the Venetian clergy) called for taxation of ecclesiastical property without reference to Rome. A gaudy symbol of the laic character of the Venetian state was the celebrated church of San Marco. Far from being Venice's cathedral, San Marco was technically the doge's private chapel where no papal bulls could be posted. Rome did not miss the implication that the Evangelist Mark's bones rested as comfortably there as St. Peter's did on Vatican hill.

An alliance between Venice and Spain, blessed by the moral and financial resources of the papacy, might have been enough to contain aggressive Islam, even though France, the Porte's anti-Hapsburg ally, and the ragtag German Empire held aloof. But mutual suspicions and antagonisms ran too deep to offer much hope for such an alignment. And over the capitals of Europe brooded the pervasive conviction that the Turks and their Barbary vassals were in any case unbeatable. Then, in the middle of the 1560s, a series of events began to unfold which dramatically opened the way for a grand concert of Christian naval power.

First came the Turkish assault upon Malta, the little island (or rather the cluster of three little islands) which guarded the eastern approaches to the straits of Sicily.[22] The crucial strategic importance of the place—dominating as it did the bottleneck between the eastern and western Mediterranean—had led Charles V to put it in the charge of the last of the military religious orders so prominent at the time of the crusades, the Knights of St. John. Throughout the winter of 1564–1565 intelligence reports from Constantinople were unanimous that the Turks were outfitting a huge armada. Not until May 18, 1565, however, when a fleet of 150 sail appeared off the southeast tip of Malta, was the Porte's objective known for certain. Within days, 23,000 Turkish troops occupied the island as the Knights withdrew to a prepared line of redoubts commanding the town and harbor of Valletta.[23] On June 23, after twenty-five days of savage bombardment, one of the key forts fell to the Turks, but the others held on and the tempo and intensity of the fighting increased. Through most of the next three months the Knights of St. John stood against the fiercest attacks the much more numerous and better-equipped Turks could mount, and except for a token force of 600 Spaniards they stood alone. By the beginning of September, when a Spanish relief column of 5,000 finally was put ashore, the Turks had had enough. Leaving behind a wilderness of ruins and heaps of their own dead—the great Dragut among them—they set sail back to Constantinople.

Amid the rejoicing over the heroic defense of Malta there was heard not a little recrimination—against the Venetians who had done nothing to help the Knights and against the Spaniards whose help had been so

22. Braudel, *La Méditerranée*, II, 319 ff.
23. The present name of the port. Jean de la Valletta was the commander of the Knights of St. John during the siege.

little and almost too late. But the dominant reaction all over Europe was an immense *sursum corda,* a happy astonishment that a major Ottoman expedition had been soundly defeated. This new optimism survived the operations of the following summer when the Turks prowled the Adriatic in great strength and without hindrance, and yet accomplished nothing substantive. Meanwhile, Suleiman raised an enormous army—perhaps as many as 300,000 men—and took the field in person to lead a massive attack on Vienna. But his last campaign went wrong from the start; the inadequate roads were soon clogged with guns and soldiers, the rivers proved impassible, the sultan was old and ill and out of heart. On September 5, 1566, Suleiman the Magnificent died of dysentery in a shabby Hungarian town. The Turkish host, after some desultory skirmishing, melted away, and by 1568 hostilities had ceased on the Austrian front.

The result of these checks to Ottoman power was a sense of rising expectations among the Christian states of the West. Perhaps the Turks were not after all unbeatable. Yet, important as this heightened morale was as a precondition for further efforts in the Mediterranean, little advantage could be taken of it unless someone should appear on the scene who could forge an anti-Moslem alliance, a persuader whom both Spain and Venice could trust.

Pope Pius V was elected after an unusually brief conclave on January 7, 1566.[24] He took the name of the immediate predecessor, whom he did not much like, out of respect for Cardinal Borromeo, Pius IV's nephew and protégé, who had swung the election to him. Such support in itself tells much about the new pope's character and aspirations. He was totally dedicated to the internal reform of the Church, and as a former grand inquisitor he suffered no qualms about using force in the service of religion. He had none of the subtlety or diplomatic skill of his predecessor—as his handling of English affairs amply proved—but in zeal and industry and sheer devotion to duty he had no peers. A bald, white-bearded, lean old man, Pius V lived with an asceticism which was itself an indictment of the softness and moral compromise of the Renaissance papacy. Instead of riding to hounds and fussing over bastards, he prayed and fasted with an enthusiasm which at first

24. See Ludwig Pastor, *History of the Popes* (London, 1932), XVII, 46 ff.; XVIII, 353 ff.

startled and then enthralled the cynical ambassadors credited to the Holy See. Not for three centuries, Granvelle told Philip II, had the Church had a better or more saintly pontiff.

And not for three centuries, he might have added, had anyone taken the word "crusade" seriously. But Pius V did. Indeed, his program was constituted of three interrelated parts: to impose the decrees of Trent upon the Catholic world at large and especially upon reluctant, fun-loving clerics; to convert heretics to mother Church or, if that failed, to destroy them; and to mobilize the kings of Christendom against that most hateful and dangerous infidel, the Turk. The latter subject became almost a papal obsession; "I am taking up arms against the Turks," he wrote in a brief of 1566 dealing with clerical morals, "but the only thing that can help me in that is the prayers of priests of pure life."

It was difficult not to be moved by such a man, particularly for a fervent Catholic prince like Philip II. Nevertheless, *el Rey Prudente,* distracted by the troubled Netherlands and in any case not disposed to hurry a decision, took his time responding to the pope's plea for a crusade. The signory of Venice did likewise, presumably with more serenity, since it had never been notable for its religious fervor. But tragic events ultimately lent strength to the pope's voice. On Christmas day, 1568, the long harried and persecuted moriscos of southern Spain exploded in rebellion.[25] The government was caught completely by surprise, as evidenced by the fact that literally no troops were available in Castile to employ against the rebels. Soon all Granada was in flame, and it was said that upwards of 150,000 Moors were ready to march on Madrid the moment sufficient arms arrived from Constantinople or North Africa. Philip's best soldiers were far away in Flanders with Alba, and not until he stripped his Italian garrisons and declared a war to the knife was the rising crushed. Even then the struggle dragged into the spring of 1570, an affair of ambuscades and massacres, fought with terrible barbarity on both sides. It showed how keen the hatred still was between Christian and Moor, a hatred born of ancient cultural and religious conflict. It also showed—and this was the lesson Philip II learned from it—that this unassimilated minority, concentrated in one

25. See Julio Caro-Baroja, *Los Moriscos del Reino de Granada* (Madrid, 1957), and Andrew Hess, "The Moriscos: An Ottoman Fifth Column in Sixteenth Century Spain," *American Historical Review,* LXXIV (1968), 1–25.

corner of the peninsula, would constitute a threat to the rest of Spain as long as it maintained its connections with the powerful Barbary and Turkish Moslems.

There was no doubt about those connections, nor about the aid the rebels had received from North Africa. The actions of the Porte had been, as usual, more mysterious, but rumors had multiplied during the summer of 1569 that a new Turkish battle fleet was about to intervene in Granada. For reasons which became clear only later, that fleet never sailed; yet the terror the stories produced in Spain was a measure of the growing conviction there that Islam was a single vast conspiracy. The massive deportation of moriscos from Granada after the revolt was one fruit of that idea, and Philip's revived interest in a crusade was another.

Venice remained unconcerned by Spain's troubles and by the news of Turkish mobilization so long as it appeared the sultan's objective lay in the western Mediterranean. Then, in March, 1570, the signory learned the bitter truth: the Turks had turned their eyes upon not Granada but Cyprus, the jewel in the Venetian imperial crown. Consternation at the sudden collapse of the long-cherished and generally successful appeasement policy swiftly gave way to a stiffening of the public will. By a vote of 199 to 21 the Venetian senate rejected the ultimatum to evacuate Cyprus. In July the Turks invaded the island, and on September 9 they captured Nicosia and put the populace there to the sword. The Venetian garrison fell back to the east coast and took up position within the strong works around Famagusta. The Turks promptly invested the city and began what promised to be a long siege.

At that moment, when the Republic of St. Mark was driven from its isolation and into the waiting arms of Pius V, the Holy League was born. Yet, in another sense, the pope's work was just beginning.[26] The negotiations which culminated in the treaty of May 20, 1571, lasted for nearly a year, and they revealed so much antipathy between Spain and Venice that a lesser man than Pius V might have given them up in despair. Twice they broke off altogether, and twice the pope got them started again. The basic disagreement had to do with strategy; for Philip II the main enemy was the one close at hand, on the Barbary coast, while for the signory the Levant was the only theater that counted. But beneath this understandable difference of opinion lay a mutual mistrust which prevented each state from accepting at face

26. See the first volume of Luciano Serrano, *La Liga de Lepanto* (Madrid, 1919).

value the good will of the other. Both were haunted by the prospect of being deserted and having to face the Turks alone.

In the midst of the talks an abortive attempt to relieve Famagusta by a joint Spanish-Venetian expedition served as an occasion for more recrimination. So the conversations went on and on, covering such points as how much the Spaniards would charge the Venetians for Sicilian grain, whether the pope would subsidize Venetian infantry, whether Venice and Madrid would secure papal agreement for extraordinary taxation of their clergies, how the lands conquered, if any, would be divided. Squads of negotiators wrangled over every detail and exhausted each other with invective. Granvelle for Spain was at his stubborn and sarcastic worst, and even the ever supple Morone, who usually spoke for the pope, had difficulty pouring oil over the constantly troubled waters. Finally, almost miraculously, fundamental agreement was reached. The triple alliance for twelve years was to furnish 300 ships and 50,000 men on a year-to-year basis. Other Catholic powers were to be regularly invited to join the League. Each spring a meeting of the allies in Rome would determine the plan of campaign for that year. If nothing could be agreed upon, each state could act independently, with the understanding that Venice would send fifty galleys to serve in the North African theater and Spain would reciprocate with aid to Venice in the Adriatic. Spain guaranteed one-half the total expense, Venice one-third, the papacy one-sixth.

On May 28, 1571, Pope Pius V walked a bareheaded penitent in jubilee procession through the streets of Rome, where solemn prayers were offered in all the churches for the success of the Holy League. Those who saw the old man that day never forgot the tears of joy rolling down his wrinkled face.

3. "DON JOHN OF AUSTRIA IS GOING TO THE WAR"

The proposal to name Don John of Austria[27] captain general of the Holy League met with relatively little debate. Since the King of Spain was willing to assume the lion's share of the costs of operations, then the King of Spain might enjoy the prerogative of selecting the com-

---

27. The best account is Felix Hartlaub, *Don Juan d'Austria und die Schlacht bei Lepanto* (Berlin, 1940). See also the first volume of P. O. von Törne, *Don Juan d'Autriche et les projets de Conquête de l'Angleterre* (Helsingfors, 1915), and the popular biography in English by Charles Petrie.

mander. Philip chose his half-brother, the bastard son of Charles V and a notoriously promiscuous German lady named Barbara Blomberg. Nor was this the first instance of Philip's brotherly solicitude; indeed, the emperor had never known the existence of Barbara Blomberg's child, and it was Philip who had rescued him from obscurity and given him a title, a suite, and a princely education. In 1571 Don John was a courtly, handsome youth of twenty-four, whose charming personality stood in marked contrast to that of his introverted and prematurely aged royal brother. But the bar sinister cast a shadow over Don John and made him touchier than the most arrogant grandee. He always suspected that people despised and hampered him because of his illegitimacy, though it was more likely that at least in Philip II's case Don John's freedom of action was limited no more than that of any other servant of the Spanish bureaucracy.

When after the usual delays his orders from Madrid finally reached him, they did contain restrictions which, Don John complained bitterly, demonstrated the king's lack of confidence in him. No doubt Philip, Pius V, and the signory of Venice expected the captain general, young and relatively untried, especially in maritime matters, to be dominated by the veteran captains who formed his council of war; and it hardly needs saying that the Venetians Veniero and Barbarigo, the Genoese Andrea Doria, the papal admiral Marcantonio Colonna, and the Spaniards Cardona and Santa Cruz contributed to the campaign a fund of invaluable experience. Yet Don John, his complaints notwithstanding, had enough discretionary authority to preside over them effectively, and his personal magnetism, his verve and boldness and sense of drama, acted like a magic paste to bind together these hard-bitten sailors—who hated each other almost as much as they hated the Turk—long enough for one grand exploit.

Don John's ignorance of warfare at sea was not a major disability, because naval tactics, hardly altered since the battle of Salamis, amounted to a simulation of land fighting.[28] The backbone of the fleet was the galley, a single-decked vessel of 120 to 180 feet in length, with a beam of up to twenty feet and a freeboard of seven. Though equipped with sails and rigging, in battle the galley depended entirely on a hundred or so rowers who could for brief spurts of time accelerate up to seven knots. A few guns were mounted in the bow, but neither these

28. See Richard Anderson, *Naval Wars in the Levant* (Liverpool, 1952).

nor the metal ramming beak which thrust out from the prow were intended to be more than auxiliaries to the business at hand. Ships were drawn into a line which bore down directly upon the enemy's line and tried to break it or outflank it. Once this basic maneuver was completed, the opposing galleys closed upon one another and the soldiers on board fought it out with harquebuses, bows and arrows, swords, and pikes. In an extensive engagement casualties could reach hideous proportions, because quarter, at least between Turk and Christian, was seldom given and retreat was impossible. Other vessels acted in support of the galley, notably the triple-masted galleon and the galeas, a huge ship propelled by both sail and oars and capable of carrying as many as seventy cannon. The future of naval warfare lay with the navigators and gunners on such ships as these, but for a little time yet, until artillery range and accuracy improved, the galley would remain the battle queen of the fleet. In 1571 the tactical problems on the water did not differ radically from those encountered in the mountain fastnesses of Granada where Don John had won his spurs putting down the morisco revolt.

It took the whole summer for the allied armada to rendezvous at Messina. Spanish warships were scattered as far away as Gibraltar, and one large Venetian squadron, on another fruitless attempt to relieve Famagusta, had to be recalled from the Levant. A critical shortage of provisions, attributable to poor Castilian harvests in 1570, caused further delay, and in the end Sicily and Naples had to supply the fleet with most of its stores of pickled pork, salt fish, biscuit, dried beans and peas, onions, garlic, cheese, and wine.

Don John sailed from Barcelona on June 20 to Genoa, where he stayed a month attending to countless details and basking in the adulation of Genoese high society. At Naples on August 9 Cardinal Granvelle formally presented him with the banner of the Holy League, and urged him in the pope's name to take decisive action. On the evening of August 13 his ship dropped anchor in Messina harbor. The next morning he saw the great host assembled for him to lead: 316 ships (208 of them galleys), 50,000 sailors and galley slaves, and 30,000 soldiers.

From the moment of his arrival Don John assumed direction of his forces with a sure hand. First he ordered that the various nationals be distributed throughout the fleet so that there would be no purely

Spanish, Venetian, or papal contingents to compete or quarrel with each other. At the same time he established a command structure which, while it stressed simple efficiency, also took due account of the sensitivities of his subordinates. The armada was organized into three tactical divisions. The center, with sixty-four galleys, Don John commanded in person with Veniero and Colonna as his lieutenants. The left wing of fifty-three galleys sailed under Barbarigo and the right, of similar size, under Doria. The vanguard of eight galleys and the rear guard of thirty were commanded by Cardona and Santa Cruz respectively. The galeases—each a floating fortress bristling with cannon—were assigned two to each division, and the galleons carrying supplies formed a separate squadron.

All this Don John settled with dispatch but also with a charm which won him affection as well as respect. When the council of war convened on September 10, he listened to various proposals, several of them advising delay, and then announced his immediate intention to seek out the Turkish fleet and destroy it. Clearly, the time for talk was over. On September 15 the sluggish galeases and galleons set sail east out of Messina, and the next day the galleys followed them. As each ship passed out of the harbor and into the open sea, the papal nuncio bestowed on it the apostolic benediction.

The Turks meanwhile had had a busy summer. Their movements had been obscured for a time by the contradictory rumors that flooded west. It was said for instance that the full brunt of attack this season would fall on Dalmatia; or that a new expedition would reduce Famagusta; or that due to a shortage of equipment and small arms the sultan had only a hundred galleys at fighting trim. In fact a fleet of 300 sail left Constantinople in June, raided its leisurely way across the Venetian outposts in the Aegean, feinted toward Cyprus, and then fell with a fury upon Crete and came within an ace of capturing the sixty-eight Venetian galleys stopping there. Next the Turks swung northwest toward Albania and devastated the coastal islands as far north as Corfu. They steered clear, however, of the entrances to the Adriatic, fearful perhaps of being bottled up by the Christian fleet reportedly assembling in Sicily. Instead they turned south, and by late September their admiral, the young and vigorous Ali Pasha, had brought them into the Gulf of Patras, to rest and regroup under the powerful batteries of the fortresses of Lepanto (the modern Naupactus).

On September 26 Don John learned at Corfu that the force that had ravaged the island shortly before had withdrawn southeast toward the Gulf of Corinth. Three days later, as his division prodded gingerly down the Albanian coast, the vanguard sent him word that not just a squadron or two but the whole Turkish fleet was anchored off Lepanto. The captain general ordered Barbarigo and Doria to join him with all speed, and on October 4 the Christian armada, at full strength except for the galleons, sailed through the waters off Preveze where Octavian had beaten Antony and Cleopatra sixteen centuries before. That same day a west-bound frigate brought news that Famagusta had fallen on August 1. The ghastly details of the sack—the Turks had among other enormities flayed the Venetian commandant alive—provided his men with precisely the food for thought on battle eve that Don John himself might have ordered.

Through October 5 and 6 the Christian fleet was stalled off the island of Cephalonia by heavy weather. No vessels were so unreliable in rough seas as galleys, and not until two o'clock in the morning of Sunday, October 7, was it safe for them to venture out again. With Doria's squadron in the lead, they sailed east by the stars, brushing the tip of Ulysses' fabled Ithaca, until they sighted the black hills crouching along the coast. Then they turned sharply south into the channel between the mainland on their left and the little island of Oxia on their right. Thanks to this maneuver they came into view of the Gulf of Patras, and any scout ships cruising there, only at the last moment.

By seven o'clock, when Don John's flagship *Réal* joined him, Doria was proceeding across the gulf's mouth to take up position on what would be the right (southern) wing of the Christian formation. A half-hour later lookouts atop the masts saw a sail come over the eastern horizon, then another, then a dozen, and soon more than they could count. Since before dawn the Ottoman fleet had been moving out of the ring of fortresses around Lepanto, and now it was less than ten miles away and closing fast. Ali Pasha, satisfied that the Christians were present in strength, had decided to meet them head-on, despite the reluctance of some of his subordinates who would have preferred more intelligence about the enemy's numbers and more rest for their own crews, fatigued after a summer's hard campaigning.

By nine o'clock, on a gloriously fine day with a soft westerly breeze blowing, the two armadas faced each other and moved slowly and relentlessly toward each other. They were about equal in size. The Christian galleys were stretched out straight from the northern shore perhaps 7,000 yards across the mouth of the gulf: Barbarigo on the left, Don John in the center, Doria on the right, Santa Cruz behind with the reserve, and Cardona paddling restlessly back and forth across the front. A half-mile or so in advance of the left and center sailed four huge galeases, their guns trained on the approaching Turks. This was the only tactical innovation[29] employed by Don John, and though it was not entirely successful—the two galeases assigned to Doria's wing never did get properly into position—it caused Ali Pasha to alter his original deployment at the cost of considerable confusion; instead of forming an enormous crescent designed to suck in the enemy's center while it turned either flank, the Turks regrouped nervously into the conventional straight line.

Just before contact was established, Don John indulged in the sort of grand gesture which he loved and at which he was so adept. He boarded a galliot and rode down the whole length of the Christian line to wave encouragement to his men and, more importantly, to inspire them with the sight of himself resplendent in his armor. The cheers that greeted him were one measure of the intense excitement which gripped the allied soldiers and sailors as the great panorama unfolded before them. Another striking sign of it followed moments later when, as though at a prearranged signal, captains, crews, and soldiers fell to their knees and, except for the prayerful droning of the chaplains, an eerie silence fell over the whole Christian fleet. By then they could hear over the water the shouts and taunts of the infidel enemy who had so often beaten and humiliated them. But in the hours ahead the religious enthusiasm of the Counter Reformation would play a part in helping these Spaniards and Italians reverse the defeats of a century, for the last battle of the last crusade was about to begin. Don John of Austria was going to the war.

About ten o'clock, the Ottoman right wing, slightly in advance of the rest of the formation, came within range of the guns on Barbarigo's galeases. The fire was not so much destructive as disconcerting, and the Turks reacted to it by veering somewhat to their right (northward). This movement coincided with their overall battle plan, which was to

29. Unless one counts removing the ramming beaks from the galleys' prow in order to achieve more fire power from the guns located there.

turn the Christian flank by forcing their way between the shore and the end of the enemy line. But they shifted farther than they had intended, and by the time they collided with the Christian left at ten thirty, a large gap had opened between them and their comrades in the center. Barbarigo seized the opportunity thus offered him, and while he repulsed the assault on his flank—only a half-dozen galleys managed to slip around and behind him—he hurled the bulk of his squadron into the breach between the Turkish right and center. Cut off from any support, the Turks of the right wing fought with their usual fury and valor, but their fate, as the Christians drove them inexorably toward the beaches, was sealed. When Barbarigo was mortally wounded, the pressure relaxed momentarily, but not for long. By a little past noon it was clear that not a Turkish man or ship would escape.

A half-hour after Barbarigo's division had become fully engaged, the galeases on Don John's front opened fire on the Ottoman center. Once again the barrage appeared to unsettle the Turks and cause them to improvise a hasty new alignment. The Christian galleys, by contrast, maintained a slow, steady stroke to the beat of their pipes and drums, and their perfect formation gave them the immediate advantage when they smashed directly into the center of the Turkish line. But no advantage lasted long in those blood-flecked waters where savage hand-to-hand fighting, not subtle maneuvers, decided the contest. Galley grappled with galley and man with man in dozens of individual combats. Ali Pasha was there himself, and as soon as he recognized it he steered straight for the *Réal*. Soon the Turk's ramming beak was entangled in the *Réal*'s rigging, and the sultan's elite janissaries stood muzzle to muzzle against the King of Spain's finest infantry. Twice the Turks boarded the *Réal*, only to be twice driven off again. The Spanish *tercios* had no better success; when they attacked they too were beaten back with heavy loss, and Don John himself was slightly wounded. For nearly two hours the fight raged around the flagships as galleys on both sides disembarked reinforcements for their respective captains general. Finally Colonna broke through the cordon of Turkish ships protecting Ali Pasha's great galley and raked its decks with gunfire. Then the Spaniards came over the side again, this time not to be denied. The janissaries, neither asking nor receiving quarter, fought until all of them were dead, and the gallant Ali Pasha too was dead. A mighty cheer went up from the Christian ranks as the Otto-

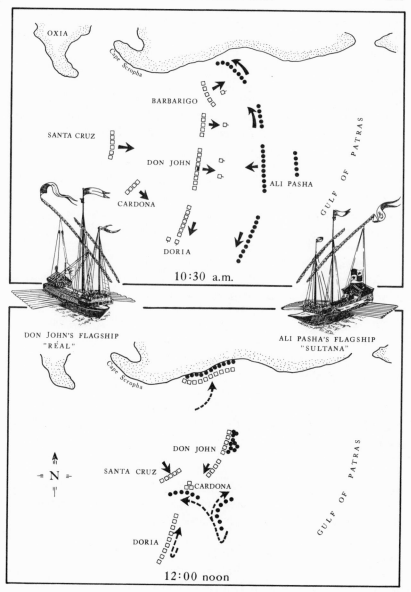

OXIA

Cape Scropha

BARBARIGO

SANTA CRUZ

DON JOHN

ALI PASHA

CARDONA

DORIA

GULF OF PATRAS

10:30 a.m.

DON JOHN'S FLAGSHIP
"RÉAL"

ALI PASHA'S FLAGSHIP
"SULTANA"

Cape Scropha

N

DON JOHN

SANTA CRUZ

CARDONA

DORIA

GULF OF PATRAS

12:00 noon

LEPANTO   October 7, 1571

man commander's head was struck from his body and lifted high on the point of a lance. This grisly trophy was a sign that now—it was almost two o'clock—the battle of the center had been won.

On the Christian right, however, the issue remained in doubt. Doria by miscalculation had allowed his squadron to be cut off from the rest of the Christian fleet, much as the Turks facing Barbarigo had done earlier in the day. To counter an apparent attempt to envelop his flank, Doria had sailed far to his right (southward), when the Turks suddenly swerved and rowed furiously toward the opening between Don John and Doria. About the time the struggle for the flagships was reaching its height, the Turks entered the gap and began to roll up Doria's sector of the line. But this superb feat of tactical seamanship was not enough to reverse Turkish fortunes. Doria, realizing his error, turned his division around with all the speed he could muster, while Santa Cruz and Cardona, commanding the reserve squadrons, raced to the rescue. The fighting here was the fiercest of the whole battle: Cardona was killed and the soldiers serving under him suffered 90 percent casualties; one papal galley was reduced to a total complement of eighteen wounded men. When, however, Don John appeared with reinforcements from the center division, the Turkish admiral knew the game was up. He cut loose his prizes and with thirteen galleys made for the open sea. With that a dreadful silence fell upon the waters of the gulf, strewn with wreckage and floating corpses.

The Battle of Lepanto, the largest engagement fought at sea up to that time and the last in which the galley played the leading role, was an almost total victory for the Holy League, paid for, however, at immense cost in human life. The casualty figures tell the tale. Thirty thousand Turks were killed outright, an unknown number drowned, and 8,000 captured; they lost 113 galleys wrecked or sunk and another 117 captured (35 ships escaped back to Lepanto). The Christians in addition took huge stores of military plunder—274 pieces of artillery, for example—and freed about 15,000 Christian galley slaves. Don John's loss in ships was trifling—a mere dozen—but more than 20,000 of his officers and men were killed or wounded.

The annihilation of the Turkish grand fleet opened many bright prospects for the future. If Don John had had his way the advantage would have been pressed immediately by storming the forts at Lepanto, but he was persuaded that the crippled condition of his own forces and the lateness of the season rendered any such project hazardous at best. So the allied armada sailed back to Sicily and dispersed until the spring. Meanwhile, a delirium of joy swept across Christian Europe. It was not just the victory—it was the magnitude of the victory and the unexpectedness of it. Bells tolled rapturously in every village, toasts were drunk and Te Deums sung in salute to the conquering heroes, and poets and painters omitted no hyperbole to celebrate the glory of this "man sent from God whose name was John." Euphoria gripped even tough-minded political professionals like Granvelle, now Spanish viceroy in Naples, who predicted that 1572 would witness crusaders once more at the gates of Constantinople. Most exultant of all perhaps was Pius V, the architect of the alliance whose lonely struggle to mount the crusade had been spectacularly vindicated by the result. Yet *il Papa Santo* himself typically gave all credit to the power of prayer and the intercession of the Virgin.

The mood of universal congratulation and good fellowship of course did not last.[30] Mercifully Pius V died (May 1, 1572) before the Holy League actually broke up, but even at that early date it was clear that old political and strategic antagonisms were reasserting themselves. When the representatives of the League met to plan the campaign for 1572, Philip II brusquely vetoed the proposed expedition to the Levant. The time had come, he said through his ambassador, to gain from this expensive alliance some benefit closer to home and more in accord with Spanish interests.

No one missed his meaning. Spanish interests were not in the Levant but in North Africa, in Algiers and Tunis, headquarters of the Barbary pirates through whom Islam menaced Spain itself. So the body of Pius V was hardly cold before the intrinsic conflict between Spanish and Venetian policy rose to the surface again. The new pope, Gregory XIII, was enthusiastic for the League, but besides lacking his predecessor's personal charisma, he shortly discovered that Pius V had played all the high papal cards: his partners were already enjoying the subsidies and clerical taxes that had been their price for joining the alliance in the first place. And he could do little to reassure the Venetians, who feared that sooner or later they would be left in the lurch to face the Turks by themselves.

Under pressure from his advisers, most notably Granvelle, Philip

30. Braudel, *La Méditerranée*, II, pp. 405 ff., summarizes the events after Lepanto.

relented for the moment, and during the summer of 1572 Don John's huge allied fleet carried out a series of strikes along the Morean coast. The results, however, were disappointing; the vague hope that the Christian population of Morea would revolt did not materialize, and the Turks, who had replaced their losses at Lepanto with astonishing speed, nevertheless refused to risk a general engagement. So the year of hope ended on a note of frustration and mutual suspicion.

The following spring the Holy League collapsed. On March 7, 1573, Venice signed a separate peace with the Porte. The signory's decision was a triumph for French diplomacy which had been intriguing for it since before Lepanto. But on a deeper level it simply expressed the dilemma Venice was in, caught between two empires so much stronger than itself. The terms of the treaty were humiliating and hardly a fit memorial to Barbarigo and the other Venetians who had died at Lepanto: Cyprus remained in Turkish hands, and tribute to the sultan was reimposed. Yet the serene republic which lived on commerce, which quite literally lived on the cereal grains imported from Turkish-held territory around the Black Sea, judged the price worth paying. Had the spice trade not dwindled in succeeding years, had their own economic institutions remained vigorous, had the plague not visited them with such a devastating effect in 1575 and 1577, the Venetians might have credited themselves with a shrewd stroke of diplomatic business. As it was, however, their withdrawal from the League made little difference to the process of retrenchment which would have gone on in any case. The internal distress that these various troubles inevitably produced was reflected in a long power struggle within the Venetian oligarchy. By 1582 a new faction had emerged which was forcefully, even truculently, anti-Spanish and antipapal. But these reformers—the *giovanni* as they were called—however much their youthful spirit enlivened Venetian art and political discourse, could not restore Venice's status as a power in the world.

The harsh accusations of treachery common in the wake of the Turco-Venetian settlement were not echoed in the dark corridors of the Escorial, even though Philip II might have considered himself the one most notably sinned against. Silent and impassive as ever, he could not in fact have been very sorry to be delivered from an impossible alliance. He now had a fleet to work his will in North Africa, and Don John, accordingly, hauled down the banner of the Holy League from the masthead of the *Réal* and sailed off to attack Tunis. Yet Philip as usual had difficulty making up his mind as to how and to what extent he wanted to proceed against the Barbary states. Meanwhile other crises began to press upon him. His finances reached their lowest ebb in nearly two decades: 1575 promised to be another bankruptcy year. And just at the moment Tunis fell to Don John, the Netherlands exploded again and Alba had to be sacked (October, 1573). Eleven months later, as if to mock Philip's irresolution, the Turks recaptured Tunis.

But this was the last dazzling Turkish incursion into the western Mediterranean. Disengagement, balance of power, spheres of influence mutually respected: these came to be gradually, almost unconsciously, standard policy in both Madrid and Constantinople. Distance, and primitive technology's inability to cope with distance, once again won out over other considerations. As the sultans worried increasingly over the Persian threat to their eastern frontier, support of their Barbary vassals, so very far away, tended to languish. Philip II for his part was more and more distracted by concerns to the north and west, especially after 1580 when he succeeded to the crown of Portugal. He was content that a series of informal truces with the Porte, lasting into the 1590s, gave him a far stronger position in the southern sea than his imperial father had ever enjoyed.

For another of that father's sons, however, the end of the crusade was gall and wormwood. Don John, a young man who dreamed dreams, retired sulking to his tent until he was dispatched a few years later to Flanders, that graveyard of eminent reputations. But no circumstance, not even his own bitterness, could diminish what he had achieved that bloody Sunday on the waters of the Gulf of Patras. Lepanto, because no decisive military operations followed it, has often been described as a victory without consequences or, at most, a moral victory, in that, as a famous participant expressed it, "all the world then learned how mistaken it had been in believing the Turks were invincible at sea."[31] But Lepanto was more than that; it was a great moment in human history because it marked the end of one era and the beginning of another. For longer than men could remember the eastern Mediterranean had been the focal point of civilized life. In skills, in resources, in the kinds of progress that define civilizations, East had stood superior to West as Egypt had to Gaul, as Athens had

31. Cervantes in *Don Quixote*.

to Rome, and, later, as Byzantine emperors and Saracen sheiks had to the rude successors of Charlemagne. But a change had begun with the Italian Renaissance, a shift subtly and, at first, barely perceptibly westward toward the Atlantic. A new world was being born which ultimately would be shaped in western Europe's image and likeness. Lepanto was a dramatic statement that the cultural domination of the East at last was over. The irony was that the hero of Lepanto should have been a knight-errant born under a troubled star and nourished with the ideals of medieval Catholicism.

> Dim drums throbbing in the hills half heard,
> Where only on a nameless throne a crownless prince has stirred,
> Where risen from a doubtful seat and half attainted stall,
> The last knight of Europe takes weapons from the wall. . . .
> In that enormous silence, tiny and unafraid,
> Comes up along a winding road the noise of the crusade,
> Strong gongs groaning as the guns boom far:
> Don John of Austria is going to the War.[32]

32. From "Lepanto" in *The Collected Poems of G. K. Chesterton,* Dodd, Mead & Company, Miss Dorothy E. Collins and Methuen Company.

Chapter Six

THE CATHOLIC OFFENSIVE

L<small>ATE</small> in 1576 a thirty-five-year-old Englishman named Gregory Martin had his first sight of Rome. An Oxford M.A. and sometime Fellow of St. John's, he had served as tutor in the household of that Duke of Norfolk executed in 1572 for complicity in the Ridolfi plot. Martin fled England a year or two before that and went to the newly founded English seminary at Douay, where he was eventually ordained priest (1573) and where he remained afterward as lecturer in Greek and Hebrew. He was a gifted linguist, a shy intellectual whom friends usually described as "learned." Already taking shape in his mind was the project which would bring him enduring fame, an English translation of the Bible, published at Rheims and Douay after his premature death in 1582 and destined to be the standard Catholic version for nearly four centuries.[1]

Martin was deeply impressed by what he saw in Rome during his eighteen-month sojourn there. It was not, however, the ancient monuments or Renaissance palaces that attracted him.

Being at Rome . . . in this time of Gregory XIII, and seeing there wonderful variety of blessed monuments, of devout persons, of godly and charitable exercises from day to day never ceasing; the churches, the martyrs, the glorious ashes of undoubted saints, the places where they prayed, preached, fasted, were imprisoned, died; when I saw moreover the good examples of all degrees, the preaching, teaching, confessing, communicating, visiting of holy places, . . . kneeling, knocking, sighing, weeping, creeping, all other manner of fervent, comely and unfeigned devotion; when I saw the alms, the religious houses, the hospitals, the colleges, the seminaries, the merciful and bountiful provision for all kind of poor and needy persons; when I saw for this purpose the confraternities and congregations, so many, so honorable, so careful of all deeds of mercy and good works. And (that which is a great cause of all the rest) when I saw the majesty of the see apostolic, his holiness among his cardinals, as Michael among the angels, . . . their solemnity in chapel, their wisdom in con-

1. A. C. Southern, *Elizabethan Recusant Prose* (London, 1950), pp. 231 ff.

sistory, audience at home and in their chambers, courtesy in all places mixed with great discretion, . . . I was in a manner rapt besides myself with admiration thereof, and said within myself very much like as [the Queen of Sheba] said to [Solomon]. It is a very true report which I have heard and read of this noble city; I did scarce think it credible till myself came and saw it with mine eyes and found that the half part was not told me.[2]

The enthusiasm of the Catholic exiled for his faith may explain the rather grotesque comparison of Pope Gregory XIII to St. Michael the Archangel, but this and similar rhetorical flourishes do not invalidate Martin's carefully documented case for Rome as the unique center of vital religion. Indeed, to one who, unlike Martin, had known the older Rome, when Medici and Farnese had jostled each other in the corridors of power and in the bedrooms of fashionable ladies, the aspect in the mid-1570s must have seemed as startling as it was edifying. The change in the papal city's character, which had begun timidly under Paul III and had accelerated with Pius IV—who, though something of a scala-wag himself, took the decrees of Trent seriously—reached a climax when the furious pieties of Charles Borromeo, Pius V, and Philip Neri were all at work at once. And fundamental was that spirit of reform common to all classes of Catholics in a generation of revivalism.

Hugo Buoncompagni remembered the old Rome.[3] The Bolognese canon lawyer was seventy when he became Pope Gregory XIII in 1572, and he had spent his whole professional life in the papal administration. Quiet and somewhat withdrawn, he lived up to his name as "good companion" only in the sense that during a long career he had managed to enjoy the regard of practically everybody, except Pius V, who could not forgive him for fathering a bastard at the age of forty-six. But under Borromeo's influence Buoncompagni experienced a conversion of his own, and by 1572 his respectability was fully established. The conclave which elected him was remarkably short; after only a day's deliberation it chose him as the moderate candidate acceptable to the three of four parties within the college of cardinals and, of crucial importance, acceptable as well to Philip II. Buoncompagni acknowledged this latter debt, and offered a hint as to the direction of his pontificate, by casting his own vote for Cardinal Granvelle.

2. George Parks, ed., *Roma Sancta* (Rome, 1969), p. 7. This is the first publication of a work Martin wrote ca. 1578–1580.

3. Ludwig Pastor, *History of the Popes* (London, 1932), Vols. XIX and XX.

Gregory XIII soon disabused those who had expected him to be merely a caretaker pope. Strong and vigorous despite his age, he ruled the Church for thirteen years, and this unusually long pontificate helped his policies to a coherence and consistency which the papacy had often lacked. His interests were extremely wide. A patron of artists and scholars in the best papal tradition, he was responsible for initiating the building program which by the end of the century transformed the face of Rome. He was not always able to pay for the grandiose projects he sponsored, and indeed fiscal administration was never his strong suit, nor was he a particularly able ruler of the Papal States. But in matters related to the universal apostolate of the Church he was conscientious and even punctilious. The missions to America and the Orient gained his enthusiastic support; education and especially seminary education, in accordance with the directives of Trent, was a top priority for him; he recodified the canon law and even reformed the Julian calendar. This latter achievement was greeted by suspicion in non-Catholic parts of Europe, where the reform was rejected as a machination of Antichrist—whom in fact Gregory resembled no more than he did St. Michael.[4] More temperate by far than Pius V, he accepted the principle of such penal institutions as the Inquisition and the Index, but sharply mitigated their practice. A white-bearded man of medium height and upright bearing, he ate and drank little, smiled seldom, and was notoriously gullible in dealing with beggars and other unforunates.

Gregory XIII had none of the glamor of his predecessors, but he possessed gifts particularly useful in a new stage of the Catholic reform movement. If the Roman Church in its attempts to rebound from the disasters of the early sixteenth century needed first Pius IV the diplomat and then Pius V the ascetic, it had now in Gregory XIII the systematizer *par excellence,* a man equipped by training and experience to organize the ecclesiastical machinery so that it would run smoothly even without charismatic leadership. He was an immensely hard worker himself, up from dawn till midnight, often omitting the sacred tradition of the siesta, and anyone who served him paid the price of matching the pope's own rigorous schedule. He was not popular among the cardinals and other curial functionaries who found him

4. The Gregorian calendar was promulgated early in 1582; October 5 became October 15. Prominent Protestant thinkers like Kepler and Brahe endorsed it.

reserved, secretive, and, except for business, scarcely approachable. He delighted in keeping them off balance; in 1583, when he heard reports that parties were forming within the sacred college for the next election, he suddenly named nineteen new cardinals and so completely upset the partisan alignments. They also resented the pope's efforts to overhaul the Curia's cumbersome procedures, and they succeeded in putting off till the next pontificate the institution of a genuine papal bureaucracy.

In the long run Gregory XIII's most lasting influence stemmed from his creation—the word is not too strong—of the papal diplomatic corps. He realized that if Roma Sancta were to function effectively as the director of the reform, if its pretensions to universal sovereignty in the Church were to be more than nominal, it needed to have permanent presence in every corner of Christendom. Nunciatures had existed before 1572, but it was Gregory who reduced papal representation abroad to a system. The new nuncios were less like the extraordinary legates of earlier times and more like modern ambassadors, and yet less concerned with political and fiscal matters and more with religious. The men the pope chose for these assignments were extraordinarily able, and to them must go the credit for linking the cause of local reform with the directive activity and prestige of Rome. They were also the sources of regular information upon which the curia based its policy decisions; indeed, the lack of just such a reliable listening post often led the papacy into grave blunders, as was the case with England. Nothing so much contributed to the solidity and ultimate centralization of the Tridentine Catholic Church than the work of Gregory XIII's nuncios. Through them the sound of Roma Sancta went out into all lands.

I. THE EASTERN MISSION

To be king of Poland in the sixteenth century meant to preside over a commonwealth that extended from Danzig to Kiev, a conglomerate of lands which included Great and Little Poland, Lithuania, parts of Silesia, Prussia, Pomerania, White Russia, and the Ukraine, a veritable empire where six languages were spoken and where disparate cultures flourished side by side.[5] This confederation of states and peoples had

5. Excellent maps in W. F. Reddaway et al., eds., *The Cambridge History of Poland* (Cambridge, 1950).

been largely the work of the Jagellon dynasty, hereditary grand dukes of Lithuania who had been regularly elected kings of Poland since late in the fourteenth century. The last of this distinguished line, Sigismund II Augustus, had made it his life's work to convert the loose, personal union between his kingdom and grand duchy into an organic one. The result of his efforts was the landmark Union of Lublin (1569) which established a single *seym* (parliament) and a common currency and foreign policy for Poland and Lithuania, though each maintained a distinct internal administration. Sigismund formally renounced his hereditary title, thus paving the way for the joint election of his successor. When he died without an heir (July, 1572), the Union proved its durability by surviving a stormy interregnum. In April, 1573, 50,000 electors converged on Warsaw and from a list of prestigious candidates chose Henry of Valois, Charles IX's younger brother, their new king and grand duke.

The logic of their choice rested upon a reluctance to elevate one from among themselves at cost to the others, or to link themselves too closely with powerful neighboring dynasts, like those of Austria, Sweden, and Russia, who all campaigned actively for the throne. France was strong but comfortably far away. A franchise so wide was itself, however, a clue to the difficulties which faced a sovereign in Poland-Lithuania. The Polish gentry—the *szlachta*—had achieved a measure of cohesiveness, at least in dealing with the king and the magnates, hardly known elsewhere in Europe, and they taught the lesson to their Lithuanian counterparts. Other hindrances also stood in the way of effective centralization: the extent of the territories, the linguistic confusion, the constant flux of peoples as culturally diverse as the Cossacks in the south and the Teutonic Knights in the north, the blurred frontiers endlessly contested by Swedes, Muscovites, Tartars, and Turks. All in all, the Jagellons had ridden herd on these problems with considerable success, but the task proved much too formidable for the slender talents of Catherine de' Medici's favorite son.

The Valois interlude did not last very long. King Henry arrived in Poland in January, 1574, was crowned in February, and with the unexpected news of his brother Charles's death fled the country secretly in June. He had done little in the meantime except amaze his subjects with his capacity for riotous living. Had the Poles been able to foresee what a dismal failure Henry would be as king of France, they might have counted themselves lucky to be rid of him. As it was, they were angry and chagrined at this repudiation of their highest honor, and some elements among the *szlachta* wanted to declare the throne permanently vacant. This view, however, did not prevail, and after a tumultuous election campaign an unlikely candidate emerged victorious. On April 29, 1576, Stephen Bátory, Prince of Transylvania, was crowned in Cracow cathedral.

The new king[6] was Hungarian by blood and, as elected ruler of the buffer state of Transylvania, had been technically a vassal of the Porte. But the sultan's writ did not mean much so far north, and it was Stephen Bátory's record as an independent, anti-Hapsburg ruler that attracted the votes of the Polish and Lithuanian gentry. Intelligent and dynamic, he might under other circumstances have been a superb administrator, but he preferred war to statesmanship, and his ten-year reign was primarily taken up with military adventures. Though they often balked at the expense, there is no evidence that his subjects, who lived, after all, on a half-tamed frontier, objected to war as such. King Stephen brought them victories over the hated Russians, and that for the moment was enough. Not until he died (1586) did they realize that those victories raised as many problems as they solved.

The Reformation caught Poland in the middle of its nation-building process. The same thing happened in other multilingual, multicultural areas—most notably in the Netherlands—to the detriment of national development. In Poland, by contrast, practical religious unanimity was achieved, even though the kingdom (and the grand duchy) harbored for a time every variety of ideological dissent, Yet, in the end, except for some Anabaptist pockets, the only churches to demonstrate staying power were the old ones, Roman Catholic and Greek Orthodox.

Such a result could scarcely have been foreseen. Lutheranism came early to Poland, first to Danzig, within a year indeed of the publication of the Ninety-five Theses, and then to the other towns where German influences were strong. After 1540 Calvinist congregations began to spring up, and soon Anabaptist groups, persecuted farther west, appeared on the scene. Remnants of the Czech Brethren settled in Poland too and ultimately merged with the Calvinists.[7] Even the Uni-

6. The standard biography is the joint effort by the Polish and Hungarian academies of science, *Étienne Bathory, Roi de Pologne, Prince de Transylvanie* (Cracow, 1935).

7. Jarold Zeman, *The Anabaptists and the Czech Brethren in Morovia, 1526–1628: A Study of Origins and Contacts* (The Hague, 1969), p. 302.

tarians, hated and proscribed by all the other sects, found a home there.[8]

Their common enemy, the Catholic Church in Poland-Lithuania, suffered from the same internal problems it did elsewhere: political bishops, ignorant priests, venal monks, pluralism, concubinage, superstition, religious foundations falling into ruin, morale wrecked apparently beyond remedy. It was little wonder that Protestantism should achieve striking gains among a people so badly served. By the 1560s Protestant communities, numbering in the many hundreds and possibly more, seemed on the verge of sweeping Romanism from the eastern European map. Yet, in an astonishing reversal of fortune, a generation later they had practically disappeared. The evangelical seed had fallen upon rocky ground.

One reason was that neither Lutheran nor Calvinist nor Anabaptist gospel gained much acceptance among the rural masses. The German associations of Lutheranism, which tended to recommend it to the mercantile classes in the towns, had the opposite effect in the countryside. Certain segments of the gentry became Calvinists, but their conversion pointed more toward an assertion of independence of a Catholic king than toward a depth of personal conviction. The Protestants failed too because of the wretched quarrels among themselves. When in 1569 the Lutherans and Calvinists asked the government to suppress the Anabaptists, one of Sigismund's entourage advised refusal on the ground that left to themselves the heretics would devour each other. To some extent so it turned out.

But also at work were the forces of revitalized Catholicism. If any one man can be said to have been responsible for the remarkable effectiveness of the Counter Reformation in Poland, it was Stanislaus Cardinal Hosius (d. 1579), who, whether in his dioceses of Chelmno and Ermeland—both located in the most protestantized areas of the kingdom—or, in his later years, as cardinal-in-curia, presided over every phase of it. As a counselor of popes and kings, as a humanist and controversialist of international reputation even before his legacy at the final sessions of Trent, Hosius was probably the most influential churchman of the Europe of his generation.[9]

He did not, however, act alone. Rome lent Polish Catholicism the

8. See G. Pioli, *Fausto Socini, Vita, Opera, Fortuna* (Modena, 1952).
9. See L. Bernacki, *La Doctrine de l'Église chez le Cardinal Hosius* (Paris, 1936).

strength of its refurbished prestige through a series of extremely able nuncios who labored hard on the one hand to enforce the canons of Trent and, on the other, to keep the Curia adequately informed of the local situation. Nowhere did the permanent nunciatures as intelligence-gathering agencies work to the papacy's better advantage than in Poland, about which popes before Gregory XIII knew as little as they did about China. The legends current in Rome in the fifteenth century,[10] which described Poles as savages and infidels, died hard, and as late as 1555 a Spanish Jesuit in Warsaw reported to St. Ignatius: "Whoever has traveled through this country has not only done penance for all his sins but has also gained a plenary indulgence." Fantasy about eastern European affairs did not altogether give way to hard information in the councils of the Curia, but a generation of nuncios helped to establish there a modicum of realism entirely missing before.

But not Hosius or the nuncios or whatever spark of life there was in native Polish Catholicism could have done without the Jesuits. At first the general sent Italians, Spaniards, and even some exiled Englishmen to the eastern mission, but these soon gave place to Polish recruits who swelled the ranks of the Society. They performed in the typically Jesuit fashion: coolly, efficiently, and with that drive of personal conviction drawn from an experience of the Ignatian *Exercises*. The most notable of them was Peter Skarga, who controverted with Protestants, founded two universities, and engaged in not a little ecclesiastical diplomacy.[11] Behind him were the squads of nameless foot soldiers who in classroom, confessional, pulpit, and even the streets demonstrated that the old religion was far from dead. Of particular importance were the Polish Jesuits' endeavors in the field of education. Many a Protestant lord sent his sons to the excellent Jesuit secondary schools and colleges, where, likely as not, they discarded the faith of their father. In these instances the Jesuits displayed a quality which was at once a strength and an occasion of much criticism (and not only in Poland): their competence as teachers or researchers or rhetoricians, their commitment to intellectual excellence, served as an allurement to impressionable young people and therefore as a means of influencing their religious opinions.

10. For an example, see Zofia Wlodek, "A Rediscovered Lampoon," *Poland* (Warsaw), No. 8 (204), August 1971, 32 f.

11. See Oscar Halecki, *From Florence to Brest* (New York, 1968), pp. 200 ff.

As the Society's erudition ministered to the classes, so the common touch and disinterested poverty of the reformed Franciscans—Bernadines as they were called in Poland—ministered to the masses. By the 1580s they were joined by increasing numbers of secular priests trained according to the Tridentine ideal in the new seminaries. By that time too there was scarcely a member of the Polish hierarchy who did not belong to Hosius's school of learned, pious, and tough-minded bishops. The Catholic restoration, if not yet complete, was well on its way to accomplishment.

The civil government watched this process with cautious approval, but it did nothing to aid it by force. Indeed, Poland was unique for the times in the measure of religious toleration to be found there. The crown had gestured toward repression when Protestantism first appeared without, however, doing anything substantive about it. Sigismund Augustus, an easygoing Erasmian when it came to religion, had made toleration of all sects his policy, and Stephen Bátory, though a more serious Catholic, maintained the same position. They both welcomed and cooperated with nuncios, Jesuits, and the other elements of the Counter Reformation—Sigismund in fact was the first secular ruler to promulgate the decrees of Trent—but neither of them had any taste for persecution. It may have been that they could not have enforced religious conformity even if they had wanted to. The aristocracy was too strong to be inhibited by the frail central government, and it was the aristocracy that found the Protestant doctrines attractive. Nor should Polish liberalism in this regard be interpreted to mean that the ordinary man chose the religion which most appealed to him. Rather the nobleman made the choice and imposed it upon his retainers and upon the villages of peasants he ruled like an absolute monarch. Yet, even with these qualifications, there remained much for Europeans at large, with their laws of uniformity and their inquisitions, to learn from the Poles, who established religious toleration as a legal principle in the Confederation of Warsaw (1573).[12] This edict was much broader than the more famous German Peace of Augsburg, in that it guaranteed freedom of conscience to all Polish gentlemen of all denominations and extended the "cujus regio, ejus religio" formula to every estate in the kingdom and grand duchy. So the Counter Reformation won a bloodless victory in Poland, which circumstance made it

12. Joseph Lecler, *Toleration and the Reformation* (New York, 1960), I, 397 ff.

perhaps the sweetest victory of all. Certainly the vicissitudes of four centuries have proved it the most complete and enduring victory.

The swift rise and fall of Polish Protestantism had a curious side effect. It helped promote a rapprochement between Catholics and Orthodox Ruthenians, who learned to compare each other to Calvin and Luther and thus were reminded of how much they had in common. The government welcomed the prospect of religious union, because, with the bulk of the Orthodox concentrated in the Ukraine, it could serve as a prop to the political union between the kingdom and the grand duchy. The Ruthenians, their ecclesiastical allegiance in disarray now that the Patriarch of Constantinople was a creature of the Porte, were eager for the connection with Rome, so long as they could avoid adopting the Latin liturgy. The papacy, for its part, looked beyond the merits of the case at hand. Might not agreement with the Orthodox in the Ukraine bring an entrée into the rest of Russia and into the greater Orthodox world? Might not Moscow be the ideal base from which to preach the Catholic and Roman faith to Persia, China, and even possibly Constantinople?

The actual event was much more modest: a decade after Gregory XIII's death and after protracted negotiations, the Ruthenians submitted to the Roman obedience. The Union of Brest-Litovsk (1596) preserved the Ukrainian rite and still secured the formal religious unity of the Polish commonwealth. Nobody then could have predicted that it would also be not a new dawn of harmony but a bone of endless contention between Rome and Orthodoxy.[13]

King Stephen Bátory did not view kindly papal illusions about the conversion of the Russians or a great opening to the East by way of Moscow, and he was neither surprised nor sorry to see the collapse of Gregory XIII's initiatives in that direction. Twice in the spring of 1582 the Jesuit diplomat Anthony Possevino interviewed the Muscovite tsar Ivan IV, only to learn that Ivan despised Catholicism and the papacy and that he richly deserved his nickname "the Terrible." The tsar had endured meeting the pope's representative because he hoped it might help extricate him from the war he was losing to the Poles, not because he was interested in evangelizing China or in a crusade against the Porte. Indeed, this last idea was at the root of all papal diplomacy in eastern Europe. Pius V had tried and failed to mobilize a Polish-

---

13. Halecki, *Florence to Brest*, tells the story in exhaustive detail.

Austrian land assault upon the Ottoman Empire in conjunction with the Holy League's campaign at sea. His successor revived the project in the form of a grand anti-Turkish alliance of Vienna, Warsaw, and Moscow. Gregory was nursing this phase of Rome's favorite obsession when he actively opposed Bátory's candidacy for the Polish throne, on the ground that the prince was too friendly with the Porte. King Stephen had turned out to be a better son of the Church than the pope had expected—perhaps in the long run one of the best royal sons the Church ever had—but he was no crusader. He trusted the infidel Turks far more than he did the Catholic Hapsburgs, and with the Orthodox Russians he fought a long, bitter war.

That conflict grew out of the extreme fluidity which prevailed among the emerging states of eastern Europe and which affected their internal composition as much as their relations to one another. Vast stretches of uninhabited land as well as the gradual disappearance of old social organizations invited competition, confusion and war. The Grand Duchy of Moscow during Ivan IV's reign (1533–1584) expanded dramatically south and east at the expense of the crumbling Tartar khanates and even pushed its sway beyond the Urals into western Siberia. To the north and west, however, where similar power vacuums existed, Muscovy was checked because there it collided with Sweden and the Polish commonwealth, which were as young and lusty and ambitious as itself. Specifically, the Russians needed a water exit to the markets of the West in order to sell their flax and hemp, hides, furs, corn, and wax. But in the north the Swedes effectively blocked their entry into the Baltic, and in the south Lithuania sprawled as far east as Kharkov and across their route to the Black Sea. Except for the trickle of trade which moved through the Arctic—Archangel was not a recognized port until 1586—the Russians were virtually encircled. To break out of this commercial encirclement Ivan the Terrible invaded the principality of Livonia in 1558 and began a quarter-century of war with Sweden and Poland.

Livonia—roughly equivalent to modern Latvia—was part of the domain of the Teutonic Knights, one of those military-monastic orders which had flourished in the Middle Ages as agents of crusade, whether against Islam or against northeast European pagans. The sovereignty of these soldier-monks had always been something of an anomaly; by the sixteenth century their own corruption, together with the ideological hostility of Lutheranism and the pressures exerted by nascent nationalism left it an impossibility and their territories attractive targets for aggression. In Livonia the Russians chose to launch their first serious thrust westward.

They failed dismally in the face of Polish and Swedish arms, and some of the blame for that failure must rest upon the strange personality of Tsar Ivan. Orphaned as a small child, the grand duke was mistreated and exploited by a regency council of boyars. He grew up brilliant but twisted, half-educated, moody, paranoid, sadistic. He did everything in excess; he passed directly from long hours of formal religious exercises to orgies of wild self-indulgence. He was extraordinarily cruel, even by the savage standards of the Muscovite court. He once sewed an archbishop who had displeased him into a bearskin and then loosed hungry dogs on him; on a vague rumor of disloyalty he massacred the population of the city of Novgorod. There is no telling how many tens of thousands of his subjects he murdered.

Yet important as the autocrat undoubtedly was, the weakness of the new Russian state had deeper causes than the quirks of Ivan the Terrible. The population which may have been as many as 17 million and as few as 4 million[14]—so sketchy is the statistical evidence—roamed through a largely empty land. The Russian peasantry migrated constantly, either by its own volition or by that of the tsar and the landlords. It was said that a peasant's hut was built to last four years. A traveler in 1553 noted a thriving village life in the area north of Moscow; another traveler, thirty-five years later, found the same territory deserted and gone back to forest. The most spectacular instance of this mobility was the rise of the Ukrainian Cossacks, roughriders who prowled between forest and steppe, who acted as the agents of the penetration of Slavic culture south and east. Some of them owed shadowy allegiance to the Grand Duchy of Lithuania, some to the Grand Duchy of Moscow, and some to nobody at all—as their name, meaning freeman or free-lance warrior, generally suggests.

Such circumstances were hardly conducive to the development of a centralized regime or of any stable institutions for that matter. Ivan confronted the same perplexing dilemma as other European monarchs, only in his case, because of the size and primitiveness of the country, on a monumental scale: the dynast could not rule without the support of

14. Richard Dunn, *The Age of Religious Wars* (New York, 1970), p. 63.

his natural competitors for power, the aristocrats. "What," asks Professor Kliuchevsky, "was the Muscovite state of the sixteenth century? It was an absolute monarchy, tempered by an aristocratic administrative personnel. . . . The supreme power had developed simultaneously and hand in hand with the very political force which now restricted it."[15]

In 1565 Ivan initiated a bold if bizarre experiment in hopes of solving the problem. He established by decree the *Oprichnina,* which he described as a special state institution designed to effect the tsar's will. The older administration—the *Zemstchina,* composed of the local magnates—functioned as before, functioned indeed as it had to given the distances involved, the communications available, the prevalent social backwardness. The council of boyars which in a loose, feudal way governed the *Zemstchina* remained, as before, nominally responsible to the tsar. The *Oprichnina,* by contrast, was his immediate executive over which he presided directly.[16]

Was the *Oprichnina* an oddity, a parody, a madness? To some extent it did reflect Ivan's paranoia in that he set it up for the same reason that he moved out of the Kremlin and established headquarters in a fortified lodge on the outskirts of Moscow: he was convinced the boyars meant to kill him. More profoundly, however, it represented an attempt at radical reform, the creation of a centralized bureaucracy at one fell swoop, without waiting for the economic and social evolution which alone could make such a bureaucracy viable. The *Oprichnina* was Ivan the Terrible's crude effort to solve the riddle of autocracy in an essentially centrifugal society.

His subjects however saw it in a more sinister light. The *Oprichniki* —some thousands strong, living on income derived from sequestered property—dressed from head to toe in black, rode black horses, and carried on their saddle pommels a dog's head and a broom, symbolic of their mandate from the tsar to sweep away the treason of the boyars. More like a private army or a secret police force than a civil service, they spread havoc across a land already wounded by a harsh nature and by human foolishness. Failure in the Livonian war, failure to effect internal reform, failure of the tsar himself: these led relentlessly to

---

15. V. O. Kliuchevsky, *A History of Russia* (New York, 1960), II, 83.
16. Michael Florinsky, *Russia, a History and an Interpretation* (New York, 1953), I, 199 ff.

deeper distress, to what Russians ever since have called the Time of Troubles.

2. THE NORTHERN MISSION

Possevino preceded his failure to interest Tsar Ivan either in the merits of the Roman Church or in the advantages of a crusade against the Turks with an even more dramatic misadventure. The scene was neighboring Sweden-Finland, which during the Counter Reformation era was ruled by Gustav Vasa's gifted but somewhat erratic sons. The monarchy, with its mixed elective-hereditary character,[17] was passing through a period of consolidation when competition for power within the estates general or Riksdag was only one of its problems. The development of Renaissance centralization was further hampered by the primitive state of the economy—barter was the rule, money the exception—and by the severe climate which turned the northern sections of the kingdom into a treeless tundra. Then too, rivalries within the new dynasty seriously diminished the authority of the king: Eric XIV (d. 1577) was hardly master in his own house, so long as his brother John—later John III (d. 1592)—remained the semi-independent Duke of Finland and his brother Charles—later Charles IX (d. 1611)—controlled the territory immediately south and west of Stockholm.

What distinguished Sweden of the late sixteenth century from the great power it was to become under Gustavus Adolphus and Charles X was the success in between of its expansion into the Baltic.[18] Eric XIV seized Reval on the Estonian coast in 1561 and thus initiated the policy which would eventually make the Baltic a Swedish lake and give Sweden the lion's share of the highly coveted Russian trade. The easterly direction taken by Eric and his equally aggressive successors was, however, dictated as much by Denmark's hostility as by Muscovy's overextension and the Teutonic Knights' weakness. Indeed, the Vasa family had mounted an independent throne only at the cost of wrecking the old Danish-dominated confederation of Scandinavian kingdoms (the Union of Kalmar), and the Danes still ruled Norway and, more important, both sides of the Sound, the straits that link the North and Baltic seas. Sweden's only exit to the west before the middle

17. See A. J. Grant, *A History of Europe from 1494 to 1610* (London, 1951), pp. 305 f.
18. And the success in the economic field. See the comparisons offered by Professor Hurstfield, *New Cambridge Modern History*, III, 129.

of the seventeenth century, when Charles X drove the last Danes off the Swedish peninsula, was a coastal stretch a few miles long at the mouth of the Gotha River. The savagely fought Seven Years' War of the North (1563–1570) did not significantly alter this balance, for while Sweden was not strong enough to break out of the Danish blockade, Denmark was not strong enough to thwart Swedish designs in the east Baltic. Successes by Denmark's mercenary soldiers—paid for largely by tolls exacted from ships passing through the Sound—were countered by successes on the sea by the fleet which Eric had exhausted his resources to build and which remained for a long time afterward a factor in European power politics.

Eric himself was not in a position to enjoy the fruits of victory, such as they were. In 1568 Queen Elizabeth's one-time suitor—handsome, cultivated, bold, and a little mad—was overturned by his nobles, certified as insane, and (probably) murdered nine years later. His successor, however, had no reason to alter the basic eastern orientation of Swedish policy. If anything John III expanded it into a vision of a Vasa empire composed of Sweden-Finland and Poland-Lithuania. Twice he was candidate for the Polish throne, and, though twice defeated, he managed to get his son and heir elected in 1587. Before that he helped the Poles conquer Livonia and annexed Estonia himself. John's wife was Polish—Catherine Jagellon, sister of Sigismund Augustus and sister also of Stephen Bátory's wife—and so, given the vagaries of dynastic politics, the dream of a confederation from the Arctic to the Black Sea did not appear to him all that far-fetched.

But if the Vasa family's pretensions in eastern Europe were to stand any chance of success, some accommodation would have to be reached with Rome.[19] John III's ambition, therefore, opened the Scandinavian door a crack to the Catholicism which had been driven out forty years before. Luther's triumph in the north had been seemingly complete. Once the kings and influential nobles adopted the Confession of Augsburg, the Mass disappeared with a swiftness which argued that it had not been particularly popular in the first place. By the same token, however, evidence was lacking a generation later that aside from certain devotional practices the new religion had taken deep root in the

19. See Oscar Garstein, *Rome and the Counter Reformation in Scandinavia* (Oxford, 1963), Vol. I. But see also the highly critical review by Vello Helk, *Revue d'Histoire Ecclésiastique*, LXI (1966), 119–131.

hearts of the people—or at least so King John might have reasoned, even while he recognized the existence of a numerous and determined Lutheran party within the country. He fancied himself in any event a kind of Henry VIII; he tinkered constantly with the state church and instructed it by way of doctrinal and liturgical injunctions which revealed an enthusiasm for, if not much knowledge of, theological lore.[20] Gradually the conviction grew on him—partly through reading the ecumenist thinker George Cassander and partly through conversations with the two priests attached to his Catholic wife's court as chaplains— that a middle way might be fashioned whereby Lutheran Swedes and Catholic Poles could walk together in harmony, perhaps under the same sovereign. The king confided to a few intimates that Catholicism might well be restored to Sweden, provided that a vernacular liturgy be maintained, that the clergy be allowed to marry, and that the Eucharist be received by the laity under both species.

By 1575 Rome had heard rumors of a new conciliatory attitude in Stockholm, and when the rumors were followed by the first of several secret delegations from King John the original skepticism gave way to guarded interest. Cardinal Hosius, the resident expert in eastern and northern European affairs, urged the pope to appoint a special commission for Scandinavia. The pope complied, though he was suspicious of the King of Sweden's intentions and remained suspicious throughout the curious negotiations of the next few years. At first the papal commission had little to do besides examining John's various proposals for reunion, which, however they were phrased, were always reducible to his three basic conditions. The more cynical among the curial officials noted that the king never failed to accompany his ecumenical schemes with a plea for the pope's intervention in another matter close to the royal heart. His wife's mother had been a member of the wealthy Sforza family, and her estate—said to be equivalent to three years of the Swedish crown's revenues—had been frozen by the Neapolitan authorities.

Under the circumstances it was not unreasonable to test John III's good will. In 1576 the Curia found the means to do so in the strange mission of Lawrence Nilsson.[21] Born in Norway about 1538 and raised

---

20. But see Toivo Hayunpao, "Liturgical Developments in Sweden and Finland in the Era of Lutheran Orthodoxy," *Church History*, XXXVII (1968), 14–35.

21. Garstein, *Scandinavia*, pp. 94 ff.

a Lutheran, Nilsson had gone to school in Copenhagen, where apparently he had had some contact with the Jesuits working secretly in the Danish capital. By 1560, he had migrated to Flanders and was enrolled at the University of Louvain; shortly afterward he became a Catholic. His was not an easy conversion—he continued for a long time to feel repelled by many Roman devotions—but it was wholehearted: in 1564 he took vows in the Society of Jesus and the next year was ordained priest. From the outset he showed himself to be a gifted writer and teacher and a very attractive if eccentric personality. What recommended him most to the Curia, however, was that he spoke Swedish. Accordingly, when it was judged appropriate to send an informal and incognito emissary to the King of Sweden, Lawrence Nilsson was chosen.

John III took the most elaborate precautions to keep the Jesuit's identity a secret, and Nilsson zestfully cooperated. He put on clerical garb, passed himself off as a Protestant theologian, and soon was the toast of Stockholm society. The king appointed him principal of a new theological college and ordered the most promising candidates for the ministry to be sent there. Nilsson devised a hybrid liturgy for his students' use, and though some of his sermons—notably one on prayer to the saints—roused the ire of orthodox Lutherans, he eluded any serious challenge and maintained his position for four years without, however, achieving much progress in converting king or kingdom.

What John III expected from this ecclesiastical charade is impossible to say. Though he was a man given to flamboyant and impracticable projects, he was shrewd enough to realize early in the game that Nilsson did not possess sufficient credentials to negotiate a settlement. Indeed, Nilsson's complete dependence on the king rendered him next to useless as a diplomat. Yet John continued to insist that he wanted reunion, and so the pope responded by naming Anthony Possevino legate to the court of Sweden. The forty-four-year-old Jesuit brought a fund of talent and experience to this delicate task. He enjoyed as well the full confidence of the curia and could speak, as Nilsson could not, authoritatively.[22] From the moment he arrived in Stockholm (Christmas, 1577) and during the five months of his stay there, King John treated him with a deference due his diplomatic rank—though he saw to it that Possevino too remained carefully disguised. The legate and

22. Pastor, *Popes,* XX, 424 ff.

the king held long conversations about religion which seemed to lead nowhere until suddenly, at the beginning of May, 1578, John declared himself convinced of the truth of Catholicism and demanded to be received into the Roman Church. Possevino put him off at first, afraid no doubt that the king acted out of romantic impulse or political calculation, but ultimately he had to give in to the royal insistence. In the greatest secrecy John III swore the Tridentine creed, went to Mass, and received the Eucharist at Possevino's hand—under the species of bread only.

Meanwhile, the unpredictable Nilsson had let it slip that he and Possevino were priests, though he had stopped short of admitting they were also Jesuits. The result was anger among the Lutheran nobles and embarrassment for the king. Possevino accordingly departed Sweden and carried to Rome the list of concessions John III claimed he needed before he would dare admit his own conversion and work for that of his people. The majority of these concessions the Scandinavian commission was prepared to grant, including the formal renunciation of ecclesiastical property confiscated since the reign of Gustav Vasa. But it refused to compromise on the matters of vernacular liturgy, celibacy, and Utraquism, and its intransigence reflected the pope's own deep feelings. More importantly perhaps, it reflected the hardening of positions which fifty years of confessional strife had brought about. None of John's three conditions involved an essential point of Catholic dogma, but each of them had come to be recognized as a public manifestation of Protestantism. The time for accommodation in such areas had passed away. Gregory XIII, not an inflexible man, declined to open Pandora's box for the sake of the Swedish king whom he did not trust anyway. Possevino for his part could only confirm the pope's suspicions of John's sincerity and urge the establishment of pontifical seminaries to train a Swedish clergy for the day when and if the king would allow them entry.

Not all hope was given up, however. Late in 1578 Possevino was confirmed as legate to Sweden and appointed vicar apostolic as well for Denmark, Russia, Saxony, and Hungary—so murky was the papal knowledge of geography. He arrived back in Stockholm on August 7, 1579, this time dressed in the habit of his order. He stayed for a year, during which the negotiations with the bitterly disappointed king went from bad to worse. Without satisfaction on his three basic conditions, the Roman connection, John said, would cost him his throne. Posse-vino argued in rebuttal that if John threw in his lot with the Catholic powers, with the papacy, with Poland, and, above all, with Spain, he would have nothing to fear from his own subjects or from the Danes and German Lutherans either. Indeed, the Jesuit had been commissioned to offer Sweden a Spanish alliance and to assure John of Philip II's brotherly concern about the Sforza inheritance. The stake here was the Swedish fleet, which Philip, with a troubled eye on the Netherlands, was anxious to use or at least to neutralize. But John remained unpersuaded and avoided all commitments, and when Possevino left Stockholm in the summer of 1580—taking with him fifteen young Swedes to be enrolled in various seminaries abroad—the disenchanted king expelled Nilsson at the same time.

After that Catholicism's last chance rested with Queen Catherine and with the crown prince, who had been raised in the old faith. But the queen died in 1583 and while Prince Sigismund was duly elected king of Poland (1587), the religion which benefited him there was his downfall in Sweden; a few years after he succeeded his father (1592) his subjects drove him from the throne and replaced him with his uncle Charles. So much for the dream of a Polish-Swedish federation presided over by the Vasa family. Possevino continued for a while, unavailingly, to negotiate for the release of the Sforza money and to perform other diplomatic chores for John III, with the faint hope that opportunity might beckon from the north once more. But it never did, and Possevino went off instead on a mission to Moscow.

The Catholic failure in Sweden showed the limits of a religious policy which concentrated almost exclusively on the person of the sovereign. No ruler was as strong in fact as he claimed to be in theory, and if, as in Sweden, the old religion aroused no significant popular support, the king could not restore it by himself. "Cujus regio, ejus religio" was at best a qualified principle of action. Even so, in the land where the "cujus regio" maxim had been coined and where it still enjoyed legal sanction, the papal approach fared rather better. Parts of Germany indeed—generally speaking, the north and northeast—had to be written off as lost to the Roman Church, and except for a diplomatic gesture or two the Lutheran heartland of Brandenburg, Mecklenburg, and Saxony did not figure seriously in Gregory XIII's plans. Elsewhere, however, prospects were much brighter, because, among other reasons, Lutheranism's evangelical fervor had been checked by its own internal tensions.

The intrusion of Calvinism into Germany—specifically into the Rhenish Palatinate, Bremen, and ultimately Anhalt and Hesse-Cassel— served to sharpen the quarrels which were already raging within the Lutheran body.[23] The storm swirled around the venerable head of Philip Melanchthon (d. 1560), whose prestige as Luther's premier disciple did not save him from the abuse of his more radical brethren. Melanchthon was too subtle and gentle a master to suit Flacius Illyricus (d. 1575) and the other so-called Gnesio-Lutherans who accused him of revisionism, of betraying gospel purity in order to accommodate Catholics on the one hand and Calvinists on the other. Melanchthon's irenic disposition and notoriously shifting views on the key issues of good works and the Real Presence in the Eucharist gave substance to such charges, and when the godly princes of north Germany took up the cudgels in support of the Philipists—Melanchthon's party—or of the radicals, a generation of strife began which threatened the very existence of the Lutheran Church.

The solution to these conflicts,[24] when it finally came, was a triumphant reassertion of Martin Luther's original vision. The struggles which preceded the *Formula of Concord*—first proposed in 1577 and ratified three years later by eighty-six state churches and by thousands of pastors—proved to have been Lutheranism's great catharsis, its coming of age, its testing time, when Melanchthon's ambivalences as well as Illyricus's primitive literalism were found wanting and definitely set aside. The *Formula* was an ingenious document, comprehensive and yet distinctively Lutheran, testifying above all to the stubborn piety of the masses of believers who were determined, whatever the intricacies of controversial theology, to follow a Christian calling which was neither Genevan nor Roman.

The conflicts which for three decades sapped the energy of Protestant Germany were bound to work to resurgent Catholicism's advantage, at least in those places where the old ecclesiastical machinery, battered as it might have been, was still intact. Having once accepted the "cujus

---

23. For some differences in attitude between Lutheran and Calvinist, see Owen Chadwick, *The Reformation* (Harmondsworth, 1964), pp. 369 f.

24. For summary and references, see Emile Léonard, *A History of Protestantism* (London, 1966), II, 11 ff.

regio" principle, the papacy could hope to exert pressure upon a prince, particularly when he saw Protestantism in retreat. A diplomatic presence was therefore important, even if all it did was demonstrate the Roman Church's viability and universality. Thus it was that the nuncios of exceptional ability—Portia, Ninguarda, Elgard, Bonhomini, Gropper—whom Gregory XIII employed in the German-speaking lands contributed to the Catholic restoration simply by performing their routine duties. And their activity was in addition to that of older ambassadors, like Delfino in Vienna, and of extraordinary legates including that of the aged but still peerless Morone, who represented the pope at the imperial Diet of Ratisbon in 1576.

As far as formal diplomacy was concerned, Germany presented certain opportunities to the forces of the Counter Reformation as well as special problems. Fragmented into hundreds of sovereign states of various sizes, it had no territorial ruler with the power of Philip II or the pretensions of John III who might want to practice caesaropapism on the grand scale. Yet at the same time the Curia found dealing with Germany a bewilderingly complex process, subject to sudden changes and reversals as petty states and conflicting interests within those states adjusted their relative positions.

A prince might indeed be swayed by genuinely religious considerations, as were the Wittelsbach dukes of Bavaria, Albert V (d. 1579) and William V (d. 1597). But even such model Catholics, upon whose support the popes staked their German fortunes, did not frame an ecclesiastical policy without a careful eye on their dynastic advantage. In this regard the difference between them and the Hapsburgs—the emperor and his archducal sons and brothers who administered the several portions of the Austrian crownlands—was one of degree rather than of kind. The Emperor Maximilian (d. 1576), for example, had marked Lutheran sympathies, but he never felt strong enough to give them free rein. His son and successor, Rudolph II (d. 1612), was by contrast staunchly Catholic; yet the Protestantism of a large proportion of the Austrian nobility led him to compromise more in religious matters than he might have liked.

Situations like these point to another parallel function of the papal nuncios which, if successful, could help win over the most reluctant prince. The sovereigns of Germany were like politicians at all times and places: they led but they also followed, in that their capacity for leadership depended upon identifying with the aspirations of their people. If the Catholic Church with its burden of decay were bound to disappear from German-speaking lands—as appeared probable before the 1570s—no moderately intelligent ruler could have been expected to gamble his throne on the Roman connection. But if popular Catholicism were somehow prodded back into life, if the old faith were to tap new springs of vitality, the prince, whatever his personal preferences, was not likely to swim against the ideological current.

To achieve such a renaissance, however, involved sweeping away huge amounts of ecclesiastical debris. The condition of the Church in Germany was doleful in the extreme, and worse perhaps than the corruption itself was the indifference to corruption prevailing in high German places. To counter an inertia so old and so encrusted by law and custom required a stimulus from the outside, and this the nuncios provided. Indeed, their work, which carried them from Silesia to the foothills of the Alps and down the Rhine to Mainz and Cologne, stands as a classic example of the universal institution coming to the rescue of one of its branches. The same might be said in another sense too, because the agents of the pope brandished the canons of Trent as weapons against rot and as criteria for reform, and Trent was a council in which German Catholics had played practically no part.

Notwithstanding many disappointments, the nuncios did by and large win acceptance for their essentially simple program. They urged as a minimum that bishops reside in and systematically visit—in the technical meaning of that word—their dioceses, and that they establish seminaries. These two provisions lay at the heart of the Tridentine reform, for what had disfigured the Church in Germany, more perhaps than elsewhere, was the chaos resulting when an episcopacy was unwilling and unable to demand an accounting from the lower ecclesiastical orders, and the failure to provide means for the moral and intellectual training of the clergy. Some bishops, caught up in the revivalist spirit of the times, cooperated with the Roman directives as fully as their resources allowed;[25] others had to be pressured, either by the threat of papal censures or by more subtle forms of persuasion, or,

---

25. For some attempts of German bishops in this regard, see M. Huber, *Die Durchführung der tridentinischen Reform in Hohenzollern, 1567–1648* (Tübingen, 1963), and E. W. Zeeden et al., eds., *Die Visitation im Dienst der kirchlichen Reform* (Münster, 1967).

often enough, by way of the territorial prince. For those groups outside the bishop's jurisdiction, like monasteries and exempt religious congregations, the nuncios used their faculties as papal visitors and subjected German monks and nuns to an embarrassingly minute inspection.

But the high-level activity of the pope's ambassadors would have achieved much less without the Jesuits. As early as 1540 St. Ignatius had sent two of his men to Germany, while he himself a few years later founded a college in Rome to train German missionaries.[26] By Gregory XIII's time hundreds of Jesuits were at work in the empire. Not all of them gained fame like the Dutchman Peter Canisius (d. 1597), who spent nearly half a century in Germany and wrote a popular catechism that went into 130 editions, started colleges at Augsburg, Munich, and Innsbruck, and exercised no small influence over the Hapsburg family. All of them, however, contributed to the familiar pattern: their zeal, their exceptional ability in all kinds of labors, and especially the quality of their schools won over the ruling classes of town and countryside.

The Society, as an arm of the refurbished papacy, represented the international Church in action, as did the Capuchins, who also did stellar work in Germany with a somewhat less genteel clientele.[27] Gregory XIII recognized the pivotal nature of the mission to Germany, and in contrast to the illusions he cherished about eastern Europe he kept very well informed about affairs there. He spared no effort to support the nuncios and the missionaries, and he gave the impression that while he valued prayer as an aid to the Catholic restoration he valued money and diplomacy no less. He enlarged the Ignatian College in Rome with the conviction that if every year forty priests imbued with *romanità* were sent back to Germany the battle would be half won. He founded a college in Milan to serve German Switzerland and endowed other seminaries in various parts of the empire. And when it came to getting results, the pope did not disdain even compromise with Tridentine principles.

The most spectacular example of this was Gregory's connivance in the accumulation of five large German dioceses by Ernest of Bavaria. Such pluralism blatantly contradicted the letter—to say nothing of the spirit—of the Council of Trent. Moreover, the Duke of Bavaria's

---

26. Hubert Jedin, *A History of the Council of Trent* (St. Louis, 1957), I, 452.
27. Cuthbert Hess, *The Capuchins* (London, 1928), I, 284 ff.

younger son was a man of notoriously bad life. Yet Ernest became lord bishop of Freising, Hildesheim, Liège, Münster, and Cologne, all at once with the pope's blessing. Indeed, the Wittelsbach family was destined to dominate the episcopacy in the lower Rhine region for the next two centuries.

The anomaly was traceable not only to the high premium Gregory placed on the good will of the Bavarian ruling family or to his own easy conscience. It stemmed also from the peculiar character of the prince-bishoprics of the Holy Roman Empire. Wide tracts of Germany lay under the jurisdiction of prelates who ruled from diocesan seats like Würzburg, Salzburg, and Trier. While the other feudal holdings evolved into dynastic dictatorships the prince-bishoprics did not, because their sovereigns, bound by celibacy, could not father a legitimate child. Instead a complicated medieval procedure, similar *mutatis mutandis* to that prevalent in the rest of Europe, continued to determine episcopal succession. The cathedral chapter—a corporation of priests responsible for certain rubrical duties in the diocesan cathedrals—had the right to elect a new bishop. Once elected, he had to obtain the formal approval of pope and emperor before he could exercise his office or enjoy its income.

If by the mid-sixteenth century much of the chapters' power had been eroded, in the prince-bishoprics their traditional mandate, with its mixed religious-political consequences, still held good. At election time their members were notoriously open to bribes and other appeals to self-interest, but this problem was dwarfed by the complications brought in with the Reformation. In north Germany, where Lutheran princes could bring their influence to bear, chapters elected Lutheran bishops; this happened at Bremen and Magdeburg, among other places. Such results not only infuriated the Catholics but also put further strain on the imperial constitution, because the "ecclesiastical reservation" clause of the Peace of Augsburg "stated specifically that any prince-bishop who turned Protestant would lose his princely dignity. . . . But Protestant princes after 1555 had argued that the reservation did not preclude the election of a Protestant to an episcopal see."[28] The upshot was that every episcopal election was potentially a contest between the two confessions and an invitation to break the peace.

28. Hajo Holborn, *A History of Modern Germany: The Reformation* (New York, 1967), p. 285.

The Catholics, by the fact that they valued the office of bishop so much *in se,* were at some disadvantage in this competition. Indeed, Trent had based its reform legislation upon a lofty conception of episcopacy which troubled none of the Protestant theologies. Yet the circumspect Gregory XIII did not hesitate to set aside the ideal if he judged that that would secure the election of a suitable candidate to a German see. Ernest of Bavaria was only one of many dubious characters with whom the papacy felt it expedient to cooperate. More often than not the papal campaigns succeeded, and Ernest's triumph in the drawn-out, often violent struggle for the key bishopric of Cologne marked a kind of turning point in the ideological struggle for Germany. By 1585 the momentum had clearly swung to the Catholic side; by then, as Ernest added Münster to his cluster of dioceses, the Protestants had lost any serious hope of tipping the overall German balance in their favor. But the Catholic Church paid for its victory dearly in money and in a certain measure of surrender to Bavarian and Austrian absolutism. And more important than either was the moral compromise involved: it was no small irony that a favorite device of the Curia during these years was the issuing of dispensations to hold multiple benefices—the very procedure which brought so much grief to the Church in the first place.

3. THE ENGLISH MISSION

"To the last, to the defeat of the Armada," observed Froude in one of those sweeping obiter dicta that made his work so provocative and so unreliable, "manhood suffrage in England would have brought back the pope."[29] No universal suffrage existed, of course, and no statistics of the kind prepared for the politician in a mass democracy survive from the late sixteenth century. But because public opinion lacked formal organs of articulation does not mean that there was no public opinion and that public opinion did not matter. Its effect indeed was felt, as it always is, on a graduated scale, much more potent in the rich and clever than in the humbler elements of society. And it could be manipulated or managed or altered by the exercise of forceful leadership. Yet even then the aspirations of the multitude could never be ignored, and if a policy dictated from on high ran directly counter to those aspirations, it was the policy that had to give way.

29. Quoted in Algernon Cecil, *Six Oxford Thinkers* (London, 1909), p. 169.

Since Froude's judgment has been concurred in at least to some degree by other historians less given than he to colorful turns of phrase, it remains pertinent to ask why the Counter Reformation failed in England as dramatically as it succeeded in Poland and western Germany. In these latter places popular will played a decisive role: if Catholicism had not shown a capacity to arouse the enthusiasm of large numbers of nameless Poles and Germans, all the endeavors of popes, nuncios, Jesuits, and assorted local statesmen would have availed nothing. What evidence there is suggests that the people of England were similarly not unsympathetic to the Catholic religion and might have been ready as late as the 1580s to bring back the Mass if not the pope. Indeed, the most striking feature of Froude's assertion was his claim that before the Armada most Englishmen would have welcomed back not just the complex doctrines and sacramental practices which had their fullest expression in the supreme Catholic good work, the Mass, but even the religious sovereignty of the Roman See, which had been unpopular in England long before Henry VIII.

Yet no such restoration occurred. The paramount reason was the success of Queen Elizabeth and her advisers, acting out of differing degrees of personal religiosity, in identifying the interests of the regime and the nation with a Protestant ascendancy. They needed skill, patience, nerve, and, at times, luck to maintain what they had set up in 1559, because that institution was never free from the attacks that all compromises are heir to. That the government was popular—and the queen particularly so—as keeper of the peace and promoter of prosperity no doubt contributed to the widespread acceptance of its religious policy. Its control of the propaganda apparatus, notably the pulpit and the printing press, worked toward the same end. During the regime's first decade, when it was at its weakest, most people obeyed the law and went to church. At the end of that time, with the Catholic name blackened by the debacle of the Northern Rising and by Pius V's excommunication of the queen, the government might well have congratulated itself on the viability of the ecclesiastical settlement it had devised.

The Established Church, however, continued to suffer from sharp internal pains. Part of the trouble was due to the stubborn continuation of those very abuses the Reformation was supposed to have rooted out. Pluralism, for example, flourished even among the more respectable members of the new hierarchy; one bishop in the 1570s accumulated seventeen benefices besides his diocese, and not a few of his brethren systematically plundered their bishoprics by selling offices or by leasing church lands at advantageous terms to their own wives and children.[30] Often enough they arrived at their exalted positions by a simoniacal route which led them to prior agreements by which they alienated ecclesiastical resources to the benefit of the queen or her friends. The court ruled the Church, and the secularist interest of the court existed side by side with much pious rhetoric and with the genuine piety of men like Cecil and Francis Walsingham. The diocese of Oxford was left vacant for twenty-seven years so that the crown could appropriate its revenues.

This disarray in high places had its counterpart among the lower orders. It took more than a generation to provide the Church of England with even a modestly educated and motivated clergy.[31] Most of the "Massing priests" of Queen Mary's days conformed after 1559, but it was no easy task to mold parsons of this new order out of men who had seen so many new orders come and go. No institutions of clerical training, like the Tridentine seminaries, were developed in England, nor were the old universities adequate for such work. Elizabethan officials complained endlessly of ignorant, venal, lackadaisical, incompetent clergymen, a few of whom on a Sunday morning would preside at the Anglican service and then, immediately afterward and for the same congregation, say Mass.

But cryptopapists were not as serious a problem as Puritans, who had their own quarrel with the settlement of 1559. Their spokesman after 1570 was the eminent Cambridge divine Thomas Cartwright (d. 1603), whose literary assaults upon the establishment, echoed in a scattering of anonymous tracts, pamphlets, and admonitions, were interrupted by several periods of exile and one of imprisonment.[32] His protests nevertheless had their effect in the House of Commons and indeed across the country, at Puritan conventicles at which fundamentalist preaching combined with covert presbyterian organizing at the grass roots. Even though Cartwright's case did not differ essentially

30. J. B. Black, *The Reign of Elizabeth* (Oxford, 1959), p. 190.

31. See W. P. M. Kennedy, *Parish Life in the Reign of Queen Elizabeth* (London, 1914), but see also Joan Simon, *Education and Society in Tudor England* (Cambridge, 1966).

32. William Haller, *The Rise of Puritanism* (New York, 1938), pp. 11 ff.

from that which had been proscribed during the vestiarian controversy, it attracted, at least in some districts, the most fervent and accomplished clergymen and thus posed a new threat to the conformity laws.

The Church fared rather badly in the ensuing pamphlet war, because until the appearance of Richard Hooker (d. 1600) and Richard Bancroft (d. 1610), it did not possess an intelligible theory with which to counter the arguments of Cartwright and his friends. Still, except for a few eccentrics—the Separatists whose leaders the government hunted down and executed—the Puritan faction wanted to belong to the establishment, with which it disagreed on organizational, not doctrinal, grounds. It went about as far as it was ready to in the late 1580s with the satirical Marprelate tracts which lampooned the bishops and exposed the theoretical poverty of a Protestant episcopate under the thumb of a royal supremacy.[33]

But the queen was never deterred by theory or the lack of it, nor was she prepared to surrender one jot of the ecclesiastical authority hers by royal prerogative—not to parliament and certainly not to a little band of dissident preachers. Catholics would conform, Puritans would conform, all Englishmen would conform, and then England would be spared the ideological conflicts which were shattering other nations. Whether or not her divines could cite appropriate scriptural texts to justify the unique blend of Erastian, Protestant, and episcopal she had wrought, that blend would be enforced nonetheless. When an archbishop of Canterbury refused out of conscience to suppress the Puritan conventicles, Elizabeth suspended him, and the conventicles were suppressed. Increasingly the queen's legal instrument was the High Commission, a permanent court which by the 1580s had evolved out of the ad hoc royal commissions appointed since Henry VIII's time to check nonconformity. Even Cecil complained at this body's spirit and procedures, which, he said, were the same as those of the Spanish Inquisition. But the High Commission functioned relentlessly despite such criticism, and for all practical purposes the Puritans went underground to await a better day.[34]

---

33. See Donald McGinn, *John Penry and the Marprelate Controversy* (New Brunswick, N.J., 1966).

34. The standard study is still R. G. Usher, *The Rise and Fall of the High Commission* (London, 1913).

The real challenge to the Elizabethan settlement came not from within but from without, not from domestic dissidents who were few and timid, but from the forces of revived Catholicism on the Continent. Simply to state this, however, leaves out of account the complexities involved in what was perhaps the most glorious and most tragic chapter in the annals of the Counter Reformation.

The facts themselves are rather easily told. Before 1570 English Catholic resistance to the religious settlement was mainly a war of words launched from refugees abroad. A large number of controversial and devotional books, many of them of a remarkably high literary quality, were written by exiled Englishmen and printed on presses in Antwerp and Louvain until in 1566-1567 Calvinist uprisings put a temporary halt to such activity.[35] It is difficult to assess how widely these proscribed works circulated in England or how much effect they had. One contemporary claimed that a total of 20,000 copies were smuggled into the country, and a missionary, fifteen years afterward, said that these "books opened the way" and "did much to bring about [a] change in men's minds";[36] the Earl of Northumberland, leader of the Northern Rising, admitted he had read some of them. At any rate, the zeal with which Elizabethan apologists answered them suggests that they were not without some impact.

But books, even very good books, could not substitute for priests in the Catholic scheme of things, for Catholicism is peculiarly dependent upon the ministrations of a priesthood which ordination endows with the unique power to confect the Mass and the sacraments. A prolonged absence of priests from a country guarantees the Catholic Church's demise, a fact well understood by the Elizabethan government. In 1568 the English Catholic exiles showed that they understood it too by founding the Collège des Prêtres Anglais in the Flemish town of Douay. The college consisted of two large houses with their adjoining gardens and four students (three of them refugees from Oxford) who lived together and took their courses in the University of Douay. Their avowed purpose was to prepare themselves for the inevitable day when the settlement of 1559 would collapse and England would need trained

35. Southern, *Recusant Prose*, pp. 60 ff., lists 41 works published by Catholics and 23 by Anglicans during the "Great Controversy," 1559–1567.

36. William Allen, quoted by John Pollen, *English Catholics in the Reign of Queen Elizabeth* (London, 1920), p. 111.

priests. One of the first Tridentine seminaries and destined to be the most famous of them all, the college sent some 440 of its graduates into England before the end of Elizabeth's reign, of whom 98 were put to death for treason.

At the head of this new venture was a thirty-six-year-old Lancashire man named William Allen (d. 1594) who was shortly to become the acknowledged leader of the English Catholics exiled for their faith. Sometime Fellow of Oriel and Principal of St. Mary Hall, Oxford, Allen appreciated the importance of appealing to the idealism of the young Englishmen who rallied to him at Douay. The regime he established there was demanding without being harsh, the scholastic requirements high and yet geared to the practical and pastoral. The college intended to train missioners, not intellectuals, but missioners with attainments of mind notably lacking both among pre-Reformation priests and among the parsons of the new dispensation. Above all Allen emphasized self-sacrifice and the nobility of the godly adventure upon which the young men and their mentors had embarked. "A little government there is and order," he said of his program, "but no bondage nor straitness in the world. There is neither oath nor statute nor other bridle nor chastisement, but reason and every man's conscience toward other."[37]

The college existed on casual handouts even after it was partially subsidized by the pope and the King of Spain, and it suffered from the violent uncertainties of Netherlands politics—from 1578 till 1593 the exiles were obliged to go into exile as the college transferred its operations to the relatively peaceful setting of Rheims. But despite these troubles Allen's experiment prospered in many other ways. Douay became the scene of a renewed literary effort on the part of English Catholics, an effort crowned by Gregory Martin's biblical translation. Increasingly the college was seen as the living symbol of resistance to the Elizabethan government, and as such it attracted many curious travelers from England; most of them went away merely charmed by the courtesy with which they were received, but others—including not a few ministers of the establishment—were drawn to Catholicism by what they experienced at Douay, and some even stayed on and matriculated at the college. Indeed, one sign that many Englishmen did not yet consider the Catholic cause lost was the necessity to found

37. Thomas Knox, *Letters and Memorials of Cardinal Allen* (London, 1882), p. 76.

seminaries in Rome, Valladolid, and Seville in order to accommodate the candidates clamoring to be enrolled at Douay.

The first three of Allen's priests were ordained in 1573. Meanwhile, in the wake of Pius V's bull, the lot of Catholics in England was growing discernibly worse. Not only did parliament pass stiffer penal laws—for instance, after 1571 to bring into the realm any papal document whatever was a treasonable offense—but execution of the older legislation assumed a new urgency. Census lists of recusants were brought up to date, and local authorities, often lenient out of deference or friendship, were pressed and sometimes superseded by the privy council into stricter enforcement of the conformity laws.[38] As always, the test was whether or not an individual went to church, and though the masses appeared no more reluctant to do so than before, the tempo of harassment toward those who did refuse quickened throughout the 1570s. The distinguished Catholic jurist Edmund Plowden (d. 1585) may have been the exception to prove the rule. After Pius V's bull he declined to attend Anglican worship any more, and he suffered thereby considerable vexation; but as the most skilled legal practitioner of his generation Plowden managed to evade the full rigor of the law. Other Catholics, less talented than he and with fewer powerful friends, trooped obediently off to the village church, content perhaps to absent themselves only from the communion service, which in most parishes occurred only four times a year.[39]

Large if unenthusiastic congregations on Sunday morning guaranteed that unless challenged on its own ground the government's gradualist policy would eventually eliminate Catholicism from England. Convinced that this was so, William Allen in 1574 reached the momentous decision not to wait for a change in regime but to send his young priests immediately into their homeland and to keep alive by their ministrations the faith of at least some of the people. So the English mission was born, and Douay became a school for martyrs. The priests arrived singly as a rule or sometimes in pairs, disguised as soldiers or merchants. Once they had slipped into an English port they

38. William Trimble, *The Catholic Laity in Elizabethan England* (Cambridge, Mass., 1964), pp. 68 ff.

39. Some of the practical difficulties involved in practicing Catholicism are summed up in Hugh Aveling, "The Marriages of Catholic Recusants," *Journal of Ecclesiastical History*, XVI (1965), 68–83.

quickly disappeared, swallowed up, as it were, by the surrounding countryside. Not long afterward they would pop up in Cornwall or Yorkshire or in any county in between, only to drop suddenly from sight again. By 1578 more than fifty seminarists—as the Douay priests were called—had joined the mission and by 1585 more than 260.

They were without question a heroic band of men, and not only because of the courage with which they faced torture and death. Other strains and tensions played upon them, most notably perhaps the complete lack of organization and leadership and the loneliness involved in their haphazard apostolate. Almost without exception they abided by Allen's stern directive not to meddle in politics, but even as they carefully restricted themselves to offering Mass and hearing the accumulated confessions of fifteen years, they could feel the cold hostility of a public opinion which considered them enemies of queen and country. And of course they realized what later apologists on both sides have found so hard to realize, that in the sixteenth century religion was inseparable from politics.

Their numbers—even when swelled by the 200 more seminarists and the handful of Jesuits[40] who came later in the reign—were insignificant in a land which counted 8,000 parishes. A difference in temper between themselves and the people they had come to serve also hampered their effectiveness. The seminarists were products of a religious revival unknown in England. English by blood, they were continental by formation, and when they preached a Catholicism in the accents of Ignatius Loyola or Philip Neri much of what they said fell on deaf ears.[41]

Yet the mission had its impact, as the Bishop of London testified in the summer of 1577 when he complained "that the papists marvelously increase both in numbers and in obstinate withdrawal from church and services of God."[42] A few months later a Douay priest was arrested near Exeter. He had on his person a papal bull—expired, ironically enough—which listed the conditions for gaining an indulgence. For this offense Cuthbert Mayne was convicted of treason and was duly hanged, drawn, and quartered on November 30, 1577.

40. The glamour of Campion, Parsons, and Southwell has led historians greatly to exaggerate the part played in the mission by the English Jesuits.

41. A thesis well argued by John Bossy, "The Character of Elizabethan Catholicism," in Trevor Aston, ed. *Crisis in Europe* (New York, 1967), pp. 242 ff.

42. Philip Hughes, *The Reformation in England* (New York, 1954), III, 303.

The Elizabethan persecution now took a bloody new turn. Between Mayne's death and her own, Elizabeth I executed 183 of her Catholic subjects and arrested, fined, imprisoned, tortured, and deported thousands more. The 183 figure does not include those actually involved in conspiracies against the government or in plots against the queen's life, nor those peripheral cases like that of Northumberland who, condemned for his part in the Northern Rising, was yet offered his life if he would renounce his religion. Of the 183, eight were Irishmen, five Welsh, one Scots, and the rest English. One hundred twenty-three of them were priests, one was an unordained friar, and fifty-nine were lay people, three of them women. Fifty-four of the 183 were converts to Catholicism, and nine of them had been clergymen in the Established Church. They represented every social class except the peerage, and forty-nine of them were products of Oxford or Cambridge.

Debate has long raged as to whether these victims of the penal laws should properly be designated as martyrs or traitors. They were indeed all convicted of treason and suffered the barbarities prescribed as punishment for that crime. But of the total, 167 were guilty of treason as defined by statutes passed in 1559, 1563, 1571, 1581, and 1585—by laws, that is, which reflected the ideological complexion of the regime. Thus five priests and seven laymen were executed for specifically denying the queen's religious supremacy, one priest for smuggling into the country copies of a book by William Allen, one layman for obtaining a papal dispensation to marry his cousin, and, under the grim statute of 1585, ninety-four seminarists and Jesuits ordained abroad for simply being in England and thirty-four lay people for assisting those priests in some way. It would be extremely difficult to demonstrate that such offenders were traitors in the ordinary sense of the word.

The remaining sixteen, all of them priests, were indeed tried and convicted under the basic treason statute of 1352; they were judged guilty, that is, of conspiring against sovereign or state at certain definite times and places and under certain definite circumstances. But in no instance were such accusations proved. On the contrary, the trials were sham affairs, mockeries of justice, with not even a pretense of fairness and due process. The Jesuit Edmund Campion's conviction in 1581 was so blatantly contrived and caused so much revulsion at home and abroad that Cecil was moved to write a pamphlet in defense of the government's actions. And after Campion's death it became standard procedure to submit to those already convicted six propositions, "most proper," Cecil said, "to try whether men are traitors or not," the last of which Catholics called "the bloody question": "if the pope or any other by his appointment and authority do invade this realm, which part [side] would you take?" The purpose of this extrajudicial interrogation, often carried on under torture, was to provide propaganda, not evidence. The victims' opinions about a future contingency, wrung from them stretched out upon the rack, where duly published and assumed stature as part of the public record.

While English Catholics were thus killed and calumniated, other Catholics, very few of them English, looked to their own personal, dynastic, or ideological advantage. It was as natural for them as for the members of Elizabeth's council to see religious unrest as a political opportunity. Gregory XIII himself during these years took up one harebrained scheme and one worthless adventurer after another in hopes of mounting an anti-Elizabethan crusade, an "enterprise of England."[43] The only fruit of his endeavors was a papal invasion force composed of one doctor of divinity and eighty soldiers who landed on the Irish coast in 1579. Other potentates, like Don John of Austria, the young King of Scots, and Henry, Duke of Guise, did not accomplish even this much as they devised complicated projects of invasion dependent upon English Catholic armies which, like Ridolfi before them, they drew out of their own imaginations. William Allen and other exiled clerics were consulted about these fantasies, encouraged them, and so revealed how out of touch they were about real conditions in England.[44] Effective foreign intervention in any event was possible only from Spain, and for the moment Philip II was too distracted to embark upon an English adventure. And when his armada finally did come at the end of the decade, the Catholics like everybody else in England rallied to the defense of queen and country.

Elizabethan apologetic, which has long dominated sixteenth-century English historiography, now admits that there was in fact no connection between the 183 Catholic martyrs and the feckless plotters on the Continent, but it contends nevertheless that the government had to resort to violent repression because Jesuits and seminarists formed a

43. Whether Gregory XIII promoted the assassination of Elizabeth is discussed in Philip Hughes, *Rome and the Counter Reformation in England* (London, 1942), pp. 210 ff.

44. Thomas Hanley, "A Note on Cardinal Allen's Political Thought," *Catholic Historical Review*, XLV (1959), 327–334.

kind of fifth column. This explanation is, however, not in accord with the evidence. It puts too much stock, first of all, in the responses to the bloody question. It presumes too that Elizabeth knew as much about the foreign plots as historians know now. It rests, moreover, upon a dubious chronology which refracts the events of 1577–1585 through the prism of 1588. The fifth column theory finally is at odds with the government's own recorded interests. The captured priests were not examined about hidden caches of arms or the plans of the Duke of Guise; they were asked rather: Where did you say Mass? Whose confessions did you hear? Whom did you reconcile to popery? The campaign against the English mission remains incomprehensible unless one admits—and historians of the post-Christian era have difficulty admitting it—that otherwise enlightened people like Elizabeth I and William Cecil really considered religious nonconformity treasonable, irrespective of its relation to external dangers threatening the state. The 183 were in fact as much victims of ideology as were the victims of Mary I, of Alba, of the Spanish Inquisition, of St. Bartholomew's Day.[45]

The campaign at any rate succeeded brilliantly. What long years of passive obedience had begun the violence carried to conclusion, and Catholicism after 1585 ceased to be a significant factor in English life. Those who clung to the old religion did so by withdrawing from society until they became a tiny, eccentric minority, isolated from the public concerns of their own country and untouched by the enthusiasms of the continental Counter Reformation. The failure of the Catholic revival in England showed how crucial was the existence and control of the ecclesiastical structure. In Germany and Poland the structure of diocese and parish, of monastery, university, and school, though shot through with corruption, was nevertheless intact, and through it the fervor of the Counter Reformation could be transmitted to the people. In the England of Elizabeth this was never the case, and so one might guess that the movement never had a chance there. One might also guess, with as much confidence as Froude guessed, that long before the armada the masses of Englishmen had given up any thought of bringing back the pope.

<hr/>

45. I follow here Hughes's argument, *Reformation,* III, 342 ff., which is often dismissed but has never been disproved or even, so far as I know, answered. The indictment for apologetic includes Pollard, Black, Conyers Read, and even Neale, and of course many lesser lights.

Chapter Seven

HIGH TIDE

TOWARD the end of 1585, just as the persecution of the young priests he had sent into England was reaching its bloody climax, William Allen went to Rome. Ostensibly, his purpose was to seek from the new pope, Sixtus V, a reinstatement of the papal subsidy which helped support his seminary at Douay and later at Rheims and which during Gregory XIII's later years had fallen into arrears. He took a small house on the Via de Monserrato, next door to the English College Gregory XIII had founded. His rooms were simple and unpretentious: a desk, a bed, a few books were their most notable furnishings. It all had the look of a temporary lodging, fit for a man who hoped soon to be going home.

That hope, more than his seminary's financial distress, had brought Allen to the Eternal City. As he wrote shortly after his arrival in a secret memorandum to the pope, the moment was ripe to put into execution the much-debated Enterprise of England. If the pope would only make the cause his own, the heretical regime of Queen Elizabeth could be overturned with relative ease. Hardly more than ten or fifteen thousand men would be needed to subdue the island, Allen argued, because the overwhelming majority of her subjects longed to be free of the wicked queen and her tyranny. Serious resistance would probably come only from the sect called Puritans, concentrated in the southern and eastern counties, but they, said Allen, would be no match for Spanish soldiers and hardy Catholic yeomen from Lancashire.[1]

It was the typical screed of the political exile: plaintive and yet proud, blurring or omitting the difficulties involved in the proposal, trying to describe conditions with which one in fact had lost contact. William Allen had not seen England for sixteen years, and now he had to experience the exile's common hard lot, to wait upon the pleasure of others, to fit one's own burning aspirations within others' strategy. There was wide admiration in Rome for William Allen, and the pope

1. Garrett Mattingly, *The Armada* (Boston, 1959), pp. 56 ff., and Ludwig Pastor, *History of the Popes* (St. Louis, 1932), XXII, 38 ff.

let it be known that he intended to make him a cardinal, as he did in 1587. But even this honor had a bitter taste for Allen, who had to wait while his former students were being hunted and killed. The Enterprise of England could happen only when Philip of Spain was ready to take it on. And Philip was not yet ready.

I. LE BALAFRÉ

If Queen Elizabeth had felt the need to justify her policy of ideological repression, she might simply have pointed across the English Channel. The Kingdom of France, distracted by sectarian pluralism and paralyzed at its administrative center, drifted ever closer to total anarchy. St. Bartholomew had changed nothing, for simultaneous with the massacre the fourth civil war had broken out. The shepherds indeed had been struck: Admiral Coligny and other senior Huguenot leaders were dead, while the young Bourbon princes, virtually prisoners at court, meekly heard Mass to the accompaniment of Catherine de' Medici's mocking laughter. But the sheep, in defiance of the biblical maxim, did not scatter. Especially in the south of France, the Protestant resistance, hesitant at first, grew apace with the realization that the savagery of St. Bartholomew did not mean the government was any less indecisive and feeble than before. The Huguenot masses, spurred on by the Old Testament rhetoric of their ministers, more than held their own in the Midi.

The conventional military operations of the fourth war, however, occurred farther north, where royalist armies besieged two of the most important Huguenot surety towns. Sancerre, after a heroic defense, fell on August 19, 1573. At La Rochelle, however, where the besieging forces were commanded by the king's brother, the Duke of Anjou, the Protestant populace survived the fierce artillery bombardments and infantry assaults until mid-summer, when Anjou learned he had been elected King of Poland. This news provided the government with an excuse to lift the siege for which it no longer had stomach; the successor of Sigismund Augustus, pledged by the Confederation of Warsaw to religious toleration in his newly acquired realm, could hardly be party to the razing of a Protestant town. So the war sputtered out with a truce which renewed the guarantees of St. Germain (1570) and therefore denied St. Bartholomew even the dubious virtue of *Realpolitik*. Meanwhile, the Huguenots in the south paid scant attention to these formalities; they asserted more forcefully than ever their practical independence by organizing themselves into a constitutional community with its own court and supported by its own taxes. It was said that this confederation, centered at Nîmes and Montauban, could put 20,000 soldiers into the field.[2]

The king's government, out of money and ideas, helplessly watched the unfolding of events over which it had no control. Charles IX had been a weakling on his best days; after St. Bartholomew he settled into a permanent state of despondency and ill health which promised an early grave. The queen mother connived as ever among the factions, but to little effect. Nor could she stop the publication of Huguenot pamphlets like Francis Hotman's *Franco-Gallia,* which, departing radically from Calvin's position, called into question the validity of an unpopular monarchy and which, incidentally, heaped particular abuse upon Catherine herself.[3] Theory thus began to catch up with practice, and the crown was too weak to do much about either. The crown was too weak even to prevent Protestant Rouen's embargo on corn passing up the Seine and Catholic Paris's embargo on wine passing down.

The next crisis arose out of a realignment of the factions. Serving with Anjou at La Rochelle had been Navarre, Condé, one of Constable Montmorency's sons, and Catherine de' Medici's youngest son, the Duke of Alençon. Their conversations in the trenches led ultimately to the formation of that party to be known as the *politiques.* At first, however, they were dubbed simply "the malcontents," a term which especially suited Alençon, who combined restless, frustrated ambition with the usual vices of the Valois family. But the Bourbon princes of the blood were unhappy too in their semi-imprisonment, and the brothers Montmorency, unburdened by their late father's old-fashioned loyalties, remembered that they were, after all, kinsmen of Coligny and ancient enemies of the House of Guise.

The *politiques* were Catholics; some, like the Bourbons, only nominal, others like Damville, the ablest of the Montmorency, rather serious Catholics. They agreed in any case that the religious problem was insoluble and that therefore the good of the nation demanded some kind of policy of confessional live and let live. But nothing of this sort could happen so long as each side was committed to the ideological

2. J. W. Thompson, *The Wars of Religion in France* (New York, 1909), pp. 454 ff.

3. Jean Mariéjol, *La réforme et la ligue* (Paris, 1904), p. 146.

conversion of the other. The solution appeared to lie in a rapprochement between the more liberal elements in both camps, not indeed as Christian believers but as Frenchmen. The *politiques* accordingly made overtures to those Huguenot leaders more interested in freedom for themselves than in a crusade in behalf of the pure gospel. The result was a merger between, so to speak, the Catholic left and the Protestant right.

The wisdom of hindsight has credited the *politique* program with more substance and credibility than it actually possessed at the time. What seems good secular sense now did not necessarily quiet ideological passions then. Besides, this agreement between warring aristocrats was viewed with deep suspicion by the rank and file of both sides who had long noted the tendency of the lords to take care of each other.[4] Even so, the maneuver might have worked had it not been compromised from the beginning by factional politics and personal ambition. Was Alençon interested in religious peace or in more power for himself? Were the Montmorency anxious to heal the wounds of the nation or to bring down the hated Guise?

Damville, governor of Languedoc and royalist commandant in the south, was at any rate the key figure. Early in 1574 he was deep in negotiations with the Huguenot confederation. Condé meanwhile escaped from court and made his way to Germany, where he sought aid from the Protestant princes. King Charles responded by clapping Alençon, Navarre, and other malcontent leaders under house arrest. Out of this series of stratagems emerged the fifth civil war, though nothing much happened before the king's death, without male issue, in May. Indeed, nothing much happened through the summer as Catherine de' Medici assumed the regency once more, and her favorite son dawdled his way home from Poland, wasting precious time with revelry in Venice and a conference with Charles Borromeo in Milan.[5] By September, when Anjou, or Henry III as he now was, finally arrived in France, the war had begun in earnest, for Damville and the Huguenots in the south had entered a formal alliance.

Against his better judgment the king marched toward the Midi only to find that he could neither sustain his army nor arouse a weary public

4. Davis Bitton, *The French Nobility in Crisis* (Stanford, 1969), p. 11.
5. For Borromeo's influence on Henry III see Frances Yates, *The French Academies of the Sixteenth Century* (London, 1947).

in support of his ill-defined cause. Individual towns and whole districts declared their neutrality and called down a plague on the soldiers of both sides. Confessional allegiances at the highest echelons tended to match the overall confusion. While d'Uzès, a notorious Protestant iconoclast, was the royalist general, the fervently Catholic Damville led the Huguenots, and Turenne, who would have preferred, he said, to be a dog than to be a Calvinist, was their field commander.[6] By the end of the year no decisive engagement had been fought, and the king retreated back across the sullen countryside, ostensibly in order to go to Rheims to be crowned and married (February, 1575), but really because he had no other military choice. A fitting conclusion to the hapless campaign was the death (December 26, 1574) of the Cardinal of Lorraine, who, as his last misguided service to the monarchy, had promoted it.

The war dragged on aimlessly in the west and south, a matter of sieges and depredations, more a contest between guerrillas than between recognizable armies. Then in September, 1575, Alençon escaped from his confinement at court (to be joined by Navarre the following February), and Condé, with English and Montmorency money, hired 6,000 Germans and 6,000 Swiss together with some *reiters* from the Rhenish Palatinate whose Elector was looking lustfully at Metz, Toul, and Verdun. On October 10 the vanguard of this host tried to cross the Marne at Dormans, sixty miles from Paris; Henry of Guise drove them off but was himself shot and severely wounded. A pistol ball mangled his left cheek and ear, leaving him hideously scarred and earning him the nickname he afterward gloried in, *le Balafré*, Scarface.[7]

With the new year of 1576, 20,000 mercenaries crossed the Meuse and headed for the Loire valley, where in March they were joined by Alençon. That young man was now in a position to dictate terms to the royal brother he hated so much. By terms of the Peace of Monsieur[8] (May, 1576) the king guaranteed complete freedom to the Huguenots (except in Paris and at court), granted them eight surety towns, granted surety towns as well to Alençon, Condé, Navarre, Damville, and almost everybody else among the *politique* hierarchy,

6. Mariéjol, *La Réforme*, p. 166. Turenne became a Protestant later.

7. Henry Sedgwick, *The House of Guise* (New York, 1938), pp. 252 f.

8. "Monsieur" was the formal title of the king's eldest surviving brother. Alençon became Duke of Anjou at this time, but in the text I continue to use his earlier name.

expressed formal regret and promised rehabilitation for the victims of St. Bartholomew, and pledged to pay the troops Condé had hired to invade the kingdom. This last humiliating provision testified to the depths to which the warlords and their ideological allies had brought the monarchy.

But the Peace of Monsieur proved no more permanent than its predecessors. Indeed, the very magnitude of the Protestant success sowed the seeds of its later defeat. However well organized and dedicated they were, however much factional support they might secure, the Huguenots still remained a minority and a rather small minority at that. And now the Catholic majority, stirred like Catholics everywhere in Europe by the various currents of the Counter Reformation, aroused itself really for the first time since the crisis had begun seventeen years earlier. One of the provisions of the Peace of 1576 gave the governorship of Picardy to Condé, with Péronne as a surety town. When the prince came to collect his spoils he discovered that neither the local commandant nor the populace at large would admit a heretic viceroy. At that moment the Catholic League was born. Or rather the first of hundreds of leagues was born, because what happened in Picardy was a local phenomenon, imitated indeed all over the country with astonishing speed and similarity, but as yet without national direction and purpose. The leagues did not at first form a party, but they might some day, and in the meantime their spontaneity and universality showed that French Catholics finally were beginning to organize.

Henry of Guise's factional instincts told him how important control of these new cadres could be. He issued a manifesto inviting the leagues to accept him as their leader in the eternal struggle against heresy. While he protested loyalty to the crown, the duke also committed himself to protect the rights of the estates general. The threat implicit in such a statement was not lost upon the king, and for one of the few times in his life he moved swiftly. Declaring himself the head of all Catholic associations, he summoned the representatives of the estates to meet him at Blois in November, 1576. So, only six months after the Peace of Monsieur, the quicksilver was running the other way. The estates, completely dominated by Leaguers, clamored for extermination of the heretics, though typically, when they adjourned in March, they had voted no money to pay for that pious project. Yet Henry III had for the moment greatly strengthened himself. In one stroke he had seized the initiative, checkmated Guise, and harnessed for his own purposes a powerful popular movement. He hastened to launch the sixth civil war.

It lasted from March to September, 1577, and consisted chiefly in a moderately successful royalist campaign in the Loire valley and the Midi, commanded by the Duke of Mayenne, Guise's less talented, less popular, and therefore, in the king's eyes, less dangerous brother. But the crown's most signal victory was the collapse of the *politique*-Huguenot alliance. Alençon, sniffing the wind of public opinion, hastily deserted his allies, and Damville, after some hesitation, did the same. Condé meanwhile quarreled with Navarre; the bourgeoisie of La Rochelle, longing for peace, quarreled with the bellicose proletariat; and the fervor of the Huguenot rank and file, compromised perhaps by association with the cynical *politiques,* appeared suddenly to wilt. Betrayed, weary, and disillusioned, the Protestants agreed with hardly a murmur to the terms of the Treaty of Bergerac, which sharply restricted their privileges and hinted at pogrom in the future. This is *my* peace, said the king exultantly, as the former one was my brother's. He thanked the Catholic leagues for their service and promptly dissolved them.[9]

He was a bewildering figure, this last ruler of the House of Valois.[10] Intelligent, charming, articulate, Henry III was also devious, cruel, perverse, and, worst of all, lazy. Days and weeks went by with no official business done, as the king wiled away the time gossiping about art and philosophy, or playing with his innumerable lap poodles, or preening himself in women's clothes, jewelry, and cosmetics. Self-respect meant nothing to him, or honor; he led his dissolute favorites, his *mignons,* through a dizzying round of exotic entertainments and then insisted they join him in equally extreme penances. Nights of exhausting pleasure were followed by days of self-flagellation, sackcloth, and ashes, because the king desired "to satisfy God and his conscience . . . without changing his heart."[11] Some saw divine retribution in the fact that like his royal brothers before him Henry had no son and that therefore the false-hearted Alençon remained his heir.

That Henry III's intentions were better than his deeds is shown in

9. J. H. Elliott, *Europe Divided, 1559–1598* (New York, 1968), pp. 253–255.
10. See Philippe Erlanger, *Henri III* (Paris, 1948).
11. Mariéjol, *La Réforme,* p. 215.

the various programs he put forward for administrative, legal, and fiscal reform. But these plans once promulgated seldom received serious implementation. Driven by his own extravagance and mismanagement, the king used any expedient to raise money. The sale of offices multiplied, including now even membership in the privy council, where of all places disinterestedness should have prevailed. In 1576 alone the government sold 1,000 patents of nobility for 1,000 livres each. It borrowed from individuals, from municipalities; it defaulted on payrolls. On one occasion it seized the treasury of the city of Paris. Extraordinary taxes were levied on the clergy; ecclesiastical lands were sold.[12] Commerce was practically ruined by the imposition of capricious duties. And still the king had hardly enough money to get from day to day. Everything he touched bore the mark of corruption: a clergy riddled by simony, a venal police, a people impoverished and lawless.

The chaos widened and deepened. Gangs roamed across the country; "armies" of one religious persuasion or other were mobilized overnight and then preyed upon communicants of both religions indifferently. The rivalries at court grew more violent than ever, with Guise challenging Montmorency and the *mignons*, brilliant swordsmen as well as foppish dandies, ready to take on all comers. Alençon quarreled with his brother again and went off to romance in England and intrigue in the Low Countries—to which places the king was happy to see him go because he was such an infernal nuisance at home. The queen mother, still a believer in personal diplomacy, had no better luck reconciling her sons than in soothing the Huguenots of the Midi when she toured the south from October, 1578, to June, 1579.

The scope of the tragedy did not exclude elements of the absurd. In November, 1579, the Prince of Condé seized the Netherlands border town of La Fère as compensation, he proclaimed, for the governorship of Picardy he had been deprived of three years earlier. This act of petulance set off the seventh civil war or "the lovers' war," so called because the jealousies of the principals' various wives and mistresses allegedly provided the driving force behind it. Fittingly enough, Catherine de' Medici tried to placate Condé by offering him marriage to the

12. See Ivan Cloulas, "Un Aspect original des relations fiscales entre la Royauté et le Clergé de France an XVIe siècle, La Conversion de l'Alienation de 1587," *Revue d'Histoire Ecclésiastique*, LV (1960), 876–901.

king's sister-in-law, but the prince apparently preferred La Fère. In the south Navarre took the field in support of his cousin and demonstrated at least his personal courage and military capacity—he captured the royal stronghold of Cahors in May, 1580. Other factional chieftains, however, notably Damville, flatly refused to fight, and Mayenne, though he campaigned a little, spent more time in secret negotiations with, of all people, the Elector Palatine. The soldiers on both sides could not be persuaded that this preposterous conflict offered them any special opportunities for loot, and so, after Condé fled to Germany and La Fère was retaken by the royalists, the war did not so much end as subside into the usual anarchy. The Peace of Fleix (November, 1580) simply confirmed the *status quo ante*.

The process of gradual disintegration probably would have continued indefinitely, as in fact it did for the next three years, had Alençon not died (June 10, 1584).[13] When he died, worn out by dissipation and failure before he was thirty, the accumulated troubles of the Kingdom of France assumed an entirely new dimension. Now Henry of Navarre, head of the House of Bourbon, was heir to the throne, and Navarre was a Huguenot. For all his indolence, Henry III was never a stupid man, and even as his brother lay dying he dispatched one of the *mignons* to Navarre's little court at Nérac with the plea that Navarre declare himself a Catholic. Otherwise, the king warned, the Catholic majority would coalesce against them both, for France would never accept a Protestant king. The only way to stop the Guise from overwhelming the dynasty was to deprive the Guise of the ideological issue. Whether Navarre saw the wisdom of this argument, whether he knew even then that some day he would have to pay for Paris by going to Mass, he was not ready yet to exchange the security given him by his Huguenot supporters for the assurances of his Valois cousin who was noted neither for truthfulness nor for fixity of purpose.

Events at any rate proved the king a good prophet. Henry of Guise, distracted during recent years by grandiose schemes to rescue his cousin, Mary Queen of Scots, and put her on the English throne, now had closer to home an opportunity suited to his immense ambition. And the instrument of coercion was also at hand: the Catholic League sprang to life again, and this time Guise, his brothers, and like-minded lords did not let control of it slip from their fingers. Assured of plenty

13. Henri Hauser, *La prépondérance espagnole* (Paris, 1948), pp. 129 ff.

of foot soldiers, they asked the pope for a blessing and Philip of Spain for money. Philip, who had disdained Guise's English adventures, found this proposal more to his liking. By the secret treaty signed at the Guise seat of Joinville on December 31, 1584, Philip promised to subsidize a program to keep Navarre off the French throne.

Independently of these proceedings, the Catholic League of Paris, egged on by the city's priests, was mounting a strident propaganda campaign against Bourbon and Valois alike.[14] Parisians had always loved the Guise, ever since the days of Duke Francis, and an alliance between them and the dashing *Balafré* was natural and inevitable. This coalition was too much for the king. Confronted by Guise's demands he squirmed and wept and sent his mother to plead, but it was no use. Guise, whose sudden power was based upon a whole nation's resources of hatred and misery, was adamant, and the king, on July 7, 1585, capitulated. By the Treaty of Nemours he agreed to abrogate all previous toleration edicts, to proscribe the Huguenots completely, to take away from them all surety towns, and to deprive them of all public functions. And he declared that the heir to the throne was the aged and safely celibate Cardinal of Bourbon. Navarre said later, when he heard the provisions of the treaty, half his mustache turned white.

2. THE FARNESE BRIDGE

Only a month after Henry III surrendered to the Catholic League at Nemours, a Spanish army captured Antwerp, and the Counter Reformation, viewed in its political and military aspects, achieved its summit. That victory also determined that out of the seventeen provinces of the Netherlands two modern nations would emerge rather than one.

The first of them began to form in 1572 when William, Prince of Orange, defeated by the Duke of Alba in the south, fled to Holland, and placed himself at the head of the Calvinist irregulars who had seized The Brill earlier that year.[15] The association was not an altogether comfortable one, because Orange did not share the ideological zeal of his lieutenants, and he worried that their fanaticism might in the long run wreck the chances of a truly national movement against

14. Nancy Roelker, *The Paris of Henry of Navarre.* (Cambridge, Mass., 1958), pp. 101 ff.

15. See above, pp. 171 f.

Spain. Yet the prince was not in a position to do more than persuade, and when his arguments went unheeded he had to accept as deplorable but necessary the looting of churches, murder of priests, and formal proscription of Catholicism that invariably accompanied the Beggars' successes. And succeed they did: before long all the towns of Zeeland and Holland, except Amsterdam, were in their hands. Orange could hardly quarrel after so many defeats with the single native Netherlands force which had actually won some victories. He acknowledged this fact early in 1573 by announcing, without notable enthusiasm, his own conversion to the reform.

The Catholic majority along this northwest coast remained by and large passive, probably because if they resented the depredations of the Beggars they feared and hated the Spaniards far more. Alba, as soon as the danger of invasion from France had passed, turned north and with his wonted efficiency and disregard for human life reduced rebel concentrations in Mechlin, Friesland, and Groningen. But Holland and Zeeland (a cluster of innumerable little islands directly south of Holland) presented an invader with special problems. These two provinces constituted "a country with unequalled natural advantages for defense and in open communication with the sea," and as such they could defy the vaunted Spanish infantry.[16] Between their dikes and their rivers they established a secure base from which the revolution could proceed.

The Spaniards, however, did not give up easily. Amsterdam, which for years stoutly resisted Orange and the Beggars, opened a bridgehead into north Holland, and much of 1573 was taken up by a Spanish siege of nearby Haarlem. The city capitulated finally, but when the Spaniards tried to move farther north, to Alkmaar, they were driven off by seawater when the Dutch opened the dikes and flooded the countryside. The campaign collapsed by the end of the year, and Alba was recalled in disgrace. The new governor, Louis de Requesens, Borromeo's former antagonist in Milan, mounted another assault upon Holland in 1575, and though the Spaniards fought with prodigious skill and bravery—one detachment in full battle gear waded at low tide through water up to the neck in order to attack a Zeeland town—the character of the country and the persistent courage of their foes were more than they could handle. Their well-deserved reputation for ferocity and cruelty also contributed to their ultimate defeat, because it

16. Pieter Geyl, *The Revolt of the Netherlands* (London, 1958), p. 120.

served to stiffen the Hollanders' resistance. This was compounded by Philip II's constant failure to pay his soldiers, which led to endless mutinies and breakdowns of discipline, and by his almost criminal folly in pursuing military objectives in such a region without adequate naval support. In conventional land warfare the Spaniards remained invincible, as they proved again in April, 1574, by crushing one more army of German mercenaries and killing its commander, Orange's brother, Louis of Nassau. But in the northwest corner of the Netherlands their defeat by 1576 was complete and final.

More a diplomat than a soldier, Requesens offered an olive branch to the provinces in the form of a repeal of the "tenth penny" and a general pardon. Overtures like these, however, had come very late in the day, and not only for Holland and Zeeland. The governor reported to Philip that the south was filled with Orange's sympathizers and that the local nobility, whatever its protestations, had no particular zeal for the Spanish and Catholic cause. It was indeed the linking of these causes that presented the gravest problem, as Requesens discovered when he attempted to negotiate directly with the states of Holland and Zeeland. Requesens died (January, 1576) before these talks accomplished anything, and at about the same sensitive moment Philip announced his government's bankruptcy. His troops, garrisoned in all the chief towns of Flanders and Brabant, responded by going on a bloody, mutinous rampage.

Madrid maintained silence about a successor to Requesens, so central authority in the Netherlands, such as it was, passed to the Council of State with its mixed Spanish and native membership. The latter element soon gained the ascendancy, and a new stage in the revolution began. In July the council declared the soldiers, still out of control, to be public enemies. In September the States-General were summoned without reference to the king-duke; at first only Flanders, Brabant, and Hainault were represented, but then one by one the other southern provinces sent delegates. The news that Don John of Austria would be the new governor did nothing to slow the accelerating forces of alienation, and though the customary ritual assurances of loyalty to crown and Church were given, the States-General proceeded to set up their own executive and to hire their own troops.

The Prince of Orange saw these developments as the best chance for Netherlands independence and unity since the recall of Granvelle fifteen years before. Here at work in the richest and most populous provinces was a grand coalition of magnates and urban oligarchs now determined to be rid of the Spaniards. It was an assertion of the venerable Burgundian spirit of liberty rather than of militant Calvinism, a spirit much more congenial to Orange than the ideology of the Beggars, whom in his heart he still considered pirates. One conviction at any rate bound the peoples of the Netherlands together: the foreign troops had to go. And on November 4, 1576, any waverers were disabused: the royal garrison at Antwerp suddenly fell upon the city it was commissioned to protect, and before the infamous "Spanish Fury" was spent thousands lay dead and injured. During the rape of Antwerp, Orange was only a few miles away, at Ghent, parleying with the leaders of the States-General. The result of their deliberations was a treaty which pledged the provinces to the expulsion of the king's soldiers and to the reduction of the king himself to a primacy of honor. The Pacification of Ghent—so called because it formally ended the state of war between Holland and Zeeland and the rest of the provinces—also committed its signatories to an extraordinary States-General which would settle all matters of detail, including the religious question. Meanwhile, the edicts against heresy were suspended, and Holland and Zeeland promised to refrain from anti-Catholic activity outside their own territories.[17]

Unhappily for the cause of Netherlands unity, religion could not long be relegated to the realm of detail. For the moment, however, Orange savored the fruits of a victory won largely by his own perseverance in the face of adversity. The forlorn figure of the hero of Lepanto testified to the apparently sweeping nature of that victory. Don John slipped into Luxembourg, the one province that had stayed aloof from the Pacification, after an incognito horseback ride across France. He brought with him neither men nor money and was armed only with a detailed list of instructions from his brother which emphasized the need for the time being to placate the natives, even to the point of recommending that the new governor not choose his mistresses from among prominent Netherlands families. As always, Don John fretted under the shadow of his illegitimacy, and he suspected that Philip acted out of spite in assigning him to the chaotic Low

17. Henri Pirenne, *Histoire de Belgique* (Brussels, 1910), II, 77 ff.

Countries instead of allowing him to indulge his own romantic plans to rescue Mary Queen of Scots.

However reluctantly, Don John obeyed orders, and in February, 1577, he formally agreed to evacuation of foreign troops in a document called, inappropriately as events soon showed, the Perpetual Edict. But not until May when the last Spanish soldier had left the country was he permitted to come to his capital at Brussels, and when he got there he saw to his chagrin the streets lined with the States-General's troops. Orange, however, was alarmed at even this modest and straitened entry of Philip's governor, and he worked hard to prevent it. It seemed that three distinct parties were struggling to emerge: two, Don John's and Orange's, which aimed in their different ways to impose a unitary regime upon the Netherlands; and a third, composed of the Catholic nobles who controlled the States-General, which intended a restoration of the older ideal of local autonomies bound in a loose confederation. But Don John soon took action which simplified the situation and narrowed the available options. During the summer of 1577 he moved restlessly from place to place, complaining loudly all the while of the machinations of Orange's agents; in June he was at Mechlin, and then, on July 24, he and his personal bodyguard seized the citadel at Namur, proclaimed martial law, and sent out a call to Madrid for troops. The response across the country to this repudiation of the Perpetual Edict was electric: provincial estates and the great Flemish towns like Brussels, Ghent, and Antwerp declared for the Prince of Orange, who, with the power of Holland and Zeeland at his back, was ready for the call.

For the next six months Don John waited in his little fortress for the *tercios* to come back. Meanwhile convulsions reminiscent of the year of the iconoclasts, 1566, shook the southern Netherlands. Social discontent joined hands again with religious fanaticism, and Calvinist preachers harangued large crowds eager to hear about the need to destroy Romish idolatry and the corrupt social order. The States-General could do nothing to stem this new militancy, and Orange could do little, because distasteful as it may have been to him, his own power base in Holland and Zeeland rested precisely on the same combination of forces. As the tempo of violence increased, doubts about the revolution spread not only among Catholics and men of property, but also among the people at large who wondered whether Protestant zealots offered a

better promise of peace and stability than the Spaniards. The suspicion
was especially pronounced in the Walloon provinces of the south
whose Celtic, French-speaking inhabitants already had reason to feel
estranged from the northern Dutch.

Early in 1578 reinforcements finally reached Don John, and at
Gembloux he put to rest forever the vacillating policy of the States-
General. Their vastly more numerous army took one look at 3,000
Spaniards and promptly ran away. Don John advanced northward and
captured several towns, but he had not sufficient force to press his
advantage and Philip refused to send him more. Yet, if the Spaniards
were reduced to marching and countermarching, internal disintegration did their work for them. Orange from his headquarters in
Antwerp watched in dismay as ideological conflict steadily undermined
the Pacification. He proposed a plan for religious peace whereby in any
district in which a hundred families requested it a second religion
would be tolerated. Though the prostrate States-General duly endorsed
this expedient, it was from the outset a dead letter, and Catholics noted
grimly that wherever the revolutionary forces had the upper hand—
even at Antwerp—Catholicism was proscribed and its adherents persecuted. Orange was confronted with a vicious circle he tried to break in
vain: the Calvinists, fearful of counterrevolution, attacked Catholics as
sympathizers of Spain, and the Catholics, once persecuted, became in
fact much more sympathetic to Spain, thus provoking a fresh outburst
of Beggar violence.

It did not help the States-General to import a bogus governor in the
person of an amiable nonentity like the Austrian Archduke Mathias,
because that gentleman, with no constituency of his own, did not bring
conventional respectability but only more confusion and ridicule on the
revolutionary regime. It did not help to hire still another army of
German mercenaries who mutinied and pillaged as soon as the English
money used to pay them ran out, and who did not have the mettle to
face the Spaniards anyway. By the end of 1578 the Pacification of
Ghent was no more than a scrap of paper, and despite Orange's furious
diplomacy the hope of a United Netherlands had faded beyond recall.
In the north Holland and Zeeland pressed for the creation of an independent Calvinist state to which were attracted like-minded elements
in the Dutch-speaking two-thirds of the country as well as those con-
tiguous towns and provinces upon which Holland and Zeeland could

exert direct military pressure. Out of this agitation emerged the Union of Utrecht, which began to function, despite Orange's protests, on January 23, 1579. A week or two earlier the Walloon lords signed a protocol at Arras by which they agreed to secede from the States-General, make their peace with Spain, maintain the Catholic religion, and organize the south into a confederation. The split into confessional blocs had come, and it was to endure. With a heavy heart the Prince of Orange did what he had to do; he threw in his lot with the Union of Utrecht.[18]

The previous October a momentous change had occurred in the cast of this drama. Don John of Austria died at age thirty-three, bitter to the end at Philip II's neglect, and was succeeded as governor by Alexander Farnese, Prince of Parma.[19] Farnese united in himself the bastard lines of two eminent houses: his father's grandfather had been Pope Paul III, who had set up the duchy of Parma as a dynastic fief for the Farnese family, and his mother, that same Margaret of Parma who had governed the Netherlands from 1559 to 1567, was the natural daughter of the Emperor Charles V. These relationships gave Farnese a station in life and opened a career for him; Philip II, after all, was his half-uncle, and Don John was too. His great-grandfather was still pope in 1545 when baby Alexander's baptism was one of the events of the Roman social season, attended by no fewer than nineteen cardinals.

Farnese spent his boyhood and youth at the Spanish court, an honored guest and relative indeed, but also a hostage for his father's good behavior as an ally of Spain. Don John and Farnese, who were the same age, were constant companions and, in some ways, kindred spirits. But whereas Don John never outgrew his youthful romanticism, Farnese tempered his with strong admixtures of shrewdness and caution. After his marriage he indulged little in the casual swordplay and womanizing expected of one of his class, and though like Don John he was always something of a knight-errant, he also displayed the characteristics of a careful man of affairs. Despite his education and early associations, he had none of the Spanish caballero about him; resourceful, supple, and yet, when the occasion called for it, hard as

18. G. N. Clark, "The Birth of the Dutch Repubic," in Lucy Sutherland, ed., *Studies in History* (London, 1966), pp. 124 ff.

19. Léon van der Essen, *Alexandre Farnèse, Prince du Parme, Gouverneur Général des Pays-Bas*, 5 vols. (Brussels, 1933–34), is the standard and very detailed biography.

steel, he epitomized rather the man of the Italian Renaissance, sprinkled over with the pieties of the Counter Reformation. He fought gallantly at Lepanto, and he led the reinforcements sent to Don John in 1577. A year later he assumed the troubled mantle himself. The man and the hour were admirably matched. No one was better suited than Farnese to take advantage of the disarray into which the Netherlands revolution had fallen.

His task was at once military and diplomatic. Yet at a deeper level he understood, as none of his predecessors did, that the arts of negotiation and war had to be judiciously employed in the service of an overall policy of reconciliation. He knew that a simple military solution of the kind Alba had tried to impose ten years earlier was out of the question. On the other hand, the excesses of the Calvinists and the inability of Orange and his allies to govern effectively offered an opportunity to win not just victories in the field but the ultimate victory of the renewed allegiance to the king on the part of most or even all the seventeen provinces. Farnese did not therefore disdain the soft word or the peruasive argument. If a bribe could capture a city for him, he paid it and saved his soldiers' energies for another day. During the fourteen years of his governorship, his charm, joviality, unassuming demeanor, and uncanny faculty for discerning other men's strengths and weaknesses were as effective weapons as the guns and pikes of his army.

The velvet glove, however, could not do without the mailed fist, and so Farnese's chances of success depended on whether he could put that army to effective use. The factor that united Netherlanders of all religions and parties was resentment against the foreign troops who had been guilty of so many outrages. The governor, who was also captain general, had at his disposal about 30,000 men of all arms—though this figure fluctuated in tune with the fiscal stability of the crown. The heart of this force were the *tercios* or regiments of the famed Spanish infantry, which constituted roughly one-third of the total. Each *tercio* was divided into ten or twelve companies (*banderos*) of 120 men commanded by the officers who had recruited them. They were professional soldiers with both the good and bad qualities that phrase implies. About eighty men in a company were armed with pikes and the rest with the heavy matchlock guns called harquebuses, a composition that determined their basic formation: a phalanx of massed pikemen with sharpshooters at front and angles to keep an enemy from thrusting at the square. The advance of the Spanish *tercios* always produced chills of terror, not only because of their formidable battlefield record but because as mercenaries they compensated themselves for any arrears in pay by preying on the local populace. In the Netherlands this habit was intensified by the Spaniards' ferocious brand of Catholicism. Though many of them were simply scoundrels and adventurers, they still saw themselves as Jesus' chosen hammers of the heretics, and they considered the relatively tolerant Netherlands Catholics as little better than heretics.[20]

It was a tribute to the fighting qualities of the *tercios* that King Philip's army in the Low Countries was always called Spanish, even though the bulk of the infantry units were Italian, German, and Walloon. Farnese also commanded separate divisions of cavalry—perhaps 3,000 horsemen—and artillery. (Custom had it that gunners were, strictly speaking, technicians rather than soldiers and hence were forbidden to participate in looting a captured town.) This motley, multilingual, multinational band of violent men could be, if properly led, the most formidable military machine in Europe. Whether it could be also an instrument of reconciliation was another and larger question.

In Farnese the soldiers found their general, their charismatic leader, and, more importantly, their master. He was tough, just, and yet respectful of their various customs, and in exchange for strict control over their potential for mayhem he gave them victory, the one thing they valued more than money. He was the kind of commander who shared every hardship endured by his men; he lived in the trenches, ate soldiers' fare, stood night watch, carried faggots in his own calloused hands when a redoubt had to be built. Ill or well—and in the uncongenial Flemish climate he was often ill—he was with them, in as much danger as they were. He made it his business to call the men in the ranks by name and to remember the little towns in Spain or Italy they had come from. They adored him, even if he was a fierce disciplinarian, punishing their depredations swiftly and harshly. More than once a gang of mutineers was reduced to obedience simply by a face-to-face confrontation with the captain general.

20. Léon van der Essen, "Croisade contre les Hérétiques ou Guerre contre des Rebelles? La Psychologie des Soldats et les Officiers espagnols de l'Armée de Flandre au XVIe siècle," *Revue d'Histoire Ecclésiastique,* LI (1956), 43–78.

With the army in hand, Farnese could proceed to implement his policy of conquest and reconciliation. His most signal advantage over his opponents was that he had a plan and the strength of will to see it through. "Cool, incisive, fearless, artful," observed the stern Congregationalist J. L. Motley with grudging admiration, "he united the unscrupulous audacity of a condottiere with the wily patience of a Jesuit."[21] The Union of Arras served him as a base of operations.[22] He cultivated the Walloon nobles, and when they demanded (1579) the evacuation of Spanish troops as a price for their collaboration, the governor smoothly agreed, aware that now back in the king's camp the Walloons would soon themselves call for help from the king's men. So it turned out, and before the end of 1580 Farnese had his *tercios* back again. And not too soon, because early in 1581, Orange in desperation revived his old dream of enlisting French help, and he persuaded the rump States-General to offer executive sovereignty to the Duke of Alençon. So the King of France's brother moved the scene of his intrigues to the Netherlands and worried Farnese through much of 1581 with the renewed danger of a strike across the French frontier into the Walloon provinces. Alencon at the head of some Huguenot freebooters did manage to capture Cambrai, which amounted more to a diversion than to the massive French intervention Orange had hoped for. The duke, however, had another arrow in his quiver; at the end of the year he rushed off to England to court Queen Elizabeth, a woman old enough to be his mother, who, if flattered by his proposal, had the good sense to reject it. By the time Alençon arrived sulking in Antwerp (February, 1582), Orange had lost considerable face among his followers for entrusting the revolutionary cause to "this tainted scion of a despised house."[23]

Farnese meanwhile almost quietly launched his great campaign. Reinforced by levies freed now from the Portuguese adventure and backed by a Spanish economy sounder than it had been in years, he was enabled to open a two-front war against the insurrection. The operations in the northeast, however, though strategically important as

21. *The Rise of the Dutch Republic* (New York, 1883), III, 372. Hopelessly biased, Motley's volumes remain the most colorful and thorough account of the struggle in the Netherlands.

22. See Charles Wilson, *Queen Elizabeth and the Revolt of the Netherlands* (London, 1970), pp. 72 ff.

23. Geyl, *Revolt*, p. 182.

a direct threat to Holland, took second place to the struggle in Flanders and Brabant, "the debatable land," as Motley was to call it, which lay between the two hostile confederations of Utrecht and Arras. Tournai, the only Walloon stronghold loyal to Orange, surrendered to the Spaniards in late 1581, and news spread quickly, as the governor intended it should, how generous his terms had been and how impeccable the conduct of his troops. Oudenaarde fell in April, 1582, and Lier in August. On each occasion the performance at Tournai was repeated; there was no sack and, aside from a preacher or two hanged, no reprisals; captured regulars received good treatment and offers of repatriation, and while religious toleration was firmly denied, Protestant inhabitants were permitted to depart with their movable property and to arrange for the sale of their real estate. The impression created by this relatively benign behavior served Philip II's cause better than another army, because it sapped the will to resist among a war-weary population and encouraged defections even in regions where the Spaniards had not yet appeared.

As Farnese probed deeper into the debatable land, paralysis gripped the leadership of the revolution. The Spaniards invested one city, one district at a time, when concerted action might have slowed them or even stopped them. Steenwyk on the border of Holland fell, and Zutphen was betrayed into Farnese's hands by its commandant. In Antwerp Alençon worried less about the Spanish advance than about the snubs he received from his Dutch subjects, who did not bother to hide their contempt for him. It was clear by now that Henry III had neither the means nor the desire to come to his brother's rescue and that therefore Orange's French policy had failed again. Alençon would have been in an impossible position even had he been a far better man than he was. In January, 1583, he resolved on the desperate gamble of coup d'état, but he proved no more adept at mutiny than at anything else. Antwerp suffered through a "French Fury"—Alençon's men ranging through the streets shouting "Vive la messe!"—before the duke ran away to die in France a year later, the most thoroughly discredited public figure of his generation.

And the Spanish offensive rolled on: Dunkirk fell, and then Eindhoven, and then Niewpoort and Audenhove. The new year of 1584 brought no respite. Farnese captured Ypres in March, Bruges in May, Dendermonde in August, and when Vilvoorde surrendered on September 7 he closed the steel net around his strategic objective, the watershed of the Scheldt. Orange meanwhile had slipped out of Antwerp and gone back to Holland, to Delft, with his new bride and fourth wife, a daughter of Admiral Coligny. The States-General soon followed them. On July 10, 1584, as he walked out of his dining room and through a crowd of petitioners, William, Prince of Orange, was shot to death by a cabinetmaker's apprentice.

On the same day a Spanish detachment seized a fortress on the bank of the Scheldt some ten miles north of Antwerp.[24] Farnese was now moving into position for the final assault. Before him lay the narrow circle of eminent Flemish cities, Ghent, Brussels, Mechlin, and Antwerp, all of them linked by the habits of centuries to the River Scheldt or its tributaries. The assassination of Orange, the evil fruit of Philip II's ban, had little effect upon what was about to happen.

Farnese's plan to invest and starve out all four cities at once involved considerable risk, in that it meant dividing an army already depleted by casualties and by the necessity to garrison areas previously conquered. The manpower problem was compounded by desertions, because Philip II chose this moment to fall behind in the military payroll. But if he could not count upon the unswerving support of his king, Farnese could by now depend on the blunders of his enemies, who once more failed to concentrate their superior numbers and so let the great cities fall into the Spaniards' hands one by one.

Ghent capitulated first, and quickly, in September, 1584. The moral impact of this victory meant much—Ghent had been the most active Calvinist center outside Holland—but the stores of matériel and equipment Farnese captured there meant more. For if Brussels and Mechlin might hopefully succumb to conventional tactics, Antwerp was another matter, and Antwerp, both as city and as symbol, was the greatest prize of all.

Direct assault was out of the question, and Antwerp, whose population of 100,000 was ten times as numerous as Farnese's striking force, appeared invulnerable to siege. The city lay on the east side of the Scheldt, perhaps twenty miles upsteam from the point where the river flowed into the North Sea amid the maze of islands of rebel Zeeland. Antwerpers were understandably confident that Farnese, practically

24. The entire fourth volume of van der Essen's *Farnèse* is devoted to the siege of Antwerp.

without ships, could never cut off their city from the north. The river was a half-mile wide and sixty feet deep at mid-channel, with tidal fluctuations up to eleven feet. Even if the Spaniards raised batteries on both banks, as in fact they did, the accuracy of cannon fire at such range was too inconsistent to inhibit the Zeeland fleets from sailing upriver loaded with provisions.[25]

The complicated system of dikes provided, if need be, another means of defense. The river itself was diked on both sides, and other connecting walls ran off at various angles to protect the land on the west (Flanders) bank and the east (Brabant) from the sea. The most important of these was the ocean dike called the Kouwenstijn, which met the Scheldt dike at a right angle about fifteen miles north of Antwerp and on the same (Brabant) side of the river. Shortly before his death Orange had argued that the Kouwenstijn should be pierced immediately, because the low, spongy land east of the river guaranteed that an inundation there would in effect bring the ocean to the gates of the city and assure its relief; the same could not be said of an inundation on the west side nor of one produced by opening only the river dikes. The Antwerpers, however, rejected this proposal as wasteful—12,000 head of cattle grazed on the pastures behind the Kouwenstijn—and in any case unnecessary, since the Spaniards could never block the river.

Yet there was a way. When Farnese first proposed to build a bridge-barricade across the Scheldt a few miles below Antwerp, his lieutenants were as skeptical as the Antwerpers themselves. The technique had indeed worked in other siege operations, but no other stream posed difficulties as formidable as the Scheldt. Farnese remained adamant; he had not come this far to have the prey elude him at the last moment. First he divided his little army in two, sending half of it across the river to occupy and fortify the Kouwenstijn. Then he scoured the Netherlands to accumulate the vast quantities of stores necessary to construct the bridge. He chose the site with care. At a bend in the river, where it was a little narrower and where, on the Flanders side, a sand bar thrust out almost to mid-channel, he threw up forts on either bank with 2,400 feet of rushing current between them. The rebels, still indifferent to the tactical importance of the Kouwenstijn, took the half-measure of opening the dikes which flooded the land west of the river. But, as Orange

25. See Mattingly, *The Armada,* pp. xvii f., for a summary of the kinds of guns available.

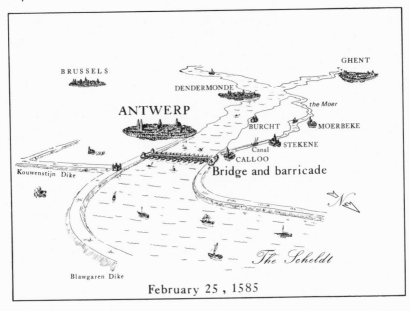

February 25 , 1585

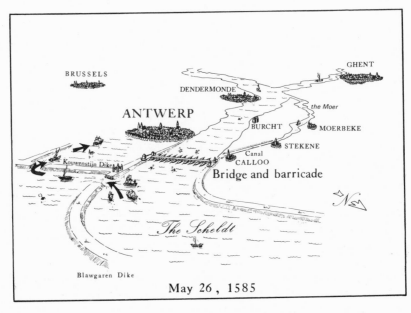

May 26 , 1585

had predicted, this device proved more a nuisance than a hindrance to the Spaniards, who made camp on high ground or simply lived in their forts on the river dike. Indeed, Farnese turned the shallow inundation to his own advantage by bringing a convoy of barges loaded with supplies down the Scheldt from Ghent and around the guns of Antwerp by way of the flooded countryside to his own camp. When the rebels countered by closing the dikes and drying up this avenue, he put to work gangs of peasants and soldiers who in a few feverish weeks dug a twelve-mile-long canal linking the bridge-site at Calloo with the town of Moerbeke and the River Moer, a Scheldt tributary to the west of Antwerp, over which the barges could float unimpeded. By these means the precious matériel piled up through the autumn: 10,000 planks, 1,500 ships' masts to reinforce the pilings, chains, cables, tar, 200,000 nails manufactured in Ghent. In November construction began when a hundred tree trunks, from 30 to 70 feet long and pointed at one end, were driven into the river bed. On February 25, 1585, the last of 32 large barks was chained and anchored into place, 10 feet from its neighbor, to form the center span where the water was too deep for pilings. The River Scheldt had been barricaded and Antwerp was doomed.

The Farnese bridge was a tribute to skill, endurance, and, above all, indomitable will. The best engineering methods of the day were employed in its construction, and the physical exertions of the men who built it were almost beyond belief. "This army," Farnese reported to Philip II, "is reduced to so pitiable a state that your majesty would be horrified. They have suffered as much as a man can suffer."[26] But in another sense the bridge was Farnese's unique achievement, because without him it would never have been attempted or, when spirits were flagging, it would have been given up. To the end the Antwerpers and Zeelanders refused to believe the project could succeed, and though they made some desultory efforts to harass the bridge builders, they gave the governor general much less trouble than ice-clogged water, tides, illness among his troops, and shortage of money. Now, with 170 guns trained up river and down from the bridge and adjacent forts, time and hunger would finish the task.

Desperation drove the besieged now to act with an energy they had neglected before. Fire ships were launched downriver, and one of them,

26. Van der Essen, *Farnèse*, IV, 29.

early in April, penetrated the outworks, blew a yawning hole in the bridge, and killed 800 Spaniards. But a missed signal meant another missed opportunity, and the followup attack, planned from Zeeland and Antwerp together, never came. Within days Farnese had repaired the damage, and the bridge stood a solid barrier again. On May 26 the rebels made their final, supreme effort. In a rare display of concerted action, they attacked the Kouwenstijn simultaneously from north and south, but after eight hours of the fiercest fighting of the war the Spaniards repulsed them. "It was a very close thing," said Farnese.

The formal surrender took place in August. By that time the hungry residents of Antwerp knew that Brussels and Mechlin had fallen, and they refused to suffer any longer for a cause which seemed irretrievably lost and for a religious ideology about which most of them felt no enthusiasm. During the negotiations, Farnese was at his diplomatic best, charming, persuasive, and benign. The terms he offered were exceedingly generous. On August 27, 1585, he rode into Antwerp, a slender, muscular, black-bearded figure, resplendent in his Milanese armor encrusted with gold and topped by an enormous lace ruff. But even at that triumphant moment he was careful not to bruise the sensibilities of those he had conquered and still hoped to reconcile. Only Walloon and German detachments accompanied him, and by his side native Netherlanders. Shortly afterward, however, he hurried back to his camp downriver for a special celebration. His beloved Spanish and Italian comrades had decked his bridge with flowers and spread on it a great feast. There, standing together above the river they had tamed, they drank a toast to the brave.

Far away at the Escorial the news reached Philip II after he had retired for the night. Courtiers who remembered how impassively the prudent king had read the dispatches from Lepanto were astonished to see undisguised joy take hold of him. He rushed out of his apartments and pounded on the door of his favorite daughter, Isabella. By the time the startled girl got her door open, her father was skipping back down the corridor. "Antwerp is ours," he was shouting. "Antwerp is ours!"[27]

27. *Ibid.*, p. 136.

Chapter Eight

CLIMAX

THE CAPTURE of Antwerp was the crest of a wave that had begun to rise six years before. At ten o'clock on the night of July 28, 1579, Antonio Pérez, Philip II's chief secretary, left his master's study after another exhausting day's work on the official correspondence. He had no inkling of the royal displeasure until, an hour later, he was arrested and charged with extortion, trading in state secrets, and suspicion of murder. Philip thus struck down without warning his closest confidant, and in so doing signaled a dramatic shift in the direction of Spanish policy. Pérez's guilt or innocence mattered less than his leadership of the faction, long dominant in the king's councils, which stood for caution, retrenchment, and peace in western Europe. Philip had now determined to repudiate these positions and their spokesman, Pérez, along with them.[1] On August 1, Cardinal Granvelle, that old warhorse among Hapsburg diplomats, appeared at court for the first time in fifteen years; he had in his pocket a letter from the king: "I have special need of your person and your help in the tasks and cares of government. . . . The sooner you come the happier I shall be."

The energetic Granvelle soon brought the administration at Madrid to a level of efficiency it had seldom achieved in the past. But the cardinal's competence was not the main reason Philip rescued him from the peripheral chores he had been performing in Italy and elevated him to the post of prime minister. Granvelle was an imperialist of the school of Charles V, under whom he had received his diplomatic training. He was not a Spaniard himself; his only loyalty was to the dynasty, and he considered the interests of Spain to be part of the internationalist Hapsburg enterprise rather than the other way around. As he had represented the hard line in the Netherlands during the early 1560s, so, two decades later, he was known as one who favored

---

1. Gregorio Marañón, *Antonio Pérez* (London, 1954), pp. 202 ff. The murder charge —the murder of Don John of Austria's secretary—came later. The king himself was deeply implicated in this crime.

bold initiatives in the north and west and who did not mind the risk of confrontation with France or England. His ascendancy meant that the prudent king had also assumed a more adventurous position.

As always with Philip the process of reappraisal was ponderous and slow. Several factors, however, which had nothing to do with his own personality or Granvelle's, combined to push him toward new ambitions and new belligerence. First among them was the unexpected prosperity of the crown of Castile. After the bankruptcy of 1575–1576, the receipts of silver from America suddenly and spectacularly increased, thanks largely to improved production methods in the Peruvian mines.[2] Over the long term this bullion flood, which continued unabated through the rest of the reign, may have helped to undermine the stability of prices and the Spanish economy generally, but for the moment it put greater strength in the king's hand than he had ever enjoyed before. Nor did he have to expend much of it in the Mediterranean area. Venice, convulsed by internal difficulties, had ceased to be a serious rival, the papacy was more or less subservient, and détente had been arrived at with the Turks: a treaty signed in 1581 and renewed at three-year intervals formalized the sullen disengagement which had been a fact almost since Lepanto. The Italian provinces could on occasion be troublesome—especially Sicily, where the tradition of violence and vendetta ran centuries deep—but by and large they remained quiet, unsure perhaps that the domination of Spain was as bad as the anarchy their grandfathers had suffered from.

The most compelling motive, however, for Philip to listen to the imperialist designs proposed by men like Granvelle and to turn from the Mediterranean toward the Atlantic was the dynastic opportunity offered him in Portugal. The stage was set in 1578 when King Sebastian died without issue and was succeeded by an aged and celibate great-uncle, the Cardinal Henry, Archbishop of Braga.[3] It was clear that within a short time the royal house of Avis, which had maintained Portugal's independence for centuries and had created a colonial empire, would be extinct and the throne vacant again. Philip II immediately began to press his claim, which according to the canons of dynastic practice was exceedingly strong. His mother had been the

2. See the table in Earl Hamilton, *American Treasure and the Price Revolution in Spain* (Cambridge, Mass., 1934), p. 34.

3. H. V. Livermore, *A History of Portugal* (Cambridge, 1947), pp. 254 ff.

cardinal-king's eldest sister, and none of the throng of candidates who declared their availability—even Catherine de' Medici discovered a royal Portuguese ancestor in her genealogy—could seriously challenge his right in blood. Within Portugal, however, there existed serious if disorganized and far from unanimous opposition to the idea of Philip's succession by those who dreaded the prospect of being absorbed politically and culturally into a Castilian superstate. Philip gave them his best assurances on this score and countered their intrigue with propaganda and bribery on a colossal scale. The affair reached a ludicrous climax when the epileptic and somewhat addled King Henry was persuaded to petition the pope for permission to marry a thirteen-year-old girl—he was sixty-seven—in hopes of producing an heir. Philip had little trouble stopping this process at Rome, and, for good measure, he dispatched some Jesuits to Lisbon to remonstrate with the old man and to harangue him on the glories of priestly celibacy.

Henry died in January, 1580, and in June 30,000 Spanish troops crossed the frontier. They were commanded by Alba, whom Philip, at Granvelle's urging, recalled from bitter retirement for one last campaign. Within four months the iron duke had stamped out the last spark of native resistance and, what eased Philip's deeper worry, garrisoned the whole country in such a way as to make foreign intervention quite unlikely.[4] In December, 1580, when Philip I of Portugal, as he now was, summoned his cortes to meet him the following spring, he was in full and secure possession of his new kingdom. And why not, he said in parody of Caesar: "I inherited it, I bought it, I conquered it."

If in fact Philip uttered so uncharacteristic a remark, its cynicism did not spill over into the final Portuguese settlement. Indeed, as Professor Lynch observes,

a sixteenth century monarch could hardly have conceded more to a conquered country. . . . He undertook never to hold the Portuguese cortes outside the kingdom and never to legislate on Portuguese affairs in a foreign assembly; the office of viceroy was to be conferred only on Portuguese or members of the royal family; administrative, military, naval and ecclesiastical appointments were to be reserved exclusively to Portuguese; the country was to be garrisoned only by Portuguese forces; for consultation on

4. Fernand Braudel, *La Méditerranée et le monde méditerranéen à l'époque de Philippe II* (Paris, 1966), II, 465.

Portuguese affairs the king was to retain . . . advisers . . . of Portuguese birth who would compose a Council of Portugal; the colonial trade was to remain unchanged, administered by Portuguese officials, conducted by Portuguese merchants and carried in Portuguese ships; finally all frontier customs between Castile and Portugal were to be abolished.[5]

Philip carefully kept these pledges, out of expediency no doubt but also out of constitutional principle. His realms were united only in his person, and he ruled each of them in conformity with its own particular traditions. The sole and fateful exception to this otherwise consistent policy was his treatment of the Netherlands. As for Portugal, the succession-conquest of 1580 resulted not in annexation but in a union of crowns which lasted for sixty years. It meant the sweet and the bitter for the Portuguese, who shared in Spain's brief golden era and then in its swift demise. Portuguese overseas possessions, for instance, benefited from incorporation into a system in which specie was plentiful; neither Brazil nor the East Indies had silver deposits like New Spain. But by the same token, when Spanish commerce began to deteriorate and to be roughly handled by Dutch, French, and English competition, the Portuguese suffered as well. With Philip as its king Portugal came to learn firsthand how mixed a blessing was *la prépondérance espagnole*.

The king resided among his new subjects until 1583, but even after he returned to the Escorial—having left his Austrian nephew the Archduke Albert in Lisbon as viceroy—his thoughts still lingered in the west. He agreed with Granvelle that the crown of Portugal had tipped the balance of power in his favor. His Iberian home base, with its long Atlantic seaboard, was now united and totally secure, his empire in America and the Orient was enormously increased, his navy had doubled in size. Perhaps the time was coming when a final blow could be struck at the heretics of England and Holland and the *politiques* of France. Meanwhile, he sent men and money to Alexander Farnese, who was dragging his siege guns into position before the great cities of Flanders and Brabant.

I. SIXTUS THE GREAT

In April of 1585, when the cardinals retired into conclave for the election of a successor to Gregory XIII, a certain amount of anxiety was evident in Rome over the increasing power and belligerency of

5. John Lynch, *Spain Under the Habsburgs* (New York, 1964), I, 309.

Spain. The Portuguese succession and Farnese's campaigns in the Low Countries were, it was widely believed, only a prelude to an attempt to impose Spanish hegemony over all of western Europe. Some curial officials, especially those most closely identified with Gregory and his policies, argued that Spain's past services to the Church should make such an eventuality welcome. But many others worried that the Catholic champion might soon grow so strong as to constitute himself a threat to the integrity of Catholicism. Orthodox and admirably pious, Philip II nevertheless practiced a blatant caesaropapism and tyrannized over churchmen in his domains as much as Queen Elizabeth did in hers. He was about as docile a son of the Holy See as William of Orange had been, or the sultan. Moreover, in an age when men commonly blurred the distinction between the sacred and the secular, Philip went further and acted as though his policies had been framed in heaven. What he wanted, God also must want; the aggrandizement of Spain and the triumph of true religion were, for him, convertible realities. This assumption was hard for a pope to gainsay, for with France prostrate there did not exist a significant political force which was Catholic and yet not Spanish. So the problem the papacy confronted was not to determine its need of Spain's friendship, because that in a dangerous world thronged with heretics and Turks went without saying. The problem, especially for the pope elected in 1585, only weeks before the fall of Antwerp, was rather how much in terms of independence Spain's friendship would cost.

Felix Peretti,[6] born (1521) into the squalor of rural poverty, proved a hard bargainer indeed; though he attained great success and eminence, there was always something about him of the eternal peasant, shrewd, grasping, wary. His father was a sharecropper, his mother a domestic servant. He came from the mountainous district northeast of Rome, where he spent a harsh childhood working in the fields and tending the family's pigs. His Franciscan uncle saw to the clever boy's basic education and no doubt influenced his choice of vocation. As a young friar Peretti relentlessly pursued the academic degrees which would open a whole new life for him; in 1548 he was awarded a doctorate in theology. His fiery pulpit oratory eventually caught the attention of Michael Ghislieri, the grand inquisitor, who brought him to Rome and

6. For Peretti's early life see Ludwig Pastor, *History of the Popes* (London, 1932), XX, 23 ff.

watched over his career. Peretti rose through the ranks of the Franciscan order, although in the process he gained many enemies due to his brusqueness and severity. But these very qualities recommended him to Ghislieri, who, when he became Pope Pius V, made Peretti a bishop and then (1570) a cardinal. He passed into eclipse, however, during the long pontificate of Gregory XIII, who disliked all friars on principle and Peretti in particular, because, among other reasons, of the high style in which the Franciscan cardinal lived once his austere patron was safely dead.

When the conclave began on April 21, 1585, Peretti was mentioned as an outside possibility; his age (sixty-four) was about right, and his enforced retirement since 1572 was a notable advantage in that it had softened earlier antagonisms toward him and had relieved him of any responsibility for the setbacks of Gregory XIII's last years. As so often happened in papal elections, the favorites checkmated each other, and after a three-day deadlock, the cardinal electors turned to Peretti, the compromise candidate, more or less acceptable to the various factions. The result left few scars, for the new pope—an ugly little man with a heavy nose, clusters of wrinkles on his high forehead, and small, piercing eyes—was not unpopular in the Curia or in the city. No one expected great things of him, but it was predicted that Sixtus V (as he called himself) would do his best to maintain the political and religious integrity of the Holy See. That may well have been the major underassessment of the century.

Sixtus V gave Rome five of the most exciting years in its long history. Felix Peretti's earlier career had provided scant warning of the imperiousness and frantic energy with which he now assaulted every papal problem. Nothing escaped his eye; no project was too big or too little to be secure from his furious intervention. He lifted the face of the ancient city, revamped the central administration of the Church, established the governmental structure of the Papal States as it was to endure for nearly 300 years. He was a peasant-pope who hoarded heaps of gold and silver in the castle of Sant' Angelo: poor princes, explained the former swineherd, are a laughingstock, especially in these wicked times when everything is accomplished by money. No one laughed for long at Sixtus, not the Roman baronage, whom he reduced to a tame court nobility, nor the Sacred College of Cardinals, of whom he made a civil service. He was a draconian legislator who defined contraception as homicide and declared adultery a hanging offense.[7] Sodomites, man or boy, he burned alive. He fought the bandits who infested his territories—as many as 20,000 of them at the end of Gregory XIII's reign—with a ruthlessness worthy of the bandits themselves.[8] Nor was he a respecter of persons: to a delegation protesting the flogging of an imperial ambassador arrested for wearing arms in the streets, the pope replied grimly that everyone in Rome would obey his laws.

Yet for all his forcefulness, for all the color of a tempestuous personality which dazzled the eyes of beholders during and since his time, Sixtus V originated hardly any of the programs for which he is remembered. He inherited policies and proposals, and the real significance of his pontificate lay in the success he enjoyed in bringing them to fruition. Not that he would himself have subscribed to such a view; he often ignored one of the most sacred canons of papal etiquette by publicly criticizing and belittling his predecessors. But Sixtus was not in fact an innovator or a creative thinker; his peculiar gift was a fund of energy and self-confidence which allowed him to overcome hesitancies and to sweep aside obstacles in achieving practical goals. The same impatience which left him incapable of serious scholarship suited him admirably as a man of action. Thus, before his election he published a critical edition of the works of St. Ambrose which abounded in textual errors due to his inclination "to dominate the manuscript [rather] than to let himself be dominated by it";[9] and as pope his unwarranted interference quite ruined the new Vulgate text of the Bible, the supreme editor going so far in one instance as to omit arbitrarily five whole verses. By contrast, in dealing with pragmatic affairs his restless drive often achieved what others had only hoped for. When, for example, experts told him that it would take ten years to execute the cupola of St. Peter's Basilica as Michelangelo had designed it decades before, the pope remarked that even engineers and architects could be hanged for thwarting the will of Christ's vicar. Twenty-two months later the world's most famous dome had been vaulted.

Under the same kind of fierce compulsion and at the same breakneck speed Rome was thrust into the age of the baroque.[10] New churches

---

7. John Noonan, *Contraception* (New York, 1967), pp. 432 ff.
8. Leopold von Ranke, *History of the Popes* (New York, 1901), I, 308 ff.
9. Pastor, *Popes*, XXI, 210.
10. See J. A. F. Orbaan, *Sixtine Rome* (London, 1911).

and palaces sprang up; old ones were repaired and enlarged. At enormous cost in money and labor the third-century aqueduct was restored to provide fresh spring water for the fountains of Rome; not one to indulge in false modesty, the pope triumphantly named it the Acqua Felice. A whole new network of streets was laid out, and hundreds of rutted roads repaved, opening the city to carriage traffic for the first time and bringing to life districts deserted for centuries. To make room for spacious piazzas and wide avenues that crossed each other at right angles, Sixtus ruthlessly tore away the city's ancient and medieval clutter and in so doing destroyed countless monuments to Rome's imperial and Christian past. Antiquarians were horrified, and genuine humanists no less so when the pope ordered the statues of the apostles Peter and Paul to be placed atop the columns of Trajan and Marcus Aurelius, and when he removed from the circus the huge obelisk Caligula had brought from Egypt and erected it, as though a trophy of paganism conquered, in St. Peter's Square. But most Romans rejoiced that their city had become more livable, that the pope's public works had created thousands of jobs, just as they rejoiced at the draining of the malarial Pontine marshes and at the various initiatives Sixtus took—with, however, only limited success—to encourage agriculture and industry. As for foreigners, they marveled at what was wrought in so short a time. "Here am I in Rome," wrote one of them about 1590, "and yet I cannot find the Rome I know, so great are the changes in the buildings, the streets, the piazzas, the fountains, the aqueducts, the obelisks and the other marvels with which Sixtus has beautified this old and ruinous city."[11]

Yet Sixtus's mammoth tasks of renovation fulfilled plans conceived and dreamed about by earlier popes; his was a triumph of will, not of intellect. But that was precisely the hallmark of Counter Reformation Catholicism, the religion of will, the religion of good works, whose vibrancy could be expessed in piles of stone and fountains gushing sweet water. The speculative problems had been settled at Trent, the theologians had fashioned their theoretical responses to Protestantism, and now had come the time for action. To Sixtus's blunt, practical mind, simple efficiency was another way to witness to revival. His predecessors had discussed the administrative reform of the Curia, and

11. Pastor, *Popes*, XXII, 305.

Gregory XIII had even initiated it. They all realized that the consistory—the weekly meeting of pope and curial cardinals at which all business was haphazardly taken up—was cumbersome and wasteful, but somehow they feared to abandon it. Sixtus felt no such qualms.[12] He fixed the number of cardinals at a maximum of seventy, assigned at least three of them to each of fifteen permanent departments called congregations—six for the government of the Papal States and nine for the business of the Universal Church—and thus established the Vatican bureaucracy which was to function virtually unchanged for centuries. The consistory continued to meet every Wednesday as before, but now only as a formality, only as an occasion for Sixtus's interminable monologues which, often as not, described how a poor peasant boy had grown up to be a very rich pope.

Sixtus V managed the feat of being a spendthrift and a miser at the same time. While he expended huge sums on his various projects, especially his buildings, he also accumulated a cash reserve which allowed him to boast that he was the richest prince in Europe. And he was in the sense that the treasure he kept at Sant' Angelo put at his disposal specie in amounts unavailable to sovereigns with much greater overall resources. The treasure—the use of which he carefully restricted to extraordinary crises like the invasion of the Papal States or a general expedition against the Turks—was the pope's all-absorbing obsession, because he was convinced that through it alone could the freedom of the papacy be guaranteed.

He was not altogether wrong, at least for the short term. But the damage this policy did to economic development by withdrawing so much capital from circulation was incalculable. The same might be said about the means Sixtus was driven to to increase his revenues. None of them was his invention, but he expanded them all drastically. More offices than ever before, honorific and administrative, were put on sale and at higher prices. The public debt grew at an alarming pace, and the annual interest due on papal bonds—Sixtus floated eight of these *monti* in five years—almost doubled. Ultimately the million and a half people who lived in the Papal States had to foot the bill. Sixtus V

12. The term "consistory" as used here should not be confused with the Genevan consistory (see p. 130 *supra*) which itself differed from the Lutheran consistory. See Owen Chadwick, *The Reformation* (Harmondsworth, 1964), p. 69.

levied eighteen new taxes on them, though not even he could get them to accept one on table wine. There were, to be sure, rigidly enforced economies within the administration, but these were never enough to balance the budget, nor enough to prevent Sixtus's new Rome, crammed with bureaucrats, grandiose monuments, and idle rentiers, from sucking up the productive lifeblood of central Italy.[13]

Sixtus practically closed one ledger of expenditures. Papal subsidies to the Catholic princes, which had soared to more than 700,000 écus during Gregory XIII's time—300,000 to Henry III, 200,000 to the Austrian Hapsburgs, 200,000 to Ernest of Cologne[14]—almost stopped under his successor. Sixtus readily used the lure of his cash reserve as a diplomatic tool, but as Philip II discovered when he was mobilizing the invincible armada, the pope subsidized only after, not before, the fact; until a venture had already achieved some success, no money to support it came from Rome.

Sixtus was as anti-Spanish as he dared to be. The restoration of France as a great power, and so as a Catholic check upon Philip II's drive toward universal monarchy, remained his major foreign policy objective, but there was little he could do directly to accomplish it. The contentions in France put him in worse than a dilemma; he had to oppose Navarre and the Huguenots, and yet he could trust neither the weak and devious Henry III nor Guise and the zealots of the Catholic League who were in the pay of Spain. When Philip's ambassador tried to bully him into excommunicating Navarre's Catholic and *politique* adherents, he flatly refused to do so. Beyond that, he had to wait for the events to sort themselves out—a posture hardly congenial to his temperament. Closer to hand he bent events to suit himself and his highly activist ideal of the Catholic revival. That might have mattered little had Spain succeeded in destroying the French and English monarchies; but as things in fact turned out, the papacy, thanks largely to Sixtus V, confronted an evolving balance of power in Europe from a base stronger than it had enjoyed since the High Middle Ages.

13. Jean Delumeau, *Vie économique et sociale de Rome* (Paris, 1954). See the same author's "Rome: Political and Administrative Centralization in the Papal State," in Eric Cochrane, ed., *The Late Italian Renaissance* (New York, 1970), pp. 287 ff.

14. To compare the value of monies of different eras is exceedingly difficult. For some idea of the value of the sixteenth century écu or crown (equivalent to three francs) see Nancy Roelker, ed., *The Paris of Henry of Navarre* (Cambridge, Mass., 1958), pp. 308 f.

2. IMPERIAL ENTERPRISE

Philip II had not opposed the election of Felix Peretti, and during the early months of Sixtus V's pontificate, when the pope granted the king a renewal of the *excusado* and other ecclesiastical taxes, a deceptive calm marked the relations between Spain and the papacy. That may have been because the pope did not know, nor did anyone else know, the plans taking shape in Philip's mind. Among the pile of documents on his desk Philip was pondering a feasibility study prepared by the Marquis of Santa Cruz, hero of Lepanto and now captain general of the Ocean Sea. Santa Cruz, fresh from two victories in the Azores over Portuguese dissidents aided by the French and (Santa Cruz thought, mistakenly) the English, reported his opinion that with a large enough force a naval attack upon England could succeed. The old sea dog's estimates were, in the king's views, excessive, quite beyond the state's capacity, but Philip was used to that in dealing with admirals and generals; they always asked for twice as much as was necessary. What mattered to him was that the best military advice confirmed his own predilections.

For Philip had decided to move at long last against England. His restraint in the face of endless provocations had been rewarded by piratical incursions upon his shipping and overseas territories and by aid given to his rebellious subjects in the Netherlands. The moment seemed ripe to punish these irritants: the power of Spain stood at its apex, while the disarray of France, which through the League Philip could turn on and off to suit his purpose, guaranteed that England would have to face the assault alone. As far as Philip cared for world opinion, he could argue that the English provocations were bolder than ever. Late in 1585 Queen Elizabeth's aging favorite, the Earl of Leicester, landed in the northern Netherlands at the head of 6,000 troops; the following February the States-General of the rebel provinces named him governor general, with fuller prerogatives than Alençon had had.[15] And about the same time Francis Drake raided his way across the Spanish Main, sacking Santo Domingo and Cartagena in the process.

The war policy had been originally Granvelle's, though the cardinal

15. An appointment which angered Elizabeth. See Charles Wilson, *Queen Elizabeth and the Revolt of the Netherlands* (London, 1970), pp. 90 ff.

did not live to see it put into execution. He was out of favor at the time of his death (September, 1586), for no better reason, apparently, than his own remarkable competence. Philip II's fatal weakness as an administrator was his inability to abide for long a gifted subordinate; Alba he treated shabbily, and then Granvelle, and ultimately Farnese, the greatest of them all, suffered the same fate. As the fleet began to assemble at Lisbon, Granvelle's talents were sorely missed, for Santa Cruz, who assumed command there, was a fighter, not an organizer. Still he did the best he could under the lash of his master's impatience, but he worried that the men, ships, guns, and stores slowly accumulating were high enough neither in numbers nor in quality to form anything like an "invincible armada."[16]

At Antwerp, Farnese—now the Duke of Parma since his father's death in 1586—learned the part he and his *tercios* were to play in the enterprise. The armada would fight its way through the channel and then conduct Parma's army across the narrow seas for a landing on the English coast. The persecuted Catholics would rise in support of the invaders, and together they would overwhelm the heretic queen and her minions. Though Parma had long believed that the Spanish conquest of the whole Netherlands would eventually involve the reduction of England, he had serious reservations about this particular plan. Like Alba before him he was not convinced that the English Catholics would rally to an invading force, whatever the protestations of William Allen, now actively lobbying for the enterprise in Rome and soon to be a cardinal. He pointed out to the king that the lack of a deep-water port could place the fleet in jeopardy, that junction with his own barges would in any case be very hazardous, that the element of surprise was almost out of the question. He begged to be allowed to finish the task in the Netherlands first and then, at leisure and with much greater safety, to attend to England.

But Philip II was adamant. The project would proceed and in all haste. The caution he had worn as a badge for so long he now discarded, as though he thought time and opportunity were running out for him. The Catholics in England would rise, he insisted, and as for a port Guise might seize one along the Norman coast or, if not, God would provide one in some other way. Parma could keep Elizabeth off her guard by gulling her through formal negotiations (which were in

16. Garrett Mattingly, *The Armada* (Boston, 1959), pp. 76 ff.

fact carried on till the eve of the armada's sailing). For the king had more in mind than a mere punitive expedition, and any doubts he may have had about its timing disappeared on February 18, 1587, when Mary Queen of Scots, victim of her own bumbling intrigues and of the inveterate hatred of secretaries Walsingham and Cecil, was executed at Fotheringay castle.[17] It was now clear that God had determined to entrust to Philip the crown of England. As a scrupulous dynast, he had been troubled at the prospect of removing Elizabeth from the English throne in favor of Mary, who, though a Catholic indeed, was also a Frenchwoman at heart. Now she was dead and her only son a heretic; who then had a better genealogical claim, dating back to John of Gaunt, than Philip himself, once the Tudors were extinct? On March 31 he ordered Santa Cruz to be ready to sail before the end of spring.

Even if it had been otherwise possible, Francis Drake, a Puritan who had his own ideas about what God intended, prevented it. From April to June he led a small but powerful squadron on a raid that set the Spanish timetable back a full year. He sailed right into Cádiz harbor and burned eighteen warships bound for rendezvous with the armada. He terrorized the Portuguese coast for weeks, destroying irreplaceable stores and even threatening Lisbon itself, and then he swung west into the open sea and captured a huge treasure carrack on its way from America to Seville.

Drake's brilliant exploit and the stiffening of resistance in the Low Counties were straws in an ill wind. Parma found 1586 a year of frustration, hardly compensated for by the betrayal of Deventer into his hands by an English Catholic officer.[18] By and large the rebels showed if anything heightened resolve after the fall of Antwerp. It was not so much Leicester's presence—before his final departure in September, 1587, he showed himself the trifler and incompetent he had always been—as the success of Holland in imposing its stubborn will upon the other six rebel provinces. Two-thirds of the States-General's revenues and the bulk of their soldiery came from Holland, where John Oldenbarneveldt was emerging as the first native Dutch leader of an Erastian, oligarchic, decentralized republic. Perhaps also the assassination of William of Orange was bearing fruit other than Philip II had expected

17. See Conyers Read, *Mr. Secretary Walsingham* (Oxford, 1925), II, 341 ff.; III, 34 ff.
18. See R. B. Werham, "Elizabethan War Aims and Strategy," in S. T. Bindoff et al., eds., *Elizabethan Government and Society* (London, 1961), p. 350.

when he put a price on that prince's head; Orange's son, Maurice of Nassau, scarcely more than a boy, had become stadholder of Holland and, under Oldenbarneveldt's guidance, was already displaying more military talent than his father ever had.[19]

But the first captain in Europe still fought on the other side, as was demonstrated again before Sluis during the summer of 1587. This town was one of the last in north Flanders under rebel control, and its port, though beginning to silt up, was ample enough to provide a juncture point for the armada coming from Spain and the royal Netherlands army, and thus solve the enterprise's gravest tactical problem. The investment of Sluis presented almost as many logistical difficulties as the more famous one at Antwerp three years before. "Never since I came to the Netherlands," Parma told Philip II, "has any operation given me such trouble and anxiety as this siege." But Sluis fell anyway on August 9, and a few weeks later reinforcements arrived by overland march from Italy to bring Parma's force to the highest number of fighting men it was ever to have. If the armada had come then instead of a year later—a year during which invasion flatboats rotted and the army dwindled from disease and desertion and the Dutch in their little flyboats learned to block the approaches to Sluis as effectively as they did to Antwerp—the enterprise might have fared differently. As it was, Santa Cruz could not sail, thanks largely to Drake's springtime depredations, and the postponement proved decisive.

Yet for all anyone could tell during the months before the fall of Sluis, the Spanish strategy appeared to be unfolding on deadly schedule. The French phase of that strategy had begun with the eighth and last of the civil-religious wars, the "War of the Three Henries," when King Henry III, under pressure from Henry of Guise and the Catholic League, had reluctantly mounted an offensive against the Huguenot state-within-a-state headed by the king's Bourbon cousin and heir, Henry of Navarre. The fighting itself was inconclusive, a victory of Navarre's over the royalists on October 20, 1587, being balanced by one of Guise's over Navarre's German Protestant allies a few weeks later. But what satisfied Philip was to have France at this moment plunged again into distraction. The only real loser was the king, if one left out of account the people of France who had not known peace for thirty years.

19. See John den Tex, *Oldenbarneveldt* (Haarlem, 1960–62), especially Vol. II.

When he returned to Paris for Christmas, Henry III heard everywhere the taunt, "Saul has slain his thousands, David his tens of thousands!" and variations of the taunt from doctors of the Sorbonne, preachers in hundreds of Parisian churches, and rabble in the streets: down with the vile, perverse Valois, friend of heretics, and *vive le duc de Guise!* When early in the new year 1588 the Spanish ambassador wanted to negotiate for ports in Picardy the armada could use on its passage up the channel, he dealt with the officers of the League, not with the hapless king. By late April the king could maintain himself in his own capital only by threatening to call in his Swiss mercenaries camped on the outskirts of the city. Spanish money meanwhile was sent to Guise with orders to keep the pot boiling.

He did so with a vengeance.[20] On May 9, contrary to Henry III's specific orders, the duke with one or two attendants rode into Paris. His handsome face, disfigured by the famous scar, was recognized everywhere, and soon the whole city knew its darling had come. A tense interview with the king followed, then a two-day war of nerves, and then the king played the only card in his hand. On May 12 he imposed martial law and ordered the Swiss to occupy the city. But the League's leaders had prepared for such an eventuality. As Swiss detachments marched stolidly through the deserted streets of early morning, barricades were suddenly thrown up before and behind them, and they were caught in a honeycomb of dead ends. Ordered not to fire upon the people, the soldiers stood fingering their weapons, bewildered and helpless, at the mercy of mobs which became uglier the more conscious they grew of their advantage. Only the personal intervention of Guise—abjectly begged for by the king—saved the Swiss from massacre. The duke rode through the streets armed only with a riding crop, and smiling broadly at the cries of *vive le roi,* conducted the mercenaries to the safety of their camps. At the end of the "Day of Barricades"—the first of many such "days" the Parisian populace was destined to have—Henry III slipped out of an unguarded gate and fled to Chartres, leaving behind his deliriously joyful capital in the charge of its uncrowned king and a revolutionary junta of sixteen district leaders of the Catholic League. Taken altogether, reported the Spanish ambassador, the situation could not be improved upon. But the Duke of Parma, when he heard that Guise out of carelessness or contempt

20. See Jean Mariéjol, *La réforme et la ligue* (Paris, 1911), p. 263.

had let Henry of Valois escape, was not so sure. "A man who draws his sword against his prince," he said, "should throw away the scabbard."

On May 9, the very moment Guise precipitated the crisis in Paris, the armada set sail from Lisbon, or rather tried to set sail. The ships of the lead squadron had barely nudged their way out of the harbor when a gale blew them back once more. Not for three weeks did the weather moderate sufficiently for another attempt at departure, and then, on May 28, the flagship *San Martín* led the flotilla of 130 vessels of all types and sizes—perhaps seventy of them first-class fighting ships—past Lisbon's protective forts and out into the Atlantic. On board were 20,000 soldiers, 10,000 sailors, enormous quantities of biscuit, bacon, cheese, wine, and water, 180 priests, and 123,790 cannon balls of various weights. These figures fell far short of Santa Cruz's estimates of the necessary minimum, but they still amounted to a mighty force and provided a grand spectacle—*la felicissima armada,* admiring observers dubbed it. And in any case Santa Cruz had died three months earlier. In his place on the deck of the *San Martín* stood the Duke of Medina Sidonia, one of the first grandees of Spain, who knew little about warfare and nothing about the sea. He had pleaded to be spared a burden for which he was so remarkably unfitted, but King Philip, privy to God's obvious design, insisted on the appointment and assured the duke that Christ himself would ride in the *San Martín*'s rigging. Later, when disaster befell the expedition, the king to his credit did not join the rest of the world in heaping abuse upon Medina Sidonia. In fact his commission was beyond human capacity; as Professor Mattingly has observed, not even Horatio Nelson could have led the Spanish armada to victory.[21]

Early in June, as he inched his way northward along the Iberian coast, the duke allowed himself some guarded optimism, and then the storms struck again, scattering his fleet and forcing it to take refuge at Corunna. On July 22, when it set out again, the weather remained fine until the 25th, when it was buffeted by still another storm. By the 29th, however, the fleet had regrouped and had entered the mouth of the English channel, a gentle southwest breeze swelling its galleons' sails. Recalling perhaps a similarly perilous moment in the Gulf of Lepanto, the admiral and his men knelt in prayer to invoke God's blessing upon

21. Mattingly, *Armada,* 201.

themselves and their cause. But whatever their fervor, as soon as the long battle started, on July 31 off Plymouth, it became cruelly apparent that Medina Sidonia was no Don John and, more important, that the present engagement would be no fight between galleys. What confronted *la felicissima armada* was indeed a new kind of naval warfare at which the Spaniards were markedly inferior. They still thought in terms of closing and boarding, but their enemy would not play that game. The English ships were longer, faster, built closer to the water, more maneuverable; they mounted more cannon which fired more accurately and at greater range. They were manned by superb crews, used to the ocean's capricious ways, and commanded by the finest sailors in the world—Drake, Martin Frobisher, John Hawkins, Lord Howard of Effingham.

The Spanish nightmare that began on the 31st continued unabated for ten days. The armada pushed relentlessly eastward, past Portland Bill and the Isle of Wight, toward the rendezvous with Parma in Flanders, and the English, seizing the windward advantage, fell in behind. It was like a bear pursued by a pack of hounds. The English refused to fight according to the only rules the Spaniards knew. When a Spanish galleon tried to close, the enemy ship drew back or to the side and then fired straight at the galleon's water line. With their superior seamanship and gunnery, the English never came near enough or stayed still long enough for the Spaniards to use the classic skills they had learned fighting the Turks in the Mediterranean. By the time it came to anchor in Calais Roads, late on the afternoon of Saturday, August 6, even though its physical losses had not been severe, the armada's ammunition was exhausted, its morale shattered, its hope gone.

The fatal weakness in Philip II's strategy now revealed itself. Without a deep-water port at its disposal the armada could not sustain itself and could not perform its prime mission of conducting the Netherlands army across the narrows to England. Parma, who had gloomily predicted the event, could do nothing to help; even if by some miracle the armada were to slip up the Flemish coast without destroying itself on the shoals, he dared not venture out to meet it in his unarmed barges so long as the Dutch flyboats—which drew so much less water than the galleons of the fleet—were there to intercept him. Medina Sidonia tried to buy supplies in Calais, but the governor—a royalist supporter of Henry III and not a Leaguer—while he offered foodstuffs for sale, courteously declined to deal in powder and ball. Meanwhile, the English fleet, heavily reinforced, drew up within cannon shot of the armada and waited for the kill.

In the tense quiet of midnight, August 7–8, Hawkins and Drake delivered the *coup de grâce*. The Spaniards caught sight of eight fire ships, driven by the tides and a stiff west wind, bearing directly toward their anchorage. For the first time in the campaign they lost their nerve and their discipline. The eerie light cast by the sputtering and exploding fire ships revealed the pandemonium as the Spaniards, cutting their cables and bouncing off one another, rushed pell-mell for the open sea. By dawn Monday, August 8, the battered *San Martin* stood off Gravelines with perhaps fifty other Spanish vessels in sight. Here the Admiral of the Ocean Sea, with that reckless valor that had overcome the Moor and conquered the new world, offered battle to the enemy now three times his size. The English happily obliged him and poured a murderous gunfire into the remnant of what had once been called the invincible armada. Then the weather, which had so often blighted the Spaniards' fortunes, suddenly intervened in their favor. A rain squall drove the two fleets apart, and after the sky cleared, the English, their own ammunition almost run out, did not renew the engagement. Instead they sailed north in the Spaniards' wake until on August 12, confident that no landing would be attempted on British soil, they turned off into the Firth of Forth.

Wild and conflicting rumors spread across Europe as the armada disappeared into the mists north of the Shetland Islands. The Spanish ambassador in Rome demanded the pope proclaim a jubilee and a solemn Te Deum in honor of his master's victory, but Sixtus V replied, with unwonted mildness, that it might be better to await further reports. Not till the middle of October, after a ghastly voyage around Scotland and west of Ireland, did the last elements of the fleet straggle into Spanish ports; half the ships and two-thirds of the men never returned at all. King Philip received the news impassively, though one bitter remark—he had sent his fleet, he said, "against men and not against the wind and the seas"—showed he did not really understand how his own uncharacteristic imprudence had contributed to the disaster. Among the other crowned heads proof of Spain's vulnerability was not unwelcome. Pope Sixtus saved the million ducats he had promised the Spaniards when and if they landed in England, and his admiration for Queen Elizabeth, of which he had never made a secret, increased considerably.

Yet anyone who thought the fate of the Spanish armada meant an end to the imperial enterprise was very much mistaken.[22] Philip II's war with England continued for another fifteen years, a fitful, inconclusive affair of raids and counterraids, which nevertheless demonstrated that English naval superiority was not a passing phenomenon. But at center stage an even more crucial phase in the struggle was about to begin. By an ironic twist his defeat in the narrow seas opened to Philip a grander opportunity.

The scene was France. Insofar as it dealt a blow to the plans of the Catholic League and to the personal ambitions of the Duke of Guise, Spain's discomfiture gave King Henry III a new lease on life. In September, 1588, he displayed unusual independence by dismissing the ministers whom his old and ailing mother, still vainly in search of accommodation, has foisted on him. When a month later the League-dominated Estates-General assembled at Blois, Guise seemed as strong, popular, and arrogant as ever. But the king was convinced that the difficulties of his rival's allies justified a bold move. On December 23, the unsuspecting Guise, in response to the king's summons, went to the royal Château at Blois, where a dozen assassins set upon him and stabbed him to death. When Catherine de' Medici heard the news, she cursed her son for a fool, turned her face to the wall, and died.[23]

"How tall he looks," said the king as he stood over Guise's bleeding corpse. "He looks taller dead than he did alive." This remark, probably apocryphal, expressed succinctly the result of the House of Valois's last miscalculation. The queen mother had read the temper of public opinion better than her son: Guise, in life a brave but vain and venal dreamer, was in death a formidable enemy. Word of his murder touched off revolts, first in Paris controlled by the Sixteen, and then in every town and district where the League had influence. The rebels formed a provisional government and appointed Guise's brother, the Duke of Mayenne, lieutenant general of the kingdom. Henry III had rid himself of an overweening subject, but instead of securing him the independence he sought the act drove him literally into the camp of his

22. See the observation of J. H. Elliott, *Imperial Spain* (London, 1963), p. 285.
23. She died January 5, 1589.

other rival, Henry of Navarre. By April, 1589, the bargain had been struck, and the little Huguenot army under the Most Christian King's own lily banners tentatively marched toward Paris.[24] In May Sixtus excommunicated Henry III and absolved Frenchmen from their allegiance, a step the wily pontiff took more readily now that it seemed unlikely that Spain would benefit from it.

But once again the assassin's knife intervened. On July 31, 1589, Henry of Valois was murdered by a Leaguer fanatic, and Navarre's soldiers promptly proclaimed him by dynastic right King Henry IV. No one denied that right, but the question remained whether he forfeited it by reason of his religion. However constitutional theorists might argue the point, the fact was that only a fraction of the nation was prepared to accept a heretic king. Henry was intelligent, courageous, attractive, a strikingly virile contrast to the Valois, and had he had the time he might have been able to allay the majority's fears. He tried the best he could; on August 4 he formally pledged to maintain the Roman Church within his dominions, and two years later he went much further, declaring Catholicism to be the religion of the state. Neither manifesto, however, excited much popular enthusiasm. The observable habits of a personal ruler weighed more than his edicts; the people of France wanted the king to go to Mass. Yet even paper concessions to the Catholics aroused Huguenot suspicions and tended to erode the narrow and ideological base of support which Henry dared not antagonize until he could count on something better. He learned very quickly the magnitude of his problem. In late September, 1589, he lured the Duke of Mayenne's relatively powerful army into Normandy and defeated it in a series of little battles near Arques. The following March he beat Mayenne again, and more decisively, at Ivry, on the outskirts of Paris. But on neither occasion was he strong enough to penetrate beyond the capital's suburbs.

The League meanwhile recognized as king the Cardinal of Bourbon—"Charles X"—whom Guise had advanced as heir presumptive during the crisis of 1584–1585. This policy suffered from the drawback that Henry IV kept his uncle, the cardinal, a prisoner, but it suited the purposes of Mayenne, who had inherited from his brother the dream of eventually snatching the crown for himself. And it suited Philip II. The King of Spain, always a stickler for dynastic protocol, had used an

24. Henri Hauser, *La prépondérance espagnole* (Paris, 1948), p. 133.

aged prelate as a stopgap in Portugal, and the same gambit, he reasoned, might well work again. For when the cardinal died, as he soon must, why should not Philip's own daughter Isabella—daughter also of Elizabeth of Valois, Henry III's eldest sister—ascend the French throne in preference to an incorrigible and lapsed heretic? Philip's imperial enterprise made some rough sort of sense only within the framework of dynastic categories, which were themselves affected by the ideological struggle of the time. In 1580 a quirk of circumstance left three royal houses headed by incumbents who had no direct heirs, and the King of Spain through blood or marriage was related to each of them. He succeeded in Portugal, where his claim was as good as his ability to enforce it, while in England his ambitions had been checked. But the very failure of the armada, by pushing Henry III into the imprudence of killing Guise and inviting retribution upon himself, seemed suddenly to have placed France, the greatest prize by far, within Philip's reach.

Not until Henry IV laid siege to Paris in the summer of 1590 did Philip fully reveal his hand. He ordered Parma's army to relieve the city, to support, for the moment, the League and Mayenne, and to add a show of force to the bribery and propaganda already being employed in France. The governor general of the Netherlands obeyed only after filing the most strenuous objections.[25] He reminded the king how the project for invading England had given the Dutch rebels an invaluable breathing space. Instead of delivering the knockout blow in 1587 or 1588 the Spaniards had spent precious time and resources preparing for an armada that never arrived. To divert their energies again could put off the pacification of the Netherlands for years or perhaps forever.

Philip, however, in the Byzantine isolation of the Escorial, remained unpersuaded. He had never appreciated a soldier's point of view, and he was in any case growing highly suspicious of the most brilliant of his soldiers. So Parma marched, crossed the frontier early in August, and by the end of the month raised the siege which had cost 13,000 Parisian lives. Even so, as he noted in his report to the king, there was depressingly little evidence in the French capital of friendliness toward Spain.

Parma got back to the Netherlands in November to find his worst

---

25. Léon van der Essen, *Alexandre Farnèse, Prince du Parme, Gouverneur-Général des Pays-Bas* (Brussels, 1934), V, 284 ff.

premonitions realized. The rebels in his absence had stormed into Brabant, captured Breda, and threatened several other key cities. The momentum had clearly passed to them. Holland, in remarkable contrast to Spanish Flanders, was booming, carrying on a lively trade with Spain, among other places, and Holland, under Oldenbarneveldt, was paying for as well as leading the United Provinces' revolution. As flourishing Amsterdam replaced Antwerp as the commercial crossroads of northwest Europe, Maurice of Nassau reorganized the States-General's army and replaced the undisciplined Beggar bands with lean, tough professional soldiers, not unduly impressed by the *tercios*. The Spaniards held the line in the south, but in a campaign of sieges that stretched over the next several years they watched their hard-won conquests in the northeast melt away. Deventer fell to Maurice in 1591, Steenwyk in 1592, Groningen in 1594. From such bases as these Parma had planned to launch the final assault upon Holland and Zeeland.

Instead in August, 1591, Philip, like a man obsessed, ordered him back into France. The King of Spain was afloat upon a sea of troubles: the English pillaged his coasts, the Dutch swarmed over his Burgundian provinces, the Aragonese were so restive and resentful of Castilian ascendancy that he had to send 12,000 men to secure his own town of Saragossa.[26] Worst of all, the Catholic League of France, his trump card in the imperial enterprise, was falling to pieces, torn apart by factional quarrels between the magnates and the radical urban leadership, between factions coming to be called *Mayennistes* and *espagnolizes*.[27] The Duke of Mayenne, his naïveté gradually dissolving, realized at last that the Spaniards were using him rather than the other way around: since January, 1591, Walloon and Neapolitan troops had been part of the Paris garrison, since March a small Spanish army had been operating in Languedoc, and since May a larger one in Brittany. The duke began to assume a hard line against Spanish sympathizers within the League, particularly against the Parisian Sixteen and their fanatical supporters among the clergy. It was one thing, he argued, to keep a heretic off the throne and quite another to deliver the throne to a foreigner or to encourage a foreigner to dismember the nation. Mayenne showed he meant business when in

26. For the part played by Antonio Pérez in the Aragonese troubles, see Marañón, *Pérez*, pp. 254 ff.

27. See De Lamar Jensen, *Diplomacy and Dogmatism* (Cambridge, Mass., 1964), pp. 175 ff.

December, 1591, he suddenly descended on Paris and hanged four members of the Sixteen.

Before that, however, Parma had come to the rescue of Rouen and chased away the Huguenots and English who were threatening the town. The campaign was yet another masterful display of generalship, but it proved to be Parma's last. On April 25, 1592, he was severely wounded and had to be carried back to the Netherlands on a litter. He languished through the summer, and when orders arrived in the autumn from Madrid to invade France a third time, he was too feeble to respond. He died on December 2, aged forty-seven, just in time to be spared the indignity of dismissal from office.[28]

In January, 1593, the French estates general, summoned by Mayenne, gathered in Rheims for the purpose of electing a monarch (the Cardinal of Bourbon had died some months earlier). The assembly was again dominated by the League, which fact did not render it altogether unrepresentative of the nation, and the League in any case was no longer a monolith, if it ever had been, as the months of wrangling amply showed. The Spanish ambassador was much in evidence, dispensing bribes and threatening members about the dire fate that would befall Catholicism and France if they failed to elect the Infanta Isabella or at least one of Philip II's archducal nephews. But the threats sounded hollower now that Parma was gone, now that the Dutch and English had formally allied themselves to Henry IV. Spain was taking on the aspect of a wounded giant, flailing this way and that with ever less effect. In June the Parlement of Paris gave its judicial verdict that by the Salic Law the Infanta was ineligible to succeed to the throne.[29]

But by that time the decisive events were occurring elsewhere. On May 17 the Archbishop of Bourges, one of Henry IV's Catholic supporters, announced his king's intention to embrace the apostolic and Roman religion of his ancestors. Two months later, at St. Denis, the son of Anthony of Bourbon and Jeanne d'Albret swore his profession of faith and received the Eucharist under the Catholic form. With that simple act dynastic and ideological interests coalesced once more, and national interests as well. The only obstacle to Henry IV, the only

28. Van der Essen, *Farnèse*, V, 383 f. "A great man has died, a great captain," said Henry IV. "His death is worth 10,000 infantry to us." To Philip II, Parma's passing was "annoying."

29. The Salic Law forbade a queen regnant and also inheritance of the throne solely through a woman.

reason left for civil strife, was gone. The rightful king now practiced the right religion, and it mattered little to the public at large whether he did so out of conviction or expediency.

Henry IV's conversion altered the state of affairs almost literally over night. Mayenne's estates general adjourned in August without pretending to elect anybody. The League, its raison d'être vanished, collapsed in confusion. One magnate after another hastened to be reconciled to the king and to participate in his coronation at Chartres in February, 1594. In March the junta meekly admitted him to Paris, and Rouen threw open its gates to him. Henry responded to every overture from his former enemies with a generosity that won him far more than his apostasy cost him among the bitterly disappointed and scandalized Huguenots.

Philip II fought a furious rear-guard action at Rome, hoping to persuade the pope of Henry's insincerity and of the necessity to deny him full communion with the Catholic Church. But the Curia was not about to refuel the faltering Spanish juggernaut, and many Romans quoted approvingly Sixtus V's scornful remark, made shortly before his death: "The Spaniards want to conquer the world and they cannot even capture Cambrai."[30] Sixtus's pious successor, Clement VIII (d. 1605),[31] was delighted that his instincts as a priest should confirm his views as a statesman. For him Henry IV was a lost sheep regained and the heaven-sent instrument to restore balance among the Catholic powers. He fussily insisted that a lapsed heretic—Henry had been nominally a Catholic during the dangerous days after St. Bartholomew —must do public penance, but once the king did so, by proxy, all was gladly forgiven. Almost as important as the pope's blessing was the reconciliation, in November, 1594, between Henry and young Charles of Guise, le Balafré's son and more heir to the mantle of Guise popularity than Mayenne had ever been. And thirteen months later Mayenne himself submitted.

In the three years' struggle that still remained, Henry IV fulfilled Coligny's dream of uniting all Frenchmen by a national crusade against Spain. The Spaniards fought with their usual skill and won not a few victories—in Languedoc, Franche Comté, Brittany, Picardy, all

30. Pastor, Popes, XXI, 368. Cambrai, seized by Alençon in 1581, was finally captured by the Spaniards in 1595.

31. Between Sixtus V and Clement (1590–1592) there were three brief pontificates.

across the Low Countries, on the high seas, and along the Portuguese and Irish coasts—but Philip II now had to pay for contemptuously dismissing the pleas of Parma to concentrate rather than to disperse his forces. In 1596 bankruptcy loomed over the Spanish state, and by November, 1597, Philip II, a dying man of seventy, sued for peace.

The Treaty of Vevrins (May 2, 1598) ended the Franco-Spanish war on terms virtually dictated by Henry IV. Four days later Philip recognized the de facto independence of the seven United Provinces by establishing for the Netherlands a regime technically detached from Spain. At the head of it he placed his daughter Isabella and her husband, Philip's nephew, the Archduke Albert.[32] By reason of some public and many secret stipulations this government of the archdukes, as it was called, gave unhappy Belgium little real freedom, but it probably went much further than Philip had dreamed of going only a few years before. In any event it provides a commentary on the fate of the imperial enterprise: Isabella, for whom her father intended first the throne of England and then that of France, ended her days at the court of Brussels, presiding over a ruined little principality.

Nothing now was left for Philip of Hapsburg except to die, and he did so with grace and courage. Afflicted by gout all his life, the king nevertheless enjoyed rather good health, at least for a man who spurned all forms of physical exercise. By the mid-1590s, however, he was suffering repeated and severe attacks of malaria, and in April, 1596, and again in September, 1597, his death was momentarily expected. Each time he rallied, though with less resilience, until he was stricken again at the end of June, 1598. Philip sensed his end was near, and he insisted that he be carried by litter from Madrid to his beloved Escorial. Scarcely there, he fell into his final illness and bore with tight-lipped patience excruciating pain before he died on September 13, 1598. With him died an epoch, a moment of gold and glory in the life of the nation he had done so much to create. "Although change is usually popular," reported the Venetian ambassador at Madrid, "yet nobles and people, rich and poor, show great grief." And many of them recounted wryly how Philip had been *el Rey Prudente* to the very last: as he lay suffering on his deathbed he planned his funeral down to the most insignificant detail.[33]

32. See Henri Pirenne, *Histoire de Belgique* (Brussels, 1910), IV, 211 ff.
33. Roger Merriman, *The Rise of the Spanish Empire* (New York, 1918), IV, 666 ff.

3. THE DEMISE OF GLORIANA

The crowds cheered at Thames-side and from the windows of London Bridge as Queen Elizabeth passed downriver on her barge from St. James's to Tilbury. It was the morning of August 18, 1588. Preliminary reports had it that the armada had been driven off, but no one yet knew how decisive the English victory had been, and no one was certain the Spaniards would not return and somehow ferry the Duke of Parma's army across the narrow seas. So the royal standard had been hoisted at Tilbury, and by the time the queen arrived perhaps 10,000 men were encamped there, spoiling for a fight with the vaunted Spanish *tercios*.

Elizabeth spent the balance of the 18th inspecting the camp, intent on seeing and even more on being seen. Next day, on the back of a white gelding and dressed all in white herself, she held a full-scale military review. The gentlemen and farmers who composed her little army saw as they marched by her a woman who looked younger than her fifty-five years. She sat slim and straight in the saddle, showing no sign of sagging flesh, and when she spoke her voice was clear and vibrant:

My loving people, we have been persuaded by some that are careful for our safety, to take heed how we commit ourselves to armed multitudes, for fear of treachery. But I assure you, I do not desire to live to distrust my faithful and loving people. Let tyrants fear. I have always so behaved myself that, under God, I have placed my chiefest strength and safeguard in the loyal hearts and good will of my subjects. And therefore I am come amongst you as you see, at this time, not for my recreation and disport, but being resolved, in the midst and heat of the battle, to live or die amongst you all, and to lay down for my God and for my kingdom and for my people, my honor and my blood, even in the dust. I know I have the body of a weak and feeble woman, but I have the heart and stomach of a king, and of a king of England too, and think foul scorn that Parma or Spain or any prince of Europe should dare to invade the borders of my realm; to which, rather than any dishonor shall grow by me, I myself will take up arms, I myself will be your general. . . .[34]

It was Gloriana's finest hour.

Armada year, the thirtieth year of her reign, was the rapturous

---

34. Quoted by Mattingly, *Armada*, 349 f.

climax of the romance between the English people and their Faerie Queene.[35] Many elements combined in that magical relationship. It depended first of all upon the sublimity of the monarchical ideal which, if a mystery to later generations, was bone and marrow of the enthusiasm on display at Tilbury. The person of the sovereign gave focus to the aspirations of a nation just beginning to be conscious of itself. The Elizabethans stood halfway between their ancestors, whose political loyalties had been expressed within a local and very personal context, and their children, who would offer obeisance to the anonymous, leviathan state.

No one was better suited than Elizabeth Tudor to articulate this nascent patriotism, to ease the rough passage of this evolutionary process. She was colorful, imperious, superbly intelligent, marvelously eloquent. She had in her veins not a drop of foreign blood, a boast, given the fashion of interdynastic marriage, no other major European ruler could make. That she did not marry herself involved succession problems worrisome to her advisers, but it endeared her to the masses of her subjects who responded to the notion that their queen loved only them. They took vicarious delight in her sumptuous court, identified readily with her wit and vitality, and when she sent Drake to singe the beard of the King of Spain, their bosoms swelled with pride. They gloried in the accounts of her manly oaths reminiscent of her father—"God's death!" was her favorite—and in the masculine vigor with which she treated bishops and other arrogant potentates—"If you, my lords of the clergy, do not amend, I mean to depose you!"[36] But they valued perhaps more her essential womanliness, her capacity for deep feeling, her unpredictability and intuitive good sense, and the proficiency with which she employed those wiles commonly called feminine.

Yet traits of character or monarchical theory cannot by themselves explain why Elizabeth should have had an era named after her. A more cogent reason is that she met and mastered, at least through the first two-thirds of her reign, the four basic challenges to a sixteenth-century dynast: she controlled the aristocracy, kept out of foreign war, avoided serious religious strife, and lived within her means. Her deal-

35. "Gloriana" was one of several titles used of Elizabeth by Edmund Spenser in his *The Faerie Queene,* the first three books of which appeared in 1590.
36. Quoted by John Neale, *Elizabeth I* (London, 1934), p. 309.

ings with the English barons were a study in the skillful use of the carrot and the stick.[37] Balance among them, and between them and the rest of the nation, was her objective, and she attained it in miniature even within her privy council, where she played off the faction headed by Leicester against that of Cecil. In religion she sought comprehension and conformity rather than doctrinal purity, and the country supported her. Though there was plenty of religious trouble, there was no religious war of the kind that scourged the Netherlands and France.

In this happy circumstance England was not unlike Spain, as Elizabeth, with her instinctive caution and procrastination, was not unlike Philip II. And when they approached old age these two antagonists came to share also similar problems in the crucial area of finance. By then Philip was long used to the dreary cycle of war and bankruptcy; for Gloriana it was a new and bitter experience.

England was no different from other evolving nation-states in that sovereign and subject both presumed that government had to be paid for out of revenues ordinarily derived from lands owned by the crown and from a variety of lesser sources, like customs duties and mineral rights. To be taxed was an exceptional thing which people would endure only to meet a particular emergency. In those halcyon days nobody yet dreamed of the state's collecting a certain portion of the gross national product in order to pay for the services it rendered. Of course, judged by later standards, it rendered relatively few services. Elizabeth's England was half an island with one sizable city, practically no roads, swarming with vagabonds and robbers, and innocent of a coherent economic or social program.[38] Parliament was the preserve of the propertied and professional classes, which passed laws on such matters as poor relief, employment regulation, land usage, and monopolistic practice in accord with their own interests. By and large they prospered in the inflationary atmosphere, while the landless and unskilled sank into ever more desperate poverty. No one thought the government had any responsibility beyond keeping the peace between the haves and the have-nots.

Occasional parliamentary subsidy was the only supplement to Eliza-

---

37. See Lawrence Stone, *The Crisis of the Aristocracy, 1558–1641* (Oxford, 1965), pp. 97 ff.

38. See, for example, John Neale, *Elizabeth I and her Parliaments, 1584–1601* (London, 1957), pp. 335 ff. and 376 ff.

beth's income, since regular property, income, and poll taxes did not exist, any more than the techniques for collecting and administering them. Sir John Neale offers some statistics which if looked at comparatively can be instructive.[39] From 1558 to 1588 Elizabeth received from ordinary sources a little more than 200,000 pounds annually, out of which she had to maintain herself and her court and perform the normal executive functions. In that same span income from parliamentary taxation—exceptional subsidies, that is, chiefly for the military—averaged about 50,000 pounds a year. Not only did the queen make do with this modest revenue; by ruthlessly cutting expenditures she was able over these three decades to devote roughly 40 percent of royal receipts to liquidation of the debt left by her predecessor and of the expenses incurred in the Scottish adventure of 1559–1560, as well as to pay off promptly the short-term, high-interest loans she occasionally had to raise in the Antwerp money market. Elizabeth paid as she went, and she resisted the temptation to imitate her peers on the Continent and mortgage the future by selling offices, floating bonds, or creating annuities. All the while she jealously guarded the intrinsic value of the English currency.

Prosaic as it may seem, this penurious, housewifely concern with solvency was the stuff of Elizabeth's statesmanship and the source of her immense popularity. The queen balanced her books, despite constantly rising prices, primarily because she kept her country at peace, and her subjects appreciated that she wasted neither their persons nor their goods. She was not an ideological pacifist; indeed, she abetted war among her neighbors as a routine diplomatic tool. But she entertained no male chauvinist illusions about military grandeur, and, like her penny-pinching grandfather, she despised war as the root of all deficits.

Elizabeth's loudest lament about armada year was that it cost her 161,000 pounds to humiliate the King of Spain, even though she delayed mobilization of the fleet as long as she dared and demobilized it with a speed that many thought was rashness. The next spring, when Francis Drake proposed a massive assault upon the Iberian coast, the queen participated not as sovereign but as investor to the tune of 20,000 pounds in what amounted to a joint-stock enterprise. She expected to turn a neat profit as she had from similar ventures in the past, and strike a blow at the Spaniards at the same time. But the dismal failure

39. Neale, *Elizabeth I*, pp. 284 ff.

of this expedition—more than half the soldiers and sailors died and no booty was taken—left her instead out of purse, as did another expensive debacle in 1595 when Drake and Hawkins led their last raid to the Caribbean. The war with Spain dragged on till the end of the reign, and though it did not absorb the nation's total resources—no war did in those days—it cost far more than the queen's exchequer could afford.

Her voracious allies helped to push her still deeper into a sea of red ink. From 1589 to 1593 she paid out a half-million pounds for military operations in the Netherlands, where an independent English force had to be supported and the States-General's army given subsidies. During the same four years Henry IV of France, who had not a sou of his own, spent 300,000 of Elizabeth's pounds; then that merry monarch became a Catholic and, not long afterward, signed a separate peace with Spain, moving the queen to call him "the Antichrist of ingratitude." But apt turns of phrase did not get the money back, and if such losses were not woeful enough, Ireland in 1595 exploded into rebellion, during the latter stages of which the Spaniards put ashore an invasion force of 3,000 men. They were eventually driven out, and the rebels crushed, but not before 1,200,000 pounds had been expended, a quarter of it in one disastrous campaign in 1599.

The steep rise in expenditures forced the queen to seek more support from the nation. By rack-renting and other dubious measures the crown's ordinary revenues were increased by roughly half, while parliamentary taxation tripled. Yet this total of about 450,000 pounds annually was not nearly enough to meet the crises brought on by foreign entanglements and intensified during the mid-1590s by four or five bad harvests in a row. In a single year the queen sold crown lands valued at more than 120,000 pounds. She hated to do this, to deplete, as it were, the monarchy's capital, just as she hated to call as many as four parliaments between 1589 and 1601, waiting indeed only until the subsidy voted by one had been collected before summoning another. Frequent parliaments meant increased dependence of the executive upon the legislature and raised a constitutional question which Elizabeth by her rigid economies had evaded for thirty years. Her policy of husbanding the resources she had instead of enlarging the crown's economic prerogative began to break down in the 1590s, and if the queen never had to face the full consequences, her successors did. The pressures of war, high prices, and hunger took much of the romance out of Gloriana's last decade and signaled the profound social and political changes to come. A sign of the unhappy times was the press gang roaming England's green and pleasant land. As Christopher Hill has said, "the great age of Elizabethan and Jacobean literature trembled on the verge of social breakdown."[40]

Armada year proved to have been the apex of the English monarchy and of Elizabeth Tudor's personal career as well. One by one her intimates passed away, just as her own strength began to fail and her troubles to multiply. The Earl of Leicester died hardly a month after he had dined with the queen at Tilbury, and so ended that ambiguous relationship. Secretary Walsingham followed in 1590 and Sir Christopher Hatton two years later. The gray and gouty Lord Burghley— William Cecil's title since elevated to the peerage—stayed faithfully at the queen's side until 1598, when his death brought to a close one of the longest and most fruitful political associations of all time. Elizabeth's own health on the whole remained good, though age was visibly taking its toll. The flattery of courtiers which she still expected had a ludicrous ring when addressed to a woman in her late sixties whose red wig perched incongruously over a rouged, wrinkled face and whose once ravishing smile revealed now only a few yellowed stumps.

But for all that she was to the end every inch the queen. Her hold on the affairs of state never relaxed. She still ruled through her council, within which the old factions survived, one led by Burghley's hunch-backed son, Robert Cecil, and the other by the dazzlingly handsome, talented, and improvident Earl of Essex. Young Essex was Elizabeth's last favorite; his animal spirits perhaps reminded her of Leicester, his stepfather, and so of her own vanished youth. Her benefactions at any rate could not quiet his vanity and recklessness, and after a series of personal and professional failures—the most spectacular one the Irish campaign of 1599—he attempted a coup d'état which, when it failed, resulted in his execution (February 25, 1601). The young man's brash ingratitude grieved the queen more deeply than any event in her long life. "Affection is false," she observed bitterly. Yet in her heart she knew better, knew that affection in a larger sense had been the cornerstone of the political edifice she had built and of the age over which she

40. Christopher Hill, *Reformation to Industrial Revolution* (London, 1967), p. 73.

had presided. Only months after Essex was beheaded she admitted as much to a delegation from the House of Commons. "Mr. Speaker," she said in part,

> we perceive your coming is to present thanks to us. Know I accept them with no less joy than your loves can have desire to offer such a present, and do more esteem it than any treasure or riches; for those we know how to prize, but loyalty, love and thanks, I account them invaluable. And though God hath raised me high, yet this I account the glory of my crown, that I have reigned with your loves. . . . It is not my desire to live or reign longer than my life and reign shall be for your good. And though you have had, and may have, many mightier and wiser princes sitting in this seat, yet you never had, nor shall have, any that will love you better.[41]

The words were truer than most epitaphs are.

This "golden speech," however, did not achieve its due place in the annals of Good Queen Bess until nostalgia had softened the harsh contours of her reign's final years. In 1603 the national mood was rather impatience that Gloriana tarried so long. Englishmen past fifty years old had not known a monarch who had not been either a child or a woman, and like the Israelites of old they yearned to be ruled by a real king. Elizabeth, according to the common opinion, "grew to be very covetous in her old days, and the people were very generally weary of an old woman's government."[42] North of the Tweed waited one willing and pathetically eager to oblige them all.

When Elizabeth I died early in the morning of April 3, 1603, the King of Scots was in his thirty-seventh year, a sandy-haired man of middle height who looked fatter than he was because of the bulletproof padding he wore beneath his clothes.[43] His overall appearance was not uncomely, though a shambling gait and a habit of slurring his speech sometimes startled those who equated royal dignity with a commanding presence. James VI had ruled Scotland in name since his mother's deposition in 1567 and in fact since he was about eighteen. Given the harsh conditions of Scottish politics, he had done very well, and it was with no ironic intent that his people spoke admiringly of King James's

41. Neale, *Elizabeth I and her Parliaments, 1584–1601*, pp. 383 ff.
42. Quoted by G. P. V. Akrigg, *Jacobean Pageant* (Cambridge, Mass., 1963), p. 17.
43. The standard biography, David Willson, *James VI and I* (Oxford, 1956), should be compared to Gordon Donaldson, *Scotland, James V to James VII* (New York, 1965), which is the third volume of *The Edinburgh History of Scotland*. David Mathew, *James I* (University of Alabama, 1967) is chatty and anecdotal.

Peace. He succeeded to a remarkable degree in taming unruly barons and Presbyterian ministers, the combination of whom had brought Queen Mary to ruin. But "in Scotland the art of kingship did not mean the art of governing the country through bureaucratic institutions. It meant the art of personal survival, of not being imprisoned, blackmailed, defeated, deposed or murdered by overmighty subjects."[44] The young king had indeed survived, mostly thanks to his own wits, because the physical resources at the disposal of the Scottish crown were practically nonexistent; it was said that in 1603 he had hardly a hundred pounds' worth of jewels and plate in his whole palace of Holyrood.

James had been schooled early as a Calvinist, and he abided by the substance of Genevan doctrine, though he had his doubts about predestination and was not unwilling later in life to be called a "Catholic" in the High Anglican sense of the word. He fancied himself a theologian and enjoyed long conversations with divines over abstruse points of Christian revelation. He gained a certain minor notoriety by engaging the eminent Cardinal Bellarmine in a literary controversy about the papacy; if he composed little of the final draft of the four pamphlets that bore his name, the ideas expressed in them were probably his. James's analytical talents were excellent and his memory prodigious, but whether in theoretical debates or in the practical business of government his staying power was limited and he had difficulty following through on any project.

His marriage to a Danish princess, though fruitful in children, was not happy; he showed little interest in women, and the parade of handsome young men he favored has led to the suggestion he was a homosexual.[45] More likely, his sole passion, besides theology, was the hunt, to which he devoted more time and energy than to any other pursuit. The uncertainties and violence of his childhood had left a mark on him in the form of timidity that amounted almost to cowardice and of an exaggerated sense of the demonic: anything he could not otherwise explain he attributed to the malevolence of witches.[46]

44. Hugh Trevor-Roper, "James I and his Bishops," in *Historical Essays* (New York, 1957), p. 132.

45. See Donaldson, *Scotland*, 186.

46. See Mathew, *James I*, pp. 75 ff.

From the moment he was old enough to realize that he was in line for the throne of England, James looked longingly toward that promised land. Queen Elizabeth never formally acknowledged his right, not even after she executed his mother—an occurrence, incidentally, that James took easily in stride. As she lay dying Elizabeth did say she expected a king to follow her and not some "rascal." There was a scattering of other claimants and several contradictory statutes about the succession, but in genealogical terms James was undoubtedly the heir, and it was in everybody's best interests to smooth his path. At least so reasoned Robert Cecil, that sensible son of a sensible father, who after Essex's fall spoke with unrivaled authority in the English privy council. During Elizabeth's last years Cecil kept carefully in touch with Edinburgh, soothing and placating James and assuring him that patience in the end would bring him all. As indeed it did: when the queen died, not a shot was fired, not a question asked, and England received James Stuart with open arms.

His procession south to London was like a Roman triumph. His new subjects welcomed him as a guarantor of stability and of an orderly transfer of power, as a man in the prime of his life with a brood of healthy children to create a dynasty, as an experienced ruler with a reputation for intelligence and thrift, as a scholar, as a good Protestant and a divine even, yet tolerant, so the Catholics hoped, and at heart a Calvinist of the stripe of John Knox, so the Puritans hoped. Disappointment was bound to come in the wake of an event which aroused so many and diverse expectations.

As for James I, as he now was, the experience brought sheer ecstasy. He exchanged the barren, violent, poverty-stricken land of his birth for the rich fields and bustling towns of England. He promised his Scottish subjects before he left Edinburgh that he planned to spend every third year in their company; as things turned out he visited them only once for a few months during the last twenty-two years of his life. No one settled into a home in a foreign country more painlessly than James; no one had his head turned more completely by good fortune than the impoverished Scot who suddenly had affluent lords and gentlemen jostling each other for his attention.

The honeymoon could not and did not last. In marked contrast to Queen Elizabeth, James, with his pathological fear of assassination, was uneasy dealing with large crowds, and people soon sensed that he disliked or distrusted them. The Scots burr in his speech and the Scots job seekers in his entourage offended various sectors of the English public. When he proposed a corporate union between his two kingdoms—Englishman and Scot should "join and coalesce together in a sincere and perfect union, as two twins bred in one belly, to love one another as no more two but one estate"—he discovered that the English considered it a plot to enrich threadbare Scots at their expense and that they would agree only to a kind of union which amounted to an absorption of Scotland by England. More dismaying still, the king discovered that English parliaments, unlike their Scottish counterparts, were genuine legislative bodies with lofty claims to integrity and freedom of speech.

The advantageous peace James concluded with Spain won him some popularity, and his stock as a reliable Protestant went soaring when a conspiracy by disaffected Catholics to blow up the houses of parliament, with king, lords, and commons inside, was uncovered in November, 1605.[47] But more fateful in the long run than the amateurish Gunpowder Plot was the conference at Hampton Court twenty months before, at which the powerful Puritan minority—dormant during Elizabeth's last years but far from dead—presented a list of grievances against the Established Church. The king presided at this meeting and showed himself more episcopal than many of the bishops, mostly because he identified the Puritans with the Scottish Presbyterians, whom he despised and feared. He presumed that the Puritans were as bent upon a theocracy as the prominent Presbyterian who back in Scotland had called the king to his face "God's silly vassal."[48] This error in judgment was typical of James's quick but superficial mind, and it was to cost the monarchy dearly in the years ahead as the ideological struggle shifted from Catholic versus Protestant to Episcopalian versus Puritan.

The bishops were probably the least-liked public men in the country, yet James cheerfully linked their fate to that of the crown. This might not have mattered so much had he appreciated other forces at work within his new kingdom, but he did not. Neither his gifts nor his experiences in primitive Scotland were equal to the complex and

---

47. A recent study is Philip Caraman, *Henry Garnet and the Gunpowder Plot* (New York, 1964).

48. Andrew Melville used the word "silly" to mean docile or subordinate.

sophisticated problems now facing him. He did not understand the common law tradition in which courts and parliaments had rights beyond the reach or gift of the king. Roman law notions of sovereignty prevailed in Scotland, and out of them had emerged the germs of James's theory of divine-right monarchy, the idea that jurisdiction flowed from God through the king into all other organs of the state. James had not been able to do more than enunciate the theory in Scotland, which was barely governable in any sense. But his new realm of England was rich and relatively literate and well ordered; here, he thought, full scope could be given to the sublime truth that kings were God's viceroys.

At issue, however, was a clash of men as well as of ideas. King James professed the divine-right theory, had even written a book about it,[49] but his practice was at odds with his theory. As an administrator he could not be bothered with the drudgery of detailed attention to the tasks of government which his theory demanded. He preferred to hunt or to argue theology. He hated London and spent as little time there as possible, dealing with his council by post or messenger. He was, in a word, lazy. He spoke of himself freely—much too freely for Puritan ears—as God's delegate, but the vigilance and sleepless care for his people which the Psalmist ascribes to the Deity were too much trouble for King James.

Ranged increasingly against him was a class of men unknown in Scotland and only of recent development in England. The country gentlemen had grown so rich that they could have bought out the peerage, it was said, three times over. They were experienced in the tasks of local government. They were allied by blood and marriage to the lawyers and other prospering professional classes. Many of them were Puritans. And when they sat in the House of Commons at Westminster, they expected to function there independent of the royal prerogative or, as James insisted, in competition to it. He may very well have been right. In any case he never learned to deal cannily as Elizabeth had with this powerful elite, mixing, as she had, cajolery with swift, unequivocal suppression when the circumstances permitted it. James instead lectured the house, hectored it, and then in the end surrendered to it and went off pouting to one of his hunting lodges.

He surrendered because he needed money. James did not live up to

49. *Basilikon Doron*, privately printed in 1599, publicly four years later.

his reputation for Scottish thrift. Thrust suddenly into what seemed to him the riches of Croesus, he was extravagant and careless, as open-handed with gold as he was with jobs. Ordinary revenues increased from 247,000 pounds in 1603 to 366,000 in 1608 because of customs duties on trade revived by peace. In the latter year, however, royal expenditures totaled 544,000 pounds and the king's debt 597,000. James had inherited part of the debt, but his own yearly deficits added regularly to it. Between 1608 and 1610 the debt was substantially reduced by selling crown lands valued at 425,000 pounds. This was an expedient which if repeated often would obviously lead to complete financial ruin. By 1610 the most rigorous management of the crown's patrimony—exercised by Cecil, James's chief minister—raised income to about 460,000 pounds, but the king was spending at the rate of almost 600,000. With a deficit of 130,000 to 140,000 pounds in the offing, a crisis was clearly at hand.[50]

The parliament of 1610, only seven years after James's joyous entry into the promised land, was the first showdown between the Stuart dynasty and the country gentlemen. Much oratory was heard about serious matters like prerogative, parliamentary liberties, and God's will, but the hard issue was one of shillings and pence. Cecil worked tirelessly for a compromise whereby the parliament would grant the crown a flat yearly subsidy of 200,000 pounds, and the king, in return, would give up such feudal rights as impositions (special customs duties) and purveyance (preemption of food and other raw goods). At first agreement on this "Great Contract" seemed likely, but then, when commons demanded the king also limit the jurisdiction of the ecclesiastical courts and lift the suspension on certain Puritan ministers, James drew back, harsh words were exchanged, and the project collapsed.[51] Parliament was dissolved with bitterness on both sides; no house, wrote the king to Cecil, except the house of hell would have treated him as the House of Commons did.

The stage was thus set for the struggle about finance, prerogative, and religion which was to occupy the next forty years. James did not live to see its solution, nor, in another sense, did his son and heir. But long before Charles I went to the block, long indeed before he came to

50. Willson, *James I and VI*, pp. 261 ff.
51. See the detailed treatment in Wallace Notestein, *The House of Commons, 1604–1610* (New Haven, 1971), pp. 255 ff.

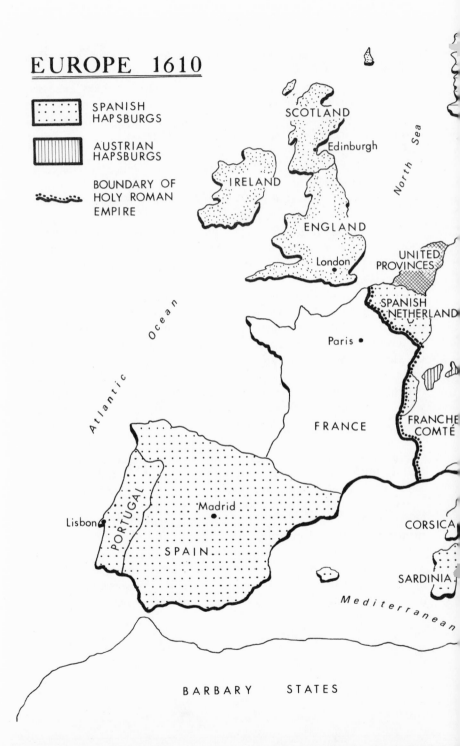

EUROPE 1610

SPANISH
HAPSBURGS

AUSTRIAN
HAPSBURGS

BOUNDARY OF
HOLY ROMAN
EMPIRE

SCOTLAND

Edinburgh

North Sea

IRELAND

ENGLAND

London

UNITED
PROVINCES

SPANISH
NETHERLAND

Ocean

Paris

Atlantic

FRANCE

FRANCHE
COMTÉ

PORTUGAL

Madrid

Lisbon

SPAIN

CORSICA

SARDINIA

Mediterranean

BARBARY   STATES

the throne in 1625, Englishmen were busy reviving and refurbishing the legend of Gloriana. That much of the tragedy which befell the Stuarts was her fault was a truth they conveniently overlooked. They preferred to remember what old Burghley had said: Elizabeth "was the wisest woman that ever was, for she understood the interests and dispositions of all the princes in her time, and was so perfect in the knowledge of her own realm that no councillor she had could tell her anything she did not know before."[52] And of course there was much truth in that too.

52. Quoted by Neale, *Elizabeth I*, p. 386.

Chapter Nine

THE LIMITS OF IDEOLOGY

"I hope God hath approved the re-entrance of His truth by such a beginning into this goodly country, which hath so long slept in error and ease." So observed Sir Henry Wotton, James I's ambassador to Venice, reporting to Robert Cecil about the quarrel which had suddenly erupted between the papacy and the Republic of St. Mark. Sir Henry, a sturdy Anglican, rejoiced "to have lived to see a pope notoriously despised by a neighbor state," and he saw in the event an opportunity to be seized by England and other Protestant powers.[1] At the moment he wrote, April, 1606, the Venetian senate lay under a sentence of excommunication and the territories of the Republic under an interdict.

The proximate cause of the breach had been the arrest of two Venetian priests, one of them for murder.[2] The fact or seriousness of the crimes committed, however, was not at issue. The Curia objected on the grounds that as clerics the accused were immune from civil jurisdiction and subject only to an ecclesiastical court. This complaint, with its quaintly medieval ring, was joined to another. Between 1602 and 1605 the Venetian government had decreed that church buildings could not be erected without special state license, that laymen could not sell or in any other way alienate land to the benefit of the clerical estate, and, finally, that property leased by laymen on long-term contracts from the Church could not revert to ecclesiastical control, because, the signory announced blandly, the lessees had presumably improved the substance of their tenancies.

Neither the arrests nor the land laws were untypical of Venetian policy over many years; in fact, the first two of the decrees mentioned above simply extended to the Republic at large what had been routine

---

1. Quoted by William Bouwsma, *Venice and the Defense of Republican Liberty* (Berkeley, 1968), p. 392.

2. A good factual summary of the interdict struggle is in Antonio Battistella, *La Reppublica di Venezia ne' suoi undici secoli di vita* (Venice, 1921).

practice in the city of Venice for generations. Mutual animosity between the Curia and the signory was of long standing, centuries old indeed, but since the collapse of the Holy League in 1573 formal relations, if chilly, had remained correct. As recently as the spring of 1605 the signory had honored the newly elected pope by conferring Venetian citizenship upon several of his nephews.

This gesture of courtesy pleased the pope, Paul V (d. 1621),[3] who was an extravagant nepotist. He was also, however, a Roman by birth, a lawyer by training, and a ruler by preference. For him the Church was first of all a structure to be governed, and a cornerstone of that structure was clerical privilege and immunity. His aggressively held conviction in this matter—less outlandish at the time than it may sound centuries afterward—brought the pontiff into direct confrontation with Venice over a relatively trivial disagreement. Trent had proclaimed the preservation of the ministerial priesthood as a distinct caste to be an essential prerequisite of genuinely Catholic reform; what therefore, asked the pope, was the Venetian challenge except the latest version of Luther's rejection of the *sacerdotium?* It provided evidence for anyone who, like Paul V, was looking for it that Venice harbored, along with its traditional anticlericalism, the remnant of Italian evangelical Protestantism.

Yet for a pragmatist like Pope Paul the most compelling argument to unleash the weapons of ecclesiastical censure may have been the remarkably successful papal record of the past forty years. Since the last pope named Paul had reigned, the papacy had satisfactorily concluded the general council, had harnessed the energies of the religious revival, had recruited legions of enthusiastic new agents, had streamlined its bureaucracy, and had put order into its finances. During that span most of Poland had been won back to the Catholic fold, as had much of Germany and at least half the Netherlands. The Turks had been checkmated, and the Protestants had fallen to fighting among themselves. Most crucial of all, France had survived the Huguenot crisis and now had a king whose Catholicism was suspect enough among his own subjects to necessitate his maintaining as cordial a connection as possible with the holy father of all Catholics. Philip II and Elizabeth I, both of them in their different ways stubbornly antagonistic to Rome,

---

3. Camillo Borghese, elected May 16, 1605. Clement VIII died on the preceding March 5, Leo XI on April 27.

had given place to weaker rulers, one of whom—despite the advice of the likes of Sir Henry Wotton and the machinations that had led to the Gunpowder Plot—talked grandly of universal religious reconciliation.[4] And very recently, in 1598, Clement VIII had shown the papacy still a power to be reckoned with in Italy by annexing the Duchy of Ferrara.[5] As heir to all these triumphs, Paul V determined to deliver a *coup de main* of his own against the troublesome city of the lagoons.

But the Venetian ruling circles at the beginning of the seventeenth century were in as truculent a mood as the pope, though for reasons opposite from his. Success had come to be an increasingly scarce commodity in Venice. The Republic's steadily deteriorating commercial situation took a grim turn for the worse between 1602 and 1605 when statistics showed conclusively that the bulk of the spice trade had passed into other than Venetian hands. The first successful intruders had been the French, who, benefiting from the friendly relations between Suleiman the Magnificent and Francis I, had had a resident ambassador in Constantinople by 1550 and consuls at Aleppo and Alexandria ten years later. These diplomatic and commercial agents were severely hampered, however, during the Wars of Religion, because France's position as the Porte's anti-Hapsburg ally was seriously weakened and because so much of the Norman and Provençal wool industry, which provided the staple for the Levant trade, was destroyed in the fighting. The pacification after Henry IV's victory restored French commercial activity in the East; it was said that by 1606 a thousand ships were engaged in a traffic valued by French merchants in the tens of millions of livres.

The Venetians took heart briefly after 1580 when Spain's annexation of the Portuguese empire seemed to promise a reduction in commerce with the Far East by way of the Cape of Good Hope and a concomitant rebound along the old routes so long their preserve. Then there might be enough business for themselves and the French, and since French textiles were notoriously shoddy in workmanship and unscrupulously misrepresented by eager salesmen, the Venetians would

4. Yet James I supported Venice. "O blessed and wise Republic," he told the Venetian ambassador, "how well she knows the way to preserve her liberty; for the Jesuits are the worst and most seditious fellows in the world." See David Willson, *James I and VI* (New York, 1956), p. 277.

5. See Romolo Quazza, *Storia Politica d' Italia: Preponderanza Spagnuola, 1559–1700* (Milan, 1958), pp. 374 ff.

have little to fear. This hope proved illusory, and in any case new and tougher competitors had arrived on the scene. The Levant Company was formed in London and confirmed by letters patent in 1581. Eleven prosperous years later the company's membership was expanded and its charter extended to include the whole Mediterranean area. The sultan received Queen Elizabeth's ambassador in Constantinople—his salary paid by the company—and granted the English monopoly a favored-nation status by fixing customs duties at a rate 2 percent less than those paid by the French and Venetians. The same boon was enjoyed by the Dutch, who, on their first appearance in the Levant in 1599, sailed under the flag of their English allies. The hard fact was that England was a wool-producing country which could manufacture and sell quality cloth at a price far below one Venice could compete with. Though the Turks also bought tin, lead, and furs from the West, their demand for woolen cloth soared more than 30 percent in the early years of the seventeenth century. The Venetians could not meet that demand at a competitive price, and so the English and the increasingly aggressive Dutch—the French practically disappeared from the market after 1610—undersold them into commercial extinction.[6]

For some time before this the signory had hedged against the collapse of the Levant trade by urging exploitation of the agricultural resources in the *terraferma,* a policy which explains to a degree the anticlerical legislation, particularly when one remembers that ecclesiastical corporations and individuals already controlled as much as 25 percent of the land in that area. But on the Venetian side other, deeper causes were also at work: the proud patricians regarded their city as the last bastion of Renaissance republicanism in Italy, the last refuge from domineering and arrogant priests.[7] And as they watched their once imperial grandeur crumble around them, their sensitivity and belligerence grew apace.

The papal censures remained in effect for a little more than a year, and they failed in their primary objective. Indeed, by the autumn of 1606 Paul V realized he had overreached himself. Even the more pious members of the Venetian senate took their excommunication in stride.

6. Alfred Wood, *A History of the Levant Company* (Oxford, 1935), pp. 11 ff., 45 f.
7. This is the thesis argued learnedly if somewhat passionately by Professor Bouwsma in *Venice and the Defense of Republican Liberty,* the subtitle of which is instructive: *Renaissance Values in the Age of the Counter Reformation.*

As for the interdict, it could be effective only if most of the priests would observe it and refuse to offer Mass and administer the sacraments. Whatever uneasiness they may have felt, a large majority of the clergy defied the pope, and the government moved swiftly against the few who displayed any hesitancy. The religious orders most closely allied to the papacy—Jesuits, Capuchins, Theatines—were expelled from the Republic, and the externals of Catholic devotion showed no significant alteration. It was said, in fact, that Venice had never witnessed as gorgeous a Corpus Christi procession as that of the summer of 1606. Many prominent people who had seldom gone to Mass before the interdict now did so with the greatest ostentation.

The pope's first peace feelers were dismissed by the Venetians, who smelled victory in the wind. They launched instead a pamphlet war against the interdict and, by implication, against all the pomps and wiles of the papacy. The protagonist in this cause was a learned Servite friar named Paul Sarpi (d. 1623), who directed the literary assault as a paid consultant to the signory.[8] Paul V was not without distinguished advocates, including the theologian Cardinal Bellarmine (d. 1621) and the historian Cardinal Baronius (d. 1607), but it soon became clear that the politicians, not the intellectuals, would settle the dispute.

The possibility that Venice and Rome might turn their quarrel into a war brought greater powers into the controversy. The petty Italian states, like Tuscany and Savoy, prepared to choose sides while they warily studied the moves of the French and the Spanish. The Protestant countries cheered Venice from the sidelines, but they could offer little real help. The key figure was Henry IV. He owed the Venetians a debt, for they had recognized him as King of France as early as 1589, when it had been hazardous to do so. Yet Henry refused to be drawn into an antipapal conflict, and above all he did not want to provoke hostilities which might give Spain an excuse to expand its already awesome holdings in Italy. In the end Henry played the broker and persuaded both sides to accept what he termed a compromise, though the settlement was far more favorable to the Venetian than to the papal position. On April 21, 1607, the censures were formally lifted and the two criminal priests were handed over to a Roman court. Jesuits,

8. See Federico Chabod, *La Politica di Paolo Sarpi* (Venice, 1962), and William Bouwsma, "Venice, Spain and the Papacy: Paolo Sarpi and the Renaissance Tradition," in Eric Cochrane, ed., *The Late Italian Renaissance* (New York, 1970), pp. 353 ff.

however, were not permitted to return to the Republic, nor was a word said about repealing the objectionable land laws.

By verbal legerdemain the French negotiators tried to save face for Paul V. Their attempt can hardly be said to have succeeded; the plain fact was that the Venetians had stood their ground and the pope had backed down. Yet in the long run many Venetians doubted they had won very much. In 1610 Sarpi, already turning over in his mind a hostile critique of the Council of Trent,[9] complained bitterly that Venice was more papal in its sympathies than it had ever been. Still, Venice's defiance in 1606–1607 perhaps did have some lasting significance; by the very fact that no pope ever again resorted to the weapon of interdict, this Venetian affair perhaps marked the outer psychological limits of the Counter Reformation. Meanwhile, far away to the east and north, geographical limits were being set as well.

I. THE TIME OF TROUBLES

The Venetian interdict proved an embarrassment even to those whose devotion to the Holy See was beyond question. The King of Poland, for instance, showed his disapproval by instructing his bishops to welcome Venetian dignitaries to all religious functions and specifically to those held at the royal court in Warsaw. Such services were frequent, because Sigismund III Vasa (d. 1632) was a remarkably pious man, so pious indeed that not a few of his subjects grumbled that he was a fanatic. They resented that the papal nuncio ranked so high among the king's advisers and that the Jesuits enjoyed so much influence over him; it appeared to many that royal policy was in some measure determined by the eminent Peter Skarga (d. 1613),[10] who during his later years deserted the field of theological controversy for that of political theorizing. At any rate, the ideological partnership between Rome and Warsaw was quite strong enough to survive Paul V's momentary rashness.

Son of the enigmatic John III of Sweden and a Jagellon princess, Sigismund experienced both profit and loss from his fervent Catholicism. If his religion had helped elect him to the Polish-Lithuanian throne in 1587, it had surely cost him the Swedish one twelve years

---

9. His highly polemical *Istoria del Concilio Tridentino*, smuggled out of Italy by English friends, was first published in London in 1619.

10. See above, p. 214.

later. He had not, however, given up hope of returning north in triumph, of ousting the usurper, his paternal uncle Charles, and of forcing the Lutheran Swedes to acknowledge his dynastic right and accept his religious faith. This plan, consistently encouraged by the king's clerical entourage, gradually assumed broader dimensions, until Sigismund envisaged a huge Catholic empire, with himself at the head of it, stretching from the Baltic to the Urals to the Black Sea. Here was a restatement of the dream his father had had,[11] only now new circumstances suggested that the shortest road to Stockholm might well pass through Moscow.

The trouble was, however, that the same centrifugal forces which left his neighbors weak enough to lend theoretical feasibility to such ideas were also at work within his own kingdom-duchy.[12] He had little effective control over the magnates and the *szlachta*, who carefully kept local administration in their own hands. He had no bureaucracy to speak of, no judicial apparatus, no predictable income. To mobilize an army of any size depended upon the cooperation of the warlords whom King Stephen Bátory had charmed by his charismatic personality and his military flair. But Sigismund was singularly lacking in gifts of this kind; moody and introspective, he preferred secret diplomacy—his critics called it intrigue—to the open-handed camaraderie Bátory had excelled in. As for soldiering, Sigismund's career as a general was a dismal failure, especially his campaigns to regain the Swedish throne.[13]

The opposition within Poland to Sigismund eventually coalesced around John Zamoisky (d. 1605), Stephen Bátory's grand hetman and chancellor, whose dashing figure recalled the glory days of the previous reign. But Zamoisky's stature rested upon more than nostalgia and upon more than his own considerable talents. He represented the resurgence in the power of the high nobility at the expense of both the gentry and the crown.[14] A cultivated man himself, he was a patron of arts and letters and founder of a university at the moment when the Polish Renaissance was manifesting itself on many intellectual levels. Such achievements were part of a developing national self-conscious-

11. See above, pp. 221 f.
12. F. Nowak, "Sigismund III," in W. F. Reddaway et al., eds., *The Cambridge History of Poland to 1696* (Cambridge, 1950), pp. 451 ff.
13. P. O. von Törne, "Poland and the Baltic," in *ibid.*, pp. 476 ff.
14. Janusz Tazbir, Emanuel Rostworowski, et al., *History of Poland* (Warsaw, 1968), pp. 223 ff.

ness among the Poles, and it may have been his realization of this that helped keep Zamoisky from allowing his differences with the king to reach a final breaking point. Still, neither he nor his fellow magnates intended to let Sigismund exploit national sentiment in order to build a unitary state wherein the monarchy could secure regular revenues and establish a standing army without reference to the parliamentary *seym*. They were dedicated rather to the constitutional arrangement Professor Halecki has called "the royal republic."[15] Zamoisky gave one indication of his feudal conception of that republic in 1600 when he raised an army on his own account and used it to invade Wallachia and Moldavia.

But this adventure revealed more than differences between the king and his magnates about the merits of centralization. The purpose of the invasion was ostensibly to unseat a prince whom the Austrian Hapsburgs had succeeded in placing upon the throne of Transylvania, but Zamoisky's deeper strategic design was to drive Poland's southern frontier to the Danube, a project dear to the heart of his late master, King Stephen Bátory. That the lands in question, nominally fiefs of the Ottoman Empire, were the objects of Austrian ambition served as no deterrent to Zamoisky and his friends, whose anti-German biases went beyond territorial competition to age-old racial and cultural tensions. Sigismund III, by contrast, was anxious to remain on cordial terms with the Hapsburgs, not because he opposed expansion but because he wanted to expand north and east rather than south. He was relieved when Zamoisky's initial victories were swallowed up in the turmoil which was the chronic condition of the Danubian area, and he assured the Emperor Rudolph that Polish and Austrian spheres of influence need not collide.[16] The result of these quarrels over strategy, compounded by quarrels over the nature of sovereignty, was to put the king and his most powerful and popular subject permanently at odds. And Sigismund III had neither the resources nor the strength of character to do much about it except wait.

His patience was ultimately rewarded, for nobody, not even a grand

15. Oscar Halecki, *A History of Poland* (New York, 1943), p. 129.

16. Sigismund displayed no anti-Germanism. In 1592 he married an Austrian arch-duchess and, when she died, her sister, even though Archduke Maximilian was contesting the 1587 election. And in 1605 Sigismund made what proved to be a fateful choice of Joachim Frederick of Brandenburg as administrator of East Prussia.

hetman, lives forever. In the spring of 1606, just as the Venetian interdict was being promulgated and, more importantly to Sigismund, just
after John Zamoisky had been laid safely in his grave, the door to the
East swung open enough for opportunity to beckon. On May 17,
Dimitry, Tsar of all the Russias, was murdered in his palace at the
Kremlin, and Muscovy exploded into civil war. The Time of Troubles
had begun; for the King of Poland it was a time rich in promise.

Actually the seeds of the trouble had been sown long before by the
recklessness and instability of Ivan IV the Terrible, who had in a fit of
rage killed his eldest son and so, at his death, had left the fortunes of
his country and dynasty in the frail hands of his other male issue, an
imbecile named Theodore and an infant named Dimitry. Theodore,
however, was blessed with a wife he loved and trusted and she with a
brother of outstanding talents. His name was Boris Godunov. He had
served Ivan IV faithfully during the dread tsar's last unhappy years,
and when the pathetic Theodore ascended the throne, Godunov assumed the reins of government. Such an arrangement suited boyars,
gentry, bourgeoisie, and peasants alike because, while they regarded the
Rurik dynasty with almost superstitious reverence, they also recognized Godunov as a man of practical sense and decisiveness.[17] He was
prudent too, prudent enough to banish Theodore's young half-brother
Dimitry to a remote provincial town where, in 1591, the boy, aged ten,
died in the midst of an epileptic seizure.

When Theodore in his turn died seven years later, Boris Godunov,
after a decent show of reluctance, succeeded to the royal title himself.
He shortly discovered that reigning in his own name presented graver
difficulties than ruling from behind the throne. The long line of Rurik
grand dukes and tsars was now extinct, and the populace was uneasy at
the accession of one who had no blood connection to that royal house.
Godunov sensed the popular mood, perhaps exaggerated it, and a kind
of panic seemed to come over him. He saw plotters everywhere. The
firm intelligence he had exhibited during his brother-in-law's reign
degenerated into cunning and cruelty. His insecurity begot a further
loss of confidence in his leadership, especially among the ever restless
boyars, who argued that, after all, the illiterate Boris Godunov was no

17. George Verdnasky, *The Tsardom of Moscow, 1547–1682* (New Haven, 1969),
pp. 175 ff.

better than themselves. Even the elements combined against him; crop failures in 1601 and 1603 led to the worst famine in memory, and the people in their unreasoning misery laid the blame at Godunov's door.[18]

About that time there appeared in Poland a young Russian who claimed to be Ivan the Terrible's youngest son Dimitry.[19] He told a story about how he had been miraculously saved from death at the hands of Boris Godunov and how he had remained in hiding since then. He made the round of Polish noble houses, encountering skepticism at first and then, little by little, attracting support. It may have been his rude energy, his good looks, his bold and charming front; it may have been the promises of land and booty he held out to magnates who had had precious little of either since the time of Stephen Bátory. What this consummate actor found, in short, was a world of people who for various reasons wanted to believe him. He gathered pledges of men and money and, to boot, a wife from one of Poland's princely families—whom he cheerfully called his tsaritsa. The enthusiasm with which he embraced the Catholic religion won over the Jesuits, to whom he assured a leading role in the task of reducing Russia to the Roman obedience. The papal nuncio enthusiastically recommended him to the pope, with whom Dimitry opened formal contacts in April, 1604. A month before that he had an audience with Sigismund III, who had remained noncommittal but very interested, as indeed Clement VIII had been.

In October, 1604, the pretender crossed the Dnieper above Kiev at the head of several thousand Polish adventurers and Don Cossacks. Armies from Moscow were sent against him, some of which he defeated and some of which defeated him. It did not matter much, because his strength did not lie in the force he could muster but in the electrifying effect his name had among the Russian people. They too wanted to believe him, and he carried off his imposture brilliantly. His advance toward Moscow was inexorable. Then, as if to prove that Dimitry was fortune's darling, Boris Godunov suddenly died (April 13, 1605) and all resistance collapsed. At the end of July the Pseudo-Dimitry was solemnly crowned tsar in the Kremlin amid delirious celebration over the revival of the old and cherished dynasty. The

18. K. Waleszewski, *La Crise Révolutionnaire, 1584–1614* (Paris, 1906), pp. 93 ff.

19. Pseudo-Dimitry's story is sympathetically recounted in Philip Barbour, *Dimitry* (Boston, 1966).

pope—by now Paul V—sent him coronation presents of a Latin Bible, a crucifix and a rosary, and a letter which began, "Beloved Son."[20]

He was beloved by all at first, but the era of good feeling lasted only a moment. The winning ways that had carried Dimitry to the throne were not enough to solve the problems of a society trembling on the edge of chaos. Perhaps the accumulated griefs, older than Dimitry, as old indeed as Mother Russia herself, defied solution; perhaps that vast, raw, mostly empty land refused to be tamed until the hatreds which pitted boyars and peasants and tumultuous Moscow townsmen against each other had first been purged with blood. Dimitry in any event, apparently oblivious to the dangers around him, gave himself over to enjoying the eminence he had won with his wits. He continued to charm those who came into contact with him, but he was careless and casual and his sexual morals were deplorable—all of which might have been forgiven him had he not also betrayed an ambiguity toward the Orthodox Church. The conversion to Catholicism which had served him so well in Poland was not widely known in Moscow, but the Polish Jesuits who had come in his train were there for everyone to see, as was his own indifference to Orthodox fasts and festivals. It was a curious error for him to have fallen into; he had needed to exploit religious ideology to get his great adventure started, yet he failed to understand that in Holy Russia, of all places, he needed to do so still.

Others were to make a similar mistake during the terrible years that followed. Meanwhile, the assassination of Dimitry on the night of May 17, 1606, acted like some infernal signal designed to let loose an orgy of violence and death.[21] The new tsar, a nondescript boyar named Basil Shiusky, never ruled much of the country outside Moscow, for the fabric of social order simply disintegrated before his eyes. Gangs of runaway slaves roamed and pillaged the countryside; armed bands of peasants and boyars battled each other. Hundreds of villages were burned to the ground. Cossacks from the Don and Volga regions rode leisurely over the land robbing and raping. Polish freebooters plundered at will, always taking special care to desecrate Orthodox churches. It was not so much a matter of armies engaged in pitched battle—the military cadres even by the standards of the time were small and scarcely organized—as it was a wild descent into anarchy. Disease

20. Ludwig Pastor, *History of the Popes* (St. Louis, 1937), XXVI, 221.
21. What follows is based on the chronology in Vernadsky, *Tsardom*, pp. 234 ff.

and hunger soon put the finishing touches to a dark picture of a people reduced to the depths of misery.

In 1607 a new pseudo-Dimitry appeared, this one not his own man like his predecessor but a creature of the Poles, the Cossacks, and the White Russians. He set up his headquarters at Tushino, only eight miles from Moscow, as if to mock Basil V's claim to be Tsar of all the Russias. Yet Dimitry had no better success asserting royal authority; his men spent their time systematically looting the neighborhood and thus inspiring waves of peasant revolts directed against the "brigand of Tushino." Early in 1609 the Swedes intervened in the north, ostensibly to help Tsar Basil but in reality to tighten and extend their hold on the approaches to the Gulf of Finland near Novgorod. The Swedish army, composed largely of French, Scots, and Spanish mercenaries, was if possible even more brutish in its behavior than the natives.

The savagery was lightened only by an occasional exhibition of the grotesque: as when Basil V engineered the canonization of the real Dimitry and promoted the cult of his bones as relics in hopes of convincing the people that Ivan the Terrible's son was in fact dead; or as when the first false Dimitry's Polish wife swore that the second false Dimitry was her husband miraculously delivered from the attempt on his life in May, 1606—though she refused to sleep with him until a wedding ceremony had been performed by a Catholic friar.

Through all these calamities Sigismund III waited his chance. On various occasions and by various factions he had been urged to intervene, but more out of timidity than craft he had held back until he was absolutely sure that Muscovy lay prostrate. In September, 1609, nearly 30,000 Polish troops crossed the ill-defined frontier and attacked Smolensk. To undertake the siege of a strong walled city rather than to strike quickly into the heart of the country was the sort of military blunder Sigismund was famous for. It appeared, however, to matter little, because from all sides supporters rushed to the King of Poland as to a messiah. The false Dimitry's partisans deserted him—he had to flee Tushino and was murdered by one of his bodyguards some months later—and Basil V watched helplessly from the Kremlin as Russian noblemen and bourgeoisie flocked to parley at the siege-camp outside Smolensk. On February 4, 1610, Sigismund announced his terms: consequent to the laying down of arms by all parties and the coronation as tsar of his fifteen-year-old son Lladislaw, he guaranteed the maintenance of the Orthodox faith, the integrity of noble and Church lands, and, as a sop to the mercantile interests, the removal of customs barriers between Muscovy and Poland-Lithuania. The Russians hesitated, but for all practical purposes the treaty was ratified on the battlefield of Klushino (June, 1610), where the Poles annihilated the last of Tsar Basil's armies. A provisional government then promptly dethroned the hapless Basil, clapped him in a monastery, and declared itself ready to accept King Sigismund's proposals. A Polish garrison occupied Moscow on the night of September 21, 1610.

Had Sigismund implemented the protocol of February 4, a union of crowns, in the best Jagellon tradition, might eventually have emerged and dramatically altered the course of east European history. But he did not, nor had he ever intended to do so. His offer of Prince Lladislaw and his soothing guarantees had been ploys to gain time or perhaps room for the serpentine maneuver he loved. He would be tsar himself, head of an immense Catholic confederation, founder of Europe's mightiest dynasty. And when, in June, 1611, his soldiers finally captured Smolensk by storm, he had reason to think he stood within reach of all his dreams.

But he was wrong, because a miracle was in the making, a miracle as wondrous as that performed in another time and place by Joan of Arc. In two short years a dizzying reversal of fortune saw the birth of the Russian nation.[22] Although the Time of Troubles was far from over, although much pain and humiliation had still to be suffered, by 1613 the danger that Muscovy should be a Polish fief or that the Latin Mass should be sung in the Cathedral of the Dormition had vanished. And if crusade means a movement fueled by the undefinable power of ideology, here was a crusade of the first magnitude. One striking sign of its character—and very significant also from a strictly military point of view—was the conversion of the Cossacks, almost to a man, from heedless marauders to defenders of Holy Russia. The same fever of dedication was felt everywhere, from Kazan to Pskov. Once Sigismund III's intentions became clear, armies sprang out of the ground, feuds were forgotten, social distinctions were set aside, and all classes and regions rallied to the cause of the Orthodox religion. By 1612 a national army had taken the field, not 100,000 strong as later enthusiastic chroniclers maintained, but large enough and disciplined enough to

22. See V. O. Kliuchevsky, *A History of Russia* (London, 1913), III, 65 ff.

hold its own against Polish and Swedish regulars. The army, which liberated Moscow in October of that year, expressed the national will whose existence heretofore had been unsuspected, and it was fitting that out of the army should evolve a representative assembly unique in Russian annals. This *Zemsky Sobor* assumed executive and legislative responsibility, collected taxes, and supervised the course of the war. Its most solemn task was accomplished in February, 1613, when 800 delegates predictably chose as tsar a native prince who claimed a personal link to the Rurik dynasty.[23] His name was Michael Romanov.

The Time of Troubles did not end in 1613, nor did the newly awakened religio-national spirit sweep everything before it. Indeed, the fighting continued in the north and west until an exhausted Russia had to settle first with Sweden (1617) and then with Poland (1618) by ceding great hunks of territory.[24] Nevertheless, from the accession of the House of Romanov, the word "Russia" came to mean a recognizable political entity rather than merely a geographical expression, and its imperial future was only just around the corner. The banners of the Counter Reformation had fluttered briefly from the spires of the Kremlin, but then—and Muscovites proud of their city might have noted the precedent—so had Persian flags for a moment flown over the Acropolis.

2. THE TROUBLED EMPIRES

The territorial losses suffered in the West by the Grand Duchy of Moscow even before Ivan the Terrible's death (1584) had been compensated for to some extent elsewhere. The Russians had forced their way into the crumbling Tartar khanates which were stretched out from the shores of the Black and Caspian seas eastward toward Asia, and though these incursions remained something less than conquests they were viewed as serious provocation by a Muscovite neighbor more powerful than Poland or Sweden. Until the 1560s Constantinople had maintained amiable if distant relations with Moscow, on the premise that the grand duchy was too weak and disorganized to pose a serious threat on the Ottoman northern frontier or, at worst, that it served as a useful counter to the ambitious Jagellon kings of Poland.

23. The new tsar's great-aunt had been Anastasia Romanovna, Ivan the Terrible's first wife. See Ian Grey, *The Romanovs* (New York, 1970), p. 2.

24. See maps and commentary in Allen Chew, *An Atlas of Russian History* (New Haven, 1967), pp. 42–45.

This policy changed gradually, not so much because the Russians proved stronger as because the buffer states in the Crimea and the Caucasus proved weaker. By 1569 the Porte had devised a plan whereby upstart Muscovy and Persia, the Ottomans' most persistent enemy, could be dealt with by a single stroke. It called for a canal to be dug between the Don and the Volga; a Turkish fleet would sail out of the Black Sea, over the canal to the Volga, and down the Volga into the Caspian. This piece of grand strategy would block Russian expansion toward the lower Volga basin, would outflank the Persians from the east, and, incidentally, would open direct trade routes between Constantinople and central Asia. Construction on the canal actually began, though before long the project was given up as impracticable. So the indefatigable Turks dragged the dismantled ships overland and launched them on the Volga, only to have them bloodily repulsed when they attacked the Russian fortress of Astrakhan, at the entrance to the Caspian Sea.[25] After this episode an informal and uneasy peace settled on the area; sultan and tsar, both heavily engaged on other fronts, had to be content for the time being with whatever security an imprecise and shifting frontier could offer.

Perhaps the most remarkable feature of the campaign of 1569 was that it had happened at all. It showed at any rate the sublime self-confidence the Turks had achieved in this heyday of their power, when no undertaking seemed beyond their capacity, when resources were presumed available for the most grandiose schemes. However, the sobering check at Astrakhan, followed shortly by the disaster at Lepanto, signaled that all was not well with the Ottoman Empire. Yet no one then would have predicted that its reversal of fortune was destined to be so swift.

Many interrelated causes contributed to the Turkish decline, which by 1610 was well on its way. Fundamentally, it was a case of a warrior people which had reached and perhaps exceeded its capacity for expansion without having learned to organize itself for nonmilitary pursuits. Agriculture was left to a despised serfdom and commerce to sharp foreign factors or to Greeks or to Jewish entrepreneurs, like the fabled Joseph Nasi, Duke of Naxos, who counted among his business enterprises a monopoly on the sale of wine within the empire and who

25. Halil Inalcik, "The Heyday and Decline of Ottoman Power," in P. M. Holt et al., eds., *The Cambridge History of Islam* (Cambridge, 1970), I, 335 f.

actually set in motion plans to convert desolate Palestine into a national homeland for Jews persecuted by Moslem and Christian alike.[26]

The sultanate reflected the nature of the Turkish crisis in a striking way. Machiavelli had observed[27] long before that the absolute character of the Ottoman autocracy made for a system relatively easy to govern. But he presumed the sultans to be first of all chieftains who could depend upon the obedience of subjects permanently on a war footing. He presumed also the sultans to have a certain minimum of intelligence and probity, which qualities, however, were not much in evidence in the vicinity of the Porte after Suleiman the Magnificent's time.[28] The sultanate had taken on some similarity to the Spanish kingship Philip II had put together: to function properly it needed to be filled by a superman, and so, human affairs being what they are, it more often than not fell victim to procrastination and unscrupulous favorites.

By the end of the sixteenth century other less personal agents were eroding the mighty Ottoman structure. The growth of population throughout the empire had not been matched by increases in the amount of land put under cultivation. The cost of bread soared as a result, and, even more ominously, a restless and violence-prone rural proletariat came into being. When in the 1580s and 1590s the full impact of cheap American silver was felt in Turkish territories, the usual inflationary ills followed: sharply rising prices, currency debasement, speculation, and usury.[29] The government's revenues remained steady, while their purchasing power plummeted as much as 60 percent. The sultans were forced into burgeoning deficits and eventually into unpopular new taxes. All this led to discontent and not infrequently to disorder, even in Anatolia, the heartland of the empire.

Among those hardest hit by the economic and social upheavals were the Moslem gentry whose ancestors had ridden to so many Turkish victories. But the incentive for conquest was no longer what it had been; plunder in the form of free land was available now only on the

26. See the works of Cecil Roth, especially *The House of Nasi, the Duke of Naxos* (Philadelphia, 1948).

27. In *Il Principe,* ch. 4.

28. See, for instances, Carl Brockelmann, *Geschichte der Islamischen Völker und Staaten* (Munich, 1939), pp. 294 ff.

29. V. J. Parry, "The Ottoman Empire, 1566–1617," in R. B. Wernham, ed., *The New Cambridge Modern History* (Cambridge, 1968), III, 370 ff.

edges of the empire, and even there its worth tended to wither away under the remorseless pressures of inflation. And the risks were greater too, because the Ottoman military apparatus was already falling behind the West in technological development. The once peerless Turkish light cavalry often found itself outgunned by heavily armed Austrian dragoons. The sultans as a consequence had to hire more troops, arm them better, and scrounge the money to do both. The character of the Turkish army changed as peasants were recruited for the first time and taught how to use muskets; often as not, after a campaign or two they went back to their home villages and fomented bread riots, or else employed their new skills with the bandit gangs that roamed unchecked over the countryside.

It was therefore from a position somewhat diminished in strength that the Ottoman Empire faced its traditional Christian enemies. The sultan, despite Queen Elizabeth's pleas and warnings that Spain was as much a danger to him as to her, resolutely maintained the policy of disengagement in the Mediterranean.[30] Instead the point of hostile contact between East and West continued to be in the Carpathian basin, where the Turks encountered an opponent in a much graver state of disarray than their own. The war that broke out on the old Hungarian battlefield in 1593 and lasted till 1606 revealed how close the Holy Roman Empire of the German Nation and the Austrian branch of the Hapsburg dynasty stood to dissolution. The fighting itself settled little, since it was desultory and inconclusive and ended with a treaty which merely confirmed the de facto frontier arrangements of fifty years' standing. The Ottomans did formally recognize the emperor as rightful king of the western strip of Hungary he actually controlled, but this concession, important a constitutional precedent as it later proved to be, was small comfort to the Magyar people, who presumably would have preferred freedom from Turk and German alike.

Indeed, some Magyars, lucky in their remoteness from the centers of power and protected by the mountain fortress nature had built them, did seize the opportunity to achieve a precarious autonomy. From 1541, when Buda capitulated to the Turks, Transylvania considered itself the remnant of free Hungary. Princes like Stephen Bátory sometimes had to acknowledge the emperor's formal suzerainty and other times to pay

---

30. Edwin Pears, "The Spanish Armada and the Ottoman Porte," *The English Historical Review*, VIII (1893), 430–466.

tribute to the sultan, but by skillfully playing off one giant against the other Transylvania eluded the domination of both and for the most part went its own way. Or rather the great lords who really ruled the country went their own way. For, predictably, mixed up with nascent nationalism were elements of noble faction and religious ideology. Protestantism, and particularly Calvinism, had flourished among the Transylvanian magnates, who, typical of their class and their time, were as interested in the political as in the spiritual uses of religion. Hapsburg expansion and Counter Reformation Catholicism had gone hand in hand for years, so that to resist the one amounted to resisting the other. The Transylvanian aristocracy might believe the Calvinist gospel to be Christ's own revelation, and still understand its value as a bulwark against German cultural and political absorption. In 1606, with their Hapsburg overlords bogged down in an unwinnable war, the Transylvanians, under a baron named Stephen Bocskay, declared their total independence of Vienna.[31] The Austrians were too prostrate to prevent this development, and the Turks, for their part, accepted it with equanimity. A militantly Calvinist Transylvania, nominally subject to themselves, could fit their overall strategic purposes, and in any event as Moslems they traditionally felt relative sympathy for Protestant Christians who, though infidels, at least did not "worship" idols as the Catholics and Orthodox did.

Pope Paul V viewed the Austro-Ottoman stalemate with undisguised bitterness. He and his predecessor had designated the war a crusade and had subsidized it lavishly, only to have it end with the bulk of Hungary still in Islam's clutches and Transylvania alienated from the Roman Church. The pope publicly denounced Austrian ineptitude and dishonesty, and as far as they went his charges were accurate: probably never had a more venal and bungling military administration presided over a more disreputable gang of mercenaries than in the Christian crusade of 1593–1606. But the deeper truth was that the Hapsburgs' failure in the war was only symptomatic of the crisis in their own affairs and in those of Germany at large. The internal settlement of 1555—the famous Peace of Augsburg—was falling to pieces.

In fact that settlement had swept many problems under the rug which, during the Turkish war, came to the surface again. Confessional hatreds had not lessened; if anything, the success of the Catholic counteroffensive produced more tension than ever. The ecclesiastical

31. See Ladislas Makkai, *Histoire de Transylvanie* (Paris, 1946), pp. 194 ff.

reservation remained the bone of fiercest contention,[32] and behind all the other disagreements was the constitutional problem of the relationship between the princes and the empire. The emperor was at once one of these princes—the hereditary or elected ruler of lands along the eastern frontier of the Holy Roman Empire—and the presiding officer of that eternally squabbling confederation. He pleaded that response to the Turkish menace was a pan-German concern, a kind of imperial imperative, because ultimately the whole empire fell under the same threat of alien invasion. But many princes retorted that the proximate and, as far as they knew, the only objective of Ottoman arms was in the East, that is, in the Hapsburg crown lands of Bohemia, Moravia, Austria, and Hungary. Why, they asked, should the resources of Germany be mobilized to rescue one prince's possessions, parts of which—notably Hungary—lay outside the boundaries of the empire? The Protestant states took the lead in advancing this argument. As early as 1594 many of them endorsed the position of the Calvinist Count Palatine, who flatly refused to grant any subsidies for the war until the ecclesiastical reservation was repealed and the centralizing pretensions of the emperor were repudiated. Nor did the Catholic princes display any eagerness to snatch Hapsburg chestnuts from the fire. At the Diet of Regensburg in December, 1597, the Archbishop of Salzburg blandly observed: "I question if the empire is in such imminent danger of falling under the Turkish yoke that it is necessary to prosecute this war, and if there were such a danger, would all the help we could contribute be sufficient in the long run?"[33] Archbishop Ratinau, a notoriously promiscuous prelate, may not have been representative of the Catholic revival, but the Duke of Bavaria, a considerably more respectable spokesman, said much the same thing.

Here was another indication that the Counter Reformation was approaching its outer limits. The uneasy alliance between the Tridentine reformers and the princely families of southern and western Germany had served both well enough, but by the beginning of the seventeenth century, among a new generation of Catholics, the conviction was growing that all the victories to be won had been won. It was more than coincidence that Protestantism rebounded from decades of reverses just as the Turkish war was grinding down to its inconclusive

32. See above, p. 81.
33. Quoted by Johannes Janssen, *History of the German People at the Close of the Middle Ages* (St. Louis, 1906), IX, p. 204.

finish. The image of the Catholic Church as an armed camp that had pushed out east and north as far as it dared was not a bad one.

And there was more than a hint of fatalism in the contention that defense of the Hungarian outposts was a concern for the Hapsburgs and not for Christendom at large. If the Turks came, they came, and, as Ratinau asked—one can almost see him spreading his fat smooth hands in a gesture of futility—what really could be done about it? Internal religious strife had finished the job begun by territorial competition: the empire was dying as an ideal and dead as a reality. One after another of the imperial techniques for keeping the peace and promoting mutual prosperity had been rejected by the contending parties. In 1608 the estates gathered again at Regensburg for a diet, and this time, after the usual confessional quarrels, the assembly broke up without bothering to declare a regular recess. This collapse of the empire's premier organ meant that opposing German leaders had given up even the possibility of speaking to each other in a neutral arena, and it was inevitably followed by the formation of new organizations along sectarian lines, the Protestant Union in May, 1609, and the Catholic League two months later. Soon both were arming.[34]

Further contributing to this process of dissolution were the rivalries within the Hapsburg family.[35] Emperor Rudolph II evolved through his long reign (1576–1612) from an eccentric into a madman. Sunk in a melancholy relieved only by ever shorter periods of frenzied activity, he was consumed by hatred of his brother Mathias—the same Archduke Mathias who had once been William of Orange's henchman in the Netherlands. The emperor lived at Prague, surrounded by seers and astrologers, completely dominated, it was said, by his valet, practically withdrawn from public life. He was beset by papal nuncios, Jesuits, Protestant noblemen, quarreling nephews and cousins, all of whom pressed him for decisions he was incapable of making either psychologically or constitutionally. By a familial coup in 1608 the childless Rudolph was stripped of all his prerogatives except the imperial title and the kingship of Bohemia, and he managed to keep the latter only by granting, in a document called The Letter of Majesty, full religious toleration to the Bohemian Protestants. Mathias, as slothful and incom-

---

34. For a summary see Hajo Holborn, *A History of Modern Germany: The Reformation* (New York, 1967), pp. 293 ff.

35. See Bohdan Chudoba, *Spain and the Empire, 1519–1643* (Chicago, 1952), pp. 189 ff.

petent as his brother was insane, succeeded to the rest of the Hapsburg patrimony, such as it was, and eventually to the imperial throne.

At this moment of wholesale disintegration Germany was suddenly confronted with the crisis of the five duchies. In March, 1609, Duke John William of Jülich, Cleves, Berg, Mark, and Ravensburg died without issue. This conglomerate of territories—not large in area but of crucial strategic significance for the lower Rhine region—immediately attracted rival claimants who in turn sought support from their respective coreligionists. A Hapsburg imperial commissioner, ostensibly dispatched to study the intricate legal problems involved in the succession, occupied part of the territory, and two Protestant princes occupied the rest. The newly formed Union and League rattled swords at each other. In short, it looked like the beginning of another dreary round of violence tempered by intrigue with which similar contests had been fought out within the empire for decades.

But this time a new element revealed itself. Foreign powers, no longer content to play an auxiliary role in German affairs—as, for example, Alexander Farnese had done at Cologne in the 1580s—now took it upon themselves to make the final decisions about war and peace. The French forbade a Hapsburg candidate in the five duchies, the Spanish would abide no Protestant, the Dutch no Catholic. And if they were determined to press their divergent policies to the extreme, then Germany would be a battlefield for foreigners as Italy had been a century before. Germans, without a semblance of unity or cohesion, without even a means of civilized communication among themselves, drifted inexorably toward a civil war they did not want and yet could not prevent. If the crisis over the five duchies should pass—as in fact it did—it would be because non-Germans for some reason were not ready to fight. Another time would come, and another crisis, when the brutal prophecy of Henry IV's intellectual friend Duplessis-Mornay would be fulfilled: "We shall set Germany afire, and we shall so manage matters that we shall reap the fruits of its death when God ordains it."[36]

3. THE GRAND DESIGN

"France and I both need to catch our breath."[37] So said Henry IV in 1598, the year of the peace treaty of Vevrins, the year of the Edict of Nantes. At forty-four the king was typical of his countrymen in that he

36. See the citation in Janssen, *History of the German People*, IX, 189n.
37. Quoted by Dunn, *Religious Wars*, p. 131.

could scarcely recall a time when his life had not been circumscribed by violence and uncertainty. He had survived the morning of St. Bartholomew, 1572, by cowering in his bride's bed and by abjuring his Protestant faith. Then he had escaped, first from the suffocating Valois court, next from his forced conversion to Catholicism, and finally from his wife, to become the vagabond King of Navarre, soldier, penniless adventurer, rebel, patriot, gambler, prodigious lover, and chief of that ideological faction whose solemn tenets caused adherents and antagonists alike to call it simply the Religion. But Henry was above all an *homme d'état,* and when his manifest destiny summoned him to do so he cheerfully switched religious hats again, thereby resurrecting a sense of national purpose sufficient to defeat the Spaniards. Now he needed a brief respite in order to get a suitably fertile wife (with the aid of an annulment of his first marriage granted by his new friend, the pope[38]) and found a mighty dynasty and lead his people into the era Frenchmen will always remember as *le grand siècle.*

Plenty of evidence, spiritual no less than physical, spoke to the kingdom's urgent want of a breathing space. Yet ruined towns and farmsteads and the cynical weariness that brooded over the land did not tell the whole story. People had learned to adjust on the local level to the national agony which forty years of religio-factional conflict had thrust upon them. Whole provinces had simply opted out of the war and gone their own way; cities had arranged truces among themselves and bribed the rival armies to stay away or go away.[39] Devastation of life and property had been immense, but the sinews of society had not been essentially damaged. A pike is not a machine gun; Western man had not yet achieved that capacity for mass destruction which was to be his dubious distinction later on. A little time of peace and good order could heal a community whose institutions, after all, were relatively uncomplicated.

Once the immediate foreign danger had passed, the first phase in the healing process had to be a solution of the ideological problem. In the famous edict signed by Henry IV at Nantes on April 13, 1598, the lines of peaceful coexistence between the two communions were laid down.[40] "Since God has not yet been pleased to allow the union of French-

38. Henry married Marie de' Medici, a distant cousin of Catherine's, in 1600.

39. See, for example, Eugène Thoison, "Un traité inconnu entre Henri IV et Mayenne," *Bulletin Historique et Philologique* (1894), pp. 452 ff.

40. Partial English text in H. Bettenson, ed., *Documents of the Christian Church* (London, 1943), pp. 302 ff.

men in one and the same form of religion," the king defined the terms whereby Huguenots should take their place among the Catholic majority "in perfect concord." Those who practiced "the so-called reformed religion (*religion prétendue reformée*)" were to enjoy equal opportunity in education and patronage, equal access to all public facilities, and equal treatment before the law. They had to restore ecclesiastical property seized during the wars, without, however, being liable for any damage it had suffered in the meanwhile. They could perform their liturgy fully and publicly in any locale in which they had done so in 1577 (the time of the Peace of Monsieur), plus two other towns to be designated later in each *gouvernement*. Protestant worship was not allowed at Paris or at court or at any site within six miles of either. While the Huguenots were permitted to build churches, they also had to pay tithe for the support of the local Catholic parish.

The Edict of Nantes was composed of four separate documents, one of which provided the key to understanding the others. The king granted that the Huguenots might consider the hundred or so towns they presently garrisoned as surety for the government's good will. In other words, the Protestants still maintained the military structure which they had no intention of dismantling and with which the king was not prepared to trifle. The edict, therefore, formally recognized the minority's continuing strength and its consequent right to exist. The arrangement reflected the realities of power rather than the emergence of a new civil enlightenment, and so it is a mistake to consider the edict an experiment in religious toleration, if by "toleration" is meant a commitment to the principle that each citizen should be free to determine his own religious choices. Henry IV intended no such concession; he was willing to acknowledge what circumstances forced him to acknowledge, a state of affairs—increasingly common across Europe—in which ideological unity was not really possible. His edict, a pragmatic, not a principled statement of policy, did not differ essentially from various plans advanced by the unlucky Valois during the wars when neither side was ready to accept them.[41] Nor did it displace the ideal of "une foi, une loi, un roi," as Henry's grandson was to demonstrate by unilaterally revoking the Huguenots' "privileges" at the moment (1685) he judged them too weak to resist.

Henry had to summon all his reserves of toughness, all the credit he

41. See Grant, *History of Europe*, pp. 549 ff., for a comparison of the provisions of the edict with those of the Peace of Monsieur.

had garnered as victor over the Spaniards and peacemaker, in order to get the Edict of Nantes endorsed. The more serious Huguenots suspected that the king, who had betrayed the true gospel once, might do so again, while the Catholics, particularly those lately associated with the League, still nursed the feeling that Navarre could never really be trusted. Even the Parlement of Paris, which had never exhibited any Leaguer sympathies, declared its orthodoxy outraged by the king's proposals. This constituted a serious threat, because without the parlement's formal registration the edict remained void in law. Early in January, 1599, the king lost patience and ordered the *parlementaires* to assemble at the Louvre, where he read them a lecture which said much about himself and about the regime he was determined to establish.

What I have to say is that I want you to verify the edict which I have granted to those of the Religion. I have done it to bring about peace. I have made it abroad; I want it at home. . . . If obedience was due to my predecessors it is due still more to me, as I have re-established the state, God having chosen me to come into this heritage. The members of my parlement wouldn't be in office without me. I know the road to sedition which led to barricades and the assassination of the late king. I'll take care that it doesn't happen again. I will root out all factions, discipline all seditious teaching. I have jumped over the walls of cities; barricades are not so high.

Don't throw the Catholic religion in my face. I love it more than you do; I am more Catholic than you are. I am the eldest son of the Church. You are mistaken if you think you have the pope on your side. He is with me instead. . . . Those who don't want the edict to pass want war. . . . I am the sole conserver of religion. I am king now, I speak as king and I will be obeyed. . . . Follow the example of the Duke of Mayenne. Some have tried to incite him to defy my will, but he replied that he was too much obliged to me. All my subjects are similarly under obligation, because I have saved France in spite of those who wanted to ruin her.[42]

The king got his way. The parlement duly registered the Edict of Nantes, and despite some grumbling and suspicion on both sides, the accommodation took effect and worked satisfactorily through Henry IV's lifetime and beyond. Perhaps only he as one who was not entirely trusted by either confessional group could have won such a compromise. His administration at any rate scrupulously observed the edict's

42. Quoted by Roelker, ed., *Paris of Henry of Navarre*, pp. 295 f.

terms so that little by little mutual animosity gave way to a wary attitude of live and let live. The nation relaxed and prospered through a generation of internal peace.[43]

Ironically enough, no institution flourished more under the new regime than the Catholic Church. The Tridentine reforms, though never officially promulgated in France, began to take hold once the religious wars ended. During the first decade of the seventeenth century both the reformed Carmelites and the Oratorians opened French houses, thus bringing across the mountains the influence of Philip Neri and Teresa of Avila. Francis de Sales and Vincent de Paul, who in their different ways represented the finest flowering of the Counter Reformation, were ordained priests in 1593 and 1600 respectively. St. Francis (d. 1622) was the elegant aristocrat turned bishop, theologian, spiritual director to the ruling classes, practitioner of *humanisme dévot* (in Bremond's phrase[44]); St. Vincent (d. 1660) by contrast was the peasant-apostle to galley slaves and riffraff and the founder of the Sisters of Charity, the first religious order of women specifically committed to ministering to the poor and sick. Meanwhile the Cistercian convent at Port Royal was attracting extraordinarily serious novices and slowly forming the center of a school devoted to the teachings of a divine named Cornelius Jansen who migrated from Louvain to Paris in 1604.[45] That same year the Society of Jesus triumphantly reentered France after a decade's exile brought about by the jealousies of the secular priests and by suspicions about its Spanish connections. The Jesuits, displaying their usual and various skills, were soon among the most enthusiastic supporters of the Bourbon monarchy.

This was a Church, however, more Gallican than ever. For as Henry told the *parlementaires* in 1599, he considered himself "the sole conserver of religion." That boast may have overstated the case, but it fit the Bourbon conception of kingship. Though he had not like James of Scotland written a book on the subject, Henri Quatre was a firm believer in divine-right monarchy. Most popular of all the French kings, his popularity rested upon his gifts and achievements, his capacity for leadership, not upon any sympathy for democratic aspirations.

43. Hauser, *La prépondérance espagnole*, pp. 166 ff.

44. Henri Bremond, *Histoire littéraire du Sentiment religieux en France* (Paris, 1916), II, *passim*.

45. See Nigel Abercrombie, *The Origins of Jansenism* (Oxford, 1936), pp. 125 ff.

He worked hard and he played hard; he had a statesman's mind and a ward politician's wily way with a crowd. He was popular because he was brave and intelligent and something of a charming rascal in his private life. After thirty years of weaklings' rule, Henry appeared a real man, worthy, it seemed to most people, to be a real king.

Henry intended to rule not only the Church but every element of French society. He did not himself say "L'état, c'est moi," but he set the stage so that his grandson could say it and mean it. The moment was propitious. The ideologies had battled to a standstill, and the great barons had either killed one another off or ruined themselves financially, or they stood disgraced in the eyes of public opinion as the villains whose greed and ambition had caused the civil wars. Events had proved that smaller units of government—cities, provinces, seignories—could not guarantee even a modicum of good order. A people weary of the hazards of liberty welcomed the imposition of authoritarian rule.

And the machinery was at hand, at least on paper. Henry IV did not feel compelled to overhaul the structure or add to it. He rather took the forms developed under Francis I (d. 1547) and Henry II (d. 1559), and admirably refined in theory by Henry III, and made them work.[46] He did not have to be reminded that the cornerstone of a successful state was its finances, that fiscal soundness outranked every other kingly priority. But an absolutist regime could not thrive if it had to secure its revenues by legislative permission. To Henry IV parliaments were anathema, and though he often promised to do so, he never convened an estates general. Instead he assumed responsibility himself for the expenses of the bureaucracy as well as for the staggering crown debt of roughly 100 million écus. Before he died in 1610 he had reduced the debt by a third, had accumulated a cash reserve of almost 5 million écus, and had staked out the government's share of France's modestly booming economy. To achieve this Henry operated within the accepted apparatus of secretaries, chancellor, councillors, *trésoriers*. The highest consultative body remained the *conseil des affaires,* but under Henry's strong hand it was much smaller and more tightly knit than its predecessors. Indeed, hardly more than a half-dozen men formed the royal inner circle. The most notable among them was Maximilien de

46. See *supra*, pp. 50 ff.

Béthune, Baron Rosny and (after 1606) Duke of Sully.[47] In him the king had a civil servant of the caliber of Granvelle and William Cecil. As a convinced Huguenot and a member of the ancient nobility—the *noblesse d'épée*—Sully was not altogether at home in a Catholic court where the new *noblesse de robe* of merchants and lawyers played such a large part. But his lineage and religion were themselves useful to the king, who by favoring Sully contributed to the reconciliation of the factions. And besides, Sully's talents were so extraordinary, his loyalty to the regime so firm—he had joined Henry of Navarre's army when he was sixteen—that he doubtless would have risen to high station in any event.

By 1596 the king discerned that Sully was much better at raising money than at soldiering, and so he withdrew him from combat and appointed him to the *conseil des finances*. Two years later Sully, at thirty-eight, became superintendent of finance, and from then until 1610 his office for all practical purposes superseded the *conseil's* functions. Henry kept a close supervisory eye upon fiscal matters, but he left the day-to-day operations to his superintendent. The royal trust was not misplaced. Sully quickly showed a genius for organizing staff and procedure and for exploiting within the limits of a cumbersome system all possible sources of revenue.[48] In 1596 the crown's expenditures were triple its receipts. In 1600 Sully presented a balanced budget, and for the rest of his years in office he was able to set aside something like 10 percent of the income for debt liquidation and for building up the cash reserve deposited in the Bastille. Much of this black ink was due simply to the peace and good times the country was experiencing. But Sully's skill in managing a small army of subordinates, his shrewd dealings with the tax farmers, his endless war against administrative waste and corruption, his policy of allocating significant sums to be spent in the localities where they were collected—these elements, and the drudgery and constant vigilance they presupposed, were enough to make the crown's new solvency Sully's personal triumph.

The superintendent did not dream any more than the king of challenging the traditional jurisdictions. He worked with what he had. He

47. For the sources see David Buisseret, *Sully and the Growth of Centralized Government in France* (London, 1968), pp. 17 ff.

48. Jean Mariéjol, *Henri IV et Louis XIII* (Paris, 1905), pp. 47 ff. This is Vol. VI of Lavisse's *Histoire de France*.

dealt differently, for instance, with those provinces—Burgundy, Brittany, Dauphiné, Languedoc, Provence—which still maintained local estates than with those where such legislatures had fallen into disuse. But whether Sully's agents acted in the *pays d'états* or the *pays d'elections,* the result was basically the same. The *taille* remained the fundamental direct tax, though receipts from it lessened somewhat in Sully's time, while those from the *traites* and the *gabelle* increased twofold. In constitutional terms the impact of Sully's accomplishment might be measured by this comparison: within a few years of Henry IV's death the *gabelle* alone, levied without parliamentary consultation, brought the King of France twice as much income as the total revenues of the King of England.

Sully's success came about through the efficiency, persistence, and overall fairness of his operation. He indulged in no radical innovations, no startling procedural changes—his clerks still kept their books in clumsy Roman numerals. No mercantilist himself, Sully nevertheless paved the way for Colbert, just as his master did for Richelieu, Mazarin, and Louis XIV.

Sully had been a soldier before he was a financier, and he carried the additional title of Master of Fortifications and Artillery. It was no secret that Henry IV adjudged peace as a time to prepare for war and that the treasure slowly accumulating in the Bastille would one day be spent for military purposes. Indeed, there had been open hostilities with Savoy in 1600, and tension with that northwest Italian principality continued at a high pitch because of France's commitment to preserve the independence of formerly Savoyard Geneva. The real enemy, however, was Spain, or rather the Hapsburg cousins in Madrid and Vienna whose combined territories still confronted France with the old danger of encirclement. Henry took one obvious way to combat this threat by supporting the United Provinces, whose enmity toward the Spanish-dominated archdukes heated up intermittently until a truce was arrived at—much to Henry's displeasure—in 1609.

In the light of these considerations, a document that survives among Sully's papers takes on a curious interest. This was the celebrated "Grand Design of Henry IV" for the organization of Europe.[49] According to this utopian scheme for a Christian Republic (wherein Catholicism, Lutheranism, and Calvinism were to enjoy equal and

49. See C. Pfister, "Les *Economies Royales* de Sully," *Revue Historique,* LIV–LVI (1894), *passim.*

exclusive status), the Continent was to be divided into six hereditary monarchies: France, Spain, Britain, Sweden, Denmark, and Lombardy;[50] five elective monarchies: the empire, the papacy,[51] Poland, Bohemia, and Hungary; and four republics: Venice, the Netherlands, Switzerland, and Italy.[52] Each of these powers was to be represented on a grand council which would settle disputes and establish "an indissoluble bond of security and friendship." The Tsar of Muscovy was to be invited to participate and, if he refused, to be deprived of his European possessions. As for the sultan, he was declared the perpetual enemy.

There is little doubt that no one, including Sully, ever took the idea of the Grand Design as a serious proposal. It may be wondered whether Henry IV ever heard of it.[53] Even so, it offers a strange insight into what was unfolding just beyond the range of men's vision in 1610. For the Grand Design was a blueprint for the era of *la prépondérance française*. Beneath its flights of rhetoric, its essential tenet was the breakup of Hapsburg power, and in that eventuality France's domination in Europe would be assured. Strip Madrid, argued Sully, of Belgium, Franche Comté, and its Italian provinces, and Vienna of Bohemia, Hungary, and the imperial crown. The Hapsburgs could be expected to resist, and if so, war would be necessary, lasting, Sully opined, about three years. But, he added, in a phrase sadly familiar, it would be a war to end war.

French preponderance in Europe was in fact just over the horizon, but the process was destined to be less neat and decorous than that outlined in the Grand Design. It began in 1609. The confessional rivalries in Germany, more or less restrained since the Peace of Augsburg, flared up again and organized themselves into two armed leagues, one Protestant and the other Catholic. At this tense moment Duke John William of Jülich, Cleves, Berg, Mark, and Ravensburg died without issue. These five duchies did not amount to much in land area, but lying just east and southeast of the Netherlands, on both banks of the Rhine, they occupied a strategic position no less important to France than to the German powers. Succession to the duchies was an intricate dynastic problem, and predictably it rapidly developed into

---

50. Savoy plus Spanish Milan.
51. Including Spanish Naples.
52. Florence and other small Italian city-states.
53. See Buisseret, *Sully*, pp. 196 f.

a contest between Catholic and Protestant claimants. The emperor intervened in a judicial capacity, as indeed was his constitutional prerogative; but neither Henry nor the Protestant German princes trusted a Catholic Hapsburg's impartiality. As Henry spoke of the dangers of further encirclement, the crisis was intensified by a ludicrous intrusion of the king's love life. The latest object of Henry's attentions, a sixteen-year-old Montmorency girl, was spirited away by her jealous husband to the court of the archdukes at Brussels. It has been argued that Henry, infuriated at this challenge to his waning prowess, decided to make the issue of succession to the five duchies a *casus belli* with the Hapsburgs of Spain and Austria.

The decision was, to say the least, uncharacteristic of the astute statesman Henry had often proved himself to be. He was without allies (except for the notoriously unreliable German Lutherans); he had no evidence that the Spanish *tercios* were any less formidable than before; his resources, despite Sully's careful husbanding, were at best limited; the overtly Protestant cause he championed was one that could well reawaken sectarian animosities in his own country. As for the alleged affront to his manhood, Henry had loved many women—his court, it was said, resembled the harem of the grand Turk—but he had never been ruled by them. Perhaps he was driven by the ambition of his youth, now long gone, to attain as much military glory as Don John of Austria had. However that may be, on the eve of the campaign, May 14, 1610, he was stabbed to death in a Paris street by an insane monk named Ravaillac.

The crisis over the five duchies subsided only to be replaced in a much more acute form eight years later. Then came a war which lasted not three but thirty years and ended with France supreme on the continent of Europe. Henry IV had nothing to do with that, and indeed Ravaillac may have spared him the ignominy of a defeat which would have altered the ultimate result substantially. No one of course can know. But this much can be said with certainty: out of the wreckage left by the religious wars Henry IV laid the foundations of a state and of a modern nation. Somehow it is summed up in the words of the courtier who brought the news of Henry's assassination to the queen. "Madame," he said, "the king is dead." Then, looking at the solemn-faced, nine-year-old boy who clung to her skirts, he added, "Long live the king."

Chapter Ten

THE QUALITY OF MIND

THE last half of the sixteenth century was a time when the nonliterary arts and the nonmathematical sciences seemed to pause to catch their breath. The universities, hardly as yet recovered from the withering attacks leveled against them by the likes of Erasmus and Rabelais, were in a phase of cautious transition. Caught up in the unfinished business of humanism or engaged in a last-ditch struggle to save their cherished Aristotelian heritage, they remained in either case elitist institutions not altogether comfortable in the real world. They concentrated on turning out squads of competent ministers, lawyers, and civil servants, but the university degree was not the ticket to eminence it once had been and would be again. Universities were sometimes troubled by religious contention and always anxious to maintain the image of orthodoxy as defined by their prince. They were not adventurous places, and they broke no new ground except in mathematics, whose very arcane language tended to heighten their aura of donnish unreality.[1]

The University of Padua[2] was something of an exception, largely because of its laic tradition, which went back to the celebrated fourteenth-century political theorist Marsiglio and which was genially supported by the anticlerical regime of the Venetian Republic, of which Padua was a subject city. The university, whose faculty of medicine had long been its pride, steered clear of theological controversy and instead promoted the sciences, particularly anatomy. Research basic to William Harvey's anatomical discoveries was carried on there, and both Copernicus (d. 1543) and Galileo (d. 1642) spent formative periods of their lives in the university, as did Harvey himself.

Even so, the serious study of human anatomy may well have begun in the artists' studios of the Italian quattrocento rather than in univer-

1. See, for instance, the early chapters of M. H. Curtis, *Oxford and Cambridge in Transition, 1558–1642* (Oxford, 1959).
2. A summary of Itailan universities in Stephen d'Isray, *Histoire des universités françaises et étrangères* (Paris, 1935), II, 3 ff.

sity lecture halls. And by 1576, when Titian died, the last of the Renaissance masters was gone, leaving behind only a reminder of past grandeur. In 1543 the Pole Copernicus published his hypothesis on the movement of heavenly bodies, and the same year the Fleming Vesalius (d. 1564) published his on the circulation of the blood. Seventy and eighty years were to pass before these seminal treatises reached fruition in the work of Galileo and Harvey. In the interval thinkers probed into this or that intellectual thicket but without any sense of urgency—soon after Vesalius wrote his landmark book he retired from research to become a fashionable court physician—and certainly without a hint that they stood on the threshold of a mighty scientific revolution.

As for the painters, sculptors, and architects, they too are remembered chiefly as transitional figures who bridged the gap between Renaissance and Baroque. The aged Michelangelo died in 1564, while Van Dyck was not born until 1599 or Rembrandt until 1606, just in time to feel the impact of the mature Rubens (1577–1640). Similarly, the masses, motets and madrigals composed by Palestrina (d. 1594) and William Byrd (d. 1623), however lovely in themselves, are nevertheless regarded primarily as prelude to opera and the Baroque cantata. A genius like El Greco (d. 1614) and a very great artist like Caravaggio (d. 1610) cannot be consigned to roles of merely passing importance, but the so-called Mannerist School of which they were the brightest ornaments proved too disparate to form an intelligible whole and, as it turned out, too fragile to resist the wave of neoclassicism which flooded the arts of the seventeenth century.[3] At any rate El Greco—born in Crete, nurtured in Venice, ripened under the hot Catholic and Moorish sun of Castile—defies the kind of comparison one might legitimately draw between, say, Leonardo and Raphael; the form, the color, the Byzantine splendor of El Greco's paintings stand outside the ordinary currents of western European tradition and leave their creator in solitary eminence.

Undefinable questions of talent aside, Mannerism is said to have been a product of the disillusionments and insecurities of the Counter Reformation era. The harmonious, reasonable, humane universe conceived of by the Renaissance artists disintegrated into a darker vision

---

3. See the articles by Jean Babelon, René Huyghe, and Rudolfo Palluchini in René Huyghe, ed., *Larousse Encyclopedia of Renaissance and Baroque Art* (New York, 1964), pp. 179 ff.

brought on by war, by inflation, and, above all, by the piercing crisis of conscience inherent in the religious upheavals. The Mannerists testified to their culture's loss of confidence in itself by shifting away from the nice balance of Renaissance perspective, by distorting light and shadow and figure, by descending sometimes through their subject matter or execution into the grotesque and bizarre. Considerable justification for this view stems from the fact that the succeeding Baroque art forms, with their own criteria of dimension and propriety, reflected a renewed sense of self-assurance, a lessening of internal tensions in a society which, after 1610, at least knew where it stood.[4]

Yet the troubles of the time seldom say enough about an epoch's quality of mind, because all times are troubled in one way or another. Rubens and Galileo, after all, flourished during the Thirty Years' War. Perhaps a better explanation for the apparent lacuna in the development of the natural sciences and the tentative character of Mannerist art can be discerned in another crisis more pervasive and in some ways deeper than the political and ideological conflicts going on at the same time. The Counter Reformation witnessed the final act in the revolt against Aristotle.

The wonder of the Aristotelianism that had dominated European thought since the twelfth century was the way it ranged across the whole spectrum of human knowledge and offered satisfactory explanations for such a multitude and variety of phenomena. Everything made sense within the Philosopher's overall world view. Logic, psychology, ethics, physics, politics, poetics, and even Christian theology all fit snugly and comfortably in the same *Weltanschauung*. But the coherence which gave strength could also be a weakness, for to discard one part of the interlocking system of ideas was to threaten the rest of it. Let it begin to unravel at one point, and there was no telling how far the process might go.

Much of the rising criticism was at cross-purposes, but eventually— toward the end of the period with which this book is concerned—it reached a destructive crescendo. The humanists who had learned to savor the purity of classical Latin reacted first against the barbarous translations in which Aristotle's work was clothed. Then, falling victim to Plato's ethereal charms, they began to describe Aristotle as a crude

4. Particularly illuminating is the essay in synthesis of Wylie Sypher, *Four Stages of Renaissance Style* (New York, 1955), pp. 100 ff.

materialist. The discovery that the ancient world they idolized had contained rivals who challenged Aristotle's doctrine at every step encouraged them to do the same. Galen the anatomist and Archimedes the mathematician took on heroic stature in their eyes. And when they needed to confirm their growing obsession, they pointed scornfully at the logic-chopping and hair-splitting to which the nominalist philosophers, in Aristotle's name, had reduced much of higher education.

The religious reformers, Catholic and Protestant, struck another blow at the grand synthesis. The mystical character of their faith had little patience with the intricate structure the scholastic theologians had built by melding the data of revelation with Aristotle's subtle art of distinction and definition. I should rather feel compassion, said the author of *The Imitation of Christ*, than to know how to define it. Thomas Aquinas will burn forever in hell, said Luther, because he smuggled that swine Aristotle into the Christian sanctuary.

The momentum of the assault quickened with the years. Mathematicians laboriously constructed a new set of meaningful symbols that went beyond the categories of the *Organon*. Mannerists painted a world of incomprehensible anguish, despite Aristotle's assurance that ultimately all things rested secure upon principles of order and reasonableness.[5] But the final and decisive battle had to come on scientific ground, where Aristotle was strongest because of his incomparable gifts as an observer and cataloguer of natural phenomena. As long as a sharp eye and common sense were the best tools available to one who would probe the mysteries of nature, Aristotelian physics and all that followed from it would hold the field.[6]

That was why Galileo's *Siderius Nuncius*, published in 1610 and based on the author's use of the telescope, marked the end of an era much more definitively than King Henry IV's assassination did a few months later. Before that could happen, however, the intellectual community—theologians, artists, humanists, as well as scientists—had to divest itself of its Aristotelian frame of reference and so prepare itself, even if unconsciously, to accept such strikingly new answers to the perennial questions. Copernicus brought the process to a head. He

5. One expression of such assurance comes at the end of the twelfth book of the *Metaphysics*: "The world refuses to be governed badly," says Aristotle. (I am indebted for this reference to my friend Professor Ralph McInerny.)

6. Marie Boas, *The Scientific Renaissance* (London, 1962), pp. 68 ff.

thrust into astronomy his heliocentric hypothesis, which explained celestial motion in a manner less complex and mathematically neater than the old Ptolemaic theory. Yet he offered no new data, and so, as Professor Butterfield observes, he suggested more perhaps than he intended: "We nowadays may say that it requires smaller effort to move the earth round on its axis than to swing the whole universe in a twenty-four hour revolution around the earth; but in Aristotelian physics it required something colossal to shift the heavy and sluggish earth, while all the skies were made of a subtle substance that was supposed to have no weight."[7]

At stake then was more than a debate about the movement of sun and stars. If the universe were not a set of transparent spheres, one on top of the other, all turning in complicated orbits around a motionless earth, perhaps matter itself was not what Aristotle conceived it to be. And maybe he had been wrong too in describing rest as the ordinary attribute of a physical body and motion as possible only so long as a moving agent is actively at work. If Copernicus were right, Aristotle's whole theory of causality came into jeopardy; without the need to invoke an efficient cause to explain motion and change, the purpose of that efficient cause—Aristotle's so-called final cause—was irrelevant. Perhaps, after all, the universe was nothing but a mindless machine. Although the culture of which they were a part shrank from the staggering implications of this possibility, men in various corners of Europe were remorselessly groping their way toward a proclamation of it. The German John Kepler puzzled over the chaotic stellar data left to him by Tycho Brahe (d. 1601), the mad Emperor Rudolph's favorite astrologer. The Italian Dominican friar Giordano Bruno speculated his way from Copernican theory to pantheism and finally to death by burning as a heretic (1600). And then, in 1609, Galileo put his eye to the telescope and saw that Copernicus indeed had been right.

The Counter Reformation was, therefore, the last age of the ancient world, not because of its religion or politics or economics, but because it was innocent of that mathematical physics which has created the modern world. Yet the essentially negative process of unraveling the Aristotelian *Weltanschauung,* crucial as it was, had little immediate effect outside a tiny community of technicians and mathematicians. Humanist scholars as a group were not friendly to science, because,

7. Herbert Butterfield, *The Origins of Modern Science* (London, 1957), p. 29.

ironically, it smacked too much of Aristotle, and the masses were blissfully unaware that nature was shortly to be reduced to hard, impersonal, mechanistic laws. For them, on the contrary, nature remained a lively and sentient thing, unpredictable as men, angels, and devils were unpredictable. Those who had read their Aristotle reasoned this way: if motion resulted only from the constant action of a mover, then invisible forces—spirits—had to be responsible for all visible phenomena. The unlettered did not bother to reason it out, and they were content that Shakespeare's "teeming earth" was less a metaphor than an appropriate statement of the real world: "tingling with anthropomorphic life, dancing, ceremonial, a festival not a machine."[8]

So the Counter Reformation's quality of mind possessed a double thrust, one of which worked below the level of popular consciousness. Perhaps the scientific precursors had the greater effect in the long run. But for the men and women of the time words meant more than numbers, and they nurtured among themselves, along with many who were merely verbose, a few of the greatest verbal craftsmen who ever lived.

I. THE COUNTRY SAGE

Though genius cannot be confined to time and place, it does work itself out within a particular setting which conditions and directs it. Montaigne's genius would undoubtedly have blossomed in other soil than the France of the late sixteenth century. Yet in fact this was where it grew, and what final form it might have taken had it grown elsewhere is impossible to say. Montaigne was heir to the ripe development of the French Renaissance, he lived through religious controversies and civil wars, he mingled with the great men of his day. These circumstances, together with the distinctive cultural heritage of the Gascon wine country, all contributed to the making of the man and of his achievement.

Michael Eyquem was born at the manor house of Montaigne in 1533.[9] He sprang on his father's side from a long line of merchants in Bordeaux, one of whom, his great-grandfather, had bought the barony of Montaigne thirty miles away. Michael, the eldest of eight surviving

8. C. S. Lewis, *English Literature in the Sixteenth Century* (Oxford, 1954), p. 4.
9. See the excellent study of Donald Frame, *Montaigne, a Biography* (New York, 1965), which is more than a biography.

children, was the first to drop the surname Eyquem in favor simply of the title which went with the estate. His mother—a stern, avaricious, and relentlessly pious woman—was a Louppes (Lopez) of Toulouse, some of whose Jewish ancestors had been burned by the Inquisition in Aragon, while others, duly christianized, had migrated to the friendlier climate of southern France in the 1480s. This may help to explain why Montaigne always displayed an unfashionable sympathy for Jewry and a lively curiosity about its rites and customs. But then he was remarkable all his life for breadth of interest, tolerance, and contempt for fashion.

His father engaged a tutor for him who spoke Latin and not French, so that Michael was six years old before he began to learn his native tongue. His fluency opened to him the world of Latin letters and gave him an arsenal of classical examples and analogies from which to draw later on. His favorite author was Plutarch, whose style and content much influenced him, but he read them all and pondered them all— Ovid, Terence, and Plautus, and, with special delight, Vergil, whose complete works he owned before he was sixteen. He grew up to be very much a man of the new learning: when he read Italian plays or French history he scribbled notes in the margins which often criticized the authors for failing to measure up to this or that canon of humanistic literature. Books at any rate, ancient or modern, became the stuff of his life. They supplied, he said, "the best provision I have found for this human journey." In a tower of the château he set up a private library which served not only as a study but as a refuge from domestic cares and as a laboratory in whose silence he might explore at leisure the riddle of himself. He liked to ride horseback, because then too he could be alone with his thoughts.

This self-absorption might have disintegrated into eccentricity or worse had it not been accompanied by a sharp eye, a rigid honesty, and a certain mocking disdain for bookish men, including the Lord of Montaigne. Even so, it had its dark and brooding side. Montaigne enjoyed only one deep friendship in the course of his life, and when that friend died he seemed reluctant to risk intimacy again.[10] Certainly he did not find a soul mate in his wife or in his one daughter (of six born) who survived infancy; indeed, his conviction that women were

10. See Marvin Lowenthal, ed., *The Autobiography of Michel de Montaigne* (New York, 1935), pp. 30 ff.

by nature incapable of any but a physical relationship with a man was as unswerving as Cicero's. He infinitely preferred conversation with the humblest tenant on his manor to the prattling of the grandest lady.

Montaigne despite his introspective tastes tried for a time to bear the responsibilities which were his as heir to a considerable name and fortune. He served for nearly fourteen years on the Parlement of Bordeaux, very likely because his father, whom he greatly admired, expected him to do so. But shortly after the father's death the son decided he had borne long enough "the servitude of the court and of public employments," and determined that having dutifully contributed his mite to the common weal, he could now with good conscience retire to his "sweet ancestral retreat" and spend the remainder of his life in the company of the Muses.[11] He was no more explicit, because at that moment—February, 1571, eighteen months before the Massacre of St. Bartholomew—he intended to be no more than a country squire pursuing intellectual hobbies. He did not know that he was about to embark upon a literary career which would eclipse all but two or three of his classical heroes.

The three books of *Essays* were written between 1571 and, if one includes the lengthy additions and emendations which appear on the "Bordeaux Copy,"[12] about 1590. Montaigne continued to tinker with his "chapters," as he called them—the term *essais* he used guardedly, though he liked it because it suggested the tentative character of his project—until the eve of his death. Generally speaking, the chapters increased in size as the years passed: Book III contained none of the one- or two-page pieces common in the earlier collections. On the other hand, the longest chapter by far appeared in Book II—written well before 1580—but this was an exceptional venture, a set academic treatise quite unlike anything that came before or after it.

More significant perhaps than the greater length was the heightened mellowness of the later essays. It was almost as though Montaigne had gradually come to terms with the depressing themes of death, pain, human frailty, and wickedness which so preoccupied him at first. As

11. From the Latin inscription mounted just outside Montaigne's library, quoted by Frame, *Montaigne*, p. 115.

12. The 1588 edition with Montaigne's handwritten marginalia. Since a careless binder cut off some of the author's glosses, the Bordeaux Copy has to be collated with the posthumous edition of 1595.

Mr. Frame points out, the specter of death was much with Montaigne in 1571; his only friend had died, then his beloved father, then his first-born child. But time and reflection, together with deeper experience, tended to soften this apprehension, and after he survived a nearly fatal riding accident in 1574 he grew wryly confident that he was at least as capable of dying well as the ancient authors who furnished his norms in this as in so many other regards. He learned also that physical pain was something he could endure and even profit from, that fear of it in his case had been really fear of the unknown. "He who dreads suffering already suffers what he dreads," was his final comment on the subject. Through his first forty years Montaigne enjoyed excellent health; later on, when he suffered from chronic headache and toothache and from the tortures of kidney stones, he discovered that his humanity had not diminished a whit. His illnesses left understanding and will, tongue, hands, and feet all intact, and they even broadened and deepened his capacity for joy. "Nature had given us pain for the honor and service of pleasure and comfort," he observed. In the relief of a kidney stone successfully passed he shared the "delicate enjoyment" of Socrates, who gratefully scratched his numb legs once the fetters were removed.[13]

Montaigne sang endlessly of himself. He brought the Renaissance cult of individual worth about as far as it could go without deteriorating into embarrassing egotism. And yet his essays do not leave the impression of inordinate self-concern, even when they delve into trivialities like the author's toilet habits or his preference for sexual intercourse in a standing position. Indeed, to Montaigne nothing human was trivial, and by exploring that human being whom he knew best he was able to discern and articulate the truth about mankind in general. "The greatest thing in the world," he wrote in 1572, "is to know how to belong to oneself." But fifteen years later he added: "The prolonged attention that I give to considering myself trains me to judge passably of others also. . . . Having accustomed myself from my youth to behold my life exhibited in the lives of others, I have acquired a thoughtful nature."[14] If such understatement were typical of him, so were his immense powers of observation and critical judgment.

13. George Ives, ed., *The Essays of Michel de Montaigne* (New York, 1946), II, 1490–1498.
14. *Ibid.*, I, 323; II, 1470.

Shrewd, earthy, skeptical, but above all candid, Montaigne moved through the bewildering tangle of human existence tasting, touching, feeling, and ultimately understanding the grandeur and shame of it all. The vehicle that carried him was his own psyche, which became, once he wrote his experiences down, a microcosm for the ages.

In 1580 Montaigne abruptly ended his life of seclusion. He went to Paris to supervise the publication of the first two books of his *Essays,* and from there he embarked on a seventeen-month tour of northern France, Switzerland, Austria, and Italy as far south as Rome. Apart from simple curiosity and the kidney ailment which led him to seek relief in watering places outside his native region, he was moved to undertake this journey by his disgust over the religious wars. Montaigne blamed both sides for the anarchy and violence, but he blamed the Huguenots more, because, he said, they raised questions which had no answers and in the process set off the bitter internecine struggle. His habitual skepticism was of a special kind; he was skeptical not about the fact of the hereafter or about the necessity of the hereafter, but about precise delineations of what the hereafter involved.[15] He was satisfied that the old church, ripe with experience, maintained in its laws, rites, and polity a decent regard for human values and a healthy respect for diversity. As one who was dubious of the human mind's capacity to find the truth, even about simple things, he shrank from a religious commitment which rested its ultimate case upon a man's naked judgment about what the deity intended. "Luther," he said, "left behind him as many schisms and dissensions—yes, more—about the uncertainty of his opinions as he himself raised about Holy Scripture."[16] Montaigne, essentially a conservative, preferred to leave such speculations to heaven. His brand of fideism, best expressed perhaps by the famous question, "Que sais-je?" was not out of tune with the spirit of the Counter Reformation.

Orthodox and practicing Catholic as he undoubtedly was, Montaigne nevertheless had no patience with the fanatics of the League or indeed with any agency which presumed to dictate to consciences. He remained on the most intimate terms with his fervently Protestant brother and sister. He kept up cordial relationships as well with

15. A point both Pascal and Newman seem to have missed. See *Grammar of Assent* (New York, 1870), pp. 298 f.
16. Ives, *Essays,* II, 1460.

Huguenot intellectuals like Duplessis-Mornay and with Henry of Navarre himself, who was his guest at Montaigne more than once and whose claim to the throne he consistently supported. He never believed that either factional chieftain, Navarre or Guise, was as interested in confessional orthodoxy as in satisfying personal ambition. He only regretted that of the two, Guise, his coreligionist, was the bolder and more ruthless.[17]

Montaigne reveled in the novel sights and sounds he encountered during the long journey of 1580–1581, and he carefully noted all his experiences down, even the number and quality of his urinations. If his kidneys functioned neither better nor worse in foreign spas, his spirits lifted immeasurably. The leisurely passage through Germany and the Tyrol lent him a new perspective, and as he approached Italy, his spiritual home, his enthusiasm knew no bounds. His traveling companions, much younger men than himself, marveled at his energy and voracious curiosity. He explored every corner of Rome, and though he was disappointed that so few of the ancient monuments remained, he liked the modern city, its cosmopolitan character and friendliness, the hope its endurance seemed to offer that France too could survive its present troubles. Pope Gregory XIII received him graciously, curial censors complimented him on the *Essays,* learned Jesuits came to pay their respects. He found Italian Catholicism more suited to his taste, more relaxed and self-assured than that of his contentious countrymen.

It was at a watering place near Florence in September, 1581, that Montaigne learned he had been elected Mayor of Bordeaux. The mandate surprised and flattered him, and by November he had returned home to assume his new duties. He served altogether for four years—his reelection to a second term, he pointed out proudly, was a rare occurrence in Bordelais history—and afterward, when critics charged that his administration had not been sufficiently vigorous, he retorted: "I never had that iniquitous and common-enough disposition that the confusion and evil plight of the affairs of the city should enhance the honor of my government; I heartily lent my aid to their being easy and facile."[18]

Whether an effective mayor or not, Montaigne applied himself to the office conscientiously, and inevitably it involved him in larger matters.

17. An unmistakable allusion in Book I, Chapter 24, of the *Essays* (*ibid.,* I, 171).
18. *Ibid.,* II, 1397.

Catherine de' Medici consulted him, as did Henry of Navarre, the latter with increasing frequency as the Wars of Religion approached their climax. In February, 1588, Montaigne went to Paris, presumably to attempt to mediate between Navarre and the king. This mysterious mission aroused the watchful attention of the Spanish and English ambassadors, as well as the suspicion of the League, whose leaders, in the wake of the Day of Barricades (May, 1588), clapped Montaigne into the Bastille. He was released after five tense hours through the personal intervention of Henry of Guise.

So the recluse in the end became an *homme d'état,* not out of preference or out of vanity, but out of the realization, which did not come to him all at once, that a man who would live true to his nature must find his unique place in the community of other men. "I enjoy private life because it is by my choice that I enjoy it, not from unfitness for public life, which is perchance not less suited to my temperament. I serve my prince in it the more cheerfully because I do it by the free preference of my judgment and my reason. . . . I hate the morsels that necessity carves out for me."[19] It was not an unworthy testament to have left behind.

2. THE POLITIQUE

John Bodin,[20] by contrast, had to eat the morsels of necessity before he died in 1596. A wide-ranging thinker of no striking depth, Bodin lacked the spark of genius which set Montaigne apart, and he was for that reason perhaps a better spokesman for the men and women of his generation. Born at Angers about 1530 of prosperous bourgeois stock, Bodin at fifteen or sixteen was professed a Carmelite friar. His order sent him for his formal education to Paris where he attended some classes at the Collège des Quatre Langues—the forerunner of the Collège de France—as well as more traditional ones within the Carmelite house.

This twofold training left a permanent mark on Bodin in that it contributed to the natural ambivalence of a man who was at once

19. *Ibid.,* 1348.

20. For biographical summaries, see introductions to M. J. Tooley, ed., *Six Books of the Commonwealth by Jean Bodin* (Oxford, n.d. [1952]), and Beatrice Reynolds, ed., *Method for the Easy Comprehension of History by John Bodin* (New York, 1945). The standard study remains Roger Chauviré, *Jean Bodin, auteur de la République* (Paris, 1914).

medieval and modern. Thus in later life he proclaimed himself a Platonist and read widely in Greek and Hebrew literature. Yet he remained deeply imbued with the Aristotelianism of the schools, and everything he wrote bore the imprint of that dialectical art which, by the late Middle Ages, had deteriorated into a rigid pedantry.

Bodin left the Carmelites at about age twenty and was dispensed from his vows. He may have had Huguenot leanings at this date and may even have spent some time at Geneva during the early 1550s, though in his mature years he gave no sign of sympathy for Calvinism as an ideology. Indeed, in his published works he carefully avoided religious controversy and instead spoke broadly of good and evil with scarcely an allusion to dogmatic labels. His obvious predilection for the Old Testament—he rarely quoted the New—and for medieval Jewish writers suggests a calculated aloofness from both competing churches (or, possibly, the unconscious influence of Calvin, who had done so much to enhance the prestige of the Old Testament).

Between 1550 and 1560 Bodin was at the University of Toulouse as student and, later, as professor of civil law. This experience served to strengthen in his mind the quaint mixture of old and new. The south of France, unlike Paris, was a stronghold of the Roman law. Moreover, Parisian lawyers, even when they used Roman law in their briefs, as they often did, took the pragmatic route of trying to fuse it upon the feudal, customary legal tradition of the north. The legists at Toulouse denounced such procedure as a barrier to the needed revision of the whole corpus of French law in accord with pure humanist theory.

Bodin was opposed to this position, represented at its best by James Cujas (d. 1590), but he was nevertheless influenced by it. He repudiated Cujas as he had Aristotle, yet both of them were present in his own work. He hankered, as they did, after systems and rationalized categories without, however, freeing himself from a simultaneous commitment to the more tentative methods of induction. He decided that the trouble with civilians like Cujas was the narrowness of their sources. So he turned to universal history as a way to an easy understanding (his own phrase in the title of a book published in 1566[21]) of accumulated human experience, and in that manner discovered "the best and most enduring forms of law." Bodin saw history not as evolutionary or developmental but as cyclical; therefore, the lessons of

21. *Methodus ad facilem historiarum cognitionem.*

history, given man's nature as a constant, admitted of direct and repeated application. Along with such fairly conventional ideas, Bodin espoused peculiar theories about the effect of climate on personality and hence on human conduct. The interpretation of mystic numbers yielded secrets to him, and he quite explicitly rejected Copernicus.

On the subject of contemporary inflation, Bodin was much more hard-headed. A book he wrote in 1568[22] and various pronouncements in subsequent years offered a curiously prophetic solution to the problem. He saw the connection between the price rise and the importation of American bullion, as well as the impact of population growth outstripping productivity. He argued that as far as France was concerned the proper program was to tax manufactures on import and raw materials on export. Austerity and native ingenuity should in time convert the realm into a self-sustaining economic unit, with floods of silver happily pouring into royal and private coffers. He advanced, in other words, a germinal theory of mercantilism seventy-five years before Mun's classic statement of it.[23] Bodin did not live to see that or even to see Sully adopt parts of his protection policy during the latter years of Henry IV's reign.

From the historical dimensions of law through economics to political science was not a difficult passage for Bodin, especially after 1571 when he joined the household of the Duke of Alençon as legal councillor. Until the duke's death twelve years later, Bodin's base was at the center of the *politique* movement. Hardly a more congenial setting could have been provided for the slightly eccentric intellectual who had no strong feelings about religion and who at the same time was convinced that society stood in desperate need of order and regularity. Not that Bodin denied the place of organized religion; he argued rather that competing ideologies left it difficult if not impossible to discern what the true religion was. Government's primary task, therefore, was to establish not true religion but a climate of mutual respect, sanctioned by law, in which both religions could be decently practiced.

The breakup of Christendom contributed directly to Bodin's theory

22. See George Moore, ed., *The Paradoxes of Malestroit and the Response of Jean Bodin* (Washington, 1946).

23. Thomas Mun's *England's Treasure by Foreign Trade* was published posthumously in 1641. See E. E. Rich and C. H. Wilson, eds., *The Cambridge Economic History of Europe* (Cambridge, 1967), IV, 524.

of the state. He did not believe that the distinction between spiritual and secular had meaning in the politics of his day. The state had to reach beyond such categories and rest its claim to obedience from its subjects upon the essence of "the commonwealth (*la république*)." "A commonwealth," he said, "may be defined as the rightly ordered government of a number of families, and of those things which are their common concern, by a sovereign power." And the sovereign power was indubitably the king, not out of divine right but out of simple expediency: monarchy, Bodin argued, worked better than other forms of political organization.

Yet the medieval part of him was not satisfied by this stark assertion of *Realpolitik*. He wanted also to see the king within a great chain of political being; he wanted to create a deducible, foolproof system in the practical order. Unlike Machiavelli, Bodin demanded high moral probity from his prince, though he proposed no means to assure it. And unlike Machiavelli he endowed the prince with a sacred character from which there could be no appeal: dynastic kings'

authority is unquestionably their own and not shared with any of their subjects. . . . It is in no circumstances permissible either by any of their subjects in particular or all in general to attempt anything against the life and honor of their king, either by process of law or force of arms, even though he has committed all the evil, impious and cruel deeds imaginable. . . . Not only is the subject guilty of high treason who kills his prince, but so also is he who has merely attempted it, counselled it, wished it or even considered it.[24]

This statement may at first glance look merely like an extravagance to be expected from a propagandist in the employ of the worst of the Valois. Actually, it was an important elaboration of the fundamental *politique* point of view. The unspoken assumption behind it was that sectarian quarrels threatened the very fabric of civilized society. From what source did rebellion and its attendant social dislocation come in the world that Bodin lived in? From religious sectaries. And what "evil, impious and cruel deeds" did potential rebels imagine their king guilty of or capable of? Those involved in persecuting the true religion of Christ as defined by themselves. And who in fact advocated revolution and tyrannicide as legitimate techniques of political change (ad-

24. Tooley, *Commonwealth*, p. 67 (Book II, ch. 5).

mittedly only in the last resort)? Huguenots and Leaguers, theologians in Geneva and Rome, fervent Calvinists and dedicated Jesuits.[25] They did so because they believed the monarch's primary obligation was to foster the mission of the Church. Bodin the *politique* tried to evade the *odium theologicum* by promoting an essentially secularist allegiance which would effectively place the sovereign above the confessional conflict. Repugnant as such a program may have been to zealots of Bodin's time and to philosophical liberals later, it was destined for a long and honorable ascendancy.

Not so honorable was its author's end. Bodin did not venture much into the public arena, except in 1576 at the Estates General of Blois, where he bearded the leaders of the Catholic League and made some powerful enemies. As a leading advocate of the *politique* position he was safe enough as long as Alençon lived. But after the duke's death in 1584 and after Bodin had retired to the obscurity of Lâon and a minor government job, the pressures on him to conform to more fashionable dogmas became intense. In the midst of the turmoil of 1588, Bodin, convinced that his life was in danger, joined the League. It was, to say the least, a sacrifice of principle.

3. DIVINE DESIGNS

Bodin's and Montaigne's diffidence about trying to justify God's ways to men was not a quality widely shared by their contemporaries. The age indeed was awash in theologians who practiced, however, a species of the theological craft different from that of both the remote and the proximate past. The serene, speculative treatises of the Middle Ages as well as the breathtaking new departures of the early sixteenth century had given place to a nervous, eclectic, belligerent science which showed itself equally suspicious of originality and speculation. A possible exception to this general rule was the Englishman Richard Hooker, who combined a measure of originality with a refreshingly serene mode of expression. But by and large theologians of every

25. The feasibility and morality of tyrannicide were at least tentatively approved by many Catholic and Protestant contemporaries of Bodin. Thus, in 1579 a Huguenot tract called *Vindiciae contra tyrannos* was published at Paris, and a year later George Buchanan wrote a similarly harsh broadside in Scotland, *De jure regni a pud Scotos*. On the Catholic side the most famous instance was the work of the Spanish Jesuit Juan de Mariana, who in his *De rege et regis institutione* (Toledo, 1598) extolled the murderer of Henry III as "aeternum Galliae decus."

persuasion agreed at least implicitly that the time had come to draw back, to regroup, to consolidate. There were no new issues, only old quarrels.

Behind such a point of view lay the conviction, also unspoken, that neither Catholic nor Protestant ideology was going to prevail universally, and that therefore the task at hand was to shore up the faith of those who already had it. This attitude cut two ways. It meant first a hardening of opposition between Catholic and Protestant blocs (and to a lesser degree between various kinds of Protestants), as the dream of a grand Erasmian synthesis, some sort of "reformed Catholicism" capable of reconciling, say, the Confession of Augsburg with the doctrinal canons of Trent, vanished in the smoke of indecisive battle.

But it meant also that within each of the great confessional camps a process of liberalization was permitted now that survival itself did not appear at stake. Theologians of the second generation after Luther and Cajetan believed deeply and cared deeply about what they believed; yet they did not feel pressed to defend the indefensible. Cardinal Bellarmine's celebrated contemporary Thomas Stapleton (d. 1598), while he devoted his whole professional life to the intellectual assault against Protestantism and titled his learned biblical commentaries "An antidote against the poison of Calvin and Beza," nevertheless just as roundly condemned the neo-Pelagian Catholic theology which, he said, had occasioned Luther's protest in the first place.[26] And when Jesuit and Dominican theologians engaged in a long and bitter dispute about the nature of divine grace—a matter of the gravest moment in the overall Catholic controversial position vis-à-vis Protestantism—Pope Paul V finally intervened (1607), declared both parties equally orthodox, and imposed on them a policy of mutual toleration.[27]

The same phenomenon was at work in different ways within the Protestant community. At the University of Leyden in Holland a professor of theology named Jacob Hermandszoon—usually latinized as Jacobus Arminius—introduced into the Dutch Reformed Church a

26. See my *Thomas Stapleton and the Counter Reformation* (New Haven, 1964), pp. 93 ff.

27. This was the controversy "de auxiliis," which had to do with the kind of aid given free will by divine intervention. It was prompted by the publication in 1598 of *De concordia liberi arbitrii cum gratiae donis*, by the Spanish Jesuit Luis de Molina. The Dominicans called the treatise Pelagian. For summary and bibliography see E. Vansteenberghe, "Molinisme," *Dictionnaire de théologie catholique*, X (1929), cols. 2094 ff.

frankly revisionist program. Arminius, though educated at Geneva under the eye of Theodore Beza, could not accept some of the rigidities of the Calvinist system, particularly those having to do with predestination. He asserted the genuine freedom of the human will and argued that Calvin's original insights had been allowed by his disciplines to degenerate into a harsh and mindless determinism. Because he also championed the prerogatives of the state as opposed to the clergy-dominated consistories, Arminius attracted the support of Oldenbarne-veldt and other powerful politicians. Indeed, Arminianism became a factor in the negotiations leading up to the truce signed with Spain in 1609,[28] and Arminius himself was accused by some ministers of aiding and abetting the enemy—a cruelly ironic charge, since his whole family had been massacred by the Spanish army. The quarrel within the Dutch Church, triggered by the statement of Arminian views in "The Remonstrance," published in 1610 (the year of Arminius's death) lasted for generations and spread far beyond Holland.[29] It proved among other things the vigor and viability of the Calvinist movement.

The Lutheran theologian Martin Chemnitz (d. 1586) was not so much a revisionist as a moderator, a peacemaker. A sometime court astrologer, and before that Melanchthon's student at Wittenberg, where he had heard Luther preach (1545), Chemnitz was instrumental in bringing about the agreement among the various Lutheran factions known as the *Formula of Concord* (1580).[30] He stood squarely in the middle of the road and displayed those qualities that might be called typical of the second-generation reformer. He espoused the essential Luther, shorn of some of the master's crudities and yet unmuddied by Melanchthon's equivocations. In dealing with his coreligionists he was quietly and courteously confident of the rightness of his cause. And he brought the same tone of moderation into his controversies with the Catholics. His *Examen concilii tridentini* (1565–1573) began as a literary exchange with the German Jesuits and ended being an article-by-article rebuttal of the pronouncements of the Council of Trent.[31]

28. Carl Bangs, *Arminius, a Study in the Dutch Reformation* (New York, 1971), pp. 284 ff.

29. For the early years of the disputes see Douglas Nobbs, *Theocracy and Toleration* (Cambridge, 1938).

30. See above, p. 226.

31. See the recent translation by Fred Cramer, *Examination of the Council of Trent* (St. Louis, 1971).

Chemnitz's masterpiece gave him the properly anti-Catholic credentials to mediate effectively the quarrels within his own communion. This may in the long run have been the most notable achievement of the *Examen*. For the time had passed when many minds were changed by controversy between two entrenched positions, even when stridency was avoided. As for content, the *Examen* demonstrated that the argument had shifted almost entirely onto historical ground.

Except for a very few extreme bibliolaters, a question of historical fact had assumed crucial importance in the now permanent debate between Protestant and Catholic. Roughly, and somewhat oversimply, stated, the question was whether the Protestant or Catholic version of Christian revelation was in accord with the belief and practice of the primitive Church. The presumption on both sides rested upon a severely static notion of historical reality. The reformers said that at some relatively early date—and they differed widely among themselves as to precisely what date—the process of Roman corruption had begun; therefore, prior to that moment, the Church still retained the pristine purity which Christ had handed over to his apostles and which the reformers now claimed it their intention to restore. The scholarly task was to prove the essential identification between, for instance, the Church at Hippo over which St. Augustine had presided at the end of the fourth century and Calvin's Church at Geneva. Often the procedure varied, though it amounted to the same thing, by taking the negative tack and trying to show that certain Roman teachings—about the Real Presence or devotion to the Virgin Mary or celibacy—were indeed corruptions of the original deposit of faith, because they had no warrant in ancient Christian documents. The Catholics proceeded in the same fashion and with the same presuppositions, only to arrive at opposite conclusions.

In either case the conclusions had been settled before the historical research began. None of the polemicists made any pretense of detachment; none of them was prepared to let the evidence speak for itself. This does not mean that they were consciously dishonest; it does mean that as they picked and chose among the documents before them the criteria of judgment they used had little to do with the canons of historical science as later generations have come to understand them. If a particular document was at odds with their preconceived theological opinion, then the document had to be spurious or it had to admit to some acceptable interpretation, however strained. This technique of collecting and analyzing literary sources represented the finest tradition of humanist scholarship and had been the theological vogue since Erasmus's day. But in less skillful, more contentious hands the method easily ran the risk of emphasizing quantitative rather than qualitative standards. For the polemicists of the late sixteenth century, Catholic and Protestant alike, understanding the texts seemed less important than accumulating and marshaling them. The overall result of this frantic cataloguing and paraphrasing and calendaring was a retreat into tediousness and, what was worse, into redundancy; an intrinsically noble debate fell by degrees to the level of wearisome pedantry.

The most influential of such historical enterprises were the famous *Centuries*,[32] published at Magdeburg in thirteen volumes between 1559 and 1574 and written by a research team under the direction of the reactionary Lutheran Flavius Illyricus (d. 1575). Each book treated the history of dogma from the first to the thirteenth century under topical headings like faith, original sin, justification, and each argued the case that in all essential points the primitive Christian community squared exactly with the conservative Lutheran churches of Germany. This format invited much repetition and a rambling style, but the centuriators compensated for faults like these by ransacking the libraries and archives of Europe and amassing a stupendous amount of documentation, which they used with unblushing prejudice.

An adequate Catholic response to the *Centuries* was a long time coming. Caesar Baronius, one of St. Philip Neri's earliest disciples, worked on his *Annals*[33] for thirty years before the last of eleven volumes was published in 1607, almost simultaneously with the author's death. The *Annals* were composed under the press of many other duties—Baronius was librarian at the Vatican, General of the Oratorians, confessor and confidant to Pope Clement VIII, eventually a cardinal, and a serious candidate for the tiara in two papal elections.

---

32. The full imposing title was *Ecclesiastica historia integram Ecclesiae Christi ideam, quantum ad locum, propagationem, persecutionem, tranquillitatem, doctrinam, haereses, caeremonias, gubernationem, schismata, synodos, personas, miracula, martyria, religiones extra ecclesiam et statum Imperii politicum attinet, secundum singularias centurias, perspicuo ordine complectens; singulari diligentia et fide ex vetustissimis et optimis historicis, patribus et aliis scriptoribus congesta per aliquot studiosos et pios viros in urbe Magdeburgica.* Note the references to sources beginning with *"singulari diligentia."*

33. Baronius was more modest at least in his title, which was simply *Annales Ecclesiastici.*

More remarkably still, he worked alone with virtually no help, in striking contrast to the joint effort which produced the *Centuries*. Baronius employed a somewhat different approach to his material. His year-by-year narrative secured a sounder chronology than that of the centuriators, though his frequent lengthy digressions qualified this advantage to some extent. As Professor Polman has said, Baronius did not exactly answer the *Centuries* of Magdeburg (but then he never claimed he did), because he wrote more a history of the institutional Church, while Flavius Illyricus and his colleagues were strictly concerned with the history of Christian doctrine.[34] But the works were similar in that they both brought before the reading public collections of documents—and, in Baronius's case, facsimiles of coins and inscriptions—long unknown or forgotten. Despite their biases and failures in critical judgment, they deserve the credit their research has earned them; they were the first serious ecclesiastical historians.

Internal synthesis and summing up, elaboration of argument, documentation within the context of controversy: these were the hallmarks of the theological scholarship of the time. And the ablest practitioner of it was a Tuscan Jesuit named Robert Bellarmine.[35] In 1570, when he was twenty-eight years old and just ordained a priest, Bellarmine joined the theology faculty in the University of Louvain. One of the Society of Jesus' strengths was the mobility of its members, who early in their careers learned to be citizens of the world—the eminent Francis Suárez (d. 1617), for example, lectured for extended periods in universities in three different countries. Bellarmine liked Louvain well enough, and he was popular there, but the climate did not agree with him and by 1576 he was back in Italy to stay. Even so, his brief interlude at Louvain, that bastion of Catholic orthodoxy set in the midst of the heretical Netherlands, had a permanent effect upon his professional life. He remained ever afterward convinced of the necessity to answer firmly and courteously each facet of the Protestant intellectual challenge. Out of the lectures he delivered at the Gregorian University from 1576 to 1588 emerged his magisterial *Controversies*,[36] first published in three thick volumes at Ingolstadt from 1586 to 1593.

34. See Pontien Polman, *L'Élément historique dans la controverse religieuse du XVI° siècle* (Gembloux, 1932), pp. 213 ff., 527 ff.

35. The standard biography is James Brodrick, *The Life and Works of Blessed Robert Cardinal Bellarmine,* 2 vols. (New York, 1928).

36. *De controversiis Christianae fidei adversus hujus temporis haereticos.*

Six years later he was named a cardinal and then Archbishop of Capua, posts which necessarily imposed on him heavy administrative duties and cut short his career as a theologian. During his last years—he died in 1621—he devoted his energies to writing works of piety and to fostering his own inner life of prayer, which led eventually to his canonization in 1930.

The *Controversies,* composed in the vigor of Bellarmine's middle age, exerted on post-Tridentine Catholic thought an influence which lasted quite literally for four centuries. The book's importance lay not so much in its content, impressive as that may have been, as in its method. Bellarmine had little taste for speculation. His mind did not respond to the categories of Aristotelian epistemology. He could not conceive of theology in the manner of the great medieval scholastics, as systems rising grandly and ineluctably from the soil of revelation. Bellarmine's logic was of a less lordly kind, more in tune with the research methods put in vogue by the humanist historians and, as he judged it, more appropriate to the circumstances of the sixteenth century.[37] He was not concerned, as Thomas Aquinas had been, to have his teaching unfold in a magnificently consistent way. He used a broadsword, not a rapier; he arranged the massed ranks of his arguments to overwhelm the enemy. As a principle of order he turned to something concrete and convenient, the Apostles' Creed. The Creed, he said at the beginning of the *Controversies,* had undergone successive heretical fire over the centuries, and perversely enough, the attacks followed a roughly chronological sequence: the first articles, dealing with God's own nature, were challenged first, then those which expressed faith in the person of Christ, and finally, from Luther's day onward, the articles at the end of the creed, "I believe in the holy Catholic Church and the forgiveness of sins."

From there it was a matter of extracting from relevant texts the arguments which substantiated the Catholic position or rebutted the Protestant. Bellarmine did this tedious job with industry, skill, and grace. He accumulated the works of the ancient Christian writers—the so-called Fathers of the Church—the decrees of councils and popes, the commentaries of exegetes, the treatises of theologians, and out of them he framed a chronicle, so to speak, of the Church's living experience.

---

37. See Edward Ryan, *The Historical Scholarship of Saint Bellarmine* (New York, 1936), especially pp. 2 ff.

What Trent had called "tradition" and had dignified as co-equal with Scripture as a source of revelation, Bellarmine spelled out by relentless induction. Explicitly and implicitly he turned the basic Protestant tenet against itself by insisting that without the testimony of living tradition the Bible remained outside its proper context and therefore was obscure, incomprehensible, and sometimes contradictory. Without the morally unanimous agreement of the Church, "no dogma," he said, "can be established with certainty."[38] And what is the Church? The Church is the assembly of men and women united by the profession of the same Christian faith and by participation in the same sacraments, under the authority of legitimate pastors, principally the Roman pontiff, who is Christ's vicar here below.

It was a modest enough assertion as Counter Reformation manifestoes went. Indeed, Sixtus V thought it showed less than the minimum regard for the prerogatives of the papacy, and he put *Controversies* on the Roman Index for a while.[39] But Bellarmine's insights outlasted that imperious pope to become the established Catholic position vis-à-vis the continuing controversy with Protestantism: without tradition, and all that tradition implies by way of continuity, consistency, and hierarchical structure, the Bible makes no sense. Here was the rock-bottom argument, the point beyond which the controversialists of the two sides could not go without one surrendering to the other.

Bellarmine's array of argumentation tried to meet his opponents' every position, but ultimately it all came back to what the Christian meant when he prayed, "I believe in the holy Catholic Church." There was nothing original about Bellarmine's work, nor were his critical faculties sharp enough to save him from falling victim now and again to bogus evidence. His erudition gained him the respect of his adversaries; he was fair-minded and even gracious to them, and he paid them the highest compliment by studying their books—so much, really, like his own—as assiduously perhaps as anyone ever did. But Bellarmine did not pretend to be a creative thinker. The *Controversies* he

38. "Non desunt tamen loca scripturae, ex quibus character collegi possit, praesertim adjuncta explicatione Patrum ecclesiae, sine qua nullum dogma ecclesiasticum omnino certo statui potest." *De controversiis*, I, 159. This remark comes in a discussion of the sacraments.

39. See Léopold Willaert, *La restauration catholique, 1563–1648* (Paris, 1960), pp. 430 f.

intended as a manual, a handbook between whose covers the Catholic would find the intellectual armament with which to defend his faith. Text would answer text and author author; and the result was stalemate. Bellarmine was the great figure of the Counter Reformation's second and formative stage, because he tacitly admitted that the movement had run its course without restoring the shattered unity of Christendom. Defense of what had been preserved would be from now on the Catholic intellectual's first duty.

St. Robert Bellarmine and his school provided this fortress mentality with a means of articulation. It came to be called in Catholic circles "positive theology," as distinct from the more cerebral "scholastic" variety. It used sophisticated techniques in linguistics and textual criticism; it represented the Renaissance consciousness of history. When skillfully practiced by the likes of a Bellarmine it could impart to ordinary believers a sense of confidence and security that the foundations of their faith were unshakable. But it remained always during its long ascendancy within the Catholic community the weapon of a beleaguered people, and as such it was hard and unyielding and somehow as unproductive as weapons usually are.

Richard Hooker's synthesis was of a different kind, primarily because the circumstances under which he put it together were different. Like Bellarmine he was a traditionalist, like Chemnitz an opponent of the extreme wing within his own communion; but like neither of them he thought and wrote against a background where static concepts of religion were harder to accept. By the 1590s, when Hooker published the first part of his classic *The Laws of Ecclesiastical Polity*,[40] the Church in England had passed through the fire of many revolutions, many expedients, many compromises. Henry VIII's Catholicism-without-the-pope had given way to the Protestant overtures sponsored by Edward VI; then had come the Roman reaction under Queen Mary—during whose reign Hooker was born, in Exeter, in 1554—and finally the practical and Erastian settlement of Elizabeth. But that last phase was under incessant attack, precisely because it bore within itself vestiges of what had gone before. A rich though deeply painful national experience supplied Hooker with data out of which he fash-

40. Only the first five of the eight books of the *Ecclesiastical Polity* were published in Hooker's lifetime.

ioned the definition of Anglican—a word, incidentally, which he never used himself.

On a more superficial level the shy and retiring Hooker, about the details of whose life very little is known,[41] carried on a running controversy with the Puritans. His disagreement with them touched on many crucial issues, but it may be reduced to one or two salient principles. Hooker, first of all, took for granted the organic growth of organizations, including the Church, and because of this he could not subscribe to the radical Protestant view which dismissed all development since the time of the apostles as popish wickedness. The only kind of Church acceptable to the Puritans was a federation of conventicles on the Calvinist pattern in which the Word of God, unadulterated by bishops and sacraments, could be preached and sinful men could be brought face to face with their Savior.[42]

Hooker argued in effect that this view oversimplified the nature of the Christian vocation. Scripture was of course the unique Word of God, but Scripture took its life within the womb of the Church, within, that is, a community of human beings as susceptible to change and development as all human groups are. Indeed, the Scripture itself grew from the Old Testament to the New, from Judaic legal prescriptions to Christ's gospel of love and fellowship. He scorned the predestinarian arrogance of the Puritans: "The Church is not the body which contains only those who are at one with Christ; it is the body which has union with Christ, but with defective members, those who do not effectively share Our Lord's Life."[43] The social and political ramifications of this distinction, so much in harmony with Queen Elizabeth's policy of religious consensus, were clear enough, but the Puritans preferred to emphasize its similarity to Roman Catholic ecclesiology. Yet from another angle Hooker was equally at odds with Tridentine Catholics who, he said, excessively glamorized and even apotheosized the Church. If he objected strenuously to the Puritans, who denied a place in the Church to bad men—bad, it should be noted, because reprobated by divine decree, through no fault of their own—he ob-

41. A not very reliable biographical sketch by Isaac Walton (1665) is reproduced in John Keble's superb three-volume edition of *Ecclesiastical Polity* (1836).

42. See above, pp. 233 f.

43. John Marshall, *Hooker and the Anglican Tradition* (Sewanee, Tenn., 1963), p. 157.

jected no less to Catholicism, which proclaimed the divinity of the Church, no matter how bad the men were who made it up.

Hooker soon discovered, as Chemnitz already had and Arminius shortly would, that the argument with the Protestant left turned on a rather stark dispute about the uses of Scripture. The Puritans maintained that anything not explicitly sanctioned by the Bible was prohibited. Hooker replied that anything not explicitly commanded by the Bible was "indifferent" and hence a matter to be settled by reason or custom or simple convenience. Thus, he dismissed the Puritan accusation that the worship forms prescribed by the Book of Common Prayer were idolatrous by observing trenchantly, "Touching God himself, hath he anywhere revealed that it is his delight to dwell beggarly?"[44] Hooker classified matters like episcopal structure, church decoration and liturgy, and even the royal supremacy as indifferent, not in the sense that they were unimportant but because Scripture said nothing definitive about them. Therefore the best guide to follow in determining these and the multitude of similarly indifferent things in the life of the Church was accumulated experience and reasoned argument. So the divines of Hooker's school—one day to be called, not quite accurately, Anglo-Catholic—made special appeal to the first four Christian centuries, not in order to establish identity with themselves but to find a guide for legitimate development.

Such a theology was anathema to the Puritans, nor did they suffer gladly the Aristotelian dialectic that lurked behind Hooker's elegant prose. The use of philosophical realism as a tool to elucidate the written revelation was a further claim that some intellectual areas were in fact indifferent in Hooker's sense of the word, that Scripture did not really settle all questions beyond debate, that the heady existentialism of justification by faith alone had to admit of some tiresome syllogistic qualifications. Hooker's *Ecclesiastical Polity* was a book more like Thomas Aquinas's *Summa* than like Calvin's *Institutes*,[45] and he himself had more in common with the Spanish Jesuit Suárez than he did with Thomas Cartwright. Yet, as a thinker, Hooker was his own man and articulated a view of Christian life and organization which

---

44. *Ecclesiastical Polity*, V, xv, 3.
45. A modern author has linked Hooker, Aquinas, and Marsiglio of Padua as medievalists. See A. P. d'Entrèves, *The Medieval Contribution to Political Thought* (London, 1939).

was different from that of Suárez or Cartwright. Perhaps the better comparison would be with Erasmus, who before the storm of the Reformation broke had hoped for a revitalized Church, stripped of its excesses and yet with its core of traditional belief intact. Richard Hooker, seventy years of bitter polarization later, hoped the same and tried to stake out an alternative road through the wreckage, a *via media* which some men travel to this day.

4. THE LAST WORD

But the last word cannot be left to the divines, however elevated their theme. The last word expressive of these fifty years came out of a mean house on a Valladolid back street, where a crippled and impoverished veteran of Lepanto told a story about a mad old man from La Mancha who read too many books on medieval chivalry; and from the stage of the Globe Theater, which stood newly built on the south bank of the Thames, where one day in 1602 (or possibly 1603) an actor looked out over a motley and boisterous audience and said, "Speak the speech, I pray you, as I pronounced it to you, trippingly on the tongue."

Cervantes and Shakespeare could hardly have been aware of each other's existence, though it is just possible that Shakespeare might have read a translation of the first part of *Don Quixote*.[46] By a striking coincidence they died on the same day, April 23, 1616, Cervantes, at sixty-nine, seventeen years the older. They both grew up under the shadow of middle-class insecurity. Cervantes's father was a ne'er-do-well surgeon who drifted from town to Castilian town trying to earn a living for his seven children, while John Shakespeare, a dreamy, illiterate man with a brood almost as large, allowed fantasy and a fondness for litigation to drive him into insolvency and then to deprive him of his coveted seat on the city council of Stratford-upon-Avon. Neither son had the advantage of a university education, and both in their youth transgressed against convention and paid the price for it: Cervantes went into exile for a time, probably because of involvement in a duel; Shakespeare compromised and then dutifully married a woman eight years his senior whom he never loved.

Yet their careers followed very different tracks. Cervantes, more adventuresome and widely traveled, never managed to escape the un-

46. Thomas Shelton's translation was published in 1612. See James Fitzmaurice-Kelly, "Cervantes and Shakespeare," *Proceedings of the British Academy*, VII (1916).

certainties of his childhood. In Italy in 1570 he joined the army of the Holy League and fought for Don John at Lepanto—"the most exalted event," he wrote years later, "of the past, the present or the future." He came away from the battle with two chest wounds and a left hand maimed for life. Four years later, still in military service, he was captured by Barbary pirates and carried off to Algiers. His repeated attempts to escape won him the grudging admiration of his captors, who were under the false impression that as a man of substance he would bring a large ransom. Freed at last in 1580, Cervantes went back to Spain, where he took up the marginal existence of an impecunious and itinerant writer. The birth of an illegitimate daughter—his only child—in 1584 did not prevent him from marrying later the same year a lady of respectable family whose dowry, however, did not deliver him from chronic insolvency. Neither did the publication, a year after that, of the beautiful pastoral romance *La Galatea*. He worked as a royal commissary for a while, purchasing supplies for the invincible armada, and later as a tax collector. Yet he never had any money or any status, and three times between 1592 and 1602 he was arrested for debt. Not even the spectacular success of the first part of *Don Quixote*, published in 1605, relieved his financial woes, thanks to his own and his publisher's carelessness.[47]

Shakespeare, by contrast, was a study in upward social mobility. From the moment he went to London about 1584, with only his wits to recommend him, he set out in pursuit of a secure place in the sun. He started out as an actor, soon was writing plays for three different acting companies, and by 1594, when he was thirty, headed a company of his own. By that time, too, he had become intimate with some of the most glamorous figures in the Elizabethan court, the golden-haired youths and dark ladies who haunt the immortal love sonnets and whose identity has been, until recently, the most tantalizing puzzle in the history of literature.[48] A noted critic testified to Shakespeare's eminence in 1598 by drawing up a catalogue of his extant plays and commenting, "The sweet witty soul of Ovid lives on in mellifluous and honey-

47. Aubrey Bell, *Cervantes* (Norman, Okla., 1947), pp. 39 ff.

48. A. L. Rowse, never one to hide his light under a bushel, announces in *William Shakespeare: A Biography* (New York, 1963), p. vii: "Proper historical method . . . has enabled me to solve, for the first time, and definitively, the problem of sonnets, which has tested so many generations and led so many people into a morass of conjecture." For his solution, see pp. 161 ff.

tongued Shakespeare." Yet this tribute probably meant less to him than the coat of arms, granted to his father two years earlier, and the title "gentleman" that went with it. "Many hundreds of Elizabethans," Mr. Rowse tells us, "signalized their move up in society by acquiring a coat of arms. But I doubt if many of them took it out in their father's name to ensure, *ex post facto,* the gentility of their birth."[49] So William Shakespeare attained the social standing he so much desired, and he confirmed it by buying the grandest, handsomest house in Stratford. In 1602, while Cervantes languished in a debtors' prison, Shakespeare, by now also part owner of the Globe, was a mogul, a theatrical entrepreneur, a friend of the mighty, and a certified country gentleman to boot.

King Lear's shrieks upon the heath and Othello's upon the battlements, as well as Hamlet's half-incestuous cry for vengeance, provide strange background music for this tale of a poor boy who made good. For Shakespeare composed these awesomely bitter tragedies between 1601 and 1605 (with *Macbeth* following shortly after) when he rested secure atop a pinnacle of fame and prosperity. And curiously enough Cervantes, the old soldier whose luck had run out long ago, who had suffered inordinately from the slings and arrows of outrageous fortune, used those same years to put the finishing touches to a funny story about a knight in rusty armor who tilted against windmills and herds of sheep. The habitual failure produced a classic of rollicking good humor, a paean to noble ideals; the "honey-tongued Shakespeare," toast of high society, laid bare the dark regions where crime and hopelessness prevail.

Of course there are hilarious moments in *Hamlet* and *Macbeth,* just as there are deeply poignant and tragic ones in *Don Quixote.* But the differences in predominant mood perhaps suggest that the personal circumstances under which the truly great artist labors tell only so much about his art. And the same might be said about the effect his times had on him and the influences that allegedly bore upon him. Certainly Shakespeare was influenced by Marlowe and Kyd, certainly his poetry reveals that Spenser and Sidney were his precursors and the young Earl of Southampton his friend. Elizabethan England was for Shakespeare the fullness of time. Similarly, Cervantes remains inconceivable outside the setting of Spain's golden age. Certainly it mattered

49. *Ibid.,* p. 277.

that he fought at Lepanto and remembered it with the same fierce pride as Aeschylus did Marathon. Certainly it mattered that his older contemporaries included mystical poets like St. Teresa and St. John of the Cross and that a younger contemporary was a dramatist of the stature of Lope de Vega.[50] It is even not without significance that he was buried dressed as a Franciscan penitent in a grave nobody now can find.

But when all this has been said, the real explanation of the artist's achievement remains untold. Some few creative spirits stand so far above their generation that they witness more properly to all times and to all people everywhere. Shakespeare and Cervantes take their place in that select company, because they probed into the heart of the human condition with a sensibility beyond the capacity of ordinary mortals. In studying them we are likely to learn more about ourselves than about those contemporaries of theirs, our ancestors. And so, as old Don Quixote said from his deathbed, "Let us proceed fairly and softly, and not look for this year's birds in last year's nests."[51]

50. See Guillermo Diaz-Plaja, *A History of Spanish Literature* (New York, 1971), pp. 155 ff.
51. *Don Quixote,* II, lxxiv.

BIBLIOGRAPHICAL ESSAY

To read all the surveys and monographs which treat of or in some way touch upon the history of Europe between 1559 and 1610 would be of course a physical impossibility. In writing this book I have studied a great amount of material only to grow depressingly aware how much there is left for me to study. It is a chastening experience. What follows, therefore, can claim to be no more than a selective, personal, and even—so some readers may think—capricious bibliography. The footnotes to the text give some indication of the authors I have consulted and the debts I have incurred. The following essay hopefully broadens that perspective somewhat. I make no particular effort to include or to exclude works cited in the footnotes, though I do try to avoid repeating titles within the essay itself.

The American Historical Association's *Guide to Historical Literature* (New York, 1961) provides the most convenient, single-volume introduction to collections of printed sources and basic secondary works, as well as various specialized treatments written in English. It might well be supplemented by the *Annual Bulletin of Historical Literature* (London, from 1911). Edith Coulter and Melanie Gerstenfeld, *Historical Bibliographies* (New York, 1935) remains useful for older works, and might be supplemented by *The International Bibliography of the Historical Sciences* (New York, from 1930), an annual publication.

There are also bibliographies related to the histories of the various nation-states. For instance, the revised edition of Conyers Read, *Bibliography of British History, Tudor Period: 1485–1603* (London, 1959), covers the reign of Elizabeth, while its companion volume, Godfrey Davies and Mary Keeler, *Bibliography of British History, Stuart Period: 1603–1714,* rev. ed. (London, 1970) includes that of James I. For French matters a useful tool is the annual *Répertoire bibliographique de l'histoire de la France* (Paris, from 1921). The venerable *Jahrenberichte für deutsche Geschichte* (Berlin, from 1878) performs the same function for Germany, along with the regular supplements, now published at Stuttgart, to the ninth edition of Friedrich Dahlman and Georg Waitz, *Quellenkunde der deutschen Geschichte* (Leipzig, 1932). D. Shapiro, ed., *A Select Bibliography of Works in English on Russian History* (Oxford, 1962), serves as an example of the kind of guide usually available for subjects in which a particular language may be a problem. The learned historical journals regularly publish articles which update the bibliographical collections. For examples relevant to the work at hand, see Perez Zagorin, "English History, 1558–1640: A Bibliographical Survey," *American Historical Review,* LXVIII (1963), 364 ff.; A. G. Dickens, "Recent Books on the Reformation and Counter Reformation," *Journal of Ecclesiastical History,* XIX (1968), 219 ff.; and Eric Cochrane, "New Light on Post-Tridentine Italy: A Note on Recent Counter Reformation Scholarship," *Catholic Historical Review,* LVI (1970), 291 ff. The last-named piece is a model of its kind.

Some multivolume histories or series, together with topical dictionaries, supply ample bibliographies as well as substantive narratives. The old *Cambridge Modern History* (1907–12) contains bibliographies. The third volume of *The New Cambridge Modern History,* R. B. Wernham, ed., *The Counter Reformation and the Price Revolution* (Cambridge, 1968), has been widely and justifiably criticized for its lack of unity and coherence as well as its lack of bibliographies. The latter fault is somewhat amended by John Roach, ed., *A Bibliography of Modern History* (Cambridge, 1968), intended to be a companion for the whole *New Cambridge* project; this manual, however, is uneven in quality and very difficult to use.

Several French series deserve mention. The advanced textbooks titled *Nouvelle Clio, L'Histoire et ses problèmes,* contain good bibliographical lists; the relevant volumes are written by Jean Delumeau (30), Henri Lapeyre (31), and Frédéric Mauro (32). Ernest Lavisse and Alfred Rambaud, eds., *Histoire générale de la France,* is an old work, but its sixth volume, J. H. Mariéjol, *La Réforme et la ligue, l'édit de Nantes, Henri IV et Louis XIII* (Paris, 1911), still is a valuable guide to further study. L. Halphen and P. Sagnac, *Peuples et Civilisations* (Paris, from 1935), is wider in scope than Lavisse-Rambaud; the relevant volume, *La prépondérance espagnole* (Paris, 1948), has excellent bibliographies. So also do L. Cristiani, *L'Église à l'époque du concile de Trente* (Paris, 1948), and Léopold Willaert, *La restauration catholique* (Paris, 1960), which are the seventeenth and eighteenth volumes of Augustine Fliche and Victor Martin, eds., *Histoire de l'Eglise.* The book by Willaert, however, is on the whole a grave disappointment; scarcely anything but a long and uncritical list of titles, it shows the pedantic depths to which bibliographical science can fall.

The articles in the *Dictionnaire de théologie catholique* (Paris, 1901–59) are written from a historical point of view and contain good bibliographies, but the later volumes are much superior to the earlier. A similar work in scope and value is *Lexicon für Theologie und Kirche* (Freiburg, 1930–38). A new *Dictionnaire d'histoire et de géographie ecclésiastique* is now in progress. The material in these massive works is particularly useful for study of an era in which religion, and notably Catholicism, played such an important role.

For the same reason, and other reasons, Ludwig Pastor, *Geschichte der Päpste* (Freiburg, 1909–29), is uniquely important. I have used volumes 15 through 25 in the standard English version published by Herder. The papacy was at the embattled center of Europe in the late sixteenth century, with interests and contacts everywhere. Pastor's unparalleled knowledge of the documents in the Vatican Archives makes him a singular authority, so that to compare his work to Ranke's much slighter study of the papacy, which is often done, is almost impudent. Indeed, Pastor's text is more often than not paraphrase and translation of primary documents. His pietistic comments can be as easily set aside as Ranke's cynical ones.

Also in a class by itself is Fernand Braudel's magisterial *La Méditerranée et le monde méditerranéen à l'époque de Philippe II*, 2d rev. ed. (Paris, 1966). A new kind of synthetic history emerges from these pages, and at the end of the second volume is a very useful critical bibliography. Harper and Row has recently published a translation of the first volume of Braudel's work, and in so doing has occasioned some analysis and adulation of the *monde braudellien* by H. R. Trevor-Roper and J. H. Hexter, as well as a short *apologia* for the *Annales* school by Braudel himself, in *The Journal of Modern History*, XLIV (December, 1972), 448–539.

There are available several general surveys of this period of varying worth. Hauser's *La prépondérance espagnole* is a good one, though it concentrates too much on matters French. Kurt Aland, *Repetitorium der Kirchengeschichte*, III: *Reformation und Gegenreformation* (Berlin, 1967), similarly treats of Germany almost to the exclusion of everything else. Better balanced is the second volume of Émile Léonard, *A History of Protestantism* (London, 1967), a translation of the 1961 French edition, which, however, shows some carelessness as to details. Henri Daniel-Rops, *L'Église de la Renaissance et de la Réforme*, Vol. II (Paris, 1955), might be read as a Catholic balance to Léonard. A. G. Dickens, *The Counter Reformation* (London, 1968), is an excellent résumé of the Catholic reform movement from its medieval sources to its baroque fulfillment; part of the Library of European Civilization Series, it also has many fine illustrations. Pierre Janelle, *The Catholic Reformation* (Milwaukee, 1949), is of little value.

Philippe Erlanger, *The Age of Courts and Kings* (New York, 1967), is interesting but unreliable, at least in this translation. Among recent surveys designed for collegiate use are Richard Dunn, *The Age of Religious Wars, 1559–1689* (New York, 1970); A. A. Parker, *The Age of Spanish Power* (London, 1970); H. G. Koenigsberger and George Mosse, *Europe in the*

Sixteenth Century (New York, 1968); and J. H. Elliott, *Europe Divided, 1559–1598* (New York, 1968). Of these the last is by far the best; Professor Elliott has become the premier among historians writing in English about this period.

I. THE QUALITY OF LIFE

Historical demography has only recently begun to penetrate into the prestatistical age of the sixteenth century. Several recent works, however, suggest that much revision of accepted views about population trends will soon be in order. Among these are E. A. Wrigley, *Population and History* (London, 1969), and the first volume of Roger Mols, *Introduction à la démographie historique des villes d'Europe du XVIe au XVIII siècle* (Louvain, 1954); the latter is exceedingly difficult for one not skilled in the science of statistics. A more wide-ranging survey is Marcel Reinhard, *Histoire générale de la population mondiale* (Paris, 1968). A brief manual with a brief treatment of Tudor times is E. A. Wrigley, ed., *Introduction to English Historical Demography* (New York, 1966). The French Société de Démographie Historique publishes its *Annales* each quarter.

The rise in population affected the economy and social structure. General studies by Heaton and by Clough and Cole are helpful here. A more specific statement of it is E. H. Phelps Brown and Sheila Hopkins, "Wage-rates and Prices: Evidence for Population Pressure in the Sixteenth Century," *Economica*, XXIV (1957), 289–306. This article followed the same authors' famous articles in the same journal in 1955 and 1956 on the price of consumables compared to builders' wages. Much of this material is conveniently presented in Peter Ramsey, ed., *The Price Revolution in Sixteenth Century England* (London, 1969), which despite its title, also includes the classic short studies of Ingrid Hammerström on Sweden and Earl Hamilton on Spain. It is profitable also to follow the debate on the price question between Y. S. Brenner and J. D. Gould in the pages of the *Economic History Review* from 1961 to 1965.

Earl Hamilton, *American Treasure and the Price Revolution in Spain, 1501–1650* (Cambridge, Mass., 1934), has been many times reprinted, most recently in 1970, as befits a work of this stature. H. Chanu and P. Chanu, *Séville et l'Atlantique* (Paris, 1955–59), 11 volumes, provides a detailed statistical analysis of Spanish commerce. The price situation in Rome, along with other economic considerations, is fully treated in the two volumes of Jean Delumeau, *Vie économique et sociale de Rome dans la seconde moitié du XVIe siècle* (Paris, 1957–59). Very useful bibliographies are provided in E. E. Rich and C. H. Wilson, eds., *The Cambridge Economic History of Europe*, IV (Cambridge, 1967), 579 ff., but the chapter by Fernand Braudel and Frank Spooner dealing with prices (374 ff.) is so obscurely written as to be practically incomprehensible.

J. H. Elliott, *The Old World and the New* (Cambridge, 1970), gives the present state of the case on the impact of American silver on the European economy, along with many other historiographical insights. J. H. Parry, *The Age of Reconnaissance* (New York, 1963), is a well-researched, lively account of commercial adventurers. Vitorino Magalhaes-Godinho, *L'Economie de l'empire Portugais aux XVᵉ et XVIᵉ siècles* (Paris, 1969), treats in the massive *Annales* style another angle of monetary and commercial history; unfortunately, it has no index. The rise of one great commercial center is described in H. van der Wee, *The Growth of the Antwerp Market and the European Economy,* Vol. III (Louvain, 1963), while the decline of others is traced in C. Cipolla, "The Decline of Italy," *Economic History Review,* Vol. V (1952), and in Philippe Dollinger, *The German Hansa* (London, 1971), translated from the French edition of 1964. Agricultural and pastoral pursuits remained of paramount importance. See, for instance, B. H. Slicher van Bath, "The Rise of Intensive Husbandry in the Low Countries," reprinted in Charles Warner, ed., *Agrarian Conditions in Modern European History* (New York, 1966), pp. 24–42, and Julius Klein, *The Mesta* (Cambridge, Mass., 1920).

Many of the above works treat of society as affected by the process of economic change. A specialized study of great importance in this area is Lawrence Stone, *The Crisis of the Aristocracy* (Oxford, 1965). Similar, but hardly comparable in scope or value, is Davis Bitton, *The French Nobility in Crisis* (Stanford, 1969), which does have an interesting bibiographical essay. J. T. Cliffe, *The Yorkshire Gentry from the Reformation to the Civil War* (London, 1970), traces a class in unevenly upward mobility. A pioneering effort to see beyond the societal elites to the masses is Robert Mandrou, *Introduction à la France moderne: Essai de psychologie historique, 1500–1640* (Paris, 1961). A. L. Rowse's contributions in the field of social history are many, the latest of which is his *The Elizabethan Renaissance* (London, 1971), in which, among other matters, the author studies continental influences in England. A companion piece might be John Murray, "The Cultural Impact of the Flemish Low Countries on Sixteenth and Seventeenth Century England," *American Historical Review,* LXII (1957), 837–854.

Reminders are plentiful that life for most people was harsh and inequities were commonplace. Brian Pullan, *Rich and Poor in Renaissance Venice* (Oxford, 1970), is one, and Gareth Jones, *History of the Law of Charity* (New York, 1969), is another. The dark and the bright side can be seen in contrasting F. G. Emmison, *Elizabethan Life: Disorder* (Chelmsford, 1970), with David Bergeron, *English Civic Pageantry, 1558–1642* (London, 1971). Bartolemé Bennassar, *Recherches sur le grandes épidémies dans le nord de l'Espagne à la fin du XVIᵉ siècle* (Paris, 1969), in a narrow area, and Erich Woehlkens, *Pest und Ruhr im 16. und 17. Jahrhundert* (Hanover, 1954), in a wider one, both measure the social dislocation caused by infectious disease.

The relation between social conditions and religious phenomena is explored by Hugh Trevor-Roper in his 1963 essay "Religion, the Reformation and Social Change," reprinted, among other places, in *The European Witch Craze* (New York, 1969). See also Keith Thomas, *Religion and the Decline of Magic* (New York, 1971), and Lawrence Stone's perceptive review article, "The Disenchantment of the World," *New York Review of Books,* XVII (Dec. 2, 1971), 17 ff.

2. THE CATHOLIC PEACE

Perhaps the best way to reconstruct the political preoccupations of the 1559 period is to consult the various national histories which are readily available. A selective list of them might include J. B. Black, *The Reign of Elizabeth,* rev. ed. (Oxford, 1959), for England; the work of Mariéjol mentioned above, as well as his biography of Catherine de' Medici, for France; the third and fourth volumes of Henri Pirenne, *Histoire de Belgique* (Brussels, from 1907), for the Low Countries; Hajo Holborn, *A History of Modern Germany: The Reformation* (New York, 1967), for German-speaking lands; J. H. Elliott, *Imperial Spain* (London, 1963), and the fourth volume of Roger Merriman, *The Rise of the Spanish Empire in the Old World and in the New* (New York, 1918), for Spain.

Less satisfactory is T. C. Smout, *A History of the Scottish People* (London, 1969), and Friedrich Heer, *The Holy Roman Empire* (New York, 1968). An enormous amount of undigested material is to be found in volumes seven and eight (translated from Ludwig Pastor's 16th German edition) of Johannes Janssen, *History of the German People at the Close of the Middle Ages* (London, 1905). The first volume of John Lynch, *Spain Under the Habsburgs, Empire and Absolutism* (New York, 1964), is learned and readable, but its almost word-for-word dependence upon Braudel in the Mediterranean sections is not properly acknowledged (see, for example, pp. 230 ff.).

Among short studies of great interest are Harold Grimm, "Social Forces in the German Reformation," *Church History,* XXXI (1962), 3–13, and Henri Pirenne, "The Formation and Constitution of the Burgundian State (Fifteenth and Sixteenth Centuries)," *American Historical Review,* XIV (1909), 477–502. A unique book of its kind is the recent translation of Jaime Vicens Vives, *Approaches to the History of Spain* (Berkeley, 1967);

in this connection consult Gabriel Jackson, "The Historical Writing of Jaime Vicens Vives," *American Historical Review*, LXXV (1970), 808 ff. The survey provided in the second volume of Denis Mack Smith, *A History of Sicily* (New York, 1968), might be studied in conjunction with the excellent monograph, Helmut Koenigsberger, *The Government of Sicily under Philip II of Spain: A Study in the Practice of Empire* (London, 1951).

Roger Doucet, *Les Institutions de la France au XVI⁰ siècle* (Paris, 1948), is a basic work, the first volume of which is relevant for the period at hand. An outstanding special study is Nicola Sutherland, *The French Secretaries of State in the Age of Catherine de' Medici* (London, 1962). The technical workings of the French administration are treated in Hélène Michaud, *La Grande Chancellerie et les écritures royales au seizième siècle* (Paris, 1967). Not so satisfactory is J. H. Shennan, *The Parlement of Paris* (London, 1969). Roland Mousnier et al., *Le Conseil du roi: De Louis XII à la Révolution* (Paris, 1970), has little directly relevant to the years 1559–1610, but it provides useful inferences.

Recent scholarship in Elizabethan history has tended to emphasize the importance of the early years of the reign. See, for instance, Mortimer Levine, *The Early Elizabethan Succession Question* (Stanford, 1966) and Wallace MacCaffrey, *The Shaping of the Elizabethan Regime* (Princeton, 1968). Even more precise in scope is William Haugaard, "The Coronation of Elizabeth I," *Journal of Ecclesiastical History*, XIX (1968), 161–170. These studies have deepened rather than contradicted the insights of the older generation of historians like Conyers Read and Sir John Neale. At the same time they manage to avoid the uncritical adulation of the queen's person, which seemed a necessity to even the most eminent older scholars; for an embarrassing example, see Conyers Read, "Good Queen Bess," *American Historical Review*, XXXI (1926), 647 ff.

3. REFORM OF HEAD AND MEMBERS

A good introduction to the reform movement within the Roman Catholic Church is Owen Chadwick, *The Reformation* (Harmondsworth, Middlesex, 1964), pp. 251 ff. This book places the movement properly within its cultural context without, however, forgetting that its primary thrust was religious. A much older work but still valuable is Martin Philippson, *Les origines du catholicisme moderne: La contre-révolution religieuse au XVI⁰ siècle* (Brussels, 1884). Beresford Kidd, *The Counter Reformation* (London, 1933), is mostly concerned with politics and lacks sympathy with the religious aspects of the subject.

The work of H. Outram Evennett deserves special notice. His one sizable book, *The Cardinal of Lorraine and the Council of Trent* (Cambridge, 1930), is a classic of painstaking research and fine writing. He subtitled it: *A Study in the Counter Reformation,* and that study remained his lifelong interest. Unfortunately, he wrote little: "The Counter Reformation," a Catholic Truth Society pamphlet (1935); "The New Orders," in G. R. Elton, ed., *The New Cambridge Modern History,* Vol. II (Cambridge, 1958); "The Counter Reformation," in Joel Hurstfield, ed., *The Reformation Crisis* (London, 1965). Evennett's Birkbeck Lectures of 1951 were published posthumously as *The Spirit of the Counter Reformation* (Cambridge, 1968). This slender volume hopefully points to future directions research in its subject will take, and anyone interested in understanding Catholicism from Trent to Vatican II must read it. It is enriched by a thoughtful bibliographical essay by John Bossy, who also edited Evennett's text.

Hubert Jedin, *Geschichte des Konzils von Trient* (Freiburg, 1947, 1957, 1970), is a monumental achievement. The first two volumes have been brilliantly translated into English by Ernest Graff. The third volume covers the sessions of the early 1550s. On the final sessions Jedin has written a brief summary, *Krisis und Abschluss des Trienter Konzils* (Freiburg, 1964). But he has also covered some of that same ground in his study of Cardinal Seripando, *Papal Legate at the Council of Trent* (St. Louis, 1947); in this instance the English edition leaves much to be desired. For a summary of Jedin's peerless researches in this area, see the second part of Erwin Iserloh, Joseph Glazik and Hubert Jedin, *Reformation, Katholische Reform und Gegenreformation* (Freiburg, 1967).

Other recent works on Trent include Giuseppe Alberigo, *I Vescovi italiani al concilio di Trento* (Florence, 1959). The same author has also written "The Council of Trent: New Views on the Occasion of Its Fourth Centenary," in *Historical Problems of Church Renewal* (Glen Rock, N.J., 1965), and has edited the most recent collection of conciliar decrees, *Conciliorum oecumenicorum decreta* (Rome, 1962). A. Durpont, "Du Concile de Trente: Reflexions autour d'un IVe centénaire," *Revue historique,* CCVI (1951), 262 ff., considers the council as a whole to be the end of something rather than a beginning. One might consult also L. Russo, *Contributi alla storia del concilio di Trento e della controriforma* (Florence, 1948).

The literature of the Society of Jesus is enormous. For a list see Willaert, *La restauration catholique,* pp. 130 ff. Among recent shorter pieces the following are of interest: Karl Rahner, "The Logic of Concrete Individual Knowledge in Ignatius Loyola," in *The Dynamic Element in the Church* (London, 1964), pp. 84 ff.; Robert McNally, "The Council of Trent, the *Spiritual Exercises* and the Catholic Reform," *Church History,* XXXV

(1965), 36 ff.; and Guenter Lewy, "The Struggle for Constitutional Government in the Early Years of the Society of Jesus," *Church History*, XXIX (1960), 141 ff. For Laynez the definitive study, in two volumes, is F. Cereceda, *Diego Laynez en la Europa de su tiempo* (Madrid, 1946). For the Jesuit part in the seminary movement see P. Delattre, "Les Jesuites et les seminaires," *Revue d'ascetique et de mystique*, Vol. XX (1953), and J. A. O'Donohoe, *Tridentine Seminary Legislation, Its Sources and Foundations* (Louvain, 1957).

The typically Counter Reformation brand of spirituality crossed confessional lines. For an instance see Louis Martz, *The Poetry of Meditation* (New Haven, 1954). L. Cognet, *De la devotion moderne à la spiritualité française* (Paris, 1958), was quickly translated into English as *Post Reformation Spirituality* (London, 1959). For the impact of Oratorian piety, see J. Dagens, *Bérulle et les origines de la restauration catholique* (Paris, 1952).

The standard work on the nunciatures as agencies of reform is H. Blaudet, *Les nonciatures apostoliques permanentes jusqu'en 1648* (Helsinki, 1910). Charles Borromeo as the great episcopal reformer is studied in a superb article, Roger Mols, "Saint Charles Borromée, pionnier de la pastorale moderne," *Nouvelle revue théologique*, LXXIX (1957), 600 ff. Mention must also be made of A. J. Roncalli and P. Forno, "Gli atti della visità apostolica de S. Carlo Borromeo a Bergamo, 1575," in *Fontes Ambrosiani* (Florence, 1936); this piece is less significant for its content than for one of its authors: Angelo Roncalli became Pope John XXIII and—so it is said by many—brought to an end within the Catholic Church the Counter Reforma-

The best work on the Spanish mystics remains the three volumes of
tion of which Charles Borromeo had been a prime founder.
E. Allison Peers, *Studies in the Spanish Mystics* (London, 1927-60). Also of interest is E. W. T. Dicken, *The Crucible of Love: A Study of the Mysticism of St. Teresa and St. John of the Cross* (London, 1963). A new and definitive biography of St. Teresa is Efren de la Madre de Dios and Otger Steggink, *Tiempo y vida de Santa Teresa* (Madrid, 1968). For St. Teresa as a reformer of the Carmelites see Idelfonso Moriones, *Ana de Jesus y la hierencia teresiana: Humanismo cristiano o rigor primitivo* (Rome, 1968).

4. RELIGION AND REBELLION

The standard biography of Beza is Paul F. Geisendorf, *Théodore de Bèze* (Geneva, 1949); it tends toward hagiography, but it is thorough, especially for its subject's early career, and replaces the older work, H. M. Baird, *Theodore Beza* (London, 1894). The best detailed account of the Colloquy of Poissy is still Evennett, *The Cardinal of Lorraine*. An old work, reproducing important documents, is Jules Delaborde, *Les Protestants à la cour de St. Germain lors du coloque de Poissy* (Paris, 1874). For Nicodemism see Carlo Ginzburg, *Il Nicodemismo: Simulazione e dissimulazione religiosa nell' Europa del 1500* (Turin, 1970). An important essay, Lucien Febrve, "Une question mal posée: Les origines de la réforme française et le problème général des causes de la réforme," *Revue historique,* CLXI (1929), 20 ff., states the thesis that the Reformation in France was less a matter of correcting abuses and more a clash of ideas.

Calvin's printed work runs to 62 large folio volumes—40,000 pages—in the *Corpus Reformatorum* series, of which 11 voumes are devoted to correspondence. Other primary sources are plentiful, especially at Geneva, and this perhaps explains the multitude of researchers who have studied Calvin from various angles and with varying results. See, for instance, Émile Léonard, "Bibliographie calvienne abrégée," in *Calvin et la réforme en France* (Aix-en-provence, n.d. [1959]), pp. 137 ff. The interest continues as sources are newly uncovered or printed; see the review article, Basil Hall, "The Genevan Tradition," *Journal of Ecclesiastical History,* XX (1969), 111 ff. Of special note is the work of Robert Kingdon, especially his *Geneva and the Coming of the Wars of Religion in France, 1555-1563* (Geneva, 1956) and his *Geneva and the Consolidation of the French Protestant Movement, 1564-1572* (Madison, Wis., 1967). A brief treatment of the Swiss background is E. Bonjour et al., *A Short History of Switzerland* (Oxford, 1952). The standard general account in English is J. T. McNeill, *The History and Character of Calvinism* (New York, 1954), which is preferable to James Mackinnon, *Calvin and the Reformation* (New York, 1936). The classic study of the relation between Calvinist Church and state is Eugene Choisy, *L'État chrétien calviniste à Genève au temps de Théodore de Bèze* (Geneva, 1902). See also W. Fred Graham, *Calvin and His City: A Study of Human Seizure of Control* (Richmond, 1970). For the Farel era in Geneva see Henri Naef, *Les Origines de la réforme à Genève,* Vol. II (Geneva, 1968). A disappointing collection is G. E. Duffield, ed., *John Calvin* (Grand Rapids, Mich., 1966).

James Westfall Thompson, *The Wars of Religion in France, 1559-1576* (New York, n.d. [1909]), is the best survey in English; the terminal date was chosen on the grounds that after 1576 the wars became "political." Lucien Romier, *Catholiques et Huguenots à la cour de Charles IX* (Paris, 1924), is less detailed; see also his *Le Royaume de Catherine de Médicis,* 2 vols. (Paris, 1922). John Neale, *The Age of Catherine de' Medici* (London, 1957), does not have the same quality as the same author's work on Queen Elizabeth. Jules Delaborde, *Gaspard de Coligny, Amiral de France* (Paris,

1882), its three volumes bulging with documents, should now be supplemented by J. Shimizu, *Conflict of Loyalties: Politics and Religion in the Career of Gaspard de Coligny, Admiral of France, 1519–1572* (Geneva, 1970). Nancy Roelker, *Queen of Navarre, Jeanne d'Albret* (Cambridge, Mass., 1968), is a superb biography which also says much about the evolution from evangelistic humanism to sectarian conflict. See also the same author's perceptive "The Appeal of Calvinism to French Noblewomen in the Sixteenth Century," *The Journal of Interdisciplinary History*, II (1972), 391 ff. The literature on St. Bartholomew is plentiful but conflicting; the result of N. Sutherland's researches on the massacre is eagerly awaited.

Pieter Geyl, *The Revolt of the Netherlands, 1555–1609*, 2d ed. (London, 1962), remains the fundamental work; I am unimpressed by the reservations on the Geyl theory as expressed in Charles Wilson, *Queen Elizabeth and the Revolt of the Netherlands* (London, 1970), pp. 6 ff. It seems to me that Geyl anticipated some of Wilson's objections in *Debates with Historians* (New York, 1958), pp. 203 ff. Useful for bibliography, especially for works in Dutch, is G. N. Clark, "The Birth of the Dutch Republic," in Lucy Sutherland, ed., *Studies in History* (London, 1966), pp. 112 ff.; Clark's lecture was originally given in 1946. For color, style, and thoroughness, if not for objectivity, the seven volumes of John Lothrop Motley on the rise of the Netherlands state are irreplaceable. A pale evocation of Motley is Edward Grierson, *The Fatal Inheritance* (London, 1969).

The best study of the Elizabethan Church's early campaign for acceptance among the intellectuals and among the masses is in Philip Hughes, *The Reformation in England*, Vol. III (New York, 1954), in which the reader will find the fullest critical apparatus. For an example of the particular difficulties of the new bishops, see M. Rosemary O'Day, "Thomas Bentham: A Case Study in the Problems of the Early Elizabethan Episcopate," *Journal of Ecclesiastical History*, XXIII (1972), 137 ff. William Haugaard, *Elizabeth and the English Reformation: The Struggle for a Stable Settlement of Religion* (Cambridge, 1968), attributes to the queen more religiosity than most authors do. The argument of Sir John Neale that sectarian struggles in Elizabethan England were analogous to ideological struggles in the twentieth century is to some degree substantiated by A. Ferguson, *The Articulate Citizen and the English Renaissance* (Durham, 1965), and Michael Walzer, *The Revolution of the Saints* (Cambridge, Mass., 1966). On Scottish affairs the best treatment by far is Gordon Donaldson, *Scotland, James V to James VII* (New York, 1965); his *The First Trial of Mary Queen of Scots* (New York, 1969) is an admirable summation of the Darnley murder and analysis of the Casket Letters. See also John Durkan,

"The Cultural Background in Sixteenth Century Scotland," in David Mc-Roberts, ed., *Essays on the Scottish Reformation* (Glasgow, 1962), pp. 274 ff. Two recent biographies, Antonia Fraser, *Mary Queen of Scots* (New York, 1969), and Jasper Ridley, *John Knox* (Oxford, 1968), though very different in style, are both excellent. An older though still useful work is J. H. Pollen, *The Counter Reformation in Scotland* (London, 1921).

5. THE SOUTHERN SEA

Braudel, *La Méditerranée,* cited above, is and no doubt will remain the basic work of synthesis. Other more specific works include Charles Monchicourt, *L'Expédition espagnole de 1560 contre l'île de Djerba* (Paris, 1913); Andrew Hess, "The Moriscos: An Ottoman Fifth Column in Sixteenth Century Spain," *American Historical Review,* Vol. LXXIV (1968); and H. G. Koenigsberger, "Decadence or Shift?" *Transactions of the Royal Historical Society,* Vol. X (1960), which is concerned with Italy. The old *Encyclopedia of Islam* contains useful articles in its four volumes; a new encyclopedia is now in progress. The conquest of Cyprus is described in George Hill, *A History of Cyprus,* Vol. III (Cambridge, 1948). The religiosity which was a cause and effect of Lepanto is touched upon in Hugh Davis, "A Rosary Confraternity of 1579 and the Cardinal of Santa Susana," *Catholic Historical Review,* XLVIII (1962), 321 ff.

The Knights of St. John who resisted the Turks in 1565 are treated most recently in Arthur Bonnici, *History of the Church in Malta,* Vol. II (Valetta, 1968). Andrew Hess, "The Evolution of the Ottoman Seaborne Empire in the Age of Oceanic Discoveries," *American Historical Review,* Vol. LXXV (1970), summarizes the growth of Turkish sea power up to the time of Suleiman. The best study of the diplomacy of the Holy League is an old one, L. Serrano, *La Liga de Lepanto* (Madrid, 1920), and the best biography of Don John is older still, William Stirling-Maxwell, *Don John of Austria* (London, 1883), both works in two volumes. Albert Lybyer, *The Government of the Ottoman Empire in the Time of Suleiman the Magnificent* (Cambridge, Mass., 1913), should be supplemented by A. D. Alderson, *The Structure of the Ottoman Dynasty* (Oxford, 1956), with its good bibliography and very detailed genealogical charts. Urban life in the conquered Balkans is discussed in a collection of monographs, Nikolaj Todorov, ed., *La ville balkanique* (Sofia, 1970). Two excellent recent books on Venice are D. S. Chambers, *The Imperial Age of Venice* (New York, 1971), and William Bouwsma, *Venice and the Defense of Republican Liberty* (Berkeley, 1968), the first an economic and political survey and the second an analysis of the Venetian intellectual tradition. The latter might well be read in conjunction with Eric Cochrane, ed., *The Late Italian Renaissance* (New

York, 1970), a collection of recent work by various scholars (including Professor Bouwsma), with very good notes and a particularly penetrating introduction by the editor.

6. THE CATHOLIC OFFENSIVE

W. F. Reddaway et al., eds., *The Cambridge History of Poland from the Origins to Sobieski* (Cambridge, 1950), follows the usual Cambridge format: different topics are explored by different experts within a rough chronological framework. Ingvar Andersson, *A History of Sweden* (London, 1955), is a popular treatment with marvelous plates. Michael Florinsky, *Russia, a History and an Interpretation,* Vol. I (New York, 1953), V. O. Kliuchevsky, *A History of Russia,* Vol. II (New York, 1960), and George Vernadsky, *A History of Russia,* Vols. IV and V (New Haven, 1968–69), give more than an adequate picture, though Kliuchevsky and Vernadsky make heavy reading. See also the review article, Michael Malin, "Backward History in a Backward Country," *New York Review of Books,* XVII (Oct. 7, 1971), 36 ff.

More specific studies include Oscar Garstein, *Rome and the Counter Reformation in Scandinavia* (Oxford, 1963), a not always reliable book based on the Kalsrud archival collections, and Jarold Zeman, *The Anabaptists and the Czech Brethren in Moravia, 1526–1628: A Study of Origins and Contacts* (The Hague, 1969), with a huge bibliography of works written in east European languages. Oscar Halecki, *From Florence to Brest* (New York, 1968), describes the relations between Catholic and Orthodox in Poland-Lithuania; the book is the last word in scholarship but mediocre from the stylistic point of view. For the great Catholic Polish reformer, see G. Gabka, "Cardinal Hosius and the Council of Trent," *Theological Studies,* VII (1946), 568 ff., and Henry Wojtyska, *Cardinal Hosius, Legate to the Council of Trent* (Rome, 1967). For Possevino see S. Polcin, *Une tentative d'union au XVIᵉ siècle, la mission religieuse du P. A. Possevino, S.J., en Muscovie* (Rome, 1959). For Skarga, see *Dictionnaire de théologie catholique,* XIV, cols. 2239 ff.

7. HIGH TIDE

This is an appropriate place to mention those scholars whose works are fundamental to an understanding of the Elizabethan era and whose fame for that reason is widely known. In the first place, Sir John Neale, for his biography of the queen, for his work on the Elizabethan parliaments, and for a host of smaller but equally perceptive pieces; next, Conyers Read, for his diplomatic and administrative histories of the reign through his exhaustive biographies of Cecil and Walsingham; then Philip Hughes, for the religious scene drawn from vast and detailed knowledge, from theological acumen and from a deeply personal commitment; then William Haller, the historian of the Puritans; and finally John Pollen, the historian of the Jesuit mission.

More recent works that bear upon the Elizabethan religious crisis include John New, *Anglican and Puritan, the Basis of Their Opposition, 1558–1640* (Stanford, 1964); W. D. J. C. Thompson, "A Reconsideration of Richard Bancroft's Paul's Cross Sermon of 9 February, 1588/9," *Journal of Ecclesiastical History*, XX (1969), 253 ff., and Paul Seaver, *The Puritan Lectureships: The Politics of Religious Dissent, 1560–1662* (Stanford, 1970). Roger Manning, *Religion and Society in Elizabethan Sussex* (Leicester, 1969), studies the enforcement of the religious laws in one county, while K. R. Wark, *Elizabethan Recusancy in Cheshire* (Manchester, 1971), does the same for another, though from a different perspective. John Bossy suggests new directions for recusant history, now that the polemical storms have passed, in two articles: "The Character of Elizabethan Catholicism," in Trevor Aston, ed., *Crisis in Europe, 1560–1660* (New York, 1967), pp. 235 ff., and in "Rome and the Elizabethan Catholics: A Question of Geography," *The Historical Journal*, VII (1964), 137 ff.

Aside from the works of Mariéjol and Romier, mentioned above, the middle stage of the French religious wars is summarized in G. Livet, *Les Guerres de religion* (Paris, 1962), and in Edward Armstrong, *The French Wars of Religion* (London, 1892). There is no satisfactory life of Henry of Guise, but see Maurice Wilkinson, *A History of the League* (Glasgow, 1929). The crucial importance of the parallel between two volatile movements is suggested by H. G. Koenigsberger, "The Organization of Revolutionary Parties in France and the Netherlands," *Journal of Modern History*, Vol. XXVII (1953).

As Alexander Farnese dominated the history of the Netherlands from 1578 to 1585 so does the five-volume biography of him by Léon van der Essen dominate the historiography for those years. But also of importance are two biographies of Farnese's opponent at Antwerp: L. van Kalken and T. Joncksheere, *Marnix de Sainte Aldegonde* (Brussels, 1952), and A. Merlo, *Marnix l'énigmatique* (Brussels, 1952), the first of which has helpful bibliographies. See also Tibor Willman, *Les Gueux dans les "bonnes villes" de Flandre (1577–1584)* (Budapest, 1969), a revisionary Marxist study of the economic and social consequences of the revolt.

8. CLIMAX

For a study of a royal secretariat as well as a tale of intrigue see Gregorio Marañón, *Antonio Pérez* (London, 1954). Martin Philippson, *Ein Ministerium unter Philipp II: Der Kardinal Granvella am spanischen Hofe* (Berlin,

1895), looks at the greatest of Philip's diplomats and bureaucrats. The background to the annexation of Portugal is conveniently found in H. V. Livermore, *A History of Portugal* (Cambridge, 1947). The opening pages of J. H. Elliott, *The Revolt of the Catalans: A Study in the Decline of Spain* (Cambridge, 1963), give a summary of Philip II's domestic troubles during his last years. A thorough if somewhat dated and tedious study of Sixtus V is J. A. Hübner, *Sixte V* (Paris, 1870), in three volumes.

The Armada campaign is described in detail and with admirable vividness in Garrett Mattingly, *The Armada* (Boston, 1959). For a more technical assessment of the naval action see Michael Lewis, *The Spanish Armada* (London, 1960). Joseph de Croze, *Les Guises, les Valois et Philippe II* (Paris, 1866), is regrettably very old, but this is compensated for somewhat by a brilliant recent study, De Lamar Jensen, *Diplomacy and Dogmatism* (Cambridge, Mass., 1964), based on the dispatches of Philip II's ambassador in Paris at the height of the League revolt. Henri Druot, *Mayenne et la Bourgogne* (Paris, 1937), studies the later fortunes of the League in Burgundy.

The long-term deterioration of Anglo-Spanish relations on a popular level is the subject of William Maltby, *The Black Legend in England* (Durham, 1971). See also Albert Loomie, "Religion and Elizabethan Commerce with Spain," *Catholic Historical Review*, L (1964), 27 ff. Frederick Jones, *Mountjoy, the Last Elizabethan Deputy* (Dublin, 1958) describes the suppression of Ireland and The O'Neil. Robert Lacey, *Robert, Earl of Essex* (London, 1969) is a competent biography. David Mathew, *The Celtic Peoples and Renaissance Europe: A Study of Celtic and Spanish Influences on Elizabethan History* (London, 1933), is an odd title for a rather odd book, but it does have some interesting things to say about Essex. A collection of essays honoring Sir John Neale, S. T. Bindoff, et al., eds., *Elizabethan Government and Society* (London, 1961), contains Joel Hurstfield, "The Succession Struggle in Late Elizabethan England," pp. 369 ff., which reveals that some die-hard Catholics hoped the Spanish Infanta would follow Elizabeth to the throne. The most important single book for the first few years of James I's reign is Wallace Notestein, *The House of Commons, 1604–1610* (New Haven, 1971), published posthumously. For James's foreign concerns in those same years see Maurice Lee, Jr., *James I and Henri IV: An Essay in English Foreign Policy, 1603–1610* (Urbana, Ill., 1970).

9. THE LIMITS OF IDEOLOGY

"All histories of sixteenth century Europe," observes J. H. Elliott (*Europe Divided*, p. 418), "will continue to look lop-sided until Ottoman history in the sixteenth century has been effectively explored." This proposition might be extended to embrace the history of central and eastern Europe and indeed Italy. There are some learned monographs but precious few satisfactory syntheses, at least in Western languages. The recent publication of *The Cambridge History of Islam* (Cambridge, 1970) is a hopeful sign. The opening chapters of an older work are also very useful: Carl von Sax, *Geschichte des Machtverfalls der Türkei* (Vienna, 1913). For western European awareness of the Turks see the opening section of H. A. R. Gibb and Harold Bowen, *Islamic Society and the West* (Oxford, 1950), as well as Samuel Chew, *The Crescent and the Rose* (New York, 1937). Erich Zöllner, *Geschichte Oesterreichs,* 2nd ed. (Vienna, 1961), is an excellent survey. Of more particular interest is Bernard Lewis, "Some Reflections on the Decline of the Ottoman Empire," *Studia Islamica,* IX (1959), 111 ff.; Jerome Blum, *Land and Peasant in Russia* (Princeton, 1961); and M. Epstein, *The Early History of the Levant Company* (London, 1935). Among other monographs might be cited Alberto Tenenti, *Piracy and the Decline of Venice, 1580–1615* (London, 1967), and Hans-Heinrich Nolte, *Religiöse Toleranz in Russland, 1600–1725* (Göttingen, 1969), which treats of the Russian government's evolving attitude to religions other than Orthodoxy. Denis Sinor, *History of Hungary* (New York, 1959), gives a sketch of the Austro-Turkish war, 1593–1606, and Bodhan Chudoba, *Spain and the Empire* (Chicago, 1952), attempts a Hapsburg synthesis which, while valuable, is not always in focus. Arturo de Carmigano, "Le part de S. Laurent de Brindes dans la ban de Donauwörth (1607)," *Revue d'histoire ecclesiastique,* LVIII (1963), 460 ff., spotlights papal diplomacy, and an unlikely papal diplomat, in increasingly troubled Germany. Dorothy Vaughan, *Europe and the Turk* (London, 1967), surveys the overall relations between East and West.

Various works of Roland Mousnier have illuminated the history of the late sixteenth and early seventeenth centuries, including *L'assassinat d'Henri IV* (Paris, 1964) and *La venalité des offices sous Henri IV et Louis XIII* (Rouen, 1945). His latest work, *Les hierarchies sociales de 1450 à nos jours* (Paris, 1970), is a brief and tentative probing into the French class structure which he finds dominated at the end of the sixteenth century by military categories. David Buisseret, *Sully and the Growth of Centralized Government in France, 1598–1610* (London, 1968), is based on a close study of manuscript sources. Nancy Roelker, ed., *The Paris of Henry of Navarre* (Cambridge, Mass., 1958), is based on the diary of *parlementaire* Pierre de l'Estoille and is enhanced by the editor's excellent notes and glossaries. A standard work on the beginnings of the Catholic revival in France is Victor Martin, *Le Gallicanisme et la réforme catholique: Essai sur l'introduction en France des décrets de Trente* (Paris, 1919).

10. THE QUALITY OF MIND

Respected surveys of European intellectual history—Crane Brinton, *Ideas and Men,* 2d ed. (Englewood Cliffs, N.J., 1963) comes to mind—give short shrift to the second half of the sixteenth century. S. J. Freedberg, *Painting in Italy, 1500–1600* (London, 1970), needs only two brief chapters to treat of artists after 1550 (except the school of Titian); for Professor Freedberg the climax of the century comes with Correggio, who died in 1534. Learned monographs, and not only those on the history of science, begin with the end of this chronological period: witness the recent two-volume analysis of printed books and who read them at Paris in H.-J. Martin, *Livres, pouvoirs et société à Paris au XVIIe siècle (1598–1701)* (Geneva, 1969); or Christopher Hill, *Antichrist in Seventeenth Century England* (Oxford, 1970), which predictably treats the 1590s as "background" for an intellectual phenomenon that blooms fully only later. Nor is this a new fashion: Henri Bremond wrote the literary history of French religious sentiment "depuis la fin des guerres de religion," from the end of the Wars of Religion. Even works which allege to merge chronological compartments are eager to pass quickly from Copernicus to Kepler, from Da Vinci to Galileo, from the humanists of Erasmus's generation to Descartes and Francis Bacon.

All of which is an apologia for the last chapter of this book. Aside from the brilliant individuals singled out there, the era does seem to be one in which the precursors and the nonsayers held the intellectual field. Whether this was because of the religious disturbances or the violent beginnings of the modern national states or the economic uncertainties, I do not know. Perhaps it was simply exhaustion of a culture which after the Renaissance needed a period of rest before the next great leap forward. More likely still, the very fact that I express such concerns reflects the frame of reference in which I write, in which a scientific marvel is expected, and taken for granted, weekly: I have watched, in living color, my contemporaries walk upon the surface of the moon; I have watched, then yawned, brushed my teeth, and gone to bed.

There are at any rate few if any satisfactory analyses of intellectual life in Europe from 1559 to 1610. But there are, especially in the burgeoning field of the history of science, enough accounts to piece together that most important phenomenon, the disintegration of the Aristotelian world view. Good introductions for nonspecialists include Herbert Butterfield, *The Origins of Modern Science, 1300–1800* (London, 1962), especially pp. 55 ff., and Marie Boas, *The Scientific Renaissance, 1450–1630* (London, 1962), especially pp. 90 ff. As Professor Boas says elsewhere (*The New Cambridge*

Modern History, III, 453), "The men of the later sixteenth century were consolidators and continuers rather than innovators. . . . Yet it was in this period that the men who were to make the scientific revolution of the seventeenth century grew to manhood and it was by the scientists and scientific literature of this age that they were trained and prepared for innovation."

And so to catch the intellectual tune of this age we have Montaigne, Bodin, Bellarmine, and Hooker, who sing for themselves and, if one listens closely, in a kind of rough harmony. For the rest we have to be satisfied with gleanings. The superb books of Frances Yates, *The French Academies of the Sixteenth Century* (London, 1947), *The Valois Tapestries* (London, 1959), and *Giordano Bruno and the Hermetic Tradition* (London, 1967), are exceptional in their richness and scope. Joseph Lecler, *Histoire de la tolerance au siècle de la réforme* (Paris, 1955), is a sort of intellectual history, with the inevitable religious bent. Gerhard Güldner, *Das Toleranz-Problem in den Nederlanden im Ausgang des 16. Jahrhunderts* (Lübeck, 1968), is a monograph along the same general lines, only it concentrates on an intellectual controversy within the Protestant camp. Robert Linder, "Pierre Viret's Ideas and Attitudes concerning Humanism and Education," *Church History,* Vol. XXXV (1965), explores the views of a prominent Swiss reformer. The deepening knowledge of Puritanism suggests that the movement had more interest in things intellectual than was formerly thought: see, for instance, K. R. M. Short, "A Theory of Common Education in Elizabethan Puritanism," *Journal of Ecclesiastical History,* XXIII (1972), 31 ff. This might be read in conjunction with Hugh Kearney, *Scholars and Gentlemen: Universities and Society in Pre-industrial Britain, 1500–1700* (London, 1970). Finally, Peter Gay, *The Enlightenment: An Interpretation* (London, 1967), is a book so broad and provocative that even the late sixteenth century receives some attention.

As for Cervantes and Shakespeare, I am presumptuous enough to suggest two books. R. O. Jones, *The Golden Age: Prose and Poetry* (London, 1971) —the second volume of the *Literary History of Spain* of which Professor Jones is general editor—says among other things that Counter Reformation Spain, allegedly a grim place crushed under the heel of the Inquisition, experienced a great boom in the publication of all sorts of light literature. And B. L. Joseph, *Shakespeare's Eden* (London, 1971), sifts the evidence and finds that those who watched Shakespeare's plays lived in a social milieu in which contradictory thought patterns and value systems existed side by side, even within the same individual. They must have been like our times, and all times.

INDEX

DATE DUE			
NO 1 4 '89			

EUROPE 1610

SPANISH
HAPSBURGS

AUSTRIAN
HAPSBURGS

BOUNDARY OF
HOLY ROMAN
EMPIRE

SCOTLAND

Edinburgh

North Sea

IRELAND

ENGLAND

London

UNITED
PROVINCES

SPANISH
NETHERLAN

Atlantic   Ocean

Paris

FRANCE

FRANCH
COMT

PORTUGAL

Lisbon

Madrid

SPAIN

CORSICA

SARDINIA

Mediterranean

BARBARY   STATES